FINANCIAL REPORTING
AND ANALYSIS

ICSA STUDY TEXT

FINANCIAL REPORTING AND ANALYSIS

THIRD EDITION

DANUSIA WYSOCKI

icsa

The Governance
Institute

First published as Financial Reporting and Analysis by David Frederick
(ICSA Publishing Limited, 2012, 2014)
Published by ICSA Publishing Limited
Saffron House
6-10 Kirby Street
London EC1N 8TS

Designed and typeset by Paul Barrett Book Production, Cambridge
Printed by Hobbs the Printers Ltd, Totton, Hampshire

British Cataloguing in Publication Data
A catalogue record for this book is available from the British Library.
ISBN 978 1860 727085

Acknowledgements

m grateful to

d Oakes and

ling support,

usia Wysocki

the first and

Foreword

Financial Reporting is an area of knowledge that ideally should be built gradually. Most qualified accountants study the subject through progressive learning, whether through the three years of their degree programme, or over the three or four year period of studying for professional examinations.

Most of those would tell you that it is all a bit of a slog – especially learning all those pesky accounting standard rules that are very precise and tend to change over time as well!

It all becomes even more difficult if you are faced with a short learning period – e.g. a few months – and your background is anything but accounting – such as law.

This demonstrates the tricky task facing the typical ICSA student who is attempting the Financial Reporting and Analysis paper. All they can do is apply themselves the best they can – and this text aims to set out all the key knowledge required in a clear and concise way.

David Oakes
Examiner, ICSA
Financial Reporting and Analysis

Acknowledgements

I would like to thank all those that supported me on this journey. In particular, I am grateful to Jon Evans for his meticulous review of draft versions with special thanks to David Oakes and Joe Adomako at London South Bank University for insight, advice and expertise.

Lastly, immeasurable thanks to Pawel, Natalia and Oscar without whose unfailing support, encouragement and considerable patience this book would not have been possible.

Danusia Wysocki

The publishers would like to acknowledge the work of David Frederick who wrote the first and second editions of this book.

Foreword

Financial Reporting is an area of knowledge that ideally should be built gradually. Most qualified accountants study the subject through progressive learning, whether through the three years of their degree programme, or over the three or four year period of studying for professional examinations.

Most of those would tell you that it is all a bit of a slog – especially learning all those pesky accounting standard rules that are very precise and tend to change over time as well!

It all becomes even more difficult if you are faced with a short learning period – e.g. a few months – and your background is anything but accounting – such as law.

This demonstrates the tricky task facing the typical ICSA student who is attempting the Financial Reporting and Analysis paper. All they can do is apply themselves the best they can – and this text aims to set out all the key knowledge required in a clear and concise way.

David Oakes
Examiner, ICSA
Financial Reporting and Analysis

Contents

How to use this study text

ICSA study texts were developed to support ICSA's Chartered Secretaries Qualifying Scheme (CSQS) follow a standard format and include a range of navigational, self-testing and illustrative features to help you get the most out of the support materials.

Each text is divided into three main sections:

- introductory material;
- the text itself, divided into parts and chapters; and
- additional reference information.

The sections below show you how to find your way around the text and make the most of its features.

Introductory material

The introductory section of each text includes a full contents list and the module syllabus, which reiterates the module aims, learning outcomes and syllabus content for the module in question.

The text itself

Each **part** opens with a list of the chapters to follow, an overview of what will be covered and learning outcomes for the part.

Every **chapter** opens with a list of the topics covered and an introduction specific to that chapter. Chapters are structured to allow students to break the content down into manageable sections for study. Each chapter ends with a summary of key content to reinforce understanding, as well as end-of-chapter examination-standard questions to test your knowledge further.

Part opening   Chapter opening

Features

The text is enhanced by a range of illustrative and self-testing features to assist understanding and to help you prepare for the examination. Each feature is presented in a standard format, so that you will become familiar with how to use them in your study.

The texts also include tables, figures and checklists and, where relevant, sample documents and forms.

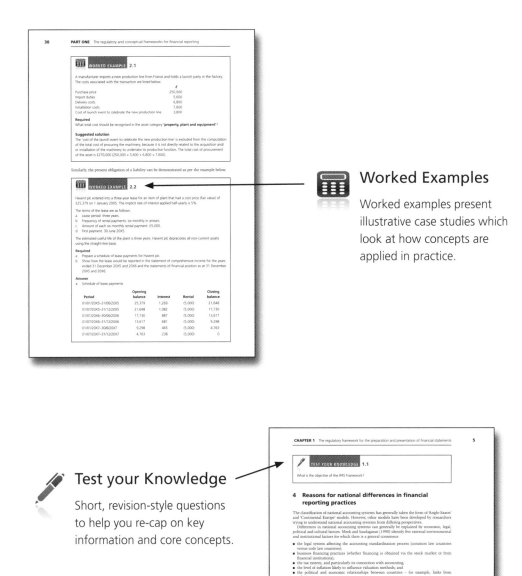

Worked Examples

Worked examples present illustrative case studies which look at how concepts are applied in practice.

Test your Knowledge

Short, revision-style questions to help you re-cap on key information and core concepts.

Definitions

Key terms are highlighted in bold on first use and defined in the end of book glossary.

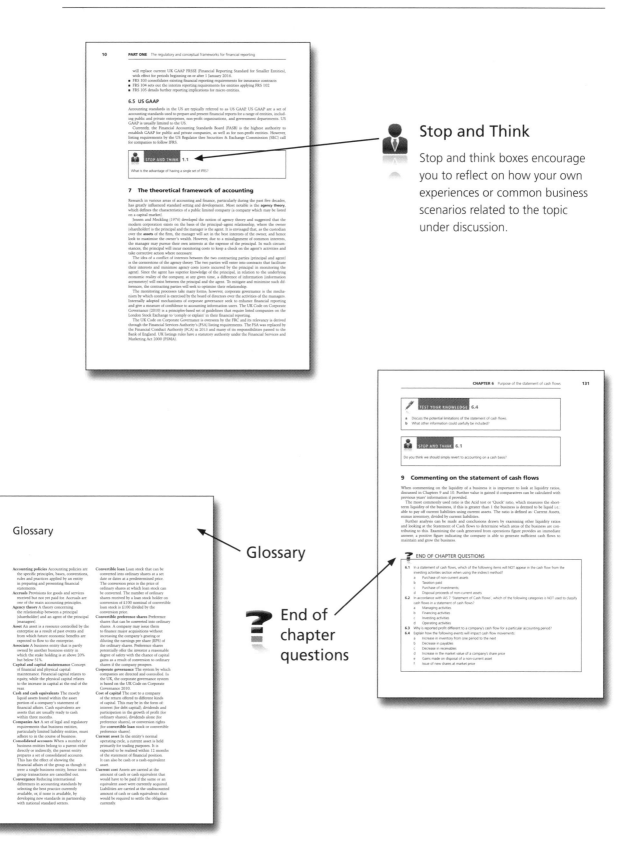

Stop and Think

Stop and think boxes encourage you to reflect on how your own experiences or common business scenarios related to the topic under discussion.

Glossary

End of chapter questions

Reference material

The text ends with a range of additional guidance and reference material.

Other reference material includes a glossary of key terms, a directory of further reading and web resources, and a comprehensive index.

Financial Reporting and Analysis syllabus

Module outline and aims

In professional practice, the Chartered Secretary has to be competent in financial accounting and reporting. In public practice and in some other organisations, the Chartered Secretary can also be called upon to fulfil the role of corporate accountant. There, the emphasis is normally on accounting for purpose rather than on detailed accounting techniques.

Chartered Secretaries need to understand the significance and relevance of accounting information and the process by which it is acquired. Core responsibilities also include compliance with legal and stakeholder requirements, including financial statements. In the boardroom, Chartered Secretaries contribute to the analysis, presentation and interpretation of corporate financial performance and results, including the implications for the organisation, shareholders and stakeholders and for effective corporate governance.

The aim of the module is to develop the knowledge and skills necessary for you to understand and supervise the execution of these professional responsibilities.

Learning outcomes

On successful completion of this module, you will be able to:

- describe and explain the language, concepts and use of financial accounts and reports;
- demonstrate a sound understanding of the significance of accounting information systems for both effective financial reporting and good corporate governance and demonstrate a systematic understanding and thorough appreciation of the regulatory framework for the preparation and presentation of financial statements;
- apply the skills necessary for the preparation and presentation of financial statements for single and group companies in compliance with legal and regulatory requirements;
- interpret and critically analyse corporate financial accounts and reports reflecting on the limitations of both published accounts and standard analytical techniques;
- describe and explain the relationship between financial reporting and corporate governance; and
- prepare reports and presentations relating to financial matters for the board and senior officers of organisations.

Syllabus content

The regulatory and conceptual frameworks for financial reporting – weighting 20%

The regulatory framework for the preparation and presentation of financial statements

- The work of the international standards setters
- Statutory framework and legal requirements
- Corporate governance and the external audit process
- Social and environmental reporting

The conceptual framework for the preparation and presentation of financial statements

- The objective and users of financial statements
- The underlying assumptions

- The qualitative characteristics that determine the usefulness of information in financial statements
- The definition of the elements of financial statements
- The recognition of the elements from which financial statements are constructed
- The measurement of assets and liabilities reported in financial statements
- Concepts of capital and capital maintenance

The preparation and presentation of financial statements for single companies in compliance with legal and regulatory requirements, including the relevant International Accounting Standards – weighting 25%

- Criteria for information appearing in published financial statements
- Income statement
- Statement of financial position
- Statement of changes in equity
- Reporting comprehensive income
- Segmental reporting
- Accounting policies
- Notes to the accounts
- Statements of cash flow
- Creative accounting
- Accounting for inventories
- Off-balance sheet finance and leasing
- Reporting the substance of transactions
- Accounting for property, plant and equipment including depreciation and impairment
- Accounting for provisions, contingent assets and liabilities, and events after the reporting period

The preparation and presentation of financial statements for groups in compliance with legal and regulatory requirements, including the relevant International Accounting Standards – weighting 25%

- Requirements for preparation of consolidated financial statements
- Consolidated statement of financial position
- Consolidated income statement
- Investment in associates and joint ventures

Analysis and interpretation of accounts – weighting 30%

- Trend or horizontal analysis
- Common size statements
- Accounting ratios and ratio analysis
- The development of XBRL
- Primary investment, operative and liquidity level ratios
- Subsidiary ratios including investment performance indicators such as price/earnings ratio
- Segmental analysis
- Inter-firm comparisons and industrial averages
- Analysing a statement of cash flows
- Earnings per share
- Limitations of analytical and interpretative techniques

Commentary on the syllabus

There are four main areas in the Financial Reporting and Analysis syllabus. What follows is an overview of each of these areas, indicating what students need to achieve in order to prepare effectively for this examination.

The regulatory and conceptual framework

Candidates will need to demonstrate an understanding of aspects of the regulatory framework responsible for the preparation and presentation of financial statements.
The candidate will be expected to be able to:

- show an understanding of the work of the International Accounting Standards Board;
- be familiar with the principal sources of legal regulations governing financial statements;
- explain the principal qualities required of external auditors if they are to contribute to effective corporate governance;
- evaluate the corporate governance implications of auditors providing consultancy services;
- list the main elements of the Eco-Management and Audit Scheme for environmental disclosure in Europe;
- reveal familiarity with the activities involved in an environmental audit; and
- outline recent developments in corporate social responsibility (CSR) reports and triple bottom line reporting.

Candidates need to be fully familiar with the content and significance of the 'Conceptual Framework for Financial Reporting' issued by the International Accounting Standards Board.
The candidate will be expected to be able to:

- explain the objective of financial statements;
- list and explain the significance of each of the qualitative characteristics of financial information;
- identify and distinguish between the elements of financial statements;
- show an understanding of the conditions that must be met to justify the recognition of assets and liabilities;
- be aware of the significance of the concepts of sufficient evidence and sufficient reliability for the recognition of assets and liabilities;
- describe how entity managers decide which measurement basis to adopt for financial reporting purposes;
- demonstrate an understanding of the concept of value to the business and of how the concept is given operational effect; and
- reveal an understanding of the existence of different concepts of capital and capital maintenance.

The preparation and presentation of financial statements

Candidates are expected to be able to prepare and present financial statements for single companies in compliance with legal and regulatory requirements, including the relevant international accounting standards.
The candidate will be expected to be able to:

- identify the criteria which must be met for information to appear in the published income statement and statement of financial position;
- construct the income statement in accordance with prescribed format 1;
- understand the effect of adopting different accounting policies on the content of the income statement and statement of financial position;
- report in the income statement the impact of discontinued operations;
- account appropriately for 'non-recurring' items requiring separate disclosure in the income statement;
- construct the statement of financial position in accordance with prescribed formats;
- show an understanding of the appropriate methods for valuing assets and liabilities;
- demonstrate familiarity with the notes that accompany financial statements;

- prepare the statement of changes in equity and explain why it must be published;
- understand the concept and be aware of the constituents of a statement of comprehensive income;
- explain the importance of segmental information and be able to prepare a segmental report;
- demonstrate familiarity with the nature of accounting policies, the significance of differences between them and the effects of changes in accounting policy;
- show an understanding of the reasons why entities are today required to publish a statement of cash flows;
- prepare a statement of cash flows in accordance with standard accounting practice;
- demonstrate an awareness of the steps entities might take to improve their accounts so as, for example, to reduce the reported gearing ratio, increase the published EPS, and strengthen the balance sheet;
- reveal a full understanding of the opportunities for subjectivity and creative accounting when preparing financial reports;
- show familiarity with the role of the audit in countering creative accounting practices;
- show an understanding of the treatment of inventories in financial statements;
- explain what is meant by off balance sheet finance and understand its significance;
- demonstrate the way in which leasing arrangements may be exploited to access the advantages of off balance sheet finance;
- outline and evaluate proposals designed to counter opportunistic behaviour by management when accounting for leases;
- distinguish between the economic substance and the legal form of a business transaction-
- demonstrate an understanding of accounting for property, plant and equipment including accounting for depreciation and accounting for impairment; and
- show familiarity with end of year accounting issues including accounting for provisions, contingent assets and liabilities and dealing with events after the reporting period.

Group accounting

Candidates need to be able to prepare and present consolidated financial statements in compliance with legal and regulatory requirements, including the relevant international accounting standards.

The candidate will be expected to be able to:

- define a reporting group in accordance with standard accounting practice;
- explain why parent companies are required to publish consolidated accounts and the circumstance in which this obligation does not apply;
- outline the circumstances in which a subsidiary company may be excluded from the consolidated accounts and the further disclosures required in such circumstances;
- explain how the idea of control is applied to decide whether another entity must be included in the consolidated accounts;
- prepare a consolidated statement of financial position in accordance with the purchase method, making appropriate adjustments for fair value;
- compute goodwill and non-controlling interest for inclusion in the consolidated statement of financial position;
- distinguish between pre- and post-acquisition profits when preparing consolidated accounts;
- make appropriate adjustments for inter-company balances and unrealised profits on inter-company sales;
- show an appreciation of the need for uniform accounting policies and reporting dates;
- explain how an investment in subsidiaries should be reported in the parent's own balance sheet;
- prepare a consolidated income statement in accordance with standard accounting practice;
- demonstrate knowledge of the definitions of an associate and of significance influence;
- identify the circumstances in which a joint venture exists;
- make calculations to enable an associate or joint venture to be reported in accordance with the equity method; and
- show familiarity with the content of a consolidated statement of cash flows.

Analysis and interpretation of accounts

Candidates need to know how to calculate the percentages and ratios used to analyse entity performance. They must also be able to display expertise in interpreting the significance of such calculations.

The candidate will be expected to be able to:

- undertake horizontal analysis of accounts between two periods based on percentage changes;
- take account of the effect of exceptional items on comparability;
- apply trend analysis to the results of a series of accounting periods;
- undertake vertical analysis based on common size statements;
- understand the nature of accounting ratios and the use that can be made of them;
- reveal an awareness of the existence of online subscription databases that reformat company accounts in standardised form for comparative purposes;
- explain what XBRL is and how it can be used;
- calculate and interpret the significance of primary investment, primary operative and primary liquidity level ratios;
- calculate and interpret subsidiary ratios: gearing, liquidity, asset utilisation, investment and profitability;
- explain the reasons for and importance of segmental accounting;
- undertake statement analysis based on segmental accounts;
- outline sources of data available for inter-firm comparisons;
- analyse and interpret the information contained in the cash flow statement;
- display an understanding of the importance of earnings per share (EPS) and its relationship with the price/earnings ratio;
- explain the calculation of the basic and diluted EPS;
- compare and contrast the uses and limitations of EPS;
- make calculations of EPS that require adjustments to the number of shares used in the basic EPS calculation;
- calculate the EPS where there has been a rights issue;
- compute and explain the significance of the fully diluted EPS;
- show familiarity with the disclosure requirements applying to the EPS; and
- explain the limitations of accounting ratios computed on the basis of the information financial statements contain.

Overview

Financial accounting and reporting is central to modern entity management 'by the numbers'. The Chartered Secretary is regularly required to fulfil the following 'accounting' functions during his/her career:

- Analyse and interpret the outputs from an entity's accounting system.
- Initiate and participate in decision-making based on accounting information.
- Initiate and suggest improvements in the entity's accounting system and its outputs.
- Provide advice on the significance for the entity of contemporary accounting developments including regulatory changes.
- Counsel senior management on the significance of (proposed) published information for external user groups.

Acronyms and abbreviations

AGM	annual general meeting
ASB	Accounting Standards Board
ASC	Accounting Standards Committee
BIS	Department for Business, Innovation and Skills
CA2006	Companies Act 2006
CFO	chief finance officer
CRM	customer relationship management
CS	chartered secretary
CSR	corporate social responsibility
EC	European Commission
EPS	earnings per share
ESG	environmental social governance reporting
EU	European Union
FCA	Financial Conduct Authority
FRC	Financial Reporting Council
FRS	Financial Reporting Standards
FRSSE	Financial Reporting Standard for Smaller Entities
GAAP	Generally Agreed Accounting Practices
GMM	gross margin method
GRI	Global Reporting Initiative
HMRC	Her Majesty's Revenue & Customs
IAS	International Accounting Standards
IASB	International Accounting Standards Board
IASC	International Accounting Standards Committee
IESBA	International Ethics Standards Board for Accountants
IFAC	International Federation of Accountants
IFRS	International Financial Reporting Standards
IPC	integrated pollution control
IPR	intellectual property rights
IR	integrated reporting
ISO	International Organization for Standardization
KPI	key performance indicators
NDAC	non-discretionary accruals
NEDs	non-executive directors
NGOs	non-governmental organisations
NPV	net present value
NRV	net realisable value
OCI	other comprehensive income
OFR	Operating and Financial Review
OROE	Operating Return on Equity
RIM	retail inventory method
ROCE	return on capital employed
ROE	return on equity
SAN	Social Audit Network
SEC	Securities and Exchange Commission
SIC	Standing Interpretations Committee
SME	small and medium-sized enterprises
SOFP	statement of financial position
TBL	triple bottom line (framework)
WTO	World Trade Organization
XBRL	eXtensible Business Reporting Language

The regulatory and conceptual frameworks for financial reporting

■ LIST OF CHAPTERS

1   The regulatory framework for the preparation and presentation of financial statements
2   The conceptual framework for the preparation and presentation of financial statements

Chapters 1 and 2 in Part One cover the syllabus section entitled 'The regulatory and conceptual frameworks for financial reporting'.

■ OVERVIEW

The International Financial Reporting Standards (IFRS) Framework describes the basic concepts that underlie the preparation and presentation of financial statements for external users.

The regulatory and conceptual **frameworks** appear to be somewhat difficult to grasp, particularly as they are not financial reporting standards. However, the frameworks are the basis for which guidance is sought in reviewing and developing new standards.

Chapters 1 and 2 introduce the various terminologies used and build upon various frameworks from around the globe and related accounting issues that are pervasive and contemporary in nature.

To put things in context, the two chapters discuss historical issues in the development of financial reporting standards and the difficulties faced in their global acceptability.

Part One contains Worked Example 2.6 on America Online (AOL). Having reviewed the material, please attempt to answer the questions that follow the AOL scenario.

■ LEARNING OUTCOMES

1 The regulatory framework for the preparation and presentation of financial statements

   ■   The work of the international standards setters

   ■   Statutory framework and legal requirements

   ■   Corporate governance and the external audit process

   ■   Social and environmental reporting

2 The conceptual framework for the preparation and presentation of financial statements

- The objective and users of financial statements

- The underlying assumptions

- The qualitative characteristics that determine the usefulness of information in financial statements

- The definition of the elements of financial statements

- The recognition of the elements from which financial statements are constructed

- The measurement of assets and liabilities reported in financial statements

- Concepts of capital and capital maintenance

The regulatory framework for the preparation and presentation of financial statements

1

■ CONTENTS

■ LEARNING OUTCOMES

Chapter 1 covers the syllabus section entitled 'The regulatory framework for the preparation and presentation of financial statements'. After reading and understanding the contents of the chapter, working through all the worked examples and practice questions, you should be able to:

- show an understanding of the work of the **International Accounting Standards Board (IASB)**;
- be familiar with the principal sources of legal regulations governing financial statements;
- explain the principal qualities required of external auditors if they are to contribute to effective **corporate governance**.
- evaluate the corporate governance implications of auditors providing consultancy services;
- list the main elements of the Eco-Management and Audit Scheme (EMAS) for environmental disclosure in Europe;
- reveal familiarity with the activities involved in an environmental audit; and
- outline recent developments in corporate social responsibility (CSR) reports and triple bottom line (TBL) reporting.

1   Introduction

The past decade has witnessed an ever-increasing volume of cross-border trade and cross-listing on the world's capital markets, due to the breakdown of trade barriers and the formation of international trade bodies such as the World Trade Organization (WTO). This, in turn, has resulted in the demand for quality cross-border financial information. International Financial Reporting Standards are the mechanism that attempt to provide a platform for financial reporting consistency and reliability, to help **stakeholders** to make informed economic decisions.

The International Financial Reporting Standards (IFRS) are the remit of the International Accounting Standards Board (IASB), which seeks to achieve global comparability and consistency in financial reporting. In developing the IFRS, the IASB relies on the regulatory and conceptual frameworks for preparing and presenting financial statements. This chapter discusses the relevant issues that underpin these frameworks.

2   The regulatory framework

IFRS for public limited companies have been used in the UK and the European Union (EU) since 2002. Students need to be aware of the **relevance** of these and the importance attached to their use and application. The IFRS Framework is fundamental to the development and application of IFRS.

The IFRS Framework refers to a principle-based approach to developing a common set of financial reporting standards. It provides a platform for accounting and financial reporting to help demonstrate to the users of general purpose financial statements the appropriate accounting treatment of common accounting matters, on the basis of International Accounting Standards (IAS) and IFRS. The former International Accounting Standards Committee (IASC) issued IAS. However, standards issued since the formation of the IASB in April 2001 are referred to as IFRS.

The objective of the framework is to set out the concepts that underlie the preparation and presentation of financial statements for external users as set out in the 'Framework for the Preparation and Presentation of Financial Statements'. It is important at the outset to understand that the framework itself is not a standard. Its primary purpose is to help the IASB to develop new or revised accounting standards, and to assist those who prepare financial statements to apply accounting standards and to deal with any issues that the standards do not cover.

The framework covers:

- the objectives of financial reporting;
- the underlying assumptions;
- the qualitative characteristics;
- recognition and measurement criteria
- the **elements of financial statements**; and
- the concepts of **capital and capital maintenance**.

These are covered in the sections on the Conceptual Framework in Chapter 2.

The IASB Framework was approved by the IASC Board in April 1989 for publication in July 1989, and was adopted by the IASB after its formation in April 2001. The section on the regulatory aspect of the framework discusses some important themes that have emerged during its development.

3   National differences in financial reporting practices

National differences in accounting and corporate reporting continue despite IFRS. Countries in which the accounting profession has developed over a long period of time (such as the UK or the US) have generally led the evolution of accounting principles. Regulations influenced by local issues have given rise to particular accounting procedures. These rules and regulations are referred to as **Generally Accepted Accounting Principles (GAAP)**.

There are many reasons for differing financial reporting practices. Some of these may emanate from cultural, economic, political, religious and other internal influences. However, the speed of change in the global business environment and the pressure for change and the **convergence** of national GAAP to the IFRS system have resulted in many countries adopting the IFRS.

Nevertheless, national implementation of IFRS differs in the degree of convergence.

Hopwood (2000) suggests that '[at] the very time when there are enormous pressures for convergence of forms of financial accounting, our insights into the factors resulting in earlier differences in such practices are still poorly developed'.

The basis for accountability through corporate financial reporting (annual accounts) is fundamental to the dissemination of financial information relevant to the economic performance of the corporation. One view of the firm (corporation) is to look at it as a 'nexus of contracts', in which the firm has legal and ethical obligations to those who provide resources (e.g. banks and creditors) and other stakeholder groups (e.g. employees and the government).

What is the objective of the IFRS Framework?

4   Reasons for national differences in financial reporting practices

The classification of national accounting systems has generally taken the form of 'Anglo-Saxon' and 'Continental Europe' models. However, other models have been developed by researchers trying to understand national accounting systems from differing perspectives.

Differences in national accounting systems can generally be explained by economic, legal, political and cultural factors. Meek and Saudagaran (1990) identify five external environmental and institutional factors for which there is a general consensus:

- the legal system affecting the accounting standardisation process (common law countries versus code law countries);
- business financing practices (whether financing is obtained via the stock market or from financial institutions);
- the tax system, and particularly its connection with accounting;
- the level of inflation likely to influence valuation methods; and
- the political and economic relationships between countries – for example, links from colonisation.

5   The classification of national accounting systems

The purpose of any accounting classification system is to show the similarities and differences in various countries' accounting systems, based on a study of either domestic regulations or business practices.

Much of the debate on international accounting has revolved around the classification of countries with similar accounting procedures and processes. This has, to a certain extent, reduced the complexity in describing accounting differences and explaining similarities.

Researchers on international accounting have tried to divide countries into groups with similar features based either on common practices, or the national regulations in force. The differences observed in information disclosure and/or application methods undermine the understanding and comparability of financial statements. This has resulted in a comparative review of national practices for work on convergence, **standardisation** and **harmonisation**.

Classifying national accounting systems is a useful exercise to identify areas of concern and helps to address such differences. However, changing and converging accounting principles has been a long and difficult process, and has given rise to new issues and problems in accounting that require constant monitoring.

Assuming that the standardisation exercise by the IASB will eventually lead to a common set of globally applicable standards for all economic entities; this will, in turn, allow a departure from national GAAP. This will itself mean that accounting information should be easier to understand from an international viewpoint and will extend the cross-border flow of capital. Nevertheless, national differences on the basis of culture, national company law and different taxations systems, etc, may be a barrier to complete global harmonisation. Issues relating to the interpretation of standards will be hampered by individual interpretation of accounting treatments at a local level. For example, the Coalition Government in the UK, led by David Cameron, announced changes to the banking system whereby UK banks will be required to keep their retail arms separate from their more risky investment activities, thereby protecting certain investments. These changes, which came into force in 2013, may create financial reporting difficulties in the future for UK banks (e.g. how would banks be required to report financial information about issues relating to group accounting?).

TEST YOUR KNOWLEDGE 1.2

Outline the benefits derived from classifying national accounting systems.

The ever-increasing use of global accounting and financial information has made it necessary to reduce the differences in the way accounting information is prepared and reported in different countries. In reducing accounting differences, standard setters use two particular approaches to standards development:

1 standardisation
2 harmonisation.

5.1 Standardisation

Standardisation is the process by which rules are developed to set standards for similar items on a global basis. Through standardisation, many technical issues relating to the treatment of accounting information have been resolved (e.g. the preparation of information relating to earnings per share (IAS 33) is now recognised globally, and is applied consistently using appropriate measures and stated on the statement of comprehensive income).

5.2 Harmonisation

Harmonisation reconciles national differences and provides those who prepare accounting information with a common framework to deal with major issues in a similar manner.

As efforts to improve comparability of financial statements have increased, the two approaches have come closer together. Attempts have been made to standardise, or at least harmonise, financial reporting to satisfy the needs of a number of different stakeholders. To make informed economic decisions, investors need clear and comparable information to assess a company's past or potential investment performance and its underlying economic reality.

Government agencies such as tax and customs authorities also have an interest in greater compatibility of information between countries to trace transactions. International accountancy firms have large numbers of multinational clients, whose accounts frequently need to be adjusted to common accounting principles before consolidations can be prepared. A reduction in national accounting differences would reduce the training costs of these firms and increase staff mobility (however, it would also limit the fees they could charge).

Companies seeking capital through cross-border listings may currently need to prepare financial statements under more than one set of regulations, to meet the needs of different stock exchanges. This is both costly and time-consuming. However, almost every stock exchange will accept accounts prepared under IFRS. A number of international bodies are involved in the processes of harmonisation or standardisation. These include organisations that may not immediately be associated with accounting, such as the United Nations (UN) and the Organization for Economic Co-operation and Development (OECD). However, the most influential organisations have probably been the IASB and the European Union (EU) via the European Financial reporting Advisory Group (EFRAG).

The process of standardisation and harmonisation through accounting standards has created an accounting environment that places an obligation on companies to disclose the **accounting policies** they have used to prepare their accounts.

This inevitably helps those who use accounts to better understand the information presented. Additionally, standards allow entities to be compared due to the consistency of accounting procedures used in the reporting of accounting information, on the basis that accounting standards:

■ require companies to disclose information in the financial statements which they otherwise would not if the standards did not exist;
■ reduce the number of choices in the method used to prepare financial statements and therefore should reduce the risk of creative accounting. This should help the users of financial statements to compare the financial performance of different entities;

- provide a platform in the accounting profession for discussion about accounting practice and to lobby the accounting setting bodies such as the IFRS and Financial Reporting Council (FRC) (UK); and
- should increase the credibility of financial statements with the users by improving the amount of uniformity of accounting treatment between companies.

6   The work of international standard setters

The major international bodies have accelerated their programmes of work and have sought greater cooperation in recent years. This section sets out something of their histories and structures, before relating the latest developments in their strategies and the effect this is likely to have on the annual reports of companies.

6.1   The International Accounting Standards Board

Following a review between 1998 and 2000, the International Accounting Standards Committee (IASC) was restructured to give an improved balance between geographical representation, technical competence and independence. The 19 trustees of the IASC represented a range of geographical and professional interests and were responsible for raising the organisation's funds and appointing the members of the Standing Interpretations Committee (SIC).

The IASB, founded in 2001, and the successor to the IASC, is responsible for the development of the IFRS.

IFRS are principles-based standards for financial reporting. They have been issued by the IASB since 2001. Many accounting standards continue to be called IAS. However, since 2001, the development of accounting standards is referred to as IFRS.

The objectives of the IASB are:

- to develop, in the public interest, a single set of high-quality, understandable and enforceable global accounting standards that require high-quality, transparent and comparable information in financial statements and other financial reporting to help participants in the world's capital markets and other users to make economic decisions;
- to promote the use and rigorous application of those standards; and
- to bring about convergence of national accounting standards and IFRS.

Convergence can be defined as:

- reducing international differences in accounting standards by selecting the best practice currently available, or, if none is available, by developing new standards in partnership with national standard setters. The convergence process applies to all national regimes and is intended to lead to the adoption of the best practice currently available.

The IASB is responsible for all technical matters including the preparation and implementation of IAS.

The process of producing a new IFRS is similar to that of national accounting standard setters. Once the need for a new (or revised) standard has been identified, a steering committee is set up to identify the relevant issues and draft the standard. Drafts are produced at various stages and are exposed to public scrutiny. Subsequent drafts take account of comments obtained during the exposure period.

The final standard is approved by the board and an effective implementation date agreed. IFRS and IAS currently in effect are referred to throughout the rest of this book. This process assists in the development of future accounting standards and improves harmonisation by providing a basis for reducing the number of accounting treatments permitted by IFRS and IAS.

Professional accountancy bodies have prepared and published translations and guidance inter-pretations of IFRS and IAS, making them available to a wide audience in a number of formats, most notably the website www.iasplus.com created by Deloitte that gives a detailed history of the standard and practical implications. The IASC has itself set up a mechanism to issue inter-pretations of the standards.

IAS and IFRS (referred to below simply as 'IAS') may be applied in one of the following ways:

- An IAS may be adopted as a national accounting standard. This can be useful where there are limited resources and an 'off the peg' solution is required (e.g. in Botswana, Cyprus and Zimbabwe). The disadvantage is that the standard may not meet specific local needs, due to the influence of the larger industrialised nations on the IAS.
- An IAS may be used as a national requirement but adapted for local purposes (e.g. in Fiji and Kuwait).
- National requirements may be derived independently, but are adapted to conform to an IAS. This is currently the procedure in the UK, although the programmes of the IASB and Accounting Standards Board (ASB) converged some years ago and work together to develop standards jointly, for example IAS 37 and Financial Reporting Standards (FRS) 12.

It is important to note that if a company wishes to describe its financial statements as comply-ing with IAS, IAS 1 requires the financial statements to comply with all the requirements of each applicable standard and each applicable interpretation of the SIC. This clearly outlaws the practice of 'partial IAS' reporting, where companies claim compliance with IAS while neglecting some of their more onerous requirements.

The old IASC had a large number of members, so it was difficult to achieve a consensus on many of the issues that the committee has addressed. Consequently, many IAS initially permit-ted a range of treatments. While this was an improvement on not having a standard at all, it was still far from ideal. In response to this criticism, the IASC began its comparability/improve-ments project in 1987, which resulted in the revision of ten standards. The IASB adopted all IAS in issue, but soon identified the need for further improvement.

TEST YOUR KNOWLEDGE 1.4

What is the role of the IASB in the process of financial reporting?

6.2 The revised structure of the IFRS/IASB

6.2.1 The Trustees of the IFRS Foundation

The IFRS Foundation (known as the IASC Foundation until 2001) appoints members of the IASB.

It is responsible for raising funding for the standards setting process.

6.2.2 The IFRS Advisory Council

The IFRS Advisory Council (previously the Standards Advisory Council) liaises with individuals who have an interest in financial reporting.

It advises the IASB regarding its agenda and priorities.

6.2.3 The IASB

The IASB was formed in 2001. It succeeded the IASC and inherited accounting standards already issued.

It is responsible for issuing IFRS.

6.2.4 The IFRS Interpretations Committee

The IFRS Interpretations Committee provides practical guidance on the application of IFRS.

Its interpretations are known as IFRIC. It replaced the Standards Interpretation Committee (SIC) in April 2001.

6.3 The European Commission

The European Commission (EC) is the EU executive body that has worked extensively in the past few years to promote IFRS particularly among member states. The work of the EC is directed towards promoting the quality, comparability and transparency of the financial reporting by companies.

In 2005, the EC took a significant step and made the use of IFRS obligatory for the consolidated financial statements of EU companies that are listed on the EU's stock markets.

In relation to listed companies, the EC work extends beyond the EU's borders and goes towards promoting the use of IFRS as the worldwide financial reporting language, thus enhancing the efficiency and transparency of capital markets throughout the globe.

To offer guidance to the EC and serve the public interest a private association was established in 2001, known as the European Financial Reporting Advisory Group (EFRAG) of which the FRC is one of eight national organisations in the 16-member general assembly.

EFRAG's purpose is 'to serve the European public interest by developing and promoting European views in the field of financial reporting and ensuring these views are properly considered in the IASB standard-setting process and in related international debates'. EFRAG ultimately provides advice to the EC on whether newly issued or revised IFRS meet the criteria in the IAS Regulation for endorsement for use in the EU, including whether endorsement would be conducive to the European public good, built on transparency, governance, due process (which may include field tests, impact analyses and outreaches), public accountability and thought leadership.

Following the result of the UK Referendum in June 2016 to leave the EU it is yet unknown the extent to which this will effect financial reporting. Initial market volatility in an uncertain political climate will certainly impact businesses within the UK with respect to opportunity and risk, investors will look for clear communication and transparency in company strategic reports to provide sufficient information upon which to base decisions.

6.4 UK GAAP

Accounting standards have their roots in various sources. In the UK, the principal standard-setting body is the ASB, which issues standards called FRS. The ASB is part of the FRC that took over from the Accounting Standards Committee (ASC), which was disbanded in 1990.

The principal legislation governing reporting in the UK is found in the **Companies Act** 2006, which incorporates the requirements of European law. The Companies Act dictates certain minimum reporting requirements for companies (e.g. it requires limited companies to file their accounts with the Registrar of Companies, which are then available to the general public).

From 2005, this framework changed as a result of European law requiring that all listed European companies report under IFRS. In the UK, companies that were not listed had the option to report either under IFRS or under UK GAAP.

6.4.1 New UK GAAP

The UK's FRC has published five standards which form the foundation of the new reporting regime:

■ FRS 100 'The Application of Financial Reporting Requirements' sets out the new reporting framework, explaining which standard apply to which entities. Certain criteria related to size of company allow reduced disclosure and classification; these will be discussed further on in the chapter.

■ FRS 101 and FRS 102 'The Financial Reporting Standard applicable in the UK and Republic of Ireland', a new financial framework specifically for small and micro entity reporting which will replace current UK GAAP FRSSE (Financial Reporting Standard for Smaller Entities), with effect for periods beginning on or after 1 January 2016.

- FRS 103 consolidates existing financial reporting requirements for insurance contracts
- FRS 104 sets out the interim reporting requirements for entities applying FRS 102
- FRS 105 details further reporting implications for micro entities.

6.5 US GAAP

Accounting standards in the US are typically referred to as US GAAP. US GAAP are a set of accounting standards used to prepare and present financial reports for a range of entities, including public and private enterprises, non-profit organisations, and government departments. US GAAP is usually limited to the US.

Currently, the Financial Accounting Standards Board (FASB) is the highest authority to establish GAAP for public and private companies, as well as for non-profit entities. However, listing requirements by the US Regulator thee Securities & Exchange Commission (SEC) call for companies to follow IFRS.

> **STOP AND THINK** 1.1
>
> What is the advantage of having a single set of IFRS?

7 The theoretical framework of accounting

Research in various areas of accounting and finance, particularly during the past five decades, has greatly influenced standard setting and development. Most notable is the **agency theory**, which defines the characteristics of a public limited company (a company which may be listed on a capital market).

Jensen and Meckling (1976) developed the notion of agency theory and suggested that the modern corporation exists on the basis of the principal–agent relationship, where the owner (shareholder) is the principal and the manager is the agent. It is envisaged that, as the custodian over the **assets** of the firm, the manager will act in the best interests of the owner, and hence look to maximise the owner's wealth. However, due to a misalignment of common interests, the manager may pursue their own interests at the expense of the principal. In such circumstances, the principal will incur monitoring costs to keep a check on the agent's activities and take corrective action where necessary.

The idea of a conflict of interests between the two contracting parties (principal and agent) is the cornerstone of the agency theory. The two parties will enter into contracts that facilitate their interests and minimise agency costs (costs incurred by the principal in monitoring the agent). Since the agent has superior knowledge of the principal, in relation to the underlying economic reality of the company, at any given time, a difference of information (information asymmetry) will exist between the principal and the agent. To mitigate and minimise such differences, the contracting parties will seek to optimise their relationship.

The monitoring processes take many forms; however, corporate governance is the mechanism by which control is exercised by the board of directors over the activities of the managers. Internally adopted mechanisms of corporate governance seek to enhance financial reporting and give a measure of confidence to accounting information users. The UK Code on Corporate Governance (2010) is a principles-based set of guidelines that require listed companies on the London Stock Exchange to 'comply or explain' in their financial reporting.

The UK Code on Corporate Governance is overseen by the FRC and its relevancy is derived through the Financial Services Authority's (FSA) listing requirements. The FSA was replaced by the Financial Conduct Authority (FCA) in 2013 and many of its responsibilities passed to the Bank of England. UK listings rules have a statutory authority under the Financial Services and Marketing Act 2000 (FSMA).

8   Arguments for and against accounting standards

8.1 The arguments for accounting standards

The corporate collapse of some well-known major international companies such as Enron (2001), Worldcom (2002), Parmalat (2003) and more recently Satyam (2009) highlighted the need for transparency in financial reporting. These corporate collapses necessitated the need for standardisation, harmonisation and convergence to protect stakeholder interests. However, these corporate collapses in large part were due to fraud, with irregularities in accounting procedures being pervasive and regulators being told untruths about the state of affairs of the various companies.

Accounting standards oblige companies to disclose the accounting policies they have used to prepare their published financial reports. This should make the financial information easier to understand and allow both shareholders and investors to make informed economic decisions.

Accounting standards require companies to disclose information in the financial statements that they might not disclose if the standards did not exist.

Accounting standards reduce the risk of creative accounting. This means that financial statements can be used to compare either the financial performance of different entities or the same entity over time.

Accounting standards provide a focal point for discussion about accounting practice. They should increase the credibility of financial statements by improving the uniformity of accounting treatment between companies.

Various EU accounting directives have sought to create minimum reporting standards so as to develop a common approach to financial reporting. The accounting directives commonly referred to are: the Fourth (Annual Accounts of Limited Companies, 1978), the Seventh (Consolidated Accounts of Limited Companies, 1983) and the Eighth (Company Law, 1984). Each directive gives separate accounting guidance on the preparation and reporting of accounting information and various elements that must be shown on the face of financial statements. The aim of the accounting directives is to facilitate the commonality and hence the transparency of accounting information across the EU member states, to help the flow of capital.

Due to the global nature of capital movement, stakeholders demand quality financial reports and accounting information which can be relied upon for consistency, commonality and overall transparency. Accounting standards try to achieve that aim, and the IASB is constantly working to reduce accounting differences.

8.2 The arguments against accounting standards

It is acknowledged that standards fulfil a valuable short-term role by ensuring that all companies adopt the best procedures, but people in some quarters believe that the standards may prove to be detrimental in the long term. Over the years, considerable improvements have been made in the form and content of published accounts, and much of this has occurred as the result of free market experiment and innovation. To place financial reporting procedures in a standardised straitjacket might, it is argued, therefore be to the longer-term detriment of those who use financial statements. In a nutshell, a major potential hazard of standards is that, although they may be intended as a floor, they end up as a ceiling.

A second problem is that, as the industry itself is not standard, it seems unlikely that the figures they produce are amenable to a large degree of standardisation. The tendency is therefore to enforce standards that are suitable for the average firm (the majority) but not for those on the margins. Many areas disagree about which method should be used (e.g. whether to use average weighted cost, last in first out (LIFO) or first in first out (FIFO) to value **inventories**, or whether to use the deferral method or the flow-through method to account for deferred taxation). The choices made by accounting standard setters, although often based on sound reasoning, can remain somewhat arbitrary.

Standards may remove the need for accountants to exercise their judgment – a crucial feature of their status as professionals. Accountants are concerned that their role will be relegated to that of a mere technician who does no more than slot figures, calculated in accordance with accounting standards, into their appropriate location. This concern seems to be exaggerated because, although numerous matters are standardised, there is still plenty of scope for accountants to exercise their professional judgment. Indeed, an important drawback of standardisation is that it gives an illusion of precision and comparability, which is totally unjustified in view of the wide range of subjective decisions that still have to be made.

A final criticism directed at the standard-setting process is that there are too many regulations. Over fifty international standards have been issued and, although several have been withdrawn, more are in the pipeline. One suggestion is that a 'plethora of principles' has been replaced by a 'surfeit of standards'.

TEST YOUR KNOWLEDGE 1.5

What are the benefits of the existence of accounting standards?

---

9   Corporate governance and the external audit process

In recent years, corporate governance and the **external audit** process has become invariably linked as bodyguards in the statutory reporting of financial performance. However, our primary concern is to understand what is meant by the term 'corporate governance' and an 'external audit'. Our secondary concern is to understand how the two concepts operate in isolation and together in the quest to safeguard the process and output of financial reporting.

9.1 The audit

The external audit is a statutory requirement enshrined in the Companies Act of the UK and other national jurisdictions. It is a process whereby an auditor appointed by the shareholders (members) provides an independent opinion on the financial statements. The auditor will provide an opinion on whether the financial statements exhibit a **true and fair view** of the company's financial performance and position, and whether it has been prepared in compliance with accepted and recognised accounting and auditing standards without any material error or omissions.

In essence, the audit process can be regarded as a process whereby the auditor examines the financial statements prepared by the company against set criteria, to provide assurance to intended users of the financial statements in the form of an opinion.

The auditor will provide an opinion of 'true and fair' if the accounts are satisfactory. Otherwise they will provide a qualified opinion, which means they are not of the opinion that the financial statements, as presented, provide a true and fair reflection of the company. An audit opinion on the true and **fair presentation** of the financial statements is required because an audit does not involve a 100% examination of the accounting records and systems but a selected sample of the accounting records and systems.

In the UK, it is mandatory for all public listed companies to have their financial statements audited by an independent auditor. Private limited companies are also subject to a company audit. However, any private limited company with a financial year end on or after 1 January 2016 can qualify for an audit exemption, if they satisfy at least two of the following conditions:

- an annual turnover of no more than £10.2 million;
- assets worth no more than £5.1 million; or
- 50 or fewer employees on average.

An audit-exempt company can have their financial statements subjected to an audit if shareholders (an individual shareholder or a group of shareholders) who own at least 10% of shares (by number or value) request an audit. The request for an audit must be made in writing and sent to the company's registered address.

The purpose of an audit is not to detect fraud, but to provide assurance to the users of the financial statements that the financial statements have been prepared in accordance with approved accounting standards. The assurance gained by the users from an audit is the increased confidence and reduction in the risks associated from the use of financial statements for their own economic decisions. The audit process is an independent examination of the accounting systems and internal controls installed by management to facilitate effective financial reporting and business performance. An audit includes an examination of evidence relevant to the amounts and disclosures in the financial statements. It also includes an assessment of the significant estimates and judgments made by the directors in preparing the financial statements. The audit is conducted in accordance with International Standards on Auditing (UK and Ireland) issued by the Audit Division of the FRC (formerly via the Auditing Practices Board).

Generally, however, auditors express an opinion of the true and fair view of the financial figures being reported. In so doing, they must have regard to the level of audit risk presented, and the level of audit work that must be carried out to enable a view to be expressed.

An external audit process ensures that a company's internal controls, processes, guidelines and policies are adequate, effective and comply with applicable legal and accounting standards, industry standards and the company's own policies and procedures. The external audit also helps ensure reporting mechanisms prevent errors in financial statements. The users of audit reports are all parties who have a vested interest in the company, such as investors, company management, regulators and business partners such as lenders, suppliers and creditors.

The external audit provides reassurance to all user groups who have a vested interest in the financial affairs of a company (e.g. company management, regulators and investors). The audit enables both the senior management and the audit committee (within plcs) of a company to determine operating breakdowns and segments showing higher risks of loss and, where necessary, to take appropriate action to safeguard the assets of the company. An auditor's job is not to comment on the efficiency and proficiency of a company's financial performance, but to verify that the financial statements are free from material error.

Regulators use audit reports to detect business trends and corporate practices and to ensure that such practices comply with the law. Investors read audit opinions to gauge a company's economic standing and management's short-term initiatives or long-term strategies.

An audit committee is a composition of the board of directors of a company, consisting of executive and non-executive directors. It has special responsibilities for both the internal and external audit functions. The audit committee has responsibility to provide the auditors with guidance, support and direction.

Despite the mandatory requirement of company audits there has been the discovery of several notable global corporate failures. Some of the notable corporate failures are set out in Table 1.1.

TABLE 1.1 Sample of global corporate failures 1991–2014

Company	Country
Colonial Life Insurance Company Limited	Trinidad & Tobago
Enron Corporation	US
Harris Scarfe	Australia
HIH Insurance	Australia
Madoff Investment Securities	US
Maxwell Corporation	UK
MCI WorldCom	US
Olympus Corporation	Japan
OneTel	Australia
Polly Peck International	UK
Satyam Computer Services Limited	India
Banco Espirito Santo (BES)	Portugal

It is evident from Table 1.1 that corporate failures are not confined to any national or regional jurisdiction. However, it is against this backdrop that the external audit has shifted and become aligned with corporate governance.

Outline the conditions that must be satisfied to allow a company an audit exemption.

9.2 Corporate governance

Corporate governance is defined in the UK Corporate Governance Code as 'the system by which companies are directed and controlled'. Corporate governance has grown in importance as the interest of the company owners (shareholders) and its agents (the officers) have grown more diverse. Companies are owned by its shareholders; however, they entrust a company's management to the board of directors (officers), who are in effect the agents. One of the principal roles of the officers is to safeguard the assets of the company plus a fiduciary responsibility. However, over the years a divergence has grown in the goals of both sides. In summary, it may be argued that shareholders possess a long-term horizon and seek to increase shareholder value, whereas the officers have a shorter-term perspective that is driven by personal goals.

The board of directors are charged with the responsibility to install systems and internal controls that ensure the effective operation of the company. Thus the board has the overall responsibility for the activities and events that a company may undertake, either directly or indirectly. Hence the chief executives or chairmen or chief operating officers will often stand down in the face of adverse activity or events that damage the reputation of their company. Similar to corporate failure, there have been numerous noteworthy such cases in the last few decades.

Corporate governance provides a supportive framework and operating environment for the reporting of corporate financial performance. The operation of best practices of corporate governance and supportive policies and procedures is a means of communicating with the company's shareholders and stakeholders to reassure them that they can rely on the financial statements and outputs from the company.

It is this assurance and reassurance of the stakeholders that brings the audit and corporate governance together.

Corporate governance may be regarded as the pillars that underpin all the features of the company that impacts upon its corporate reporting and behaviour, whereas the external audit is merely one of the pillars, with the sole focus upon the financial statement's adherence to best accounting and auditing practices.

The growth of the role of corporate governance across the globe has increased the prominence of social and environmental reporting, as entities begin to embrace their impact upon the environment, and the recognition of costs that is not imputed in our neo-classical model of business and the price mechanism for goods and services.

10   Environmental reporting and sustainability

10.1   Environmental Protection Act 1990

Environmental law can be traced as far back as the 1860s, when controls on air pollution from industrial units and factories necessitated legislation due to the release of harmful substances in the air. The Environmental Protection Act 1990 consolidated older laws into more relevant legislation. The Act gave rise to legal implications for directors of companies. They could be prosecuted if it could be proved that they had neglected their duty to protect the environment. The Act was a major development in environmental protection in the UK.

10.2   Industry initiatives

ISO 14000 (International Organization for Standardization – Standard 14000) is a voluntary code that addresses environmental management and prevention. It is an industry-led standard that requires companies to abide by certain conditions relating to environmental issues. ISO 14000 requires companies to document and work towards reducing or eliminating pollution and processes that can be harmful to the environment. ISO 14000 was the basis on which the Environmental Management System (EMS) was developed. EMS is a management system designed to achieve organisational directives and policies regarding the environmental impact of an organisation's activities.

10.3 Economic consequences for environmental reporting

Pressures on corporations and the demand for environmental-related information have led to a plethora of disclosures on environmental reporting. However, environmental disclosures have economic implications for the company. Environmental reporting can be defined as:

> [t]he process of communicating externally the environmental effects of an organisation's economic actions through the corporate annual report or a separate stand-alone publicly available environmental report.

Invariably, disclosures would relate to the policy, procedures and processes and environmental audit in a company's environmental report. Consequently, users will assess (on the basis of information provided) the economic and reputational impact of such policies. Expenditure and benefits that transpire will be assessed for **sustainability**. A report by the ACCA (Association of Chartered Certified Accountants) on Singapore firms that disclose environmental matters looked at the impact of environmental reporting and identified ten important issues that have an economic impact on company environmental disclosures:

1 *Risk management* – in areas of financial, legal and reputation implications.
2 *Marketing strategy* – public image, brand enhancement such as through receiving environmental awards.
3 *Legal needs* – to keep in pace with/anticipate regulations.
4 *Competition* – to get ahead of/stay with competitors.
5 *Ethics* – individual commitment, commitment to accountability and transparency.
6 *Accounting requirements* – in compliance with financial reporting requirements and providing a link between financial and environmental performance/reporting.
7 *Investors' interests* – demands of green (ethical) investors.
8 *Employees' interests* – attracts right staff from the labour market.
9 *Value-added reporting* – to add value to corporate reports and communicate to a wider range of stakeholders, addressing their environmental concerns.
10 *Certification needs* – to indicate compliance with ISO 14000 and other environmental regulatory guidelines.

Various emerging regulations and the implications for financial reports indicate that there is a move towards **'integrated reporting'** on CSR (corporate social responsibility) and environmental issues that allow interactivity on web-based publication of such reports. Web-based facilities would enhance user perceptions and that of the company by allowing users to extract specific information that will help them to make economic decisions.

10.4 Stand-alone environmental reporting

There is now an expectation that businesses should operate in a way that reduces any adverse impact on the environment to an absolute minimum. Measuring the impact that a company has on the environment presents challenges to accountants. While some of the increased emphasis on all things environmental may be due to genuine concern, some is driven by market forces, as businesses that are considered environmentally irresponsible are likely to lose market share.

Stand-alone environmental reporting is primarily web-based disclosure. It is usually separate from a company's annual report and other company publications devoted to issues on the impact of company operations on the environment. The quality and quantity of environmental reports partly depend on the nature of the business in which a company operates. Industries such as pharmaceuticals, chemical, petroleum and gas have attracted the most attention on environmental issues. These industries have led the way in environmental reporting. Some countries make it mandatory to publish environmental reports: Denmark, Sweden, Norway and Holland all require environmental reports by law, particularly from environmentally sensitive industries.

10.5 Sustainability

The term sustainability was first coined in the Brundtland report (1987) where the World Commission on Environment and Development was asked to formulate a 'global agenda for change' by the General Assembly of the UN. Brundtland defined sustainable development as:

'Development that meets the needs of the present without compromising the ability of future generations to meet their own needs.'

Forming part of corporate governance codes of practice and linked closely to CSR businesses are now called upon to report on the inherent sustainability within their strategic and operational business practices, also referred to as the three P's of sustainability or triple bottom line (TBL): people (social), planet (ecological) and profit (economic).

TEST YOUR KNOWLEDGE **1.7**

Explain the term 'corporate governance'.

11   Eco-Management and Audit Scheme (EMAS)

11.1   What is an environmental audit?

An environmental audit is a tool that a company can use to identify the full extent of its environmental impact. It enables a company to determine its level of compliance with relevant legislation and with its own environmental policies, thus enabling users of the report to understand achievements and shortcomings in company environmental practice.

11.2   EMAS

The EMAS is an audit tool specifically designed for eco-management audits. It allows a company to determine both its environmental impact and determine ways to improve, or reduce, such impact. As greater numbers of companies realise that not taking part in environmental reporting has economic consequences, the EMAS assists companies to report in more or less a standardised fashion.

The EMAS was first made available as far back as 1995, with a particular emphasis on companies in the industrial sector. However, the scheme has now been extended to all businesses.

In 2009 the EMAS Regulation was revised and modified for the second time. Regulation (EC) No. 1221/2009 of the European Parliament and of the Council of 25 November 2009 on the voluntary participation by organisations in a Community EMAS was published on 22 December 2009 and entered into force on 11 January 2010.

The main elements of the EMAS tool require the disclosure of the following information.

a Conduct an environmental review
The organisation needs to conduct a verified initial environmental review, considering all environmental aspects of the organisation's activities, products and services, methods to assess them, the organisation's legal and regulatory framework and existing environmental management practices and procedures.

b Adopt an environmental policy
Registration to EMAS requires an organisation to adopt an environmental policy and to commit itself both to compliance with all relevant environmental legislation and to achieving continuous improvement in its environmental performance.

c Establish an EMS

Based on the results of the environmental review and the policy (objectives), an Environmental Management System (EMS) needs to be established. The EMS is aimed at achieving the organisation's environmental policy objectives as defined by the top management. The management system needs to set responsibilities, objectives, means, operational procedures, training needs, monitoring and communication systems.

d Carry out an internal environmental audit

After the EMS is established, an environmental audit should be carried out. The audit assesses in particular if the management system is in place and in conformity with the organisation's policy and programme. The audit also checks if the organisation is in compliance with relevant environmental regulatory requirements.

e Prepare an environmental statement

The organisation needs to provide a public statement of its environmental performance. The environmental statement lays down the results achieved against the environmental objectives and the future steps to be undertaken in order to continuously improve the organisation's environmental performance.

f Independent verification by an EMAS verifier

An EMAS verifier accredited with an EMAS accreditation body of a Member State must examine and verify the environmental review, the EMS, the audit procedure and the environmental statement.

g Register with the Competent Body of the Member State

The validated statement is sent to the appropriate EMAS Competent Body for registration and made publicly available.

h Utilise the verified environmental statement

The environmental statement can be used to report performance data in marketing, assessment of the supply chain and procurement. The organisation can use information from the validated statement to market its activities with the EMAS logo, assess suppliers against EMAS requirements and give preference to suppliers registered under EMAS.

Source: http://ec.europa.eu/environment/emas/pdf/leaflet/emasleaflet_en.pdf

11.3 The environmental audit process

The format and procedural activities of an environmental audit will vary depending on the nature of the business, geographical location and the level of environmental impact. The environmental audit will take into account external factors such as the target audience and level of disclosure.

Generally, environmental audits involve the collection, collation, analysis, interpretation and presentation of information. This information is then used to:

- assess performance against a list of pre-set targets, related to specific issues;
- evaluate and assess compliance with environmental legislation as well as corporate policies; and
- measure performance against the requirements of an EMS standard.

To facilitate a successful environmental audit, the audit process requires progression through the following three stages:

1 Pre-audit stage
   - full management commitment;
   - setting overall goals, objectives, scope and priorities; and
   - selecting a team to ensure objectivity and professional competence.
2 Audit stage
   - on-site audit, well defined and systematic using protocols or checklists;
   - review of documents and records;
   - review of policies;

- interviews; and
- site inspection.
3 Post-audit stage
- evaluation of findings;
- reporting with recommendations;
- preparation of an action plan; and
- follow-up.

STOP AND THINK   **1.2**

What would the economic impact for companies be if they did not report on their environmental and social activities?

The three stages provide the general framework or an environmental audit. However, depending upon the size and nature of the entity some areas may require a more in-depth investigation. This will, in most cases, involve specialist advice, independent verification and co-operation, and action on any shortcomings identified during the audit stage.

12 Social accounting

Social accounting (also known as corporate social responsibility or CSR) is the formal process by which business entities communicate the impact of their economic activity to stakeholders who have a vested interest in the entity. However, it has and is continuing to become recognised that the wider community has a direct and indirect involvement in CSR and the behaviour of entities. For example, the impact of the Deepwater Horizon oil spillage in 2010 has had more than just a financial impact upon British Petroleum.

Social accounting seeks to create a balance between a company's business activities and how it discharges its social and environmental responsibilities. However, it is a broad term that can mean different things to different people. In the example of BP and the Deepwater Horizon oil spillage in 2010, a variety of stakeholders have been and continue to be affected. Some have lost their livelihoods, while others have had to move out of their homes.

The range of reporting a company can engage in with a view to reporting on social accounting can include:

1 recycling of waste;
2 education;
3 environment/pollution emission/chemicals;
4 regeneration, social inclusion and community investment;
5 workforce issues;
6 responsible behaviour in developing countries;
7 agriculture;
8 pharmaceuticals/animal testing/drug development; and
9 regeneration issues etc.

The process involves undertaking regular evaluation of what an organisation does through consultation/audit. Using feedback from relevant stakeholders, a company can monitor, adjust and plan its activities. Future performance can be more effectively targeted to achieve an organisation's objectives. From a broader perspective, social accounting is a mechanism that adds value to a company's financial report by providing information about non-financial activities and the related costs of business behaviour in society.

The Social Audit Network (SAN) is an entity that supports non-governmental organisations (NGOs) and charitable organisations both in the UK and internationally. The SAN has well-defined objectives to help social organisations to attain an understanding of the environment in which these organisations operate. These should be:

- *multi-perspective*: encompassing the views of people and groups that are important to the organisation;
- *comprehensive*: inclusive of all activities of an organisation;
- *comparative*: able to be viewed in the light of other organisations and addressing the same issues within same organisation over time;
- *regular*: done on an ongoing basis at regular intervals;
- *verified*: checked by people external to the organisation; and
- *disclosed*: readily available to others inside and outside of the organisation.

When information is available, discerning and risk-averse investors can put pressure on companies to change or enhance their business practices to recognise the social agenda. This can only be achieved when there is a consistent flow of relevant and useful information over a sustained period of time.

Social accounting can be viewed from two competing perspectives: management control and accountability, allowing organisations to pursue profits as well as social objectives for a sustainable future.

Management exercises control over the resources and assets of a business. Social accounting can help management to facilitate internal corporate planning and objectives. All entities can obtain the following benefits from implementing social accounting and reporting:

- commensurate sharing of information on business activities;
- precise transfer of costs to the consumer;
- reputational and corporate legitimacy;
- increased market presence and awareness;
- investor-friendly image; and
- awareness of social responsibilities.

Since the management control perspective is inward-looking, social accounting can be meaningful through external party participation which can verify organisational commitment to society. Some of these external parties include independent social audit, certification on standards and compliance and periodic and consistent reviews by independent persons or organisations.

TEST YOUR KNOWLEDGE 1.8

Explain the meaning of social accounting.

---

13 Integrated reporting (IR)

An integrated report is a 'concise communication about how an organisation's strategy, governance, performance and prospects lead to the creation of value, over the short, medium and long term.' As defined in the International Integrated Reporting Framework developed by the International Integrated Reporting Council (IIRC). Integrated reporting (IR) combines social, ethical, environmental and economic aspects of accounting to provide stakeholders with a holistic view of the organisation's performance to allow stakeholders to make a more informed assessment of the future value creation ability of the firm.

The two essential concepts of integrated reporting are 'capitals' and the 'value creation process', explained in the International Integrated Reporting Framework as:

'The capitals are stores of value that are increased, decreased or transformed through the activities of the outputs of the organization. They are categorized in this Framework as financial, manufactured, intellectual, human, social and relationship, and natural capital, although organizations preparing an integrated report are not required to adopt this categorization or to structure their report along the lines of the capitals. The ability of an organization to create value for itself enables financial returns to the providers of financial capital. This is interrelated with the value the organization creates for stakeholders and society at large through a wide range of activities, interactions and relationships. When these are material to the organization's ability to create value for itself, they are included in the integrated report. (IIRF)'

Integrated Reporting is currently a hotly debated topic in the financial accounting arena, as to its need and use there can be little doubt. The IIRC produced a discussion paper in 2011, including feedback from large companies already piloting (IR) demonstrating overwhelming support and of most beneficial use to investors.

14   The changing role of the accountant

14.1   The modern corporation

Today's accountant is no longer the isolated, unconnected bean counter in the back room. The role and practice of the accountant is now very much integrated at the forefront, driving and steering the business through unchartered waters, some which are shark infested!

The accountant is now a key player in the strategic development of an entity and no longer reports solely on financial performance to a narrow audience. Today's accountant has a central and direct role in the process of business. They communicate a wide range of accounting and financial information to internal and external stakeholders and as such, core skills on the growing list of professional competencies attributable to accountants in business, must be related to clear, concise and effective communication.

 ## END OF CHAPTER QUESTIONS

1.1 What are the objectives of the IASB?

1.2 Why is there a need for the existence of accounting standards?

1.3 What is the purpose of the external audit?

1.4 What is the role of corporate governance in financial reporting?

1.5 How can an entity benefit from social accounting and reporting?

The conceptual framework for the preparation and presentation of financial statements

■ CONTENTS

■ LEARNING OUTCOMES

Chapter 2 continues our coverage of the syllabus section entitled 'The regulatory and conceptual frameworks for financial reporting'.

In this chapter, we focus on the conceptual framework for the preparation and presentation of financial statements.

After working through this chapter, you should understand and be able to explain:

■ the objective and users of financial statements;
■ the underlying assumption of going concern;
■ the qualitative characteristics that determine the usefulness of information in financial statements;
■ the definition of the elements of financial statements;
■ the recognition of the elements from which financial statements are constructed;
■ the measurement of assets and **liabilities** reported in financial statements; and
■ the concepts of capital and capital maintenance.

1 Introduction

The joint development of the Conceptual Framework for Financial Reporting 2010 by the International Accounting Standards Board (IASB) and US Financial Accounting Standards Board (FASB) was the end of the first phase in the development of an improved conceptual framework for International Reporting Standards and US Generally Accepted Accounting Principles (GAAP). This is another staging post in the ongoing journey in the development and evolution of an internationally recognised and agreed framework for financial reporting.

The conceptual framework considers the theoretical and conceptual issues of financial reporting to develop a consistent platform to underpin the development of accounting standards.

Financial statements are prepared and presented for external users by many entities around the world. Although such financial statements may appear similar from country to country, there are differences which have arisen from a variety of social, economic and legal circumstances, and by different countries having in mind the needs of different users of financial statements when setting national requirements.

These different circumstances have led to the use of a variety of definitions of the elements of financial statements: for example, assets, liabilities, equity, income and expenses. They have also resulted in the use of different criteria for the recognition of items in the financial statements and in a preference for different bases of measurement. The scope of the financial statements and the disclosures made in them have also been affected.

The IASB is committed to narrowing these differences by seeking to harmonise regulations, accounting standards and procedures relating to the preparation and presentation of financial statements.

It believes that further harmonisation can best be pursued by focusing on financial statements that are prepared for the purpose of providing information that is useful in making economic decisions.

The Board believes that financial statements prepared for this purpose meet the common needs of most users. This is because nearly all users are making economic decisions, for example:

a   to decide when to buy, hold or sell an equity investment;
b   to assess the stewardship or accountability of management;
c   to assess the ability of the entity to pay and provide other benefits to its employees;
d   to assess the security for amounts lent to the entity;
e   to determine taxation policies;
f   to determine distributable profits and **dividends**;
g   to prepare and use national income statistics; and
h   to regulate the activities of entities.

The IASB recognises that governments, in particular, may specify different or additional requirements for their own purposes. These requirements should not, however, adversely affect the usability of the financial statements for any group of users.

Financial statements are most commonly prepared in accordance with an accounting model based on recoverable **historical cost** and the nominal financial capital maintenance concept. These concepts are discussed later in this chapter. Other models and concepts may be more appropriate in order to meet the objective of providing information that is useful for making economic decisions although there is at present no consensus for change. The conceptual framework has been developed so that it is applicable to a range of accounting models and concepts of capital and capital maintenance.

The Conceptual Framework for Financial Reporting 2010

This conceptual framework sets out the concepts that underlie the preparation and presentation of financial statements for external users. The purpose of the conceptual framework is:

a   to assist the Board in the development of future IFRS and in its review of existing IFRS;
b   to assist the Board in promoting harmonisation of regulations, accounting standards and procedures relating to the presentation of financial statements by providing a basis for reducing the number of alternative accounting treatments permitted by IFRS;
c   to assist national standard-setting bodies in developing national standards;
d   to assist preparers of financial statements in applying IFRS and in dealing with topics that have yet to form the subject of an IFRS;
e   to assist auditors in forming an opinion on whether financial statements comply with IFRS;
f)   to assist users of financial statements in interpreting the information contained in financial statements prepared in compliance with IFRS; and
g   to provide those who are interested in the work of the IASB with information about its approach to the formulation of IFRS.

The conceptual framework is not an IFRS and hence does not define standards for any particular measurement or disclosure issue. Nothing in the conceptual framework overrides any specific IFRS.

The Board recognises that in a limited number of cases there may be a conflict between the conceptual framework and an IFRS. In those cases where there is a conflict, the requirements of the IFRS prevail over those of the conceptual framework.

As, however, the Board will be guided by the conceptual framework in the development of future IFRS and in its review of existing IFRS, the number of cases of conflict between the conceptual framework and IFRS will diminish through time.

The conceptual framework will be revised from time to time on the basis of the Board's experience of working with it.

2   The scope of the conceptual framework

The conceptual framework addresses the preparation and presentation of financial reports for external user groups. The conceptual framework deals with:

a   the objective of financial reporting;
b   the qualitative characteristics of useful financial information;
c   the definition, recognition and measurement of the elements from which financial statements are constructed; and
d   concepts of capital and capital maintenance.

The conceptual framework is the foundation for addressing the emerging challenges in accounting and its financial reporting. The conceptual framework provides the nature, boundaries and functions for the effective financial reporting of accounting information.

The framework clearly recognises the general purpose of financial reporting as follows:

'The objective of general purpose financial reporting is to provide financial information about the **reporting entity** that is useful to existing and potential investors, lenders and other creditors in making decisions about providing resources to the entity.'

The framework also recognises the general purpose of financial statements:

'General purpose financial reports provide information about the financial position of a reporting entity, which is information about the entity's economic resources and the claims against the reporting entity. Financial reports also provide information about the effects of transactions and other events that change a reporting entity's economic resources and claims. Both types of information provide useful input for decisions about providing resources to an entity.'

In addition, the framework also clearly states what purpose financial reports are *not* designed to perform or provide:

'General purpose financial reports are not designed to show the value of a reporting entity; but they provide information to help existing and potential investors, lenders and other creditors to estimate the value of the reporting entity.'

The qualitative characteristics of useful financial information are addressed within the conceptual framework identified as the fundamental and enhancing qualitative characteristics of information.

2.1   The emergence of a conceptual framework

Is there a need for a conceptual framework? Practitioners and academics alike have debated this question over the years. Without subscribing to any camp, it is necessary to examine the position that existed within the world of accountancy and financial reporting without conceptual frameworks:

1   Accounting standards evolved without much consistency or connectivity.
2   Standards had a tendency to evolve in a reactive rather than a proactive manner. Consider the rise and fall in the accounting for changing prices and latterly corporate failures (scandals).
3   The lack of consistency often gave rise to the same theoretical issue being addressed across multiple standards.

4   The lack of balance on some standard setting boards resulted in standards being skewed in one particular direction.

However, the absence of a conceptual framework gave rise to a rules-based prescriptive approach to financial reporting. Despite the prescriptive nature, the twin benefits that arise are consistency and comparability in financial reporting. This contrasts with the principles-based approach that comes from the conceptual framework evolution. The result of a financial reporting based upon an agreed conceptual basis may be the decline in consistency and comparability for users who rely on the information to make economic decisions.

3   Users of financial information

Within the conceptual framework, potential investors, lenders and creditors are identified as the primary users to whom general purpose financial reports are directed. The conceptual framework also highlights that users' needs are different and may conflict.

'Individual primary users have different, and possibly conflicting, information needs and desires. The Board, in developing financial reporting standards, will seek to provide the information set that will meet the needs of the maximum number of primary users. However, focusing on common information needs does not prevent the reporting entity from including additional information that is most useful to a particular subset of primary users.'

Despite the identified primary group of three within the conceptual framework, the users of financial reporting information will be widened to encompass the seven users first identified in the 1975 Corporate Report by the Accounting Standards Steering Committee (ASSC). These are the following.

1   *Investors*: The providers of risk capital are concerned with the risk inherent in, and return provided by, their investments. They need information to help them determine whether they should buy, hold, or sell. They are also interested in information which enables them to assess the ability of the enterprise to pay dividends.
2   *Lenders*: They are interested in information that enables them to determine whether their loans, and the interest attaching to them, will be paid when due.
3   *Employees*: Employees and their representative groups are interested in information about the stability and profitability of their employers. They are also interested in information which enables them to assess the ability of the enterprise to provide remuneration, retirement benefits and employment opportunities.
4   *Suppliers and other trade creditors*: They are interested in information that enables them to determine whether amounts owing to them will be paid when due. Trade creditors are likely to be interested in an enterprise over a shorter period than lenders (unless they are a major customer).
     Customers: They have an interest in information about the continuance of an enterprise, especially if they have a long-term involvement with, or are dependent on, the enterprise.
6   *Government agencies*: Governments and their agencies are interested in the allocation of resources and, therefore, the activities of enterprises. They also require information to regulate the activities of enterprises, determine taxation policies and to serve as the basis for determining national income and similar statistics.
7   *The public*: Enterprises affect members of the public in a variety of ways. For example, they may make a substantial contribution to the local economy in many ways including the number of people they employ and their patronage of local suppliers. Financial statements may assist the public by providing information about the trends and recent developments in the prosperity of the enterprise and the range of its activities.

TEST YOUR KNOWLEDGE 2.1

a   Identify four user groups of financial information.
b   Outline the uses for each of the four user groups.

4   Qualitative characteristics of useful financial information

The conceptual framework (paragraph QC3) asserts that the qualitative characteristics of useful financial information are not restricted to the reporting of information in the financial statements.

'The qualitative characteristics of useful financial information apply to financial information provided in financial statements, as well as to financial information provided in other ways.'

The qualitative characteristics of information are classified into two tiers to meet their usefulness: fundamental and enhancing.

4.1 Fundamental characteristics

The conceptual framework outlines two fundamental characteristics for useful financial information: relevance and **faithful representation**.

4.1.1 Relevance

Financial information is relevant when it is capable of making a difference in the decisions made by its users. Financial information would still be relevant if some decision-makers chose not to use the available information. Financial information is relevant in the decision-making process of the user when it can be used to help predict the outcomes of future events, or to confirm the outcome of a past event. In summary, the reported financial information can provide predictive and confirmatory values for the decision-making process of the decision-maker. For example, profit information reported in a company's current year financial statement may be used to help predict future profit performance and to compare with previous predictions for the current year. This demonstrates the interrelationship of the predictive value and confirmatory value of financial information.

The relevance of the financial information is also dependent upon the degree of materiality embedded in the information. Information is regarded as material if its omission or misstatement would affect the decisions made by the users. Consider the following example: Enfield Islands Plc, a large company, has a warehouse in the Thames River Basin District. The warehouse is destroyed as a result of severe flooding and after a lengthy battle with the insurance company, the company reports an extraordinary loss of £20,000. The company has net income of £20,000,000. The materiality concept states that this loss is immaterial because the average stakeholder would not be overly concerned with an item that is 0.1% of net income.

If, in the example above, the company is a small or medium-sized enterprise (SME) with net income of £100,000 the loss has a significantly greater impact at 20% of net income. This is deemed a substantial loss for the company and considered material, possibly causing some concern to stakeholders

4.1.2 Faithful representation

Faithful representation is explained in paragraphs QC12–QC16 of the conceptual framework as the concept that the financial statements accurately reflect the condition of a business. For example, if a company reports in its statement of financial position that it had a current asset of £43,201 as accounts receivable as at the end of June, then that amount should indeed have been evident on that date.

The concept of faithful representation must encompass all elements of the financial statements, including the results of operations, financial position, and cash flows of the reporting entity. Financial statements that faithfully represent these aspects of a business should have the following three attributes:

■ *Complete*: All information that a reader of financial statements needs in order to form a clear picture of the results, financial position, and cash flows of a business are included in the financial statements. This means that no information is omitted that lead a reader to form a different opinion of, or make an alternative decision about, the business. For example, a business could report that it had a £200,000 loan as at the statement of financial position date, but this would not be considered complete unless additional information about the loan were provided, such as its maturity date.

- *Neutral or free from bias*: The financial statements represent the actual state of an organisation, without trying to amplify its results unnecessarily or present an unfavourable picture. For example, biased financial statements could be used to give an overly optimistic view of a business in order to encourage a prospective buyer to pay a higher price for it. Conversely, financial statements could be manipulated report a worse position in order to reduce the related income tax liability.
- *Free from error*: The financial statements should contain no errors, the information contained within them presents a true and fair view of the organisation. Frequent and regular errors in the statements reduce stakeholder confidence and in some cases can lead to fraudulent financial reporting.

4.2 Enhancing characteristics

The fundamental characteristics are supported by four enhancing characteristics that make reporting financial information useful for its users: comparability, verifiability, timeliness and understandability.

4.2.1 Comparability

Users of financial information often want to make a comparison between time periods or within the same time period for similar companies. Comparability is the qualitative characteristic that enables users to identify and understand the similarities in, and differences among, items in their comparative analysis. Comparability does not relate to a single item. Consistency, although related to comparability, is not the same. Consistency refers to the use of the same methods for the same items, either from period to period within a reporting entity or in a single period across entities. Comparability is the goal, whereas consistency is the methodology to achieve that goal.

Comparability is not uniformity. For information to be comparable, similar things must look similar and different things must look different. This will be further demonstrated when undertaking comparative financial analysis and the use of ratio analysis.

4.2.2 Verifiability

Verifiability is the quality that helps to assure users that the reported financial information faithfully represents the economic phenomena it purports to represent. Verifiability would permit two or more different knowledgeable and independent observers to reach consensus that a particular depiction is a faithful representation. Verifiability may be regarded as underpinning the granting of a true and fair view audit opinion for any set of company financial statements. Verification can be direct or indirect. Direct verification may arise from the process of direct observation, such as the end-of-year stock count.

Indirect verification is the process of checking using a calculation model or technique to verify the financial information. An example of the indirect verification is the use of the cost of sales model (opening stock plus purchases less closing stock) to verify any of the elements therein.

4.2.3 Timeliness

Timeliness is the provision of the information to decision-makers with sufficient time to allow the information to influence their decisions. Financial information such as company financial reports should be made available to decision-makers in a timely manner to allow them ample time to make their decision about the company.

4.2.4 Understandability

Information should be classified, characterised and presented clearly and concisely to facilitate understanding by users. The users of financial information are deemed to have a reasonable knowledge of business and economic activities such that the exclusion of a complex phenomenon should not occur to ease understanding. The advantage gained from the ease of understanding would result in the information being incomplete, misleading and not a full representation.

In summary, to be useful to its users reported financial information must be relevant and faithfully represented. Neither a faithful representation of an irrelevant phenomenon nor an unfaithful representation of a relevant phenomenon helps users to make good decisions.

A single or collection of the enhancing qualitative characteristics cannot make irrelevant information useful or faithfully represented.

TEST YOUR KNOWLEDGE 2.2

List and explain the role of qualitative characteristics in the preparation of financial reports.

4.3 Constraints on the provision of information

The conceptual framework recognises that cost is a constraint on the ability to provide useful financial information. In view of the costs of reporting, it is necessary that the benefits gained from the reported financial information is greater than the costs incurred in the reporting. The providers of financial information expend time and money in the collecting, processing, verifying and dissemination of financial information. Consequently, the trade-off for users of financial information is fewer returns as the costs being incurred become greater.

Furthermore, it is not possible for general purpose financial reports to provide all the information that every user requires.

5   The underlying assumption

The **going concern** concept is the only underlying assumption identified in the conceptual framework. This is a departure from the IFRS twin bedrock accounting principles of going concern and **accruals**.

The assumption as set out in the conceptual framework para 4.1 is as follows. The financial statements are normally prepared on the assumption that an entity is a going concern and will continue in operation for the foreseeable future. Hence, it is assumed that the entity has neither the intention nor the need to liquidate or curtail materially the scale of its operations; if such an intention or need exists, the financial statements may have to be prepared on a different basis and, if so, the basis used is disclosed.

Practical examples of the application of the going concern assumption:

■ Assume Banana Plc, a large multi-million-pound corporation, is in the process of suing a small communications company for copyright violation over its latest mobile phone design. Since this phone is the only line the communications company produces, losing this lawsuit would be significantly detrimental to their business. There is a 97% expectation that Banana Plc will win the lawsuit. The small communications company is not a going concern because it is probable they will be out of business after the lawsuit is settled.
■ In 2011, Gibson Guitar Factory, was under scrutiny by the US Justice Department for illegally smuggling endangered wood into the country. The Justice Department took more than $250,000 worth or Gibson's inventory and charged them with large fines for violating international laws. Gibson is still considered a going concern, because it is not likely the fines and punishment will stop its operations (www.investors.com).

6   Elements of financial statements

The financial statements in the form of the statement of financial position (the balance sheet) and the statement of profit or loss and other comprehensive income (the income statement) are respectively reporting on changes in an entity's financial position and measurement of its performance. Both these statements classify their elements to provide information to enable users to make their economic decisions.

The five elements that are classified in the financial statements are shown in Figure 2.1 are:

a   income;
b   expenses;
c   assets;
d   liabilities;
e   equity.

Financial statements

Statement of financial position (Measure of financial position)	Statement of profit or loss and other comprehensive income (Measure of performance)
1. Assets 2. Liabilities 3. Equity	1. Income 2. Expenses

FIGURE 2.1 The classification of elements in financial statements

The conceptual framework provides the following definitions for the five elements of financial statements.

1   An *asset* is a resource controlled by the entity as a result of past events and from which future economic benefits are expected to flow to the entity.
2   A *liability* is a present obligation of the entity arising from past events, the settlement of which is expected to result in an outflow from the entity of resources embodying economic benefits.
3   *Equity* is the residual interest in the assets of the entity after deducting all its liabilities.
4   *Income* is an increase in economic benefits during the accounting period. Income takes the form of inflows or enhancements of assets and decreases of liabilities that result in increases in equity (other than those relating to contributions from equity participants).
5   *Expenses* are decreases in economic benefits during the accounting period. Expenses take the form of outflows or depletions of assets or incurrences of liabilities that result in decreases in equity (other than those relating to distributions to equity participants).

🖋 **TEST YOUR KNOWLEDGE** **2.3**

Identify and distinguish between the elements of financial statements.

---

7   Recognising the elements of financial statements

Elements of financial statements become recognised when they are included in the financial statements: the statement of financial position (the balance sheet) and the statement of profit or loss and other comprehensive income (the income statement). To be recognised, elements must satisfy the following conditions:

a   It is probable that any future economic benefit associated with the item will flow to or from the entity.
b   The item has a cost or value that can be measured with reliability.

Thus recognition introduces the concepts of probability and measurement reliability. The producers of financial statements have to make an assessment on the probability of any future economic benefit flowing from an item. Such is often the case with the decision to write off a **debt** as a bad debt or the making of a provision for a doubtful debt, (allowance for receivables). The application of a reliable estimate in financial reporting does not serve to render the financial statement unreliable in content. The estimate of the useful life of a non-current (fixed) asset does not invalidate the statement of financial position (the balance sheet) and the statement of profit or loss and other comprehensive income (the income statement) – although both financial statements are affected by the estimate used to calculate the annual depreciation charge.

Where an essential element is unable to meet the criteria for recognition, its disclosure is not dismissed. Disclosure of the element may occur in the form of explanatory notes to the financial statements when knowledge of the item would be relevant to the assessment of the financial statements and the economic decision by the users of financial statements.

8 Measuring the elements of financial statements

Items and elements recognised within financial statement reporting are measured by the assignment of monetary units. The measurement basis most commonly applied in the preparation of and reporting in financial statements is the historical cost. However, historical cost often co-exists with other measurement bases. The conceptual framework outlines in para 4.55 the following basis for the measurement of elements recognised within financial statements.

- **Historical cost**. Assets are recorded at the amount of **cash or cash equivalents** paid or the **fair value** of the consideration given to acquire them at the time of their acquisition. Liabilities are recorded at the amount of proceeds received in exchange for the obligation, or in some circumstances (for example, income taxes), at the amounts of cash or cash equivalents expected to be paid to satisfy the liability in the normal course of business.
- **Current cost**. Assets are carried at the amount of cash or cash equivalents that would have to be paid if the same or an equivalent asset was acquired currently. Liabilities are carried at the undiscounted amount of cash or cash equivalents that would be required to settle the obligation currently.
- **Realisable (settlement) value**. Assets are carried at the amount of cash or cash equivalents that could currently be obtained by selling the asset in an orderly disposal. Liabilities are carried at their settlement values – that is, the undiscounted amounts of cash or cash equivalents expected to be paid to satisfy the liabilities in the normal course of business.
- **Present value**. Assets are carried at the present discounted value of the future net cash inflows that the item is expected to generate in the normal course of business. Liabilities are carried at the present discounted value of the future net cash outflows that are expected to be required to settle the liabilities in the normal course of business.

TEST YOUR KNOWLEDGE 2.4

Explain the economic consequences of different accounting practices under **current cost**, realisable cost and **present value** approaches.

8.1 Valuing assets and liabilities

International Accounting Standard (IAS) 1 states: 'An entity shall present separately each material class of similar items. An entity shall present separately items of a dissimilar nature or function unless they are immaterial.' Typically, items on the face of the statement of financial position are presented as 'assets' or 'liabilities' in the form of current and non-current assets and liabilities. IAS 1 further states that it is not permitted to **offset** assets or liabilities or income and expenses unless required or permitted by an IFRS.

WORKED EXAMPLE 2.1

A manufacturer imports a new production line from France and holds a launch party in the factory. The costs associated with the transaction are listed below.

	£
Purchase price	250,000
Import duties	5,600
Delivery costs	6,800
Installation costs	7,600
Cost of launch event to celebrate the new production line	3,800

Required
What total cost should be recognised in the asset category **'property, plant and equipment'**?

Suggested solution
The 'cost of the launch event to celebrate the new production line' is excluded from the computation of the total cost of procuring the machinery, because it is not directly related to the acquisition and/or installation of the machinery to undertake its productive function. The total cost of procurement of the asset is £270,000 (250,000 + 5,600 + 6,800 + 7,600).

Similarly, the present obligation of a liability can be demonstrated as per the example below.

WORKED EXAMPLE 2.2

Havent plc entered into a three-year lease for an item of plant that had a cost price (fair value) of £25,379 on 1 January 20X5. The implicit rate of interest applied half-yearly is 5%.

The terms of the lease are as follows:
a   Lease period: three years.
b   Frequency of rental payments: six monthly in arrears.
c   Amount of each six monthly rental payment: £5,000.
d   First payment: 30 June 20X5.

The estimated useful life of the plant is three years. Havent plc depreciates all non-current assets using the straight-line basis.

Required
a   Prepare a schedule of lease payments for Havent plc.
b   Show how the lease would be reported in the statement of comprehensive income for the years ended 31 December 20X5 and 20X6 and the statements of financial position as at 31 December 20X5 and 20X6.

Answer
a   Schedule of lease payments

Period	Opening balance	Interest	Rental	Closing balance
01/01/20X5–31/06/20X5	25,379	1,269	(5,000)	21,648
01/07/20X5–31/12/20X5	21,648	1,082	(5,000)	17,730
01/01/20X6–30/06/20X6	17,730	887	(5,000)	13,617
01/07/20X6–31/12/20X6	13,617	681	(5,000)	9,298
01/01/20X7–30/6/20X7	9,298	465	(5,000)	4,763
01/07/20X7–31/12/20X7	4,763	238	(5,000)	0

⊞ **WORKED EXAMPLE** **2.1** *continued*

b   Havent plc statement of comprehensive income for the year ended 31 December 20X6:

	20X5	20X6
	£	£
Depreciation (25,379/3 years)	8,460	8,460
Interest	2,351	1,568

Havent plc statement of financial position as at 31 December 20X6:

	20X5	20X6
Non-current assets	£	£
Property, plant and equipment-cost	25,379	25,379
Accumulated depreciation	8,460	16,920
	16,919	8,459
Liabilities		
Lease obligation	17,730	9,298

⊞ **WORKED EXAMPLE** **2.3**

Edgar Ltd is evaluating an investment opportunity and expects the future cash flows arising as in the table below. Edgar requires a return of at least 10% on its investments. The expected life of the investment is expected to be five years with no residual value.

Year	Cash flow
0	(250,000)
1	80,000
2	80,000
3	72,000
4	68,000
5	45,000

Required
Calculate the **net present value** of all future cash flows and comment on the viability of the investment.

Answer

	Year	Cash flow	Calculation of PV	Discount factor	PV
Investment in year 0	0	(250,000)	$250,000/(1+0.1)^0$	1	(250,000)
Cash inflow in year 1	1	80,000	$80,000/(1+0.1)^1$	0.9091	72,727
Cash inflow in year 2	2	80,000	$80,000/(1+0.1)^2$	0.8265	66,116
Cash inflow in year 3	3	72,000	$72,000/(1+0.1)^3$	0.7513	54,095
Cash inflow in year 4	4	68,000	$68,000/(1+0.1)^4$	0.6830	46,445
Cash inflow in year 5	5	45,000	$45,000/(1+0.1)^5$	0.6209	27,942
Net present value (NPV)					17,325

Since the net present value of the initial investment and future cash inflows is positive, we know the project exceeds the target 10% return. The investment opportunity should be accepted.

WORKED EXAMPLE 2.4

Tanner Ltd runs a nationwide convenience store business with many stores around the country. Recently the company re-valued its chain of stores on a fair value basis. The fair value assessment revealed an increase in the value of land and building by £40 million in 20X6. See extract of statement of financial position for 20X5 below:

	20X6 £m
Non-current assets	
PPE	412
Land and buildings	602
Equities and liabilities	
Equity	1,200
Revaluation reserve	0

Required

Assuming all other assets and liabilities remain the same, reflect the amended information in the extract of the balance sheet for Tanner Ltd.

Answer

Extract from the statement of financial position for Tanner Ltd as amended to reflect the changes in value to land and buildings. Land and buildings would increase by £40 million, while a revaluation reserve would be created in equity and liabilities:

		ADJUSTED
	20X5 £m	20X6 £m
Non-current assets		
PPE	412	412
Land and buildings (602 + 40)	602	642
Equities and liabilities		
Equity	1200	1200
Revaluation reserve	0	40

8.2 Impairment of assets and value-in-use

IAS 36 Impairment of Assets (as discussed later in Chapter 4) addresses the impairment of assets and aims 'to ensure that assets are carried at no more than their recoverable amount, and to define how recoverable amount is determined'. IAS 36 further states that **value-in-use** is the discounted present value of the future cash flows expected to arise from the continuing use of an asset, and from its disposal at the end of its useful life.

The standard gives further guidance on testing assets for impairment in relation to their carrying amount. The calculation of value-in-use should reflect the following elements:

- an estimate of the future cash flows the entity expects to derive from the asset;
- expectations about possible variations in the amount or timing of those future cash flows;
- the time value of money, represented by the current market risk-free rate of interest;
- the price for bearing the uncertainty inherent in the asset; and
- other factors, such as illiquidity, that market participants would reflect in pricing the future cash flows the entity expects to derive from the asset.

WORKED EXAMPLE 2.5

Solar Ltd suspects its printing press, with a net book value (after depreciation) of £280,000, is impaired. However, in the absence of a market price, Solar carries out value-in-use exercise. Its **cost of capital** is 10%. Solar has determined the future cash flows arising from the continued use of the asset as:

Year	Cash flow
1	100,000
2	86,000
3	76,000
4	68,000
5	52,000

Required
Determine if the asset is impaired based on current book value of the asset and its value-in-use.

Answer

Year	Cash flow	Discount factor 10%	PV
1	100,000	0.9091	90,910
2	86,000	0.8264	71,070
3	76,000	0.7513	57,099
4	68,000	0.6830	46,444
5	52,000	0.6209	32,287
Net present value			297,810
Value-in-use of the asset:			297,810
Net book value of the asset (NBV)			280,000
Carrying amount = NBV			280,000

Since the value-in-use of the asset is greater than the book value, the asset is deemed not to be impaired and the book value remains at £280,000 net of depreciation.

TEST YOUR KNOWLEDGE 2.5

Describe three ways in which an asset or a liability can be measured.

9   Capital and capital maintenance

Two concepts of capital are in existence: a financial concept of capital and a physical concept of capital. The former is usually applied in the preparation of financial statements. The financial concept of capital is synonymous with the net assets or equity of a company, whereas the physical concept of capital, such as operating capability, concerns the productive capacity of a company, often determined upon by its daily production or output.

The two concepts of capital generate two concepts of capital maintenance as outlined in para 4.59 of the conceptual framework.

1 *Financial capital maintenance.* According to this concept, a profit is earned only if the financial (or monetary) amount of the net assets at the end of the period exceeds the financial (or monetary) amount of net assets at the beginning of the period, after excluding any distributions to, and contributions from, owners during the period. Financial capital maintenance can be measured in either nominal monetary units or units of constant purchasing power.

2 *Physical capital maintenance.* According to this concept, a profit is earned only if the physical productive capacity (or operating capability) of the entity (or the resources or funds needed to achieve that capacity) at the end of the period exceeds the physical productive capacity at the beginning of the period, after excluding any distributions to, and contributions from, owners during the period.

WORKED EXAMPLE 2.6

The following example relates to two American listed companies, America Online (AOL) and Time Warner (TW). AOL was engaged in internet services (i.e. provision of internet-based applications). TW was an entertainment company engaged in films and other entertainment products.

It is not typical of an examination in financial reporting and analysis, however, its purpose is to highlight how larger companies can make detrimental mistakes.

In 2000, the merger between AOL and TW was seen as one of the biggest corporate collaboration in recent times. TW's strategy for the future seemed clear and straightforward; by tapping into AOL, TW would have an established customer base of millions of home subscribers. AOL and TW could merge each other's resources in a marriage of convenience with high-speed cable lines to deliver to the new companies. This would have created 130 million subscription relationships.

With the advent of the worldwide web and upcoming dot.com companies, and steep demand for online services, the growth and profitability of the AOL division declined sharply, due to advertising and subscriber slowdowns due mainly to the burst of the dot.com bubble and the economic recession after September 2001. The value of the AOL division dropped significantly, not unlike the market valuation of similar independent internet companies that drastically fell. This forced a **goodwill** write-off, causing AOL-TW to report a loss of $99 billion in 2002 – at the time, the largest loss ever reported by a company. The total value of AOL stock subsequently fell from $226 billion to about $20 billion.

Consequently there followed great upheaval within AOL, with internal politics being played out among competing executives.

When the AOL-TW merger was announced in January 2000, the combined market capitalisation was $350 billion. It subsequently fell dramatically. Even by the time the merger was approved by the relevant supervisory bodies, a year later on 11 February 2001, the company's market capitalisation had plummeted to $208.6 billion. By 2009, the company's value had tumbled even further, to just $65.7 billion, or approximately one-sixth of its value at the height of the dot.com bubble era when the deal was announced.

The expected synergies between AOL and TW divisions never materialised, as most TW divisions were considered to be independent companies that had rarely cooperated prior to the merger. A new incentive programme that granted options based on the performance of AOL TW, replacing the cash bonuses for the results of their own division, caused resentment among TW division heads, who blamed AOL for failing to meet expectations and dragging down the combined company. AOL TW chief operating officer (COO) Pittman, who expected to have the divisions working closely towards convergence, instead found heavy resistance from many division executives, who also criticised him for adhering to optimistic growth targets for AOL TW that were never met.

WORKED EXAMPLE 2.6 *continued*

For the fiscal year 2002, the company reported a $99 billion loss on its income statement because of $100 billion in non-recurring charges, almost all from a write-down of the goodwill (intangible asset) from the merger in 2000. This loss is one of the largest in corporate history. The value of the AOL portion of the company had dropped sharply with the collapse of the Internet boom, in the early twenty-first century. On 4 February 2009, TW posted a $16.03 billion loss for the final quarter of 2008, compared with a $1.03 billion profit for the same three months of 2007.

AOL-TW was criticised by analysts for its aggressive accounting methods and the quality of its reported earnings figures. This was mainly related to the capitalisation of certain marketing costs; these marketing costs, which were substantial in size, should have been expensed and hence impacted upon the earnings figures.

Required

Having read the related issues, answer the questions that follow:

Issue: Substantial marketing costs, measuring millions of dollars, such as subscriber acquisition (costs related to securing new and retaining old customers) and costs of subscriber kits (costs in respect of distributing hardware and software to customers) and direct marketing expenses were capitalised. Subscriber costs were charged to the income statement over the average lifetime of subscriptions. This practice was seen as unusual in common accounting practice under GAAP.

1 How should the marketing and subscriber-related costs be treated by AOL?
2 What impact would the practice of capitalisation by AOL have on reported earnings?
3 What possible impact would there be on reported earnings and **earnings per share (EPS)** if AOL had charged marketing expenses to the income statement in the first place?
4 Discuss the flexibility the framework allows a reporting entity in the choice it makes when using accounting choices.
5 Under the agency theory, what factors could potentially influence managers' choice of accounting policy?
6 How should AOL be more transparent in its deliberation of accounting choices from a qualitative perspective?
7 What accounting concepts should AOL declare in its annual reports to allow users of financial information to make informed accounting decisions?

10 Accounting policies and the significance of differences between them

10.1 Nature of accounting policies

Accounting policies essentially refer to specific accounting principles and the methods of applying those principles adopted by a business entity in the preparation and presentation of financial statements. However, there is no single list of accounting policies that applies to every situation.

Companies operate in a diverse and complex marketplace. Choosing the appropriate accounting bases and the methods of applying those principles requires a certain degree of judgment on the part of management.

Regulatory requirements together with IFRS guidance on preparing and presenting financial statements have reduced the number of options available to management. With the level of convergence set to increase further, particularly between IFRS and US GAAP, these alternatives will be further eroded, with the result that greater transparency will be achieved in financial statements. Nevertheless, the availability of alternative accounting practices of applying those principles is not likely to be eliminated altogether in view of the differing circumstances faced by the enterprises that may transpire over time or because of regional issues.

TEST YOUR KNOWLEDGE 2.6

Explain what is meant by the nature of accounting policies, and how different companies can treat assets and liabilities differently.

10.2 The significance of differences in accounting policies

The following are examples of the areas in which different accounting policies may be adopted by different business entities:

- impairment of assets;
- methods of depreciation, depletion and amortisation;
- treatment of expenditure during construction;
- conversion or translation of foreign currency items;
- valuation of inventory;
- treatment of goodwill;
- valuation of investments;
- treatment of retirement benefits;
- recognition of profit on long-term contracts;
- valuation of fixed assets; and
- treatment of contingent liabilities.

Changes to accounting and measuring procedures of assets and liabilities from one period to the next may blur reality and present misinformation for users. Business entities must ensure that economic reality is faithfully represented and that accounting and reporting principles are followed.

As an example, if a company changes its accounting policy on the way it measures depreciation on assets, this must be declared in the notes to the financial statements narratives and an explanation provided as to why the changes have occurred. The change may have a material impact on the book value of the assets.

WORKED EXAMPLE 2.7

Potter Ltd is engaged in the mining of coal. It has an item of plant, which originally cost £300,000. This has been depreciated over five years on a straight-line basis. At the start of Year 4, Potter Ltd decides to switch to the reducing-balance method to calculate depreciation.

Required
Calculate the impact of Potter Ltd switching to the reducing-balance method at the start of Year 4 and its impact on the financial statements assuming a depreciation rate of 20%.

Calculation for depreciation on straight-line basis:

Year	Cost £	Depn £	NBV £
0	300,000		
1		60,000	240,000
2		60,000	180,000
3		60,000	120,000
4		60,000	60,000
5		60,000	0

WORKED EXAMPLE **2.7** *continued*

Calculation for depreciation on reducing-balance basis:

Year	Cost £	Depn £	NBV £
0	300,000		
1		60,000	240,000
2		60,000	180,000
3		60,000	120,000
4		24,000	96,000
5		19,200	76,800
NBV of asset after five years			76,800

(*Note*: NBV = Net Book Value/Carrying Amount)

On a straight-line basis, Potter Ltd would report a depreciation charge of £60,000 per annum in the statement for comprehensive income and a reduction in the same amount on the carrying value of the asset in each subsequent year. After five years, the asset will have a nil residual value. The net book value of the asset in the statement of financial position at the end of Year 4 would be £60,000.

If Potter Ltd switches to the reducing balance method at the start of Year 4, the depreciation charge to the statement for comprehensive income in Year 4 would only be £24,000, thus inflating income for Year 4 by £36,000. At the end of Year 4, the asset would have a carrying amount in the statement of financial position of £76,800.

The directors of Potter Ltd would have to declare the change in accounting estimate for depreciation and demonstrate why the change was necessary in the narratives.

IAS 8 'Accounting Policies, Changes in Accounting Estimates and Errors' states that the effect of a change in an accounting estimate should be recognised prospectively by including it in profit or loss in:

- the period of the change, if the change affects that period only; or
- the period of the change and future periods, if the change affects both.

IAS 8 further states that:

- entities that exercise a change in accounting estimates must further disclose the nature and amount of a change in an accounting estimate that has an effect in the current period, or is expected to have an effect in future periods; or
- if the amount of the effect in future periods is not disclosed because estimating it is impracticable, an entity shall disclose that fact.

❓ END OF CHAPTER QUESTIONS

2.1 Outline the general purpose of financial reporting.

2.2 True or false?

a Financial reports are designed to show the value of a reporting entity.

b Financial reports provide information to help existing and potential employees negotiate a pay increase.

c Financial reports provide information to help existing and potential investors, lenders and other creditors to estimate the value of the reporting entity.

d The qualitative characteristics of useful financial information are restricted to the reporting of information in the financial statements.

e Relevance and faithful representation are the two fundamental characteristics for useful financial information.

f Four bases for the measurement of elements recognised within financial statements are outlined in IAS 1.

2.3 State the four enhanced characteristics that make reporting financial information useful for its users.

2.4 Identify and explain the underlying assumption identified in the conceptual framework.

2.5 Identify two financial statements in the form of the statement of financial position (the balance sheet) and the statement of profit or loss and other comprehensive income (the income statement).

2.6 Identify and explain the two concepts of capital maintenance.

The preparation and presentation of financial statements for single companies in compliance with legal and regulatory requirements

■ **LIST OF CHAPTERS**

■ **OVERVIEW**

Chapters 3, 4, 5 and 6 deal with the preparation and presentation of financial statements for single companies in compliance with legal and regulatory requirements, including the relevant international accounting standards.

3 Financial accounting and the preparation of financial reports

■ LEARNING OUTCOMES

Chapter 3 covers the preparation and presentation of financial statements for single companies. After reading and understanding the contents of the chapter, and going through all the worked examples and practice questions, you should be able to:

■ understand and explain the purpose of financial information and accountability;
■ understand the purpose and uses of financial information and the role of accountability;
■ explain financial accounting and name the principal reporting entities;
■ identify and explain the purpose of the principal accounting statements;
■ understand and explain the uses of accounting information;
■ demonstrate both how financial statements are presented and the prescribed format for the financial reports;
■ understand and apply the concept of measurement and recognition of **revenue**, expenses assets and liabilities; and
■ use additional information in the financial reports.

1   Introduction

There are numerous definitions of accounting, however, most definitions attempt to describe the same basic purpose of accounting. The American Accounting Association (1966) defines accounting as:

> 'the process of identifying, measuring, and communicating economic information to permit informed judgments and decisions by users of the information.'

For the purposes of further discussion, it would be useful to analyse the terminology used in the above definition:

■ It suggests that accounting is about providing information to others. Accounting information is economic information – it relates to the financial or economic activities of the business or organisation.

- Accounting information needs to be identified and measured in a systematic manner. This is done by way of a set of accounts, based on a system of accounting known as **double-entry bookkeeping**. The accounting system identifies and records accounting transactions.
- The measurement of accounting information is not a straightforward process. Accounting involves making judgments about the value of *assets* and *liabilities* owed by a business. It is also about accurately measuring how much profit or loss has been made by a business in a particular period. As we will see, the measurement of accounting information often requires subjective judgment to come to a conclusion.
- The above definition identifies the need for accounting information to be communicated. The way in which this communication is achieved may vary. There are several forms of accounting communication (e.g. annual report and accounts, management accounting reports) each of which serve a slightly different purpose. The communication need is about understanding *who* needs the accounting information and *what* they need to know!

1.1 What are the purposes of the financial statements?

Accounting information is communicated using financial statements. Financial statements have two main purposes:

1   to report on the financial position of an entity (e.g. a business, an organisation); and
2   to show how the entity has performed (financially) over a particularly period of time (an 'accounting period').

The most common measurement of 'performance' is profit. It is important to understand that financial statements can be historical or relate to the future.

TEST YOUR KNOWLEDGE 3.1

a   What is meant by 'accounting'?
b   Demonstrate the purpose of financial statements.

---

2   Accountability

Accounting is about *accountability*. Most organisations are externally accountable in some way for their actions and activities. They produce reports on their activities that will reflect their objectives and the people to whom they are accountable.

The table below provides examples of different types of organisations and how accountability is linked to their differing organisational objectives:

All of these organisations have a significant role to play in society and have multiple stakeholders to whom they are accountable. All require systems of financial management to enable them to produce accounting information.

3   How accounting information helps businesses to be accountable

As described in the introductory definition, accounting is essentially an 'information process' that serves several purposes. It:

- provides a record of assets owned, amounts owed to others and monies invested;
- provides reports showing the financial position of an organisation and the profitability of its operations;
- helps management to manage the organisation;
- provides a way of measuring an organisation's effectiveness (and that of its separate parts and management);
- helps stakeholders to monitor an organisation's activities and performance; and

■ enables potential investors or funders to evaluate an organisation and to make any necessary decisions.

TABLE 3.1 Accountability of different types of organisation

Organisation	Objectives	Accountable to (examples)
Private or public company (e.g. Barclays Bank, Tesco)	Profit creation of wealth	Shareholders Other stakeholders (e.g. employees, customers, suppliers)
Charities (e.g. Age Concern)	Achievement of charitable aims Maximise spending on activities Value for money	Charity commissioners Donors Volunteers
Local authorities (e.g. Liverpool City Council)	Provision of local services Optimal allocation of spending budget	Local electorate Government departments
Public services, such as transport or health (e.g. NHS, Prison Service)	Provision of public service (often required by law) High quality and reliable services	Government ministers Consumers
Quasi-governmental agencies (e.g. Data Protection Registrar, Scottish Arts Council)	Regulation or instigation of some public action Coordination of public sector investments	Government ministers Consumers

There are many potential users of accounting information, including shareholders, lenders, customers, suppliers, government departments (e.g. HM Revenue and Customs (HMRC)), employees and their organisations, and society at large. Anyone with an interest in the performance and activities of an organisation is traditionally called a stakeholder.

For a business or organisation to communicate its results and position to stakeholders, it needs a language that is understood by all in common. Hence, accounting has come to be known as the 'language of business'. There are two broad types of accounting information:

■ Financial accounts are geared toward external users of accounting information.
■ Management accounts are aimed more at internal users of accounting information.

Although there is a difference in the type of information presented in financial and management accounts, the underlying objective is the same: to satisfy the information needs of the user. These needs can be described in terms of the following overall information objectives:

TABLE 3.2 Information objectives

Objective	Description
Collection	Collection in money terms of information relating to transactions that have resulted from business operations.
Recording and classifying	Recording and classifying data into a permanent and logical form. This is usually referred to as book-keeping.
Summarising	Summarising data to produce statements and reports that will be useful to the various users of accounting information – both external and internal.
Interpreting and communicating	Interpreting and communicating the performance of the business to the management and its owners and users of financial information.
Forecasting and planning	Forecasting and planning for future operation of the business by providing management with evaluations of the viability of proposed operations. The key forecasting and planning tool is the budget.

The process by which accounting information is collected, reported, interpreted, and actioned is called financial accounting. Taking a commercial business as the most common organisational structure, the key objectives of financial management would be to:

- create wealth for the business;
- generate cash; and
- provide an adequate return on investment, bearing in mind the risks that the business is taking and the resources invested.

In preparing accounting information, care should be taken to ensure that the information presents an accurate and true view of the business performance and position. To impose some order on what is a subjective task, accounting has adopted certain conventions and concepts which should be applied when preparing accounts.

For financial accounts, the regulation or control of the kind of information that is prepared and presented goes much further. UK and international companies are required to comply with a wide range of accounting standards. These define the way in which business transactions are disclosed and reported. These are applied by businesses through their accounting policies.

TEST YOUR KNOWLEDGE 3.2

a   On what basis is accounting information prepared?
b   Summarise the five principals for whom accounting information is prepared.

---

4   What is financial accounting?

A conventional division of the discipline of 'accounting' is into what are labelled 'financial accounting' and 'management accounting'. Under the two classifications, the following explanation is used to describe both types of approaches to accounting:

- Financial accounting: accounting information prepared for external users, such as investors and lenders. Financial accounting information may influence the economic decisions external users make and is prepared under International Financial Reporting Standards (IFRS) or Generally Accepted Accounting Practice (GAAP).
- Management accounting: accounting information for internal users. Accounting information for management use is prepared for internal monitoring and control in making the most efficient use of limited resources.

5   Reporting entities

Providers of accounting information include the following entities (these are listed in no particular order of priority).

5.1 Sole traders

These are businesses where the sole trader and the entity are the same person. The individual is responsible for all the risks and receives all the reward. Operations are usually on much smaller scale than limited companies. Accounts are prepared primarily for the sole trader to help establish the amount of income tax due to HMRC. The sole trader makes little use of accounting statements for business decisions, which are instead based on knowledge obtained as a result of direct contact with all aspects of business activity.

5.2 Partnerships

These exist where two or more individuals join together to undertake some form of business activity. The partners share ownership of the business and the obligation to manage its operations between them. Professional people, such as accountants, solicitors and doctors, commonly organise their business activities in the form of partnerships. Accounting statements are required as a basis for allocating profits between the partners and, again, for agreeing tax liabilities with HMRC.

5.3 Clubs and societies

There are many thousands of clubs and societies in Britain, organised for recreational, educational, religious, charitable and other purposes. Members pay an annual subscription and management powers are delegated to a committee elected by the members. The final accounts prepared for (usually large) societies are often controlled by statute. For a local club or society, the form of the accounts is either laid down in the internal rules and regulations or decided at the whim of the treasurer. Conventional accounting procedures are sometimes ignored in a small organisation. The reasons for this are lack of expertise, the meagre quantity of assets belonging to the organisation and the fact that the accounts are only of interest to the members.

5.4 Limited companies

A limited company is usually formed by registering with the Registrar of Companies under the provisions of the Companies Act 2006 (CA2006) and complying with certain formalities. The company may be private (indicated by the letters Ltd at the end of its name), or public (in which case the designatory letters are 'plc'). The main significance of the distinction is that only the latter can make an issue of shares to the general public. In the case of public companies, there is a further distinction between quoted companies, whose shares are listed and traded on the stock exchange, and unquoted companies. In general, public companies are larger than private companies and quoted companies larger than unquoted.

The directors of all limited companies are under a legal obligation to prepare and publish accounts, at least once in every year, which comply with the requirements of the CA2006. A limited company may, alternatively, be formed by either a private Act of Parliament or a Royal Charter. Before registration under the Companies Act became possible (prior to 1844) these were the only methods of incorporation available, but they are rarely used today. Companies formed in this way are called statutory and chartered companies, respectively. The form of their accounts may be regulated by their charter or statute and they normally comply with the general requirements of the CA2006. Additionally, the CA2006 also applies to charities that trade, public sector bodies such as hospital trusts and universities, local authorities and quasi-government agencies (companies that are private yet supported by the government). These types of organisations can be considered as reporting entities.

✎ TEST YOUR KNOWLEDGE 3.3

a   Define financial accounting.
b   Distinguish between partnerships and sole traders.

5.5 Financial reporting requirements in relation to size of company

5.5.1 Company size thresholds

Following the latest revision to the CA2006 (effective 6 April 2015), reflecting provisions in the EU Accounting Directive related to the preparation of financial statements for small companies and micro entities, one of the most notable changes was the increase in size thresholds, effecting the financial reporting requirements and related necessary disclosures and seeing approximately 11,000 businesses drop from medium sized to small company classification (Department for Business, Innovation and Skills (BIS)). See table 3.3 for classification thresholds.

TABLE 3.3 Company classification thresholds

Classification	Turnover	Balance Sheet Total	Average no. of employees
Micro-entity	< £632,000	< £316,000	< 10
Small company	< £10.2m	< £5.1m	< 50
Small group	< £10.2m net *OR* < £12.2m gross	< £5.1m net *OR* < £6.1m gross	< 50
Medium-sized company	< £36m	< £18m	< 250
Medium-sized group	< £36m net *OR* <£43.2m gross	< £18m net *OR* < £21.6m gross	< 250
Large company	£36m or more	£18m or more	250 or more
Large group	£36m net or more *OR* £43.2m gross or more	£18m net or more *OR* £21.6m gross or more	250 or more

6   Principal accounting statements

IAS 1 'Presentation of Financial Statements' is the basis by which the primary financial statements are prepared. Limited liability companies prepare annual reports consisting of a complete set of financial statements that include narratives which help to further explain the financial figures. IFRS prescribed standard formats, including IAS 1.10 'Complete Set of Financial Statements', are used to prepare financial reports. These include:

- a statement of profit or loss and other comprehensive income;
- a statement of financial position;
- a statement of change in equity;
- a statement of cash flows; and
- explanatory notes.

The narrative expands upon particular aspects of the financial reports and helps users to make a further qualitative review of the underlying economic reality of the company.

The purpose of financial accounting statements is mainly to provide a report on the financial position of an entity at a particular point in time and to show how that entity has performed during the accounting period.

A statement of financial position (SFP), which replaces the balance sheet for all companies subject to compliance with IFRS, shows what resources are controlled (usually) owned by a business – it's Assets at a particular point in time and what it owes to other parties – its Liabilities. It also shows how much has been invested in the business and what the sources of that investment finance were.

As it is synonymous with the balance sheet, the statement of financial position is a snapshot of the financial position of the entity at a specific point in time. However, while this is a useful picture to have, the snapshot will change every time an accounting transaction takes place.

By contrast, the statement of profit or loss and other comprehensive income (SPLOCI) which is the new name for the profit and loss account or income statement for IFRS-compliant companies provides a review of the performance of the entity during the accounting period. The statement of profit or loss and other comprehensive income is usually for a period of one year, but it may be produced for shorter accounting periods. The statement of profit or loss and other comprehensive income reveals the financial transactions that took place during the accounting period and the overall performance as a result of the financial transactions. The performance of the entity during the accounting period is measured by the accounting profit earned in the accounting period. Accounting profit is the amount by which income receivable for the period (sales revenue/turnover or income) exceeds the expenses incurred in the period.

The range of financial information published by reporting entities varies according to the nature and purpose of their operations. We will now consider the practice of limited companies.

6.1 The statement of profit or loss and other comprehensive income

Revenues are generated and costs are incurred as a result of undertaking business activity. These are summarised in the statement of profit or loss and other comprehensive income. When total revenue exceeds total expenses, the business has made a profit. If total revenue is the same as total expenses, the business 'breaks even'. If total revenue is less than total expenses, the business suffers a loss. From the statement of profit or loss and other comprehensive income, users gain obtain information about:

a   whether a profit (or loss) was made in the period;
b   the amount of the profit (or loss);
c   the level of corporation tax payable;
d   the amount payable to providers of finance;
e   the amount payable to shareholders; and
f   the residual amount of profit retained by the company.

6.2 The statement of financial position

The statement of financial position (previously known as the balance sheet) sets out the financial position of the company at a particular point in time, the end of the accounting period. A key difference between the statement of profit or loss and other comprehensive income and the statement of financial position is that whereas the former reports inflows and outflows of resources over a period of time, the latter sets out the assets and liabilities at a particular point in time.

It is for this reason that the statement of financial position has been likened to a financial photograph of a business. Like all photographs, the position just before or just afterwards may be entirely different. This provides scope for management to undertake cosmetic exercises that present the company's position in the best possible light. For example, it might borrow money just before the year end in order to inflate the cash balance and then repay it on the first day of the next accounting period. Such devices are called 'window dressing' and it is part of the auditor's job to ensure that decision makers are not misled by such procedures.

6.3 The statement of changes in equity

Equity is the residual interest in the assets of the entity after deducting all its liabilities, as defined in 4.4 of the Conceptual Framework for Financial Reporting 2010. Equity may be subclassified in the statement of financial position of a corporate entity into funds contributed by shareholders, **retained earnings**, reserves representing appropriations of retained earnings and reserves.

The statement of changes in equity is an important component of financial statements, since it explains the composition of equity and how has it changed over the year.

The statement of changes in equity summarises the movement in the equity accounts during the year, namely:

■ share capital;
■ share premium;
■ retained earnings;
■ revaluation surplus;
■ unrealised gains on investments;
■ issue and redemption of share capital;
■ transfers between reserves;
■ profit after tax; and
■ dividends.

6.4 The statement of cash flows

This summarises all the cash inflows and outflows that have occurred during the accounting period under review (this is normally a year). Chapter 12 shows that the cash flows are classified under headings designed to maximise their informative value. Because it is based on 'hard cash', the cash flow statement is considered to be less susceptible to manipulation than the other main financial reports. As a result, it is likely to provide important insights concerning business performance during a particular accounting period (e.g. whereas the statement of profit or loss and other comprehensive income may show a healthy figure for operating profit, the cash flow statement could cast doubt on the quality of reported profit if it communicates a decline in the actual cash flow from operating activities).

7   Users and uses of accounting information

Financial statements are important, as they help show how a business has performed and provide some indication of likely future performance. A wide range of users, both inside the business and outside it, use the financial reports to help them make decisions.

We have seen that people who use accounting information can be classified into those within the firm and those outside. Users within the firm include managers, at any level of responsibility ranging from the shop floor to the board of directors, who use information for one or more of the following purposes:

- *Planning* – to assess the financial effects of possible alternative courses of future action.
- *Decision making* – for example, to decide which project to undertake or whether to reallocate resources from one use to another.
- *Assessment and control* – to monitor the performance of personnel, departments and products.

External users also use accounting information to make decisions. In the case of an investor, for example, they may use financial reports to assess past performance and predict future performance to help decide whether to make an initial investment in the business, purchase more shares or dispose of an existing holding. Historically, the principal external users of accounting information were seen as comprising only the shareholder and the creditor groups, but for some time this has been recognised as too narrow a view.

We can, therefore, see that external users require accounting information for a range of purposes. The principal accounting statements are of interest to both internal and external users but, when presented to the latter, they will normally be in a condensed form. The main factor affecting the amount of detail contained in the accounts is the requirements of the user group. In general, external users wish to assess the overall performance of the entity, so an enormous amount of detail is inappropriate, both because it is of little interest and because it is likely to obscure important trends. It is mainly for this reason that information is presented in a highly summarised form in the published accounts. However, disclosing too much detail may be useful to competitors when analysing a company's strengths and weaknesses.

Financial statements prepared for management contain much more detail. Shareholders base their decision to sell shares, retain their investment or buy more shares mainly on the level of reported profit and dividends declared. Management, in contrast, has a keen interest in the costs and revenues that make up the profit figures. They are responsible for taking decisions such as:

- whether to expand or contract production;
- whether to substitute one material for another, or one type of worker for another;
- whether to replace labour-intensive production methods by machinery;
- whether to acquire property instead of renting it; and
- which type of power supply to use etc.

These decisions influence individual items of revenue and expenditure. In many instances, reports must be specially prepared to help reach these decisions, and appraisal techniques have been developed to help the management process. After the decisions have been made, the outcome is monitored to see the extent to which expectations have been fulfilled.

8   Presentation of financial statements

This is the subject of IAS 1 'Presentation of Financial Statements'.

8.1   Objectives of IAS 1

IAS 1 prescribes the basis for the presentation of general purpose financial statements, to ensure comparability with: the entity's financial statements of previous periods; and the financial statements of other entities.

8.2   Concepts and guidelines

IAS 1 sets out some of the basic concepts and other guidelines that that should be complied with when preparing and presenting statements. These concepts have been covered above when considering the content of the framework, namely: going concern; accruals; consistency; and materiality.

8.3   Offsetting

It is important that both assets and liabilities and income and expenses, when material, are reported separately so that users can make a proper assessment of the progress and financial position of the entity. It is for these reasons that IAS 1 states that assets, liabilities, income and expenses are not to be offset unless required or permitted by an IFRS.

Offsetting in either the statement of profit or loss and other comprehensive income or the statement of financial position is required or permitted where it reflects the substance of the transaction or event. The reporting of assets net of valuation allowances (e.g. obsolescence allowances on inventories and doubtful debts allowance on receivables) is therefore permitted.

8.4   Comparative information

Comparative information is disclosed for all amounts reported in the financial statements, unless an IFRS requires or permits otherwise.

8.5   Criteria for items that must be reported

The financial statements that constitute the annual reports of a company, prepared on the basis of IFRS, must declare a minimum number of items. The prescribed format in the presentation of the statement of profit or loss and other comprehensive income and the accompanying financial statements must include items that are included in the various standards. These items must also be calculated in a consistent and recommended manner.

Once a company has selected the manner and format in which it will report its financial figures, it must use that format consistently. In the UK, companies that do not follow the IFRS system of accounting must comply with CA2006 as well as with UK GAAP. These give comprehensive guidance on what items must be reported on the face of the financial statements with an appropriate set of narratives.

9   Prescribed format for the statement of profit or loss and other comprehensive income

IAS 1 allows entities to choose between two formats for reporting income and expenses. All items of income and expense recognised in a period must be included in profit or loss unless a standard or an interpretation dictates otherwise (IAS 1.88).

Some differences exist between the US GAAP understanding of revenue and the IFRS version. In the UK, for listed companies, the IFRS version takes precedence. As an example of interpretation and understanding, here is the distinction in revenue recognition between US GAAP and IFRS:

- *Earned*: The earnings process must be complete and the value of the transaction can be measured.
- *Realisation*: The revenue must have been collected OR there must be some assurance that it will be collected.

The most popular method of reporting on the face of the statement of profit or loss and other comprehensive income in the EU is Format 1. Format 1 analyses expenses by function (e.g. by cost). Format 2 analyses expenses by type (e.g. employee benefits, similar type of operating expenses). For the purposes of this manual, we will illustrate income and expense using Format 1.

WORKED EXAMPLE 3.1

NRG plc – statement of profit or loss and other comprehensive income for the years ended 31 December:

	Notes	2016 £,000	2015 £,000
Income from continuing operations			
Revenue	1	550,000	470,000
Cost of sales	2	(420,000)	(370,000)
Gross profit		130,000	100,000
Selling & distribution costs	3	(12,000)	(8,000)
Administrative expenses	4	(24,000)	(18,000)
Other operating expenses		(9,000)	(6,000)
Profit from operations	5	85,000	68,000
Interest payable	6	(500)	(300)
Profit before tax		84,500	67,700
Tax	7	(25,350)	(20,310)
Profit for the period from continuing operations		59,150	47,390
Discontinued operations			
Loss for the period from discontinued operations	8	(6,200)	(4,500)
Total comprehensive income		52,950	42,890
Attributable to ordinary equity holders		42,360	34,312
Attributable to minority interest		10,590	8,578
Earnings per share	9	11	9

10 Measurement and recognition of revenue

IFRS 15 specifies how and when reporting entities should recognize revenue from the sale of goods and provision of services. Revenue is referred to by a variety of different terms including: sales, fees, interest, dividends, royalties and rent and is recognized when a customer obtains control of a good or service and has the ability to direct the use of and obtain the benefit from the good or service being provided.

The core principle of IFRS 15 is that an entity should recognize revenue to depict the transfer f promised good or services to customers in an amount that reflects the consideration to which the entity expects to be entitled in exchange for the goods or services. There are a number of steps to take when applying the core principles of IFRS 15 to determine revenue recognition – these will be outlined in detail in the next chapter.

WORKED EXAMPLE 3.2

NRG plc is in the business of supplying electricity to commercial customers. NRG plc typically enters into contracts that are worth at least £1 million and last for a minimum of two years. NRG recently acquired two new customers. Customer A entered into a contract with NRG for the supply of electricity for four years at a contract price of £5 million. Customer B had a similar arrangement, but with a contract price of £8 million over eight years. The annual contract values are paid in advance by both customers.

NRG plc has a policy to give discounts to longer running contracts.

Required
State the revenue NRG plc will recognise in relation to the contracts with customers A and B.

Answer
The revenue NRG plc will recognise in relation to the contracts for customers A and B are as follows:

Customer A
£5 million/4 years = £1.25 million (annualised charge to revenue)

Customer B
£8 million / 8 years = £1 million (annualised charge to revenue)

Total annualised charge to revenue for customers A and B are:

Customer A	£1.25 million
Customer B	£1.00 million
	£2.25 million

Under IFRS rules and IAS 1, the above calculations are measurable and reliable. The calculations will meet the criteria for prescribed revenue recognition whereby 'the gross inflow of economic benefits arising from the ordinary operating activities of an entity' would have been met. Additionally, the recognition to revenue would have met the criteria for revenue measurement at 'fair value of the consideration'.

Further, revenue is being recognised on an *accruals basis*. NRG is being paid in advance of the annualised contract value; hence it will defer revenue recognition to the statement of financial position and introduce monthly charge to revenues. The proportion of annualised contract not yet expended will be a liability to NRG plc.

11 Reporting comprehensive income

The Financial Accounting Standards Board (FASB) (US) describes comprehensive income as:

'the change in equity (net assets) of a business enterprise during a period from transactions and other events and circumstances from non-owner sources. It includes all changes in equity during a period except those resulting from investments by owners and distributions to owners.'

As such, comprehensive income is the total of profit or loss and other items that are not recorded through the statement of profit or loss and other comprehensive income due to their nature, including items such as unrealised holding gain or loss from available-for-sale securities and foreign currency translation **gains or losses**. These items are not part of profit or loss; nevertheless, if they are material they should be included in comprehensive income, thus allowing users a more comprehensive understanding of organisational performance.

Items included in comprehensive income, but not profit or loss, are reported under the accumulated other comprehensive income section of a shareholder's equity. Comprehensive income paints a better picture when measured on a per-share basis. This in turn reflects the effects of events such as dilution and options. Comprehensive income mitigates the effects of equity transactions for which shareholders would be indifferent: dividend payments, share buy-backs and share issues at market value.

12 Prescribed format for the statement of financial position

IAS 1 (paragraph 54) specifies the minimum line item disclosures on the face of, or in the notes to, the statement of financial position, the statement of profit or loss and other comprehensive income, and the statement of changes in equity.

12.1 General format

Both current and non-current assets and current and non-current liabilities are presented as separate classifications on the face of the statement of financial position. These distinctions are required because the extent into the future that assets and liabilities are to be realised has clear implications for an assessment of the financial position and solvency of an entity. Any assets and liabilities not falling within the definitions of 'current', as indicated below, are to be classified as non-current.

A **current asset** is one that:

- is expected to be realised, or is intended for sale or on consumption, in the entity's normal operating cycle;
- is held primarily for trading purposes;
- is expected to be realised within 12 months of the statement of financial position date; or
- is cash or a cash equivalent asset.

A **current liability** is one that:

- is expected to be settled in the normal course of the entity's operating cycle; or
- is due to be settled within 12 months of the statement of financial position.

A format that covers most of the information that one might expect to appear in an entity's statement of financial position is given below.

TEST YOUR KNOWLEDGE 3.5

a   What is meant by a current asset and current liability?
b   Explain the process of recognising revenue under IAS 15.

WORKED EXAMPLE 3.3

NRG plc – Statement of financial position at 31 December:

	20X2 £,000	20X1 £,000
Assets		
Non-current assets		
Property, plant and equipment	607,000	602,000
Accumulated depreciation	(134,000)	(119,000)
	473,000	483,000
Goodwill	11,000	11,000
Accumulated impairment	(5,000)	(4,000)
	6,000	7,000
Other intangible assets	13,000	9,000
Investments in **associates**	9,000	9,000
Available-for-sale investments	13,000	6,000
Total non-current assets	35,000	24,000
Current assets		
Inventories	34,000	24,000
Trade receivables	24,000	18,000
Cash and cash equivalents	22,000	21,000
Total current assets	80,000	63,000
Total assets	594,000	577,000
Equity and liabilities		
Share capital	50,000	50,000
Other reserves	63,000	63,000
Retained earnings	225,000	172,050
	338,000	285,050
Non-controlling interest	103,000	92,410
Total equity	441,000	377,460
Non–current liabilities		
Long-term borrowings	52,000	56,000
Deferred tax	11,000	9,000
Long-term provisions	5,000	5,000
Total non-current liabilities	68,000	70,000
Current liabilities		
Trade and other payables	13,000	26,540
Short-term borrowings	36,000	68,000
Current portion of long-term borrowings	6,000	6,000
Taxation	25,000	20,000
Short-term provisions	5,000	9,000
Total current liabilities	85,000	129,540
Total liabilities	153,000	199,540
Total equity and liabilities	594,000	577,000

13 Additional information on the statement of financial position

IAS 1 paragraph 54 provides the minimum line items to be included on the face of the statement of financial position.

Additional line items, headings, and subtotals shall be presented on the face of the statement of financial position if these are relevant to understanding the entity's financial position. There is no prescribed order or format in which items are to be presented; however, the guidelines are as follows:

- Line items are included when the size, nature or function of an item or aggregation of similar items is such that separate presentation is relevant to an understanding of the entity's financial position.
- The descriptions used and the ordering of items or aggregation of similar items may be amended according to the nature of the entity and its transactions, to provide information that is relevant to an understanding of the entity's financial position.

14 Statement of changes in equity

Changes in shareholders' equity between statement of financial position dates are, of course, equal to the increase or decrease in net assets during that period. The change comprises three basic elements:

- capital injections by the shareholders;
- withdrawals in the form of repayment of capital and dividends; and
- recognised gains and losses.

The general rule, as noted above, is that gains and losses should go through the statement of comprehensive income. The reasons for this are two-fold:

1 Gains and losses, whatever their source, have an identical impact on the financial position of the enterprise.
2 The impact of a gain, or perhaps more likely a loss, is not 'played down' by relegating it to a position outside the primary financial statements.

It was noted in section 11, however, that accounting standards require a restricted range of gains and losses to be excluded from the statement of profit or loss and other comprehensive income, but shown as other comprehensive income such as gains and losses on sale of an asset. These, together with the profit for the year reported in the statement of profit or loss and other comprehensive income, are reported in the statement of changes in equity. The content of this report will depend on the nature of gains and losses arising during the year.

14.1 Other items appearing in the statement of change in equity

Transactions that are material in nature may also be reported through the statement of changes to equity and may include items such as transfer between reserves (e.g. revaluation reserve) and issue of shares and prior period adjustments (discussed in Chapter 4).

- *Transfers from reserves*: When an asset held for sale is eventually disposed of any gain that transpires may be transferred to the equity. Any such transfer will simply be shown in the statement by a minus in one column and a plus in another.
- *Share issues*: companies often issue shares in various forms that have a material impact on the capital structure. These include bonus shares, **rights issues**, new share issues and occasionally companies will buy back their own shares (in the US these are known as treasury shares). Any share issue below the market price will have a dilutive effect on shareholder wealth.
- *Prior period adjustment*: If prior period mistakes or errors are material, IAS 8 'Accounting Policies, Changes in Accounting Estimates and Errors' allows such misstatements to be included in the statement of changes as adjusting item(s) brought forward from those years. For instance, a research and development expense wrongly capitalised will have a subsequent reducing impact on retained earnings and assets (see below).

WORKED EXAMPLE 3.4

Statement of changes in equity for the year ended 31 December 20X2:

	Share capital £,000	Other reserves £,000	Translation reserve £,000	Retained earnings £,000	Total £,000
Balance at 1 January 20X2	x	x	x	x	x
Change in accounting policy (IAS 8)				x	x
Restated balance at 1 January 20X2				x	x
Changes in equity during the year					
Other comprehensive income					
Gain/loss on property revaluation (IAS 16)		x			x
Exchange differences (IAS 21)					x
Available for sale investments (IAS 39)		x			x
Tax on above items (gains or losses) recognised directly in equity		x			
Total other comprehensive income		x	x		x
Profit for the period				x	x
Total recognised income and expenses for the period	x	x	x	x	x
Dividends				(x)	(x)
Issued share capital	x				x
Balance at 31 December 20X2	x	x	x	x	x

 WORKED EXAMPLE 3.5

	Share capital £m	Share premium £m	Revaluation reserve £m	Retained earnings £m	Total £m
Balance at 1 January 20X2	350	50	20	640	1,060
Change in accounting policy (IAS 8)				10	10
Restated balance at 1 January 20X2				650	1,070
Changes in equity during the year					
Other comprehensive income					
Gain/loss on property revaluation (IAS 16)		–	10		10
Transfer on realisation		–	(7)	7	0
Tax on above items (gains or losses) recognised directly in equity		–	(3)		(3)
Total other comprehensive income	350	50	20	7	7
Profit for the period				20	20
Total recognised income and expenses for the period				27	27
Dividends				(6)	(6)
Balance at 31 December 20X2	350	50	20	671	1,091

STOP AND THINK **3.1**

Do we really need a defined and constantly evolving standard setting process?

? END OF CHAPTER QUESTIONS

3.1 Briefly discuss the principal statements and their purpose that constitute a complete set of financial statements.

3.2 The statement of changes in equity includes reconciliation between:
  a   the carrying amount of retained earnings at the beginning and the end of the period;
  b   the carrying amount of total equity at the beginning and the end of the period; and
  c   the carrying amount of each component of equity at the beginning and the end of the period separately disclosing changes resulting from:
      ■ profit or loss;
      ■ each item of comprehensive income; and
      ■ the amounts of investments by, and dividends and other distributions to, owners.
  From the above statements, select which answer best reflects the statement of changes in equity.

3.3 The following items were extracted from the records of Sigma plc on 31 December 20X4.

	£,000
Goodwill	400
Capitalised development expenditure	200
Brand	100
Property, plant and equipment	900
Trade and other receivables	950
Inventories	300
Cash and cash equivalent	200
Trade and other payables	300
Short term financial asset	100
Other receivables (due to be received 20X7)	300
Investments in subsidiaries	200
Deferred tax liabilities	100
Current tax payable	100
10% bond payable 20X8	60
Provision for decommissioning of nuclear plant in 20x8	50
Revaluation reserve	150
Retained earnings	300
Retirement benefit obligations	120
Capital redemption reserve	80
Share capital – £1 ordinary shares (balancing item)	?

Required
Prepare the statement of financial position of Sigma plc on 31 December 20X1. The statement should be prepared in accordance with IAS 1.

? **END OF CHAPTER QUESTIONS** *continued*

3.4 Opal Ltd is a company which operates a number of retail shops, some of which it owns and others it rents. The following is the company's trial balance at 31 December 20X2:

	Note	£,000	£,000
Sales revenue			5,100
Purchases		2,500	
Accounts payable			212
Accounts receivable		208	
Inventories at 1 January 20X2	6	250	
6% debenture loan	5		200
Administration expenses	3	924	
Equipment at cost	2	600	
Accumulated depreciation at 1 January 20X2			120
Selling & distribution costs	4	540	
Ordinary shares	7 & 8		2,200
Share premium account at 1 January 20X2	7 & 8		250
Retained profit at 1 January 2012			850
Bank			15
Final dividend for 20X1 paid in July 20X2		35	
Freehold property at cost	1	3,890	
		8,947	8,947

You are given the following additional information:
1. The company does not depreciate its freehold property.
2. The equipment was purchased on 1 January 20X2, at which time they were expected to have a ten-year life and a zero residual value.
3. Six months' rent of £26,000, included in administration expenses, was paid in advance on 1 October 20X2.
4. An invoice of £5,000 for advertising during 20X2 was received in January 20X3, and is not reflected in the above trial balance.
5. The **debenture** interest due for 20X2 has not yet been paid or accrued.
6. The value of inventories at 31 December 20X2 was £270,000.
7. The company had issued share capital of 1.75 million ordinary shares of £1 each at 31 December 20X1.
8. On 30 June 20X2 the company issued, for cash, 250,000 shares. The entire proceeds of this issue have been recorded as part of the balance of £2.2 million on the ordinary shares account.
9. It is estimated that the corporation tax charge for 20X2 will be £300,000 and has not been paid.
10. The directors intend to declare an ordinary dividend of 4 pence per share on each share in issue at 31 December 20X2.

Required
Prepare the following financial statements of Opal Ltd for 20X2 in accordance with the provisions of IAS 1 'Presentation of Financial Statements':
1. Statement of profit or loss and other comprehensive income using function of expense format.
2. Statement of changes in equity.
3. Statement of financial position.
4. Provide definitions for the following concepts/terminologies:
   a. Fair value in accordance with IFRS 3 'Business Combinations' (Past ICSA question).
   b. Measurement and recognition of revenues in accordance with IAS 18 'Revenues'.
   c. Other comprehensive income.
   d. Reporting entities.

Accounting policies 1

4

■ **CONTENTS**

■ **LEARNING OUTCOMES**

At the end of this section, you will be able to:

■ demonstrate familiarity with the nature of accounting policies, the significance of differences between them and the effects of changes in accounting policy;
■ show an understanding of the treatment of inventories in financial statements;
■ demonstrate an understanding of accounting for property, plant and equipment including accounting for depreciation and accounting for impairment; and
■ show familiarity with end-of-year accounting issues including accounting for provisions,
■ contingent assets and liabilities and dealing with events after the reporting period.

1   Introduction

The objective of financial reporting is to provide financial information to users of financial statements to make their own economic decision. This is expressed in the Conceptual Framework as follows:

'The objective of general purpose financial reporting is to provide financial information about the reporting entity that is useful to existing and potential investors, lenders and other creditors in making decisions about providing resources to the entity. Those decisions involve buying, selling or holding equity and debt instruments, and providing or settling loans and other forms of credit.'

The importance of the output from financial reporting serves as a constant reminder to management and their appointed agents why due care must be exercised with the process.

Moreover, accounting is somewhat short of being an exact science despite some of the traits; thus the need for clarity on the accounting of items included and presented in financial statements. The move towards clarity and enhanced usefulness is derived from the accounting policies.

2   Accounting policies

Accounting policies are defined in International Accounting Standard (IAS)8 'Accounting Policies, Changes in Accounting Estimates and Errors' as 'the specific principles, bases, conventions, rules and practices applied by an entity in preparing and presenting financial statements'.

Our definition reveals the multiplicity and breadth of the features of accounting policies. These features are applied in the two stages, the preparation and the presentation of financial statements. Implicit in the definition is to provide useful information to the users who use the financial information to make economic decisions.

The definition gives rise to two feature concerns governing the application of the accounting policies. These twin concerns are:

1 the selection and application; and
2 the consistency of accounting policies.

2.1 Selection and application of accounting policies

The determinant for the selection and application of the appropriate accounting policy is the application of the standard and/or guidance issued by the International Accounting Standards Board (IASB). However, an IASB standard does not exist to address every transaction or item or activity to be reported by management. In such cases the concerns for the users of reported financial information will be how they can be assured that the reported financial information will meet their needs.

In such instances, management must display judgment in selecting accounting policies that are relevant and reliable, as stated in IAS 8.

'In the absence of a Standard or an Interpretation that specifically applies to a transaction, other event or condition, management must use its judgment in developing and applying an accounting policy that results in information that is:
a relevant to the economic decision-making needs of the users; and
b reliable.'

2.2 Consistency of accounting policies

Accounting policies should be applied consistently for similar transactions, other events and conditions. The only exception is where an IASB Standard permits or requires item categorisation and the application of different policies.

The most common example found in financial statements is the accounting for non-current assets. Property, plant and equipment are depreciated and this is shown in the statement of financial position. However, non-current assets may be categorised and have a particular depreciation policy applied to each class rather than across the whole group.

3 Accounting for inventory (IAS 2)

Inventories have a significant position in the financial statements. Firstly, they are used in the computation of the gross profit on the statement of profit or loss and other comprehensive income and secondly, they are held as current assets and displayed on the statement of financial position. Therefore the identification and measurement of inventory can have a material impact on the reported performance and position of an entity. IAS 2 (Accounting for inventories) provides the framework and policy guidance.

Inventories are defined as assets that may exist in the following three conditions:

■ held for sale in ordinary course of business;
■ in the process of production for such sale; and
■ in the form of materials or supplies to be consumed in the production process or in the rendering of services.

IAS 2 applies to all inventories with the exception of:

■ construction contracts (IAS 11 'Construction Contracts');
■ financial instruments (IAS 32 'Financial Instruments: Presentation' and IFRS 9 'Financial Instruments'); and
■ biological assets (IAS 41 'Agriculture').

Similarly, IAS 2 does not apply to measurement of inventories held by:

■ producers of agricultural and forest products;
■ minerals and mineral products; or
■ commodity brokers.

The standard outlines what items are included as inventories and which items are excluded. The comparative outline is shown in Table 4.1.

TABLE 4.1 Comparative list of costs included and excluded from inventories

IAS 2 Inventories include:	IAS 2 Inventories exclude:
■ Costs of purchase, including non-recoverable taxes, transport and handling ■ Net of trade volume rebates ■ Costs of conversion ■ Other costs to bring inventory into its present condition and location.	■ Abnormal waste ■ Storage costs (unless necessary for the production process) ■ Admin overheads not related to production ■ Selling costs ■ Interest cost (where settlement is deferred)

The basis for the valuation of inventories is the lesser of historical cost and net **realisable value** (NRV), where the NRV is the estimated selling price in the ordinary course of business, less the estimated costs of completion and the estimated costs to make the sale.

To ensure that full provision is made for foreseeable losses, IAS 2 requires the comparison between cost and net realisable value to be based on individual items of stock, with the proviso that groups of similar items may be compared where the comparison of individual items is impractical.

WORKED EXAMPLE 4.1

The following information is provided in respect of a group of items of inventory belonging to Banbury Ltd:

Item of inventory	Cost	Net realisable value (NRV)
	£	£
A	500	580
B	300	370
C	250	330
D	760	600

Required:
Calculations of the total value of Banbury's inventories, based on the lower of cost and net realisable value, assuming that cost is compared with net realisable value:

a on an individual item basis;
b on a group basis.

Answer

a Individual item basis:

Item of inventory	Cost	NRV	Lower of cost and NRV: individual item basis
	£	£	
A	500	580	500
B	300	370	300
C	250	330	250
D	760	600	600
			1,650

b Group basis:

Item of inventory	Cost	NRV	Lower of cost and NRV: group basis
	£ £	£	
A + B + C + D	1,810	1,880	1,810

> **WORKED EXAMPLE** **4.1** *continued*
>
> Comparing cost with the NRV of individual items results in a lower inventory value (£1,650 as compared with £1,810) and therefore a lower profit figure. This is because the comparison of total figures for cost and NRV results in a foreseeable loss of £160 on item D (£760 cost – £600 NRV) being offset by total unrealised gains of £230 on items A–C (£1,280 NRV – £1,050 cost). Method a being the preferred method under IAS 2.

The principal situations in which NRV is likely to be below cost are where there has been:

- a fall in selling price;
- physical deterioration of inventories;
- obsolescence of a product;
- a decision, as part of an entity's marketing strategy, to manufacture and sell products for the time being at a loss (so-called 'loss-leaders'); and
- miscalculations or other errors in purchasing or production.

In practice, any one of the above is unlikely to apply to more than a small proportion of the company's inventories. For the remainder, NRV will exceed cost and can be ignored when valuing inventories for inclusion in the accounts. However, the problem will remain of deciding how to compute cost.

There are two basic areas of difficulty:

1 Whether to value inventories on the marginal cost or the total cost basis (see section 3.1 below).
2 How to identify purchases with issues to production and match finished goods with sales, i.e. a choice has to be made between, for instance, first in first out and last in first out (see section 3.2 below).

> **TEST YOUR KNOWLEDGE** **4.1**
>
> Identify the principal situations in which NRV is likely to be below cost and explain the appropriate accounting treatment of the discrepancy.

3.1 Marginal cost or total cost

The main difference between these two methods is their treatment of fixed factory costs, and it is therefore a problem that is primarily confined to manufacturing companies. The marginal cost basis includes only the variable costs associated with producing a single extra unit of output, whereas the total cost basis also includes a proportion of fixed factory costs. The main arguments for and against the total cost basis, which are the reverse of the arguments for and against the marginal cost basis, are as follows:

For total cost:
1 Each unit manufactured benefits from the provision of facilities that result in fixed costs being incurred, and a proportion of their cost should therefore be included in the value of inventories.
2 The accruals concept requires costs to be matched with related revenues, and the total cost of inventories unsold at the statement of financial performance date should therefore be carried forward and matched against revenue arising during the following accounting period.

Against total cost:
1 Fixed costs are a function of time rather than of production, and should therefore not be carried forward, but should be charged against the revenue arising during the period when they are incurred.
2 The valuation of inventories and, therefore, the level of reported profit fluctuate depending on the level of production. This is because the quantity manufactured determines the proportion of fixed cost attributed to each item, e.g. a low level of output causes each unit to be charged with a high element of fixed cost.
3 Fixed costs cannot be directly related to particular items of inventory and are therefore apportioned on an arbitrary basis.

IAS 2 requires companies to use the total cost basis for external reporting purposes. It defines total cost as costs 'incurred in bringing the inventories to their present location and condition'. This normally means that the valuation should include a share of factory overheads (based on normal capacity of the production facilities), but not distribution costs or administrative expenses. The problem, implicit in the second argument against the use of total cost, listed above, is avoided by the requirement that the calculation of the overhead element should be based on the 'normal level of activity, taking one year with another'.

Worked example 4.2 illustrates the difference between the marginal cost and total cost bases of inventory valuation.

WORKED EXAMPLE 4.2

At the beginning of 20X1 Deer Ltd was incorporated. The company manufactures a single product. At the end of the first year's operations, the company's accountant prepared a draft statement of profit or loss and other comprehensive income that contained the following financial information:

Statement of profit or loss and other comprehensive income: Deer Ltd for 20X1

	£	£
Sales (200,000 units)		600,000
Less: Marginal cost of units manufactured during 20X1 (500,000 units):	800,000	
Deduct closing inventories(300,000 units x £1.60 each)	480,000	
Marginal cost of goods sold(200,000 units x £1.60 each)	320,000	
Fixed costs:		
Factory expenses	200,000	
General expenses	100,000	(620,000)
Net loss		(20,000)

Additional finance is required, and the directors are worried that the company's bank manager is unlikely to regard the financial facts shown above as a satisfactory basis for a further advance. The company's accountant made the following observation and suggestion:

'The cause of the poor result for 20X1 was the decision to value closing inventories on the marginal cost basis. An acceptable alternative practice would involve charging factory expenses to the total number of units produced and carrying forward an appropriate proportion of those expenses as part of the closing inventories value.'

Required:
a A revised statement of profit or loss and other comprehensive income, for presentation to the company's As original formatting in current version of text book bank, valuing closing inventories on the total cost basis suggested by the company's accountant.
b Assuming that, in 20X2, the company again produces 500,000 units, but sells 700,000 units, calculate the expected profit using each of the two inventories valuation bases. Assume also that, in 20X2, sales price per unit (£3) and costs incurred will be the same as for 20XI.

WORKED EXAMPLE **4.2** *continued*

c   Comment briefly on the accountant's suggestion and its likely effect on the bank manager's response to the request for additional finance.

Answer

a   Statement of profit or loss and other comprehensive income for 20X1 – total cost basis

		£000	£000
Sales			600
Less:	Marginal costs	800	
	Factory expenses	200	
	Total cost of manufacture	1,000	
	Deduct closing inventories (W1)	600	
	Cost of goods sold	400	
	General expenses	100	(500)
Net profit			100

W1. The company produced 500,000 units but sold only 200,000 units, and so it had 300,000 units in stock. The total cost basis therefore results in a inventories valuation of (£1,000,000 ÷ 500,000) x 300,000 = £600,000.

b   Forecast statement of profit or loss and other comprehensive income for 20X2

	Marginal cost		Total cost	
	£000	£000	£000	£000
Sales		2,100		2,100
Less: Opening inventories	480		600	
Marginal costs	800		800	
Factory expenses	–		200	
	1,280		1,600	
Deduct closing inventories (W2)	160		200	
	1,120		1,400	
Factory expenses	200		–	
General expenses	100	(1,420)	100	(1,500)
Net profit		680		600

W2. Opening inventories comprise 300,000 units and 500,000 units are expected to be manufactured during 20X2. Assuming 700,000 units are sold, 100,000 units will remain in stock at the end of 20X2. The closing inventories valuations are therefore:

Marginal cost basis: (£800,000 ÷ 500,000) x 100,000 = £160,000
Total cost basis: (£1,000,000 ÷ 500,000) x 100,000 = £200,000

c   Total cost is an acceptable basis for valuing inventories; indeed it is the method required for external reporting purposes by IAS 2. Provided the resulting valuation does not exceed net realisable value, it should be used. The use of different valuation bases does not, of course, alter the underlying financial facts, but it can affect the allocation of profit between consecutive accounting periods. Use of the total cost basis, which relates indirect manufacturing costs to output rather than time, produces 'higher' profits than the marginal cost basis when production exceeds sales. Three-fifths of the fixed factory costs (£200,000 X 3/5 = £120,000) are added to the value of closing inventories for the purpose of preparing the revised statement of profit or

WORKED EXAMPLE **4.2** *continued*

loss and other comprehensive income for 20X1, and this converts a reported loss of £20,000 into a reported profit of £100,000. The situation is reversed when sales exceed production (see forecast results for 20X2 above). The company's bank manager should, but may not be, aware of the effect of different accounting policies on reported profit. Therefore, it is difficult to say whether or not the bank manager will be influenced by changing to a method that reports the underlying facts more favourably.

TEST YOUR KNOWLEDGE **4.2**

Explain the difference between marginal cost and total cost.

3.2 FIFO, AVCO and LIFO

The price at which goods are purchased normally increases during the year and, consequently, items on hand at the year-end will have been purchased at different prices. In theory, the accruals concept requires the cost of items sold to be matched individually against their sales proceeds and, where such an approach is practical, it should be adopted. Usually, however, this is impracticable because of the large number of 'interchangeable' items bought, perhaps processed and then sold during an accounting period. To simplify the matching process, assumptions are made concerning the flow of goods through the firm. The eligible cost formulas for this purpose are usually considered to be first in first out (FIFO), last in first out (LIFO) and weighted average cost (AVCO).

- *FIFO*: This assumes that the items that have been held longest are used first, and inventories in hand represent the latest purchases or production. The effect is that, during a period of rising prices, cost of sales is reported at a low figure, reported profit is maximised and the statement of financial performance figure for inventories represents most recent purchase prices.
- *LIFO*: This assumes that the items purchased or produced most recently are used first, and the quantities of inventories on hand represent earliest purchases or production. The result is that cost of sales is higher than under the FIFO assumption, and reported profit is correspondingly lower. In the statement of financial performance inventories are valued at a relatively low figure, representing prices ruling weeks, months or even years earlier.
- *AVCO*: This method produces results which fall somewhere between the above two extremes.

All three approaches have their advocates. For example, some argue that FIFO is superior because it is more likely to approximate the actual flow of goods through the company. Supporters of LIFO argue that their method works better during a period of inflation, because it produces a more realistic measure of profit. Although acknowledging the latter argument, IAS 2 rejects LIFO on the grounds that it fails to produce a statement of financial performance figure for inventories which bears a reasonable relationship to actual cost. The two eligible cost formulas are therefore FIFO and AVCO.

4 Accounting policy and changes (IAS 8)

Consistency is one of the two desirable principles of accountancy and requires that there is uniformity of accounting treatment of like items within each accounting period and between periods. Consistency provides for comparable analysis and the ability to examine or monitor trends over time.

4.1 Change in policy

In accordance with IAS 8, a change in accounting policy can be undertaken if:

1   required by an IFRS, or
2   a change will provide more relevant and reliable information.

Where a change in accounting policy is the result of a change in an accounting standard or its interpretation, transitional provisions should be applied. If there are no transitional provisions, the change should be made retrospectively unless it is impractical and the new policy would require significant disclosure.

A retrospective change requires that everything changes and reporting as though the change had always been in place. IAS 8 provides the following guidance on retrospective change:

> 'when a change in accounting policy is applied retrospectively ... the entity shall adjust the opening balance of each affected component of equity for the earliest prior period presented and the other comparative amounts disclosed for each prior period presented as if the new accounting policy had always been applied.'

A change in policy as a result in a change in accounting standards require full disclosure that addresses each of the following at the end of the first accounting period in which the change was introduced:

- the title of the accounting standard or interpretation that was responsible for the change;
- the nature of the change in policy;
- a description of the transitional provisions;
- for the current period and each prior period presented, the amount of the adjustment to:
  a) each line item affected, and
  b) earnings per share;
- the amount of the adjustment relating to prior periods not presented; and
- if retrospective application is impracticable, an explanation and description outlining how the change in policy was applied.

 **WORKED EXAMPLE 4.3**

The following balances relating to 20X1 have been extracted from the books of Oldham plc:

	£,000
Turnover	11,170
Cost of sales	(7,721)
Profit on the sale of shares in Preston Ltd	500
Administration expenses	(621)
Distribution costs	(133)
Interest payable	(26)
Final dividend paid in respect of 20X0	(600)
Interim dividend paid for 20X1	(250)
Retained profit at 31 December 20X1	3,875

The following additional information is provided:

1   Shares in Preston Ltd were sold during the year. These shares were purchased ten years ago and were the only investments owned by the company. It is estimated that attributable tax payable will be £150,000.
2   The company's cost of sales includes a £200,000 write-off of uninsured inventories damaged by fire.
3   After the above balances were extracted, the directors decided to adopt the policy of depreciating the company's freehold building that has been owned for some years. This decision requires the opening carrying amount of the building to be reduced by £700,000, and a charge for 20X1 of £114,000 must be added to cost of sales.

📟 **WORKED EXAMPLE** **4.3** *continued*

4 Corporation tax on profits from normal trading operations is estimated at £1.2 million.
5 Oldham plc's issued share capital amounted to £10 million throughout 20X1.

Required
The statement of profit or loss and other comprehensive income and statement of changes in equity of Oldham plc for the year ended 31 December 20X1 in 'good form', and complying with standard accounting practice so far as the information permits.

Note: Assume all amounts are material.

Answer
Revised cost of sales for Oldham plc 20X1

	£,000
Cost of sales	7,721
Add: Additional depreciation	114
Adjusted cost of sales	7,835

Statement of profit or loss and other comprehensive income for Oldham plc 20X1

	£,000
Turnover	11,170
Cost of sales (Note 1)	(7,835)
Gross profit	3,335
Distribution costs	(133)
Administration expenses	(621)
Operating profit	2,581
Other income (Note 2)	500
Finance costs	(26)
Profit before tax	3,055
Taxation (1,200 + 150)	(1,350)
Profit for the year 2011	1,705

Statement of changes in equity of Oldham plc for 20X1:

	Share capital £,000	Retained earnings £,000	Total £,000
Balance at 1 January 20X1	10,000	3,875	13,875
Change in accounting policy (Note 3)		(700)	(700)
Balance at 1 January 20X1 as restated	10,000	3,175	13,175
Changes in equity during the year			
Profit for the year 20X1		1,705	1,705
Dividends		(850)	(850)
Balance at 31 December 20X1	10,000	4,030	14,030

Notes to the accounts
1 Cost of sales includes a £200,000 write-off of uninsured inventories damaged by fire. Material amount requires disclosure.
2 During the year the company realised a profit of £500,000 on the sale of its shareholdings in Preston Ltd purchased some years ago and also requires disclosure in view of the material amount involved.
3 The directors have decided to change Oldham's accounting policies so as to depreciate the company's freehold building, purchased some years ago, in order to give a fairer presentation of the results and financial position of the company.

4.2 Change in accounting estimates

Financial reports are not always produced with absolute results. Often, there is a need to include estimates because there is no certainty about an activity or an item within the financial statements. A common example of this activity is the provision for doubtful debt (PDD). It is impossible to measure or predict or forecast the level of trade receivables who may be unable to meet their debt obligations. Under such conditions, it is common practice to apply an estimate of the level of doubtful debt based upon a combination of factors such as professional judgment, historical behaviour and current information and sector analysis. It may be the case that the level of the PDD may be revised downwards or upwards over two accounting periods. However, revising the PDD is not a change in accounting policy but an example of a change in accounting estimate.

In IAS 8, a change in accounting estimate is defined as:

'an adjustment of the carrying amount of an asset or a liability, or the amount of the periodic consumption of an asset, that results from the assessment of the present status of, and expected future benefits and obligations associated with, assets and liabilities. Changes in accounting estimates result from new information or new developments and, accordingly, are not corrections of errors.'

Changes in accounting estimates do not require retrospective adjustments in financial reports. All changes in accounting estimates require a prospective adjustment. Our earlier revision of the PDD will require a prospective adjustment, as the revised PDD will only be reported in the current period's financial report.

WORKED EXAMPLE 4.4

You have been asked to explain when a prospective and a retrospective application should be made in financial statements to comply with IAS 8.

Solution

A retrospective application is required when there is the application of a new accounting policy or the correction for a material prior period error. The retrospective application will require the restatement of the comparative financial statements for each prior accounting period that is being presented to account for the new accounting policy and/or the material error.

For completeness, the details of the changes must be disclosed in the notes to the financial statements.

However, IAS 8 does allow for the prospective application of both a change in accounting policy and material prior period errors to be carried out if it is impracticable to perform the retrospective adjustment.

- An example of a retrospective application would include a material over/understatement of sales or inventory or other expenses.
- A prospective application is required when there is a material change in an accounting estimate. In such cases, the change would be disclosed in the notes to the financial statements.
- Examples of a prospective application would include:

a a change in the estimated lifespan of a non-current asset; or
b a change in the estimate used in the calculation of the provision of doubtful debtors.

The disclosure requirement for a change in accounting estimate is less onerous than the disclosure for a change in accounting policy. The only disclosure required for a change in accounting estimate is the nature and amount of change that has an effect in the current period (or expected to have in future). There is an absence of disclosure of the effect of future periods because it is impractical.

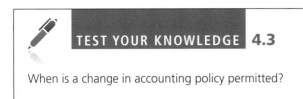

TEST YOUR KNOWLEDGE 4.3

When is a change in accounting policy permitted?

4.3 Accounting errors

Financial information may not be comparable or useful for users because of material prior period errors.

'Prior period errors are omissions from, and misstatements in, an entity's financial statements for one or more prior periods arising from failure to use/misuse of reliable information that:
a was available when the financial statements for that period were issued
b could have been reasonably expected to be taken.'

The prior period errors may have arisen from:

1 mathematical mistakes;
2 mistakes in applying accounting policies;
3 oversights and misinterpretation of facts; or
4 fraud.

Errors should be corrected retrospectively in the first set of financial statements after the discovery of an error. Secondly, a restatement of the comparative amounts for prior periods in which the error occurred should be made or, if the error occurred before that date, the opening balance of assets, liabilities and equity for the earliest period presented should be restated.

The disclosure required to address the discovery of a material prior period error must be made in the first set of financial statements for publication following the discovery and should provide the following:

- An explanation of the nature of the prior period error.
- For each prior period presented, if practicable, disclose the correction to:
  a each line item affected; and
  b earnings per share (EPS).
- Highlight the amount of the correction at the beginning of earliest period presented.
- If retrospective application is impracticable, explain and describe how the error was corrected. An example of a prior period error that requires retrospective application is shown in Worked Example 4.4.

WORKED EXAMPLE 4.5

During the process of preparing the financial statement for the year ended 30 June 20X7, the bookkeeper at ZeeZee Retail discovered the inventory at 30 June 20X6 had been understated by £40,000.
   A summary of the draft financial statement for the year ending 30 June 20X7 is shown as follows:

	20X7 £,000	20X6 £,000
Turnover	800	650
Cost of goods sold	(430)	(350)
Gross profit	370	300
Operating expenses	(320)	(260)
Profit before taxation	50	40
Taxation at 20%	(10)	(8)
Profit after tax	40	32

WORKED EXAMPLE **4.5** *continued*

Required
You are required to prepare:
a   a restated financial statement as at 30 June 20X6; and
b   a financial statement for the year ended 30 June 20X7.

Solution

	b)	a)
		Restated
	20X7	**20X6**
	£,000	*£,000*
Turnover	800	650
Cost of goods sold	(470)	(310)
Gross profit	330	340
Operating expenses	(320)	(260)
Profit before taxation	10	80
Taxation at 20%	(2)	(16)
Profit after tax	8	64

The restated financial statement shows that the annual gross profit has increased by the £40,000 understatement. Consequently, the gross profit in 20X6 increased by 50%. Conversely, the profit levels in 20X7 decreased by £40,000 and the level of taxation.

TEST YOUR KNOWLEDGE 4.4

When should an entity amend any errors discovered in their financial statements?

5   Accounting for events after the reporting period (IAS 10)

It is not uncommon for a material event to occur between the reporting date and the issuance date of the financial statements. Examples of such events may include:

- damage to a production plant by a fire, flood or other disaster;
- pollution of the environment, such as an oil spillage;
- disposal or acquisition of an asset;
- an announcement to discontinue an operation;
- material change in the net realisable value of inventories held at reporting date; and
- discovery of fraud in the financial statements.

The problem that arises from these events is deciding how to report them in the financial statements, since the reporting date has passed. The litmus test for determining how to account for such events is as follows:

1 Did the condition exist at the reporting date?
2 Did the condition exist after the reporting date?

IAS 10 'Events after the reporting period' provides us with guidance to determine when an adjustment is necessary in the financial statements for events after the reporting date. Where the condition existed at or prior to the end of the reporting period, an adjustment is made to the financial statements. In these cases, such events are adjusting events because the condition was in existence at or prior to the end of the reporting period.

Where the condition arose after the reporting date, there is no adjustment to be made in the financial statement. However, if the event is material, a disclosure is required in the financial statement before it is issuance date. The content of the disclosure is as follows:

■ state the nature of the event that is being disclosed;
■ provide an estimate of the financial effect of the event; or
■ when it is not possible to provide a financial estimate, provide a statement to that such estimate cannot be made.

WORKED EXAMPLE 4.6

Bar-Zee Plc's financial statements for the year ended 30 June 20X7 included several retail outlets and depots with a net book value of £350 million. It has always been company policy to issue its financial statements in week two of October. However, on 12 July 20X7, one of Bar-Zee's main customers went administration owing Bar-Zee £1.23m and the tax authority over £96m. Over ten years of trading, Bar-Zee had never made any contingencies for doubtful debts, as all buyers went through a rigorous vetting process before being granted credit. The company was struck by more bad news on 15 August. A disgruntled ex-employee had managed to set fire to the company's main depot and damage estimated at around £0.975m was caused to the building.

Required
How should Bar-Zee account for these two events in their financial statements for the year ended 30 June 20X7?

Answer
The entry into administration of its main customers is an adjusting event, although the event occurred on 12 July – after the end of the reporting period. The absence of any provision made and given the immateriality of Bar-Zee's debt in comparison to the tax authority means that the debtors' balance at the end of the reporting period has been overstated by £1.23m. Therefore the £1.23m debtors' balance should be written off in the statement of profit or loss and other comprehensive income for the year ended 30 June 20X7.

The fire damage on 15 August should be reported as a non-adjusting event in the financial statement. As at 30 June, all the buildings were in existence at £350m. The fire damage should be reported by way of a disclosure in the financial statements. The reporting of the fire should clearly state that the event that gave rise to the note was a fire on 15 August 20X7, and it should also include the estimated cost of damage.

In summary, when a material event occurs at the end of the reporting period prior to the issuance of the financial statement, the route to its treatment in the financial statement is shown in Figure 4.1. It is important to note here that the going concern concept needs application in cases where management determine, post reporting date, either that it intends to liquidate the entity or cease trading; hence adjusting events.

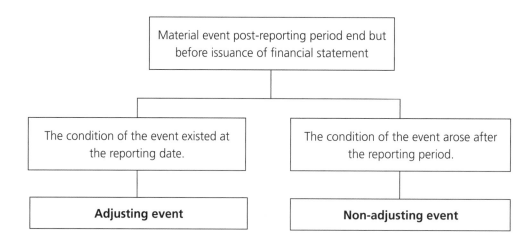

FIGURE 4.1 Adjusting or non-adjusting event

6   Fair value measurement (IFRS 13)

The measurement of fair value is addressed in IFRS13 (Fair Value Measurement). Fair value is an almost pervasive concept embedded in international financial reporting standards. It is defined as 'the price that would be received to sell an asset or paid to transfer a liability in an orderly transaction between market participants at the measurement date'. Fair value is essentially an exit price that is applicable to assets and liabilities. It may be regarded as the cost to receive a liability or the cost to exit the ownership of an asset. At the heart of the standard is a hierarchy of fair value and it is non-entity specific based value. The fair value definition is applicable across all other IFRS that requires a measure of fair value with notable exceptions within IAS 2 (Inventories), IAS 36 (Impairment of assets) and IAS 17(Leases).

6.1 Features of fair value

There are four primary operational features embedded in the definition of fair value.

6.1.1 Asset/liability

When measuring fair value of an asset or liability, the specific characteristics of the item will be taken into consideration. Consideration will be given to the existing condition of the item, its location and any restriction on its use or sale. These considerations are not uncommon as they are already operating when acquiring or disposing of an asset or liability.

6.1.2 Transaction

Transactions are deemed to take place orderly in the principal market for the asset or liability.

An orderly transaction occurs when the item of sale has been exposed to the market for a reasonable time period that is appropriate for the asset or liability. For example, the disposal of inventory may need to be exposed to its market for a shorter period than the disposal of land and buildings. The sale transaction is not a forced sale and sufficient time has been allowed for participants to conduct their information gathering and search process to establish the competitive price and their willingness to pay.

The principal market is the market where trade for the item normally takes place. For example, the principal market for the sale or purchase of equities is the stock market.

In the absence of a principal market, transactions are deemed to occur in the in the most advantageous market for the asset or liability. The most advantageous market is the market that would maximise the amount received for the sale of an asset or the exit from a liability. It should be noted that although any transaction costs are recognised in the determination of the most advantageous market, transaction costs are not a cost in the determination of fair value. The transaction costs are invariably a characteristic of the transaction and not the asset or liability. For example, the cost of transportation is a characteristic of the location of the asset or liability and not the asset or liability itself.

6.1.3 Market participants

The fair value measurement of an asset or a liability is synonymous to that used by individual market participants in their pricing of an asset or liability when acting in their own economic interest. The market participants must satisfy four characteristics:

1 *Independent* – They must be independent and not related.
2 *Knowledgeable* – Market participants must possess reasonable understanding of the asset and liability with respect to all available information.
3 *Able to transact* – Market participants must be able to engage in the transaction.
4 *Willing to transact* – Market participants must be willing to engage in the transaction.

6.1.4 Price

Fair value is the price that would be received from the sale of an asset or paid to exit or transfer a liability in an orderly market transaction in the principal or most advantageous market, at a measurement date under current prevailing market conditions. This price is an exit price for the asset or liability and does not need to give any consideration to any other prevailing prices that may arise from any alternative known or observed or estimated measures.

6.2 Fair value hierarchy of inputs

The determination of fair value is based upon on a hierarchy of inputs used by the market participants. Three actual levels of inputs are deemed to exist.

Level one inputs exist when there is an active market for the asset or liability with observable quoted prices available. For example, the fair value for office furniture could be established using inputs from level one because there is an active market for items of office furniture, with observable and quoted prices readily available in catalogues or obtainable from suppliers of office furniture. When a market exists with level one inputs, these are used in the determination of fair value.

Level two inputs arise when there is a need to use adjusted quoted prices as a result of non-observable prices for the asset or liability and there may not be an active market in existence. This may be the case for an obsolete item. In such cases adjustments need to be made to prevailing prices for similar or near similar items to derive a fair price.

Level three inputs are non-observable quoted prices used in the determination of fair value. Such unobservable values may arise from projections or internally generated values by a company.

In determining fair value, entities should seek to maximise the use of level one inputs and minimise the use of level three. However, it is noteworthy that a company making use of its own internally generated values in the determination of fair value is not excluded within IFRS 13. Nevertheless, this practice should not be promoted, as level three is the least reliable and substantiated input into the fair value determination process.

 **WORKED EXAMPLE** **4.7**

Louigee Plc is seeking to establish the fair value for several assets and has presented you with the following information:

a An item of plant has been valued primarily on the basis of the discounted value of the sales revenue over the next five years.
b A total of 1,000 ex-rental computers no longer available on the market were valued with reference to a similar brand of computers.
c The portfolio of UK equities were valued at the closing price on the last day of trading on the London Stock Exchange.

You are required to comment on the inputs, as classified above, level 1, 2 or 3, used to determine the fair value of each item.

WORKED EXAMPLE **4.7** *continued*

Suggested solution

Item a) has used level three inputs; item b) has used level two and item c) has used level one inputs to derive the respective fair values.

On that basis, the valuation of item c) has used the most reliable inputs and item a) the least reliable inputs to derive their fair values.

6.3 Valuation

IFRS 13 recognises that the objective of using a valuation technique is to estimate the price at which an orderly transaction to sell the asset or to transfer the liability would take place between market participants and the measurement date under current market conditions.

The fair value measurement for a non-financial asset is its highest and best use. This should take into consideration a market participant's ability to generate economic benefits from their use of the asset in its highest and best use, whether the asset is used as a standalone item or in combination with other assets.

Three valuation techniques are recognised and identified in IFRS 13:

1 *market approach* – uses prices and other relevant information generated by market transactions involving identical or comparable (similar) assets, liabilities or a group of assets and liabilities (e.g. a business);

2 *cost approach* – reflects the amount that would be required currently to replace the service capacity of an asset (current replacement cost); and

3 *income approach* – converts future amounts (cash flows or income and expenses) to a single current (discounted) amount, reflecting current market expectations about those future amounts.

TEST YOUR KNOWLEDGE **4.5**

What is the meaning of fair value?

7 Accounting for property, plant and equipment (IAS 16)

Property, plant and equipment are non-current assets and they are defined in IAS 16 as:

'tangible items that are held for use in the production or supply of goods or services, for rental to others or for administrative purposes; and are expected to be used during more than one period.'

For the purpose of clarity and IAS 16 provides the definitions for the following terms:

■ *Cost* – The amount of cash or cash equivalents paid or the fair value of the other consideration given to acquire an asset at the time of its acquisition or construction or, where applicable, the amount attributed to that asset when initially recognised in accordance with the specific requirements of other IFRS.

■ *Impairment loss* – The amount by which the carrying amount of an asset exceeds its recoverable amount.

- *Carrying amount* – The amount at which an asset is recognised after deducting any accumulated depreciation and accumulated impairment losses.

The cost of an item of property, plant and equipment are only recognised as an asset if they meet the following two conditions:

a   it is probable that future economic benefits associated with the item will flow to the entity; and

b   the cost of the item can be measured reliably.

7.1 Initial measurement

The measurement to be applied for the initial recognition of property, plant and equipment is their cost. The initial recognition cost of property, plant and equipment would include the following three elements:

a   the cost price of the asset;

b   any costs that may be required to get the asset to its destination or operational state as deemed intended; and

c   any estimated costs of dismantling, removing and restoring the site where the asset is located, providing these cost obligations are incurred on acquisition of the asset.

WORKED EXAMPLE 4.8

On 28 February 20X7, ZeZe industrial manufacturing company received a formal quotation from a supplier for a new item of plant which ZeZe's Production Executive had seen at a recent exhibition. The detailed quotation read as follows:

		£
a	Machinery cost price	350,000
b	Delivery fee	2,750
c	Annual servicing	20,000
d	Installation fee	15,750
e	VAT @ 25%	97,125
f	Total cost	466,200

ZeZe's financial year end is 31 March and they are VAT registered.

Required
Determine the actual cost of the new plant for the Production Executive in accordance with the requirements of IAS16.

Solution
The only items of the received quotation that will be included in the cost of the new plant to comply with IAS 16 is as follows:

a   Machinery cost: £350,000
b   Delivery charge: £2,750
d   Installation fee: £15,750

Thus a total cost of £368,500

The servicing charged is a revenue expense and should be charged to the accounts in accordance with the accruals concept.

    The VAT should not be considered because as a VAT-registered company it is an expense that ZeZe can recover in its accounting for VAT.

The accounting and reporting for property, plant and equipment is important in financial reporting because over last two decades there has been some catastrophic corporate failures centred around fraudulent accounting of property, plant and equipment. One of the least discussed cases is Waste Management in US, where over a five-year period a range of inappropriate accounting treatments were used. These included not depreciating their waste collection vehicles by assigning unsupported and inflated salvage values and extending their useful lives, and assigning arbitrary residual values to other assets that previously had no residual value.

STOP AND THINK 4.1

ZeZe acquired a new plant at a cost of £5m. The legal fees incurred were 1% of the purchase price, and the combined buildings and contents insurance were £25,650.

What would be the cost that of plant recorded in the books of ZeZe to comply with IAS 16?

a £5,000,000

b £5,050,000

c £5,075,650

7.2 Subsequent measurement

IAS 16 provides us with two methods of measuring property, plant and equipment after its initial recognition. The two methods are the cost model and the revaluation model.

The cost model measures property, plant and equipment after initial recognition on the basis of the cost of acquisition less accumulated depreciation and any impairment losses.

The revaluation model measures property, plant and equipment after recognition on the basis of its fair value revaluation based fair value less any accumulated depreciation and any impairment losses.

However, when applying the revaluation measurement, it is necessary to take some considerations into account.

When applying the revaluation model to any item of property, plant and equipment, the revaluation must be applied to the entire class of items. If one item of machinery or one building is being revalued, then all machinery and buildings must be revalued.

All items of property, plant and equipment in the same class must be revalued at the same time. This provides consistency in valuation dates and prevents the selective revaluations of items at sporadic revaluation dates. Furthermore, to ensure that the fair value and the carrying amount of property, plant and equipment are not materially different, revaluations should be undertaken at sufficient regularity. IAS 16 does not state frequency of property, plant and equipment revaluation. However, it does state that 'the frequency of revaluations depends upon the changes in fair values of the items of property, plant and equipment being revalued'. It is usually the case that property has a tendency to experience more frequent changes in its fair value than plant or equipment, therefore the revaluation of property, plant and equipment may be driven by rate of change in the fair value of property. It may be sufficient to undertake annual revaluations, but in exceptional circumstances (such as in inflationary or deflationary periods), a shorter time interval may be selected.

7.3 Revaluation gains and losses

IAS 16 paragraphs 39 and 40 provides guidance on the accounting treatment of any revaluation gains or losses arising from the revaluation of items of property, plant and equipment.

'If an asset's carrying amount is increased as a result of a revaluation, the increase shall be recognised in other comprehensive income and accumulated in equity under the heading of revaluation surplus. However, the increase shall be recognised in profit or loss to the extent that it reverses a revaluation decrease of the same asset previously recognised in profit or loss.

If an asset's carrying amount is decreased as a result of a revaluation, the decrease shall be recognised in profit or loss. However, the decrease shall be recognised in other comprehensive income to the extent of any credit balance existing in the revaluation surplus in respect of that asset. The decrease recognised in other comprehensive income reduces the amount accumulated in equity under the heading of revaluation surplus.'

WORKED EXAMPLE 4.9

Cud-Joe reporting year is 31 March and on 1 April 20X3 purchased a property for £950,000. On 31 March 20X5 the property was revalued at £800,000 and Cud-Joe decided not to sell. On 31 March 20X7, the property was revalued prior to its disposal and it was revalued at £1,050,000. Cud-Joe always uses the revaluation model for all property, plant and equipment.

Required

a How should Cud-Joe account for the revaluation of the property in 20X5 and 20X7?

b What additional advice would you offer the company?

Suggested solution

a 31 March 20X5
   The £150,000 decrease should be recognised as an expense in the profit or loss for 20X5.
   31 March 20X7
   The £250,000 increase should be credited to a revaluation reserve and shown as other comprehensive income in the statement of profit or loss and other comprehensive income.

b Cud-Joe should be advised that in compliance with IAS 16, all other property held should have also been revalued at the same dates.

Any increase in the carrying amount arising from the revaluation of property, plant and equipment is credited to a revaluation reserve and shown reported as other comprehensive income. Such treatment of an increase in revaluation is to ensure that the revaluation is not treated as revenue in line with the IAS 18 definition of revenue (see next section). Secondly, as the revaluation has arisen is an unrealised gain it is not distributable as dividends

7.4 Depreciation

Depreciation is defined in IAS 16 as the systematic allocation of the depreciable amount of an asset over its useful life. In addition, IAS 16 provides clarity with the accounting and understanding of depreciation with the definition of the following elements of depreciation:

- *Depreciable amount* – 'the cost of an asset or other amount substituted for cost, less its residual value'.
- *Residual value* – 'the estimated amount that an entity would currently obtain from disposal of the asset, after deducting the estimated costs of disposal, if the asset were already of the age and in the condition expected at the end of its useful life'.
- *Useful life* – 'the period over which an asset is expected to be available for use by an entity; or the number of production or similar units expected to be obtained from the asset by an entity'.

When depreciating property, plant and equipment, each part of an item of property, plant and equipment with a cost that is significant in relation to the total cost of the item shall be depreciated separately. A modified extract from the 'John Lewis annual reports and accounts 2015' shown below demonstrates this components approach.

Consolidated	Land and buildings £m	Fixture and fittings £m	Assets in course of construction £m	Total £m
Cost				
At 25 January 2014	4,034.6	1,738.0	192.7	5965.3
Additions	0.00	1.4	512.17	514.1
Transfers	331.0	210.8	(541.8)	0.00
Disposals	(77.9)	(135.3)	(6.2)	(219.4)
At 31 January 2015	4,287.7	1,814.9	157.4	6,260.0
Accumulated depreciation				
At 25 January 2014	833.4	1,144.7	0.00	1,978.1
Charges for the year	116.6	165.1	0.00	281.7
Disposals	(25.3)	(134.6)	0.00	(159.9)
At 31 January 2015	924.7	1,175.2	0.00	2,099.9
Net book value at 31 January 2015	3,363	639.7	157.4	4,160.1

The annual depreciation charge is charged to the profit or loss, unless it is included in the carrying amount of another asset.

7.5 Depreciation methods

The depreciation methods used to depreciate property, plant and equipment should reflect the pattern in which their future economic benefits are expected to be consumed by the entity.

The depreciation method applied should be reviewed at least at the end of each financial year and, if there has been a significant change in the expected pattern of consumption of the future economic benefits embodied in the asset, the method should be changed to reflect the changed pattern. Any such a change should be accounted for as a change in an accounting estimate in accordance with IAS 8. It is necessary to review the useful life and residual values at least once per annum.

IAS 16 states that 'a variety of depreciation methods can be used to allocate the depreciable amount of an asset on a systematic basis over its useful life'. The three main methods of depreciation identified in IAS 16 reflect the consumption pattern of the future economic benefits of the assets are:

- straight-line method;
- reducing balance method; and
- units of production method.

The straight-line depreciation charge for an accounting period is the depreciable amount of property, plant and equipment spread over their useful life. This provides a constant depreciation charge per accounting period.

The reducing balance depreciation charge for an accounting period is a fixed percentage applied to the carrying amount of the property, plant and equipment. Unlike the straight-line method, this method produces a reducing depreciation charge per accounting period.

The units of production depreciation charge for an accounting period is derived by applying a depreciation consumption rate to the annual level of production. The depreciation consumption rate is determined by spreading the depreciable amount over the asset's lifetime productive capacity.

WORKED EXAMPLE **4.10**

A manufacturing company is planning on purchasing a new machine at the start of the financial year commencing 1 April 20X7 for £67,876. The machine is expected to produce 120,000 units over its five-year life span and to have a residual value of £7,876. The production for the five years is as follows.

Year	Units
1	24,000
2	26,000
3	34,000
4	24,000
5	12,000

Required

You are required to calculate the annual depreciation charge for the life of the new machine using the following depreciation methods:

a) units of production;
b) reducing balance at 35% per annum; and
c) straight line method ay 20% per annum

Answer

Depreciable amount = 67,876 − 7,876 = 60,000
In previous years, the company has depreciated similar items using a reducing balance basis.

a Units of production

The depreciation consumption per unit of production is **£0.50**

$$\frac{\text{Depreciable amount}}{\text{Units of production}} = \textbf{£0.50}$$

Year	Units of production	Annual depreciation at £0.50 per unit £
1	24,000	12,000
2	26,000	13,000
3	34,000	17,000
4	24,000	12,000
5	12,000	6,000

b Reducing balance

Year	Carrying amount b/f	Annual depreciation at 35% £	Carrying amount c/f £
1	67,876	23,757	44,119
2	44,119	15,442	28,678
3	28,678	10,037	18,640
4	18,640	6,524	12,116
5	12,116	4,241	7,876

c Straight-line method

$$\frac{\text{Depreciable amount}}{\text{Life span}} = £12,000 \text{ per annum}$$

IAS 16 also provides clear guidance on the treatment any accumulated depreciation following the revaluation of property, plant and equipment. IAS 16 states that any accumulated depreciation at the date of the revaluation should be treated in one of the following ways:

a   Restated proportionately with the change in the gross carrying amount of the asset so that the carrying amount of the asset after revaluation equals its revalued amount. This method is often used when an asset is revalued by means of applying an index to determine its depreciated replacement cost.

b   Eliminated against the gross carrying amount of the asset and the net amount restated to the revalued amount of the asset. This method is often used for buildings.

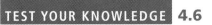 **TEST YOUR KNOWLEDGE 4.6**

Identify and explain the three methods of depreciation in IAS 16.

---

8   Accounting for revenue (IFRS 15)

8.1 Revenue from contracts with customers

Revenue is often the first figure that readers of financial statements look at. This may be associated with the fact that it is the first figure that appears in the statement of profit or loss and other comprehensive income. Despite its presence in financial statements and reporting, it is necessary to establish what revenue *is*. IFRS 15 provides an operational definition of revenue:

> 'Revenue is the gross inflow of economic benefits during the period arising in the course of the ordinary activities of an entity when those inflows result in increases in equity, other than increases relating to contributions from equity participants.'

For the purposes of the preparation of financial statements and the subsequent reporting of financial statements, it is necessary to understand fully and be able to determine and separate revenue from all the inflows into an entity. Monies collected or received on behalf of third parties, such as sales taxes or value added taxes, are not economic benefits that flow to the entity and do not result in increases in equity. Therefore these items should never be included as part of the revenue of a company's financial reporting.

This distinction between gross sales and revenue is clearly evident when reading financial reports such as the John Lewis Partnership plc consolidated income statements. The John Lewis consolidated income statements (unlike many other companies' consolidated income statement) begin with the gross sales. The second line of the John Lewis consolidated income statement is the revenue, gross sales less VAT.

In addition to sales tax, where there is an agency relationship such that a company acting as an agent collects monies on behalf of its principal, the amounts collected on behalf of the principal are not revenue. Revenue is only the commission due and payable to the agent.

WORKED EXAMPLE 4.11

For the year ended 31 December 20X6, a tour operator's gross fees from its holiday sold during the year was £2.4m. The tour operator receives commission equal 32% of holiday sales plus 20% sales tax from the travel companies.

Required
What is the revenue that the tour operator should recognise in the financial year ended 31 December 20X6?

Suggested solution
Revenue recognised = gross sales × 32%
= £2.4m × 32%
= £768,000

> ▦ **WORKED EXAMPLE** **4.11** *continued*
>
> The gross sales less the commission is the money that is collected on behalf of the principal – in this case, the travel companies.
>
> The sales tax, £153, 600 (20% × £768,000), is money repayable to the government and this is also excluded from the revenue of the tour operator.

8.2 Revenue recognition

As mentioned previously IFRS 15 specifies how and when reporting entities should recognize revenue from the sale of goods and provision of services. Revenue is referred to by a variety of different terms including: sales, fees, interest, dividends, royalties and rent and is recognised when a customer obtains control of a good or service and has the ability to direct the use of and obtain the benefit from the good or service being provided. The core principle of IFRS 15 is that an entity should recognise revenue to depict the transfer of promised good or services to customers in an amount that reflects the consideration to which the entity expects to be entitled in exchange for the goods or services. There are a number of steps to take when applying the core principles of IFRS 15 to determine revenue recognition:

Revenue is recognised when a customer obtains control of a good or service.

Step 1: Identify the contract(s) with a customer.
A contract is defined as an agreement between two or more parties that creates enforceable rights and obligations. Ingredients of a valid contract under IFRS 15 include:

- Approval and commitment of the parties.
- Identification of the rights of the parties.
- Identification of the payment terms.
- The contract has commercial substance.
- It is probable that the entity will collect the consideration to which it will be entitled in exchange for the goods or services that will be transferred to the customer.

Step 2: Identify the performance obligations of the contract.
A performance obligation is a promise by an entity to transfer a good or service to the customer. If an entity promises in a contract to transfer more than one good, or service, to the customer, the entity should account for each promised good or service as a separate performance obligation. Each performance obligation is 'distinct', being either a good or service from which the customer can benefit on its own (or in combination with other readily available goods and services). However, two or more distinct goods and services (such as the supply of construction material and labour) are combined if, in reality, they represent one overall obligation.

Step 3: Determine the transaction price.
The transaction price is the amount of consideration (for example, payment) to which an entity expects to be entitled in exchange for transferring promised goods, or services, to a customer. To determine the transaction price, an entity should consider the effects of:

a **Variable consideration** – If the amount of consideration in a contract is variable, an entity should determine the amount to include in the transaction price by estimating either the expected value (that is, probability- weighted amount) or the most likely amount, depending on which method the entity expects to better predict the amount of consideration to which the entity will be entitled.

b An entity should adjust the consideration for the effects of the **time value of money** if the timing of the payments agreed upon by the parties to the contract provides the customer, or the entity, with a significant benefit of financing for the transfer of goods or services to the customer. IFRS 15 states that entities can ignore time value of money if the period between transfer of goods or services, and payment is less than one year.

Entities might agree to provide goods, or services, for consideration that is dependent on certain future events occurring, or not occurring.

Examples include refund rights, performance bonuses and penalties. According to IFRS 15, an estimate of variable consideration should be included in the transaction price, if it is highly probable that the amount will not result in a **significant revenue reversal**, if estimates change.

Step 4: Allocate the transaction price to the performance obligations in the contract.

Entities that sell multiple goods or services in a single arrangement must allocate the consideration to each of those goods or services. To allocate an appropriate amount of consideration to each performance obligation, an entity must determine the standalone selling price, at contract inception, of the distinct goods, or services, underlying each performance obligation.

Step 5: Recognise revenue when the entity satisfies a performance obligation.

An entity should recognise revenue when (or as) it satisfies a performance obligation by transferring a promised good or service to a customer.

A good or service is transferred when (or as) the customer obtains control of that good or service.

It must be noted that reporting entities are required to disclose qualitative and quantitative information about the following:

- its contracts with customers;
- the significant judgments, and changes in the judgments, made in applying the guidance to those contracts; and
- any assets recognised from the costs to obtain or fulfill a contract with a customer.

WORKED EXAMPLE 4.12

Java Plc sells cloud-based accounting and integrated client costing and CRM systems to small legal practices at the cost of £20,000. Law firms are given the opportunity to pay in three annual instalments of £8,000 in year one and £6,000 on the anniversary in one and two years' time respectively. For the split payment terms, Java's appropriate **discount rate** is 7% per annum.

If a new law firm purchases a system on 15 March 20X4, how much revenue should Java recognise on sale?

Answer

The revenue recognised on 15 March 20X4 is £18,848 as shown below is the present value of the revenue inflows over the annual anniversaries for the three years.

Students should note that the difference, £1,152, is the notional interest recognised by Java.

Date	Revenue £	Discount factor	Present value £
15 Mar 20X4	8,000	1.0000	8,000
15 Mar 20X5	6,000	0.9346	5,608
15 Mar 20X6	6,000	0.8734	5,240
Total	20,000		18,848

Some transactions between parties involve the exchange of similar or dissimilar goods/services, i.e. a barter or a swap. In such cases there is a two-part test. The test is based upon whether the goods/services that are the subject of the exchange are of a similar nature and value.

Where the items are similar in nature and value, the exchange is not regarded as a revenue generating transaction. However, if the items are dissimilar in nature and value, a revenue generating transaction is deemed to have taken place. In such cases, the revenue is measured at its fair value basis. The revenue is measured at the fair value of the goods or services received, adjusted by the amount of any cash or cash equivalents transferred.

When the fair value of the goods or services received cannot be measured reliably, the revenue is measured at the fair value of the goods or services given up, adjusted by the amount of any cash or cash equivalents transferred.

 **WORKED EXAMPLE 4.13**

On 15 September 20X3, a training company with a financial year ended 30 June secured a new 18-month contract to deliver 15 days (135 hours) external training from 1 November 20X3 to 30 April 20X5, assume training is 7.5 hours per month. The value of the 18-month contract is £324,000.

Required
How should the training company recognise the value of the contract in their financial statements?

Suggested answer
The total contract value of £324,000 is apportioned to each financial year on the basis of the number of training days within each financial year ended 30 June.

Year ended	Income recognised
30 June 20X4	1 Nov 20X3 – 30 Jun 20X4
	$= \dfrac{15 \times 8 \times £324,000}{15 \times 18}$
	$= £144,000$
30 June 20X5	$= £324,000 - 144,000$
	$= £180,000$
To check 30 June 20X5	$= \dfrac{15 \times 10 \times £324,000}{270}$
	$= £180,000$
	£180,000 + £144,000 = £324,000

---

9 Accounting for provisions (IAS 37)

Provision is a word commonly found within financial reports – provision for doubtful debt, annual provision for depreciation and provision for an unknown liability. Examples of provisions for unknown liabilities are monies set aside by UK banks for payment protection insurance (PPI) claims, or the provisions made by Microsoft several years ago as it awaited the outcome of a US anti-trust court case.

Despite these three forms of reference to provisions in financial statements, IAS 37 provides clarity on the meaning of a provision.

IAS 37 provides a definition of a provision and the conditions under which it should be recognised. A provision is defined as 'a liability of uncertain timing or amount'. It should only be recognised when all of the following three conditions are satisfied:

a an entity has a present obligation (legal or constructive) as a result of a past event;
b it is probable that an outflow of resources embodying economic benefits will be required to settle the obligation; and
c a reliable estimate can be made of the amount of the obligation.

IAS 37 is therefore not concerned with a provision for a doubtful debt or annual provision for depreciation. These are primarily the reduction in an entity's asset and not a liability. It is not unusual to have these types of provisions termed as allowances.

A provision is only possible because of a past event that has given rise to the provision. Such past events are known as obligating events. An example of this is the BP oil spillage off the coast of the US.

A past event becomes an obligatory event for an entity if either of the following conditions are satisfied:

a the obligation is legally enforceable; or
b a constructive obligation was created as a result of the event.

IAS 37 defines constructive obligation as:

'an obligation that derives from an entity's actions where:

a by an established pattern of past practice, published policies or a sufficiently specific current statement, the entity has indicated to other parties that it will accept certain responsibilities; and

b as a result, the entity has created a valid expectation on the part of those other parties that it will discharge those responsibilities.'

Furthermore, the requirement for an obligatory event resolves use of the word 'provision' in relation to the provision for a future activity. It is set out in IAS 37 that a provision cannot be made for an unknown or known future activity or cost.

 **WORKED EXAMPLE 4.14**

Zorex Motors sold 24,000 cars during the year to 31 March 20X4. It is customary for the industry to recall 5% of its sales. A historic trend of recalls has revealed that the cost of recalls exhibit the following behaviour:

Cars recalled %	Average repair bill €
20	200
25	150
55	100

Required
Calculate the Zorex Motors provision for the year ended 31 March 20X4.

Suggested solution
The provision for the year is as follows:

Recalled cars 24,000 × 5% = 1,200

Cars	€	€'000
240	200	48
300	150	45
660	100	66
1,200	Total	159

Zorex Motors provision for the year ended 31 March 2004 should be €159,000.

The solution in the above example demonstrates an important feature of the recognition of a provision as outlined in IAS 37. The amount of a provision should be the best estimate of expenditure required to settle the present obligation at the end of the reporting period. In Worked Example 4.14, Zorex Motors has historic trend information on the maximum repair costs and the percentage of recalls within each expenditure class. Therefore this information provides the best estimate for the computation of the provision. However, it may be questioned whether the past is any guide to the future. In the absence of any additional information, the available information is sufficient to provide the best estimate for the computation of the provision.

The use of the statistical estimation technique, expected value, as applied in Worked Example 4.14, is recognised in IAS 37 as applicable to handle uncertainties in the determination of the provision where there is a large population of data.

Where it is not possible to provide a reliable estimate for a present obligation liability, the liability must be disclosed as a contingent liability. The inability to determine a reliable measure of the liability is only one element of a contingent liability. Furthermore, a contingent liability arises where there is not expected to be any outflow of economic benefits to meet an obligation. For example, where there is a joint obligation and one part is to be met by a third party, that element which a third party meets is a contingent liability. IAS 37 does not permit the recognition of contingent liabilities in the statement of financial position. IAS 37 states:

'unless the possibility of any outflow in settlement is remote, an entity shall disclose for each class of contingent liability at the end of the reporting period a brief description of the nature of the contingent liability and, where practicable:

a) an estimate of its financial effect,
b) an indication of the uncertainties relating to the amount or timing of any outflow; and
c) the possibility of any reimbursement.

In addition, for each class of provision, the following disclosures are required:

a) a brief description of the nature of the obligation and the expected timing of any resulting outflows of economic benefits;
b) an indication of the uncertainties about the amount or timing of those outflows. Where it is necessary to provide adequate information, an entity shall disclose the major assumptions made concerning future events, as addressed in paragraph 48; and
c) the amount of any expected reimbursement, stating the amount of any asset that has been recognised for that expected reimbursement.'

In contrast to a contingent liability, under IAS 37, a contingent asset usually arises from unplanned or other unexpected events which may give rise to the possibility of an inflow of economic benefits to the entity. The example from IAS 37 is as follows, a claim that an entity is pursuing through legal processes, where the outcome is uncertain.

Contingent assets are not recognised in financial statements, as they may give rise to the recognition of income that an entity may never realise. However, IAS 37 states clearly: 'when the realisation of income is virtually certain, then the related asset is not a contingent asset and its recognition is appropriate.'

In such circumstances, the same disclosure rules are applicable to contingent assets as contingent liabilities.

 **TEST YOUR KNOWLEDGE** 4.7

Outline the conditions that must be satisfied to allow the recognition of a provision.

10 Accounting for intangible assets (IAS 38)

An intangible asset is defined in IAS 38 as 'an identifiable non-monetary asset without physical substance'. Embedded in this definition is a complexity of issues for the reporting entity and the reader of financial reports.

An intangible asset is identifiable when it can be separated from an entity and moved to another either via sale, transfer, licence or rent. This gives rise to a challenge for the popular concept of goodwill that generally arises from and is associated with the reputation and status of the entity, because goodwill is thus not separable from the entity. Goodwill is fully covered in Chapter 7, section 6.1.

Intangible assets by their nature are non-monetary, as monetary assets by definition are financial assets. Furthermore, intangible assets have no physical substance or existence unlike items of plant property and equipment, which one is able to view and touch in their physical format.

Underpinning all of the above, intangible assets must meet the base condition for an asset: the ability to generate future economic benefits to the entity and controllable by entity. This condition provides clarity or not on whether certain items are creating an intangible asset for the entity. It is sometimes mooted that, in some sectors, employees are the intellectual property of the entity. However, when exposed to the test of entity control, it is self-evident that an entity cannot really exercise any control over the movement of its workforce, irrespective of the monies spent on their development and the expectation of the entity. However, an entity has and can exercise control over its trademarks, patents and copyrights.

The recognition of an intangible asset is only possible if satisfies the following two conditions outlined in IAS 38:

a   it is probable that the expected future economic benefits that are attributable to the asset will flow to the entity; and
b   the cost of the asset can be measured reliably.

IAS 38 provides guidance on the measurement of intangible assets. The initial measurement of an intangible fixed asset should be its cost. Its cost is either the cost incurred on acquisition or the cost incurred in its generation where the intangible asset has been internally generated.

Intangible assets may arise from three sources: acquired separately; via a business combination; or internally generated. It is the latter that presents the greatest challenge. An individual acquisition or through a business combination will have resulted in a price being paid for the asset, therefore the expectation is a future economic benefit will flow to the entity. However, the internally generated intangible asset presents a greater test, especially as IAS 38 states: 'internally generated goodwill shall not be recognised as an asset' (see Chapter 7). Goodwill usually arises during the course of a business combination, when one entity acquires another entity.

10.1   Internally generated intangible assets

To address the problem of internally generated goodwill, IAS 38 requires the separation of internally generated assets into a research and a development phase.

An intangible asset cannot be born out of the research phase because this is the exploratory phase when all the planning and investigation occurs. IAS 38 lists examples of the research phase as follows:

a   activities aimed at obtaining new knowledge;
b   the search for, evaluation and final selection of, and applications of research findings or other knowledge;
c   the search for alternatives for materials, devices, products, processes, systems or services; and
d   the formulation, design, evaluation and final selection of possible new or improved alternatives.

Consequently, all such expenditure is written off as an expense when incurred by an entity.

Activities in the development phase go beyond the foundation-laying activities and as such can give rise to the generation of an intangible asset. However, an intangible asset is only recognised from the development stage if all of the following conditions are satisfied:

a   The technical feasibility of completing the intangible asset so that it will be available for use or sale.
b   The entity intends to complete the intangible asset and use or sell it.
c   The entity's ability to use or sell the intangible asset.
d   The intangible asset will generate probable future economic benefits.
e   The availability of adequate technical, financial and other resources to complete the development and to use or sell the intangible asset.
f   The entity can measure reliably the expenditure attributable to the intangible asset during its development.

If all these conditions are satisfied, the expenditure incurred should be capitalised. However, if any of these six conditions are not met, the expenditure must be written off as an expense.

WORKED EXAMPLE 4.15

Piton Plc spent £900,000 during the year to 30 June 20X4 on two internal projects, Acezar and Beezar. Acezar consumed 60% of the total expenditure and £216,000 total expenditure was incurred on pure research plus an additional £18,000 was spent on staff training. The remainder of Acezar's expenditure was applied to the development phase. The expenditure on Beezar was for the development phase of a prototype. However, new information has cast a doubt over whether Piton Plc will be able to sell the Beezar.

Required

How should Piton Plc account for the £900,000 expenditure on:

a Acezar

b Beezar?

Suggested solution

a Acezar

£900,000 × 60% = £540,000

R & D	216,000	
Staff Training	18,000	excluded from development phase
Total	234,000	
Residual	306,000	

Piton should write-off the £234,000 to its statement of profit or loss and other comprehensive income for the year ending 30 June 20X4.

The residual £306,000 should be capitalised and recognised as an intangible asset if Acezar can satisfy all the six conditions.

If all the six conditions are not satisfied, the £306,000 should be expensed to its SOCI for the year to 30 June 20X4.

b Beezar

£900,000 × 40% = £360,000

The expenditure on Beezar should not be capitalised and recognised as an intangible asset if Piton Plc cannot meet the six conditions of the development phase, including if the item cannot be used internally or sold.

If Piton Plc cannot sell the asset, but can use it internally and it will generate future economic benefits to the company, the £360,000 should be capitalised and Beezar recognised as an intangible asset for the year ended 30 June 20X4.

The uncertainty of a possible sale is not sufficient on its own to prevent Beezar from being classified as an intangible asset. IAS 38 provides for an entity's ability to sell or use the asset internally among its six conditions test at the development phase.

Similar to IAS 16, IAS 38 outlined the same two models for the subsequent measurement of an intangible asset. Furthermore, the guidance for the accounting treatment of revaluation for gains or losses of an intangible asset is identical to the treatment for property, plant and equipment outlined in IAS 16.

WORKED EXAMPLE 4.16

During the accounting period ended 31 December 20X4, Zolvix plc spent £265,000 on research and development costs of a new multimedia project as follows:

a   Feasibility study: £30,000
b   Overhead costs: £50,000
c   Domain name: £10,000
d   Software development: £75,000
e   Maintenance costs: £25,000
f   Web page development: £40,000
g   Administration costs: £35,000

Required

How should the £265,000 research and development costs be accounted for in Zolvix plc financial statement at the end of the accounting period 31 December 20X4?

Suggested solution

The following £140,000 research and development costs should be charged to the statement of profit or loss and other comprehensive income:

a   Feasibility study: £30,000
b   Overhead costs: £50,000
c   Maintenance costs: £25,000
d   Administration costs: £35,000

The residual £125,000 of research and development costs should be capitalised and recognised as intangible assets in the statement of financial position, if each item can satisfy all six conditions set out in IAS 38.

a   Domain name: £10,000
b   Software development: £75,000
c   Web page development: £40,000

If any of the six conditions cannot be satisfied by any of the above three items, they should also be charged to the statement of profit or loss and other comprehensive income.

STOP AND THINK 4.2

What were the two models for the subsequent measurement of property, plant and equipment identified in IAS 16?

IAS 16 provides for the depreciation of property, plant and equipment. However, IAS 38 does not provide for the depreciation of intangible assets. Instead, intangible assets are amortised.

10.2 Amortisation

Amortisation is the equivalent to the depreciation of property, plant and equipment, but for intangible assets. Amortisation is defined as the systematic allocation of the depreciable amount of an intangible asset over its useful life. However it is only applicable to intangible assets with finite lives. Therefore it is necessary to be able to determine the useful life of an intangible asset. IAS 38 set out a list of seven factors to be considered and assist in the process of determination of the useful life of a finite intangible asset. The list from IAS 38 is set out below:

a   the expected usage of the asset by the entity and whether the asset could be managed efficiently by another management team;

b   typical product life cycles for the asset and public information on estimates of useful lives of similar assets that are used in a similar way;

c   technical, technological, commercial or other types of obsolescence;

d   the stability of the industry in which the asset operates and changes in the market demand for the products or services output from the asset;

e   expected actions by competitors or potential competitors;

f   the level of maintenance expenditure required to obtain the expected future economic benefits from the asset and the entity's ability and intention to reach such a level;

g   the period of control over the asset and legal or similar limits on the use of the asset, such as the expiry dates of related leases; and

h   whether the useful life of the asset is dependent on the useful life of other assets of the entity.

The determination of whether an asset has a finite or indefinite life is determined by whether there is a foreseeable limit to the period over which the asset is expected to generate net cash inflows for the entity. Where there is no foreseeable limit, the intangible asset will be deemed to have an indefinite life. Conversely, all other assets will have a definite useful life, as there will be a foreseeable limit to the period over which the asset is expected to generate net cash inflows for the entity.

It suffices to assert that the accounting for amortisation mirrors that of depreciation accounting for plant, property and equipment. The useful life of an intangible asset that is not being amortised shall be reviewed each period to determine whether events and circumstances continue to support an indefinite useful life assessment for that asset. Any change in the useful life assessment from indefinite to finite shall be accounted for as a change in an accounting estimate in accordance with IAS 8.

TEST YOUR KNOWLEDGE 4.8

When can an entity capitalise its expenditure on research and development?

END OF CHAPTER QUESTIONS

4.1   Alibi Ltd bought (and capitalised as a non-current asset) an 'off-the-shelf' computer system at a cost of £1 million. A few months later, the manufacturer dropped the price of the same system to £700,000.

- What accounting action should Alibi Ltd take as a result of this action?

    a   Increase the depreciation of the computer system.

    b   Impair the carrying amount of the computer system.

    c   Recognise the reduction as an impairment indicator and carry out an impairment test.

    d   No action required.

4.2   Reporter plc, a newspaper publisher, entered into a four-year lease agreement with Admac plc for a printing machine on 1 January 20X3, on which date the machine being leased was delivered and a deposit of £38,211 paid to the lessor. The initial direct cost incurred in negotiating the lease amounted to £4,000.

The lease agreement provides for four equal payments of £230,010 due on 31 December annually, with the first payment due on 31 December 20X3. The fair value of the machine on 1 January 20X3 was £800,000. The estimated useful life of the machine is four years.

Ken Wood is expected to insure and maintain the printing machine over the lease period. Ken Wood's similarly owned assets are depreciated on a straight-line basis. The implicit interest rate within the lease is 8%.

Required

Using the information given above, calculate the amounts to be shown in the financial statements of Reporter plc for the years ended 31 December 20X3 and 20X4.

4.3 The broad principles of accounting for tangible non-current assets involve distinguishing between capital and revenue expenditure, measuring the cost of assets, determining how they should be depreciated and dealing with the problems of subsequent measurement and subsequent expenditure. IAS 16 'Property, plant and equipment' seeks to improve consistency in these areas.

Required

Explain:

a how the initial cost of tangible non-current assets should be measured; and

b the circumstances in which subsequent expenditure on those assets should be capitalised.

4.4 Alphabet Ltd secures a long-term loan agreement from its bankers. The purpose of the loan is to invest in the land and buildings owned by the company to bring them within the requirements of the relevant health and safety legislation. The loan is for £1.5 million over 13 years with an annual payment (in arrears) of £160,000; however, the final payment in year 13 will be a reduced amount of £154,396. The implied rate of interest is 5%.

Required

Prepare a schedule of repayments clearly showing capital and interest payments and the balance reducing after each annual payment.

4.5 Explain the difference between an adjusting and a non-adjusting event to comply with IAS 10.

4.6 During the preparation of the financial statement for the year ended 31 December 20X3, Simpark

uncovered a fraud that had taken place, which had resulted in errors in the financial statements for the year to 31 December 20X2. The company's sales had been overstated by £150,000 as a result of several ex-employees' attempts to manipulate their bonus payments, and a non-approved supplier had been paid for an invoice totalling £45,000. The retained earnings at 31 December 20X1 were £85,000.

A draft of an extract from the statement of profit or loss and other comprehensive income for the year to 31 December 20X3 is shown below.

	20X3 £,000	20X2 £,000
Sales	850	750
Cost of goods sold	365	300
Gross profit	485	450
Expenses	460	335
Pre-tax profit	25	115
Taxation @ 20%	5	23
Profit after taxation	20	92
Dividends distribution	5	12

Required

a Produce a revised statement of profit or loss and other comprehensive income for the year to 31 December 20X3 after the amendment showing a restatement of the statement of profit or loss and other comprehensive income for the year to 31 December 20X2.

b Show the closing retained earnings as at 31 December 20X3.

Accounting policies 2

5

■ **CONTENTS**

■ **LEARNING OUTCOMES**

At the end of this section, you will be able to:

- demonstrate an understanding of accounting for property, plant and equipment including accounting for depreciation and accounting for impairment;
- demonstrate the way in which leasing arrangements may be exploited to access the advantages of off-statement of financial position finance;
- outline and evaluate proposals designed to counter opportunistic behaviour by management when accounting for leases;
- distinguish between the economic substance and the legal form of a business transaction;
- report in the statement of profit or loss and other comprehensive income the impact of **discontinued operations**;
- show an understanding of the appropriate methods for valuing assets and liabilities;
- explain the importance of segmental information and be able to prepare a **segmental report**;
- demonstrate familiarity with the nature of accounting policies, the significance of differences between them and the effects of changes in accounting policy;
- demonstrate an awareness of the steps entities might take to improve their accounts so as, for example, to reduce the reported gearing ratio, increase the published earnings per share (EPS), and strengthen the statement of financial position;
- reveal a full understanding of the opportunities for subjectivity and creative accounting when preparing financial reports;
- show familiarity with the role of the audit in countering creative accounting practices;
- show an understanding of the treatment of inventories in financial statements; and
- explain what is meant by off-statement of financial position finance and understand its significance.

1   Introduction

This chapter will examine seven additional accounting policies with reference to the appropriate international accounting standards to enable a greater understanding of the financial statements. The accounting policies that will be discussed throughout this chapter are as follows:

- Income taxes
- Leases
- Financial instruments
- Earnings per share
- Impairment of assets
- Non-current assets held for sale and discontinued operations
- Operating segments

2   Income taxation (IAS 12)

Taxation and the level of income tax paid by entities has become a global subject in recent years, particularly after the financial crisis that began in 2007. Even before this increase in profile, taxation was recognised as an important issue by those who prepare financial statements and those who rely on them.

UK readers may be familiar with the distinction in the UK tax system between income tax (which is levied upon individuals) and corporation tax (which is levied on companies). However, for our purposes, when we refer to 'income tax' we are referring to the taxation levied on the profit of an entity, rather than the narrower UK interpretation of income tax.

This fits with the definition provided in International Accounting Standard (IAS) 12. Current tax is defined as 'the amount of income taxes payable (recoverable) in respect of the taxable profit (tax loss) for a period'.

It should be noted that the taxable profit (loss) for a period is not synonymous with the accounting profit (loss) for a period. IAS 12 provides guidance on this matter and defines taxable profit (tax loss) as 'the profit (loss) for a period, determined in accordance with the rules established by the taxation authorities, upon which income taxes are payable (recoverable)'.

Income tax is an expense that, in accordance with IAS 1, is reported within the statement of profit or loss and other comprehensive income. Any income tax unpaid at the end of the period is reported as a liability in the statement of financial position.

 WORKED EXAMPLE 5.1

A global company generated an accounting profit of £900,000 in the period ended 30 September 20X6. The accounting profit for the period included £25,000 of expenditure, which is not allowable for income tax purposes and excluded £150,000 expenditure on plant, property and equipment, which is an allowable income tax expense for this year only. During the year, the company made four quarterly income tax payments of £25,000 each. The prevailing income tax rate in the region is 20%.

Required
Calculate the following for the company:

a the income tax liability for the year; and
b the income tax liability reported in the statement of financial position.

Suggested solution
a The income tax liability for the year is £155,000. The computation is as follows.

	£
Accounting profit	900,000
Plus non tax deductible expense	25,000
Less expenditure on PPE	(150,000)
Taxable profit	775,000
Annual income tax @ 20%	155,000

This is the amount that is shown in the company's statement of profit or loss and other comprehensive income.

b The income tax liability that is reported in the statement of financial position is the total income tax that is still unpaid due and payable at the end of the year. The income tax unpaid at the year-end reported in the statement of financial position is £55,000. The computational workings are as follows:

	£
Income tax liability for the year	155,000
Income tax paid £25,000 × 4	(100,000)
Income tax unpaid at year end	55,000

As previously stated and demonstrated in Worked Example 5.1, an entity's tax payable for an accounting period is always based upon its taxable profit and not its accounting profit.

Accounting profit is profit or loss for a period before deducting tax expense. Please note that IAS 12 defines accounting profit as a before-tax figure (rather than the more common after tax figure), to remain consistent with the definition of a taxable profit.

Taxable profit (or taxable loss) is the profit (or loss) for a period determined in accordance with the rules established by the taxation authorities upon which income taxes are payable.

The differences between accounting and taxable profit arise from two sources:

1   The statement of profit or loss and other comprehensive income will include 'disallowable items'. These are expenses incurred but not allowable for taxation purposes. These items generate what is known as a 'permanent difference' between accounting and taxable profit. Permanent differences are not reversed in any future accounting periods.

2   There may be items in the statement of profit or loss and other comprehensive income that incur a different treatment for accounting purposes than the treatment they receive for taxation purposes. The most common example is the treatment or accounting for non-current assets. For accounting purposes, depreciation is applied to non-current assets, but for income taxation purposes, capital allowances are applied. No adjustment is required if depreciation charges and capital allowance charges are the same. However, they do often differ. These differences give rise to 'temporary differences'. Temporary differences are reduced to nil over the life of an asset, but the financial statements will reflect the differences between the two treatments at reporting date. The annual distortion from temporary differences will impact upon any accounting ratio that utilises the post-tax figure (see Chapter 10), and if not adjusted, would give an incorrect impression of performance. Deferred tax is an accounting measure used to match the tax effect of transactions with their accounting impact and thereby produce less distorted results.

2.1 Deferred tax

In accordance with IAS 12, deferred tax is the amount of income tax payable in future periods in respect of taxable temporary differences. This can be illustrated with the following worked example.

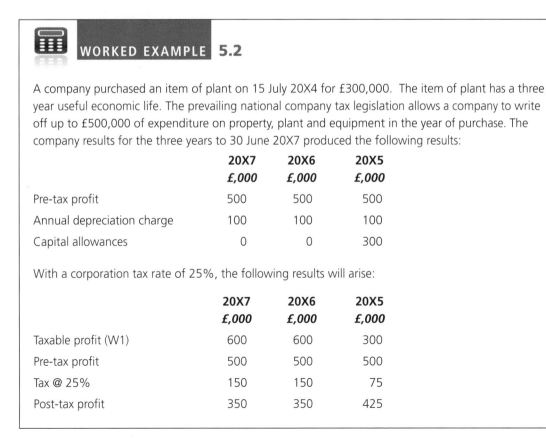

WORKED EXAMPLE 5.2

A company purchased an item of plant on 15 July 20X4 for £300,000. The item of plant has a three year useful economic life. The prevailing national company tax legislation allows a company to write off up to £500,000 of expenditure on property, plant and equipment in the year of purchase. The company results for the three years to 30 June 20X7 produced the following results:

	20X7 £,000	20X6 £,000	20X5 £,000
Pre-tax profit	500	500	500
Annual depreciation charge	100	100	100
Capital allowances	0	0	300

With a corporation tax rate of 25%, the following results will arise:

	20X7 £,000	20X6 £,000	20X5 £,000
Taxable profit (W1)	600	600	300
Pre-tax profit	500	500	500
Tax @ 25%	150	150	75
Post-tax profit	350	350	425

WORKED EXAMPLE 5.2 *continued*

W1 Taxable profit is the pre-tax profit plus the annual depreciation charge. The annual depreciation charge is not a tax deductible expense, therefore it must be added back to the pre-tax profit to enable the derivation of the taxable profit.

In 20X5, the pre-tax profit is £300,000 because the total amount of the cost of acquisition is a tax deductible expense.

Worked Example 5.2 demonstrates the impact of the temporary timing differences. Over the three years, despite the company pre-tax profits and annual depreciation charges being constant, the company has shown a reduced level of post-tax profit.

It is evident that this distortion has been the result of the temporary difference as a result of the different accounting and taxation treatment of the new plant purchased in 20X4–X5. The temporary differences between the accounting and taxation treatment of property, plant and equipment in accordance with IAS 12 is accounted for as follows:

a   When there is a periodic temporary difference that gives rise to a taxable profit greater than the accounting profit, the income tax reported in the statement of profit or loss and other comprehensive income should be reduced by a transfer from the deferred tax account.
b   Conversely, when there is a periodic temporary difference that gives rise to a taxable profit less than the accounting profit, the income tax reported in the statement of profit or loss and other comprehensive income should be increased by a transfer to a deferred tax account.

2.2 Tax base

Under IAS 12, at the end of each reporting period, the tax base and carrying amount of each asset and liability should be calculated. A deferred tax adjustment will be required when the tax base and carrying base are not equal.

The tax base of an asset/liability is defined in IAS 12 as 'the amount attributed to that asset or liability for tax purposes'. The carrying amount is the amount shown for each item in the financial statements.

The differences between the two bases are temporary differences in accordance with the following definitions as set out in IAS 12, where it states that temporary differences are differences between the carrying amount of an asset or liability in the statement of financial position and its tax base. Temporary differences may be either:

a   taxable temporary differences, which are temporary differences that will result in taxable amounts in determining taxable profit (tax loss) of future periods when the carrying amount of the asset or liability is recovered or settled; or
b   deductible temporary differences, which are temporary differences that will result in amounts that are deductible in determining taxable profit (tax loss) of future periods when the carrying amount of the asset or liability is recovered or settled.

WORKED EXAMPLE 5.3

Yazzu plc's statement of financial position for the year ended 31 December 20X6 had plant at a cost of £50,000 and accumulated depreciation to date of £24,000. The written-down value of the plant for tax purposes was £16,000. The plant had a residual value of nil at the end of its useful life. The prevailing tax rate is 25%.

Required
a   Determine the carrying amount of the plant as at 31 December 20X6.
b   Determine whether a temporary tax difference exists.
c   Calculate the level of any deferred tax.

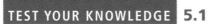

WORKED EXAMPLE **5.3** *continued*

Suggested solution

		£
a	Plant at cost	50,000
	Accumulated depreciation	24,000
	Carrying amount	26,000
b	Tax base	16,000
	Temporary difference (26,000 – 16,000)	10,000
c	Tax provision at 25%	2,500

TEST YOUR KNOWLEDGE **5.1**

What is deferred tax?

3 Accounting for leases (IFRS 16 – replacing IAS 17)

A lease is a legal contract between a supplier or 'lessor' (the party that grants the lease) of an item and a user of an item, the 'lessee'. International Financial Reporting Standard (IFRS) 16 defines a lease as 'a contract that conveys to the customer (lessee) the right to use an asset for a period of time in exchange for consideration.' An entity assesses whether a contract contains a lease on the basis of whether the customer has the right to control the use of an identified asset for a period of time.

It is important to understand that under the previous standard, IAS 17, leases were sub-classified as either a **finance lease** or an operating lease. IFRS 16 eliminates the classification of leases as either operating leases or finance leases, and introduces a single lessee accounting model, establishing principles for the recognition, measurement, presentation and disclosure of leases, with the objective of ensuring that lessees and lessors provide relevant information that faithfully represents those transactions (IFRS 16:1).

Essentially a finance lease was a lease that transferred substantially all the risks and rewards incidental to the ownership of an asset, title may or may not eventually have been transferred, the assets then being included on the company's statement of financial position and so clearly visibly disclosed in the Financial Statements.

By contrast some leases were termed **operating leases** whose term was short compared to the useful life of the asset, and commonly used to acquire equipment on a relatively short-term basis and thus included as an expense on the income statement. Classification of the lease as operational reduced the disclosure of any subsequent liability related to the leasing contract and was known as off 'balance sheet financing'. The classification of a lease as 'finance' or 'operating' was previously determined not by the contract but by the substance of the contract and this remains unchanged for lessors in IFRS 15. In essence, the transfer of 'risks and rewards' to the lessee was denoted as the principal difference between a finance and operational lease, thus determining the difference in accounting treatment.

IFRS 16 introduces numerous measurement simplifications such as:

- The exclusion of *variable* lease payments from the measurement of lease assets and liabilities, any such costs being recognised in profit or loss in the period in which they are incurred.
- Any inflation-linked payments are measured, based upon current contractual payments, entities are not required to forecast future inflation.
- Leases containing clauses that relate to uncertain optional payments are excluded from the measurement of lease assets and liabilities.

3.1 Identifying the lease

Under IFRS 16 the assumption is made that all leases result in a company (the lessee) obtaining the right to use an asset at the start of the lease, recognising possible financing implications if periodic lease payments are made. Accordingly, IFRS 16 eliminates the classification of leases as either operating leases or finance leases as is required by IAS 17 and, instead, introduces a single lessee accounting model. Applying the model, a lessee is required to recognise:

a   the present value of assets and liabilities for all leases with a term of more than 12 months in the statement of financial position, exemptions apply if the underlying asset is of low value; and

b   depreciation of leased assets separately from interest on lease liabilities in the income statement.

WORKED EXAMPLE 5.4

A catering company Eliss plc enters into a 4-year contract to rent 20 cubic metres of storage space in a climate controlled warehouse. The proprietor of the warehouse proposes two options:

1   Ellis plc will occupy 20 cubic metres but the actual space will be determined by the proprietor based upon his usage of the warehouse and storage space available.

2   Ellis plc will occupy Unit A, a 20 cubic metre space, in the first quadrant on the ground floor, assigned specifically to, and solely for the use of, Ellis plc for the duration of the contract.

Required

Identify if either or both options would be classed as a lease under IFRS 15 and advise Eliss plc on the accounting implications of the two options proposed.

Solution

In order to advise Eliss plc firstly determine whether these contracts contain a lease as defined in IFRS 16, assess whether an underlying asset can be identified. If no asset can be identified, then assume no lease.

1   The first contract does not contain any lease, because no asset can be identified. The reason being the supplier can exchange one place for another and you lease only certain capacity. Therefore, you would account for rental payments as expenses in the statement of profit and loss and other comprehensive income.

2   The second contract does contain a lease, because an underlying asset can be identified – you are leasing a specific space (asset) unit A, a 20 cubic metre space, in the first quadrant on the ground floor. Therefore, you need to account for this contract as for the lease, recognising the asset and a liability in your statement of financial position.

3.1.1 Recognition exemptions

IFRS 16 allows recognition exemptions when identifying leases that (i) have a lease term of 12 months or less and contain no purchase options, (determined by class of underlying asset); and (ii) leases where the underlying asset has a low value when new (such as personal computers or small items of office furniture). Both elections of which can be made on a lease-by-lease basis. In this instance the lessee may elect to account for lease payments as an expense on a straight-line basis over the lease term or alternative systematic basis, either an actuarial or sum of digits method.

TEST YOUR KNOWLEDGE 5.2

Describe the two types of lease that may be exempt from applying the recognition requirements of IFRS 16.

3.2 Separating components of a contract

The leasing of assets often involves the provision of additional services by the lessor such as maintenance, cleaning, repairs etc. Given a combined contract under the terms of IFRS 16 the lease payments must be spilt into lease element and non-lease element based on relative stand-alone prices, in order to:

i   Account for the lease element as for a lease if recognition criteria are met under IFRS 16; and

ii Account for a service element as before an expense in the statement of profit or loss and other comprehensive income.

 WORKED EXAMPLE 5.5

Cundy plc, a marketing consultancy business, enters into a 3-year contract with Tate ltd to lease an industrial printing and laminating machine. Annual rental payments are £12,000 including maintenance services, payable in arrears. Cundy plc were also given the opportunity to lease a similar machine without maintenance services for £9,000 per annum but would have to pay £3,500 for this service separately. Assume an appropriate discount rate of 5% and adoption of straight-line depreciation method.

Required
Advise Cundy plc as to the accounting treatment of the contract in the above scenario.

Suggested solution
Accounting under IFRS 16:

Step (1): Establish if there is a lease as recognizable under IFRS 16
Adopt the single lessee model of accounting for leases and recognize the machine as a 'right-of-use' asset and liability

Step (2): Separating components of the contract if there are multiple elements

Lease element: recognise in the statement of financial position

$$\frac{9,000}{(9,000 + 3,500)} \times 12,000 = 8,640$$

Maintenance element: Account for this in the statement of profit and loss and OCI

$$\frac{3,500}{(9,000 + 3,500)} \times 12,000 = 3,360$$

Step (3): Determine how to measure and recognize the elements per IFRS 16 at commencement and subsequently.

At Commencement:
- recognize the right to use the asset in the amount equal to the lease liability
- calculate the lease liability as present value of lease payments over lease term

$$P\left[\frac{1 - (1 + r)^{-n}}{r}\right] \text{ for Cundy plc where } P = £8,640, r = 5\% \text{ and } n = 3 \text{ years}$$

P = Periodic Payment
r = rate per period
n = number of periods
Present Value = £23,529

WORKED EXAMPLE **5.5** *continued*

Subsequently: At the end of each reporting period recognise the depreciation of the right-of-use asset and corresponding re-measurement of lease liability in include interest:

Depreciation: 23,529/3 yrs = 7,843

Year	Lease Liability B/f	Interest at 5%	Lease Payment	Lease Liability C/f
1	23,529	1,176	(8,640)	16,065
2	16,065	803	(8,640)	8,228
3	8,228	411	(8,640)	0
Total	N/A			N/A

Cundy plc Accounting entries at the end of year 1

At commencement:
Dr   Right-of-use-Asset   £23,529
Cr   Lease liability   £23,529
To record the lease at commencement

At the end of Year 1:
Dr   Interest   £1,176
Cr   Lease Liability   £1,176
To record the interest element of the lease

Dr   Lease liability   £8.640
Dr   P/L Maintenance Expenses   £3,360
Cr   Cash   £12,000
To record machine rental for the year

Dr   P/L Depreciation Expense   £7,843
Cr   Right-of-use asset   £7,843

3.2.1 Sale and leaseback transactions

Per IFRS 16 to determine whether the transfer of an asset is accounted for as a sale, an entity applies the requirements of IFRS 15 (Revenue Recognition) for determining when a performance obligation is satisfied (IFRS 16:99).

If an asset transfer satisfies IFRS 15's requirements to be accounted for as a sale the seller measures the right-of-use asset at the proportion of the previous carrying amount that relates to the right of use retained. Accordingly, the seller only recognises the amount of gain or loss that relates to the rights transferred to the buyer (IFRS 16:100a).

If the fair value of the sale consideration does not equal the asset's fair value, or if the lease payments are not market rates, the sales proceeds are adjusted to fair value, either by accounting for prepayments or additional financing (IFRS 16:101).

 WORKED EXAMPLE **5.6**

Menawethan Ltd (the lessee) enters into a four-year lease of the first floor of a building, with an option to extend for four years. Lease payments are £500,000 a year during the initial term and £600,000 per year during the optional period, all payable at the end of each year. To obtain

WORKED EXAMPLE 5.6 *continued*

the lease, Menawethan Ltd incurs initial direct costs of £120,000 (£90,000 to the former tenant occupying the floor and £30,000 to the estate agents). The lessor agrees to reimburse the lessee the estate agent's commission of £30,000 and provide £50,000 for leasehold improvements.

At the commencement date, the lessee decides that they are not 'reasonably certain' that they will exercise the option to extend the lease. Therefore the lease term is four years. The rate of interest implicit in the lease is 5% per annum.

Required
Produce relevant extracts from the financial statements of Menawethan showing how the above transaction would be reported in the statement of profit of loss for years 1, 2, 3 and 4 and the statements of financial position at the end of years 1, 2, 3 and 4.

Suggested solution
Menawethan Ltd
Calculation of the lease liability
Implicit rate of interest: 5%

	Payments	DF	PV
Year 1	500,000	0.952	476,000
Year 2	500,000	0.907	453,500
Year 3	500,000	0.866	433,000
Year 4	500,000	0.823	411,500
			1,774,000

Initial recognition at the beginning of Year 1

	Dr	Cr
Dr Right of Use Asset	1,774,000	
Cr Lease Liability		1,774,000
Dr Right of Use Asset	120,000	
Cr Cash		120,000
Dr Cash	30,000	
Dr Right of Use Asset		30,000

Hence, the initial cost of the right of use asset will be calculated as follows:

	£
Lease liability	1,774,000
Initial Direct Costs	120,000
Reimbursement of initial direct costs	– 30,000
	1,864,000
Annual Depreciation	1,864,000
	4
	466,000

Lease Liability Amortisation Table

Year	Amount Owing at the beginning of the year	Interest	Rental	Amount Owing at Year End
1	1,774,000	88,700	– 500,000	1,362,700
2	1,362,700	68,135	–500,000	930,835
3	930,835	46,542	– 500,000	477,377
4	477,377	22,623	–500,000	–0

📟 **WORKED EXAMPLE** **5.6** *continued*

Menawethan Ltd
Statement of Profit or Loss for the year ended...

	Year 1	Year 2	Year 3	Year 4
Depreciation	466,000	466,000	466,000	466,000
Interest	88,700	68,135	46,542	22,623

Menawethan Ltd
Statement of Financial Position at the end of

	Year 1	Year 2	Year 3	Year 4
Asset				
Right of Use Asset	1,864,000	1,864,000	1,864,000	1,864,000
Accumulated Depreciation	–466,000	–932,000	–1,398,000	–1,864,000
	1,398,000	932,000	466,000	–
Liabilities				
Current				
Lease liability	431,865	453,458	477,377	
Non-Current Liabilities				
Lease liability	930,835	477,377		

Martino Plc is a large, multi-national entity with approximately £30 billion annual turnover. Martino entered into a contract to lease one floor of an office building in London for an annual lease rental of £30,000. The lease period is 4 years. On the same date, Martino leased 400 Magnifico laptops for its employees. The annual lease rental for each laptop is £500. The retail price for each laptop is £1,300. The lease period for each laptop is 4 years.

In addition to the above contracts, Martino entered into a contract with Nelson which requires Nelson to transport a specified quantity of goods by using a specified type of vehicle in accordance with a stated timetable for a period of five years. The timetable and quantity of goods specified are equivalent to Martino having the use of 10 vehicles for four years. Nelson supplies the vehicles, driver and engine as part of the contract. The contract states the nature and quantity of the goods to be transported (and the type of vehicle to be used to transport the goods. Nelson has a large pool of similar cars that can be used to fulfil the requirements of the contract. Similarly, Nelson can choose to use any one of a number of vehicles to fulfil each of Martino's requests, and vehicle could be used to transport not only Martino's goods, but also the goods of other customers. The vehicles are stored at Nelson's premises when not being used to transport goods.

Required
Explain how the above contracts should be accounted for in the books of Martino Plc.

a   The lease of the office building should be capitalised and treated as a Right of Use Asset.
b   The lease of each laptop qualifies as a lease of a low value item. Hence, Martino Plc can claim the exemption for low value items under IFRS 16 and expense the rental amount of each laptop.
c   The vehicles are kept in the Nelson's premises. Since Martino has a large pool of similar cars and substitution costs are not likely to be high, it appears the company's right of substitution is substantive. Hence, the arrangement does not contain a lease.

4   Financial instruments (IAS 32 / IFRS 7 / IFRS 2)

As the banking collapse of the first decade of this century showed, financial instruments are not only very technical but can result in financial catastrophe if misused and misunderstood. The former Governor of the Bank of England was attributed with the statement:

the most alarming fact that arose when the system collapsed was the fact that some banking and financial institutions only then began to understand the complex financial instruments in which they had invested, as they literally collapsed overnight!

IAS 32 seeks to provide clarity where none previously existed and defines a financial instrument as follows: 'any contract that gives rise to a financial asset of one entity and a financial liability or equity instrument of another entity'. This is further enhanced by the defining of a financial asset as any asset that is:

a cash;
b an equity instrument of another entity; or
c a contractual right to receive cash or another financial asset from another entity or to exchange financial assets or financial liabilities with another entity under conditions that are potentially favourable to the entity.

Consequently, it is self-evident that virtually all business transactions give rise to a financial instrument, from a cash or credit sale to the raising of capital via new issues.

Conversely, a financial liability is defined as any liability that is 'a contractual obligation to deliver cash or another financial asset to another entity; or to exchange financial assets or financial liabilities with another entity under conditions that are potentially unfavourable to the entity'.

Financial instruments may be further separated into equity instruments or liabilities. A financial instrument is only an equity instrument if the following two conditions are fully satisfied:

a The instrument includes no contractual obligation:
   i   to deliver cash or another financial asset to another entity; or
   ii to exchange financial assets or financial liabilities with another entity under conditions that are potentially unfavourable to the issuer.
b The instrument will or may be settled in the issuer's own equity instruments.

This definition of equity instrument provides a clarity that enables a clear separation of items commonly considered within a single group. For example, ordinary shares and **preference shares** are by definition not in the same class, on account of the simple fact that a preference share imposes a contractual obligation to deliver cash in the future renders it a liability and not an equity instrument.

STOP AND THINK 5.1

Explain why a credit sale and a credit purchase give rise to a financial instrument.

4.1 Variations in issue value, redemption value and coupon rate

The accounting treatment of capital instruments sometimes needs to reflect the following circumstances:

- Where the issue proceeds are less than nominal value due to the issue having being made at a discount and/or because there are material issue costs which, in accordance with required practice, must be deducted from issue proceeds (see Worked Example 5.6).
- Where interest is payable in some years but not in others.
- Where interest is payable at different rates in different years (see Worked Example 5.7).

In all cases, the difference between the net issue proceeds and the amount payable to the supplier of debt finance represents the total interest cost which must be allocated between years in order to achieve the two following objectives:

1 Interest must be charged at a constant rate based on the carrying amount – that is, the actuarial method must be applied.

2   At the debt redemption date, the carrying amount must be equal to the amount payable at that time.

 **WORKED EXAMPLE 5.7**

On 1 January 20X5, Bergerac plc issues a debt instrument for £475m which is repayable at its nominal value of £500m at the end of four years. Interest is payable at 8% per annum on nominal value. The costs incurred in issuing the securities totalled £30m. The effective rate of interest is 11.59% per annum.

Required
Calculate for each of the years 20X5–X8:

a   the annual finance charge to be debited to the statement of profit or loss and other comprehensive income; and
b   the carrying value of the liability in the statement of financial position.

Note: Calculations should be to the nearest £0.1m.

Answer

Year	Interest paid, 8% £m	Interest charge in the statement of profit or loss and other comprehensive income, 11.59% £m	Carrying value in the statement of financial position £m
			445.0
20X5	40.0	51.6	456.6
20X6	40.0	52.9	469.5
20X7	40.0	54.4	483.9
20X8	40.0	56.1	500.0

 **WORKED EXAMPLE 5.8**

On 1 January 20X0, Castlenaud plc issues non-equity shares for £50m which are redeemable for the same amount at the end of ten years. Dividends are payable of £4m per annum for the first three years, £5m for the next three years and £6.5m for the remaining four years. The actuarial rate of return over the issue period is 10.06% per annum.

Required
Calculate for each of the years 20X0–20X9:

a   the annual amount to be debited to the statement of profit or loss and other comprehensive income; and
b   the carrying value of the non-equity shares in the statement of financial position.

Note: Calculations should be to the nearest £m.

WORKED EXAMPLE 5.8 *continued*

Answer

a   b

Year	Interest paid £m	Interest charge in the statement of profit or loss and other comprehensive income, 10.06%* £m	Carrying value in the statement of financial position+ £m
			50.0
20X0	4.0	5.0	51.0
20X1	4.0	5.1	52.2
20X2	4.0	5.2	53.4
20X3	5.0	5.4	53.8
20X4	5.0	5.4	54.2
20X5	5.0	5.5	54.6
20X6	6.5	5.5	53.6
20X7	6.5	5.4	52.5
20X8	6.5	5.3	51.3
20X9	6.5	5.2	50.0

* The non-equity shares meet the definition of a liability – obligation to transfer economic resources – so return on the securities should be charged to the statement of profit or loss and other comprehensive income above the line.
+ Difference due to rounding.

IAS 32 does not address the recognition or measurement of financial instruments. These are embodied in IAS 39, where the initial measurement for financial assets and liabilities should be measured at fair value. IAS 39 provides four classifications of financial assets after their initial recognition. These four classes are reduced to just two by the later standard IFRS 9. The two classes of financial assets are those measured at amortised cost and those measured at fair value. The classification into these two classes should take place when the financial asset is initially recognised. After its initial recognition, IFRS 9 confirms IAS 39 two measurement classification of fair value through profit or loss (FVTPL) and amortised cost. Financial liabilities held for trading are measured at FVTPL, and all other financial liabilities are measured at amortised cost unless the fair value option is applied.

IAS 32 requires the interest and dividends payable to financial instruments to be recognised as an expense in an entity's statement of profit or loss and other comprehensive income. Consequently, unpaid dividends to preference shareholders are deemed to be accrued expenses.

5 Earnings per share (IAS 33)

Earnings per share is a ratio used to analyse the comparative performance of an entity and/or groups of entities. The use of EPS to compare performance of different entities requires that the measure is calculated the same way each time to ensure consistency.

To this end, IAS 33 provides a prescriptive measurement for users and readers of financial statements. The basic EPS is a ratio calculated as follows: the profit or loss attributable to ordinary equity holders of the parent entity divided by the weighted average number of ordinary shares outstanding during the period. EPS is calculated as follows and is examined in greater depth in Chapter 10, section 6.1.

$$\frac{\text{Earnings}}{\text{No of \textbf{equity shares} in issue}}$$

WORKED EXAMPLE 5.9

The following information has been extracted from the financial statements of Gee company for the year ended 31 December 20X3:

Profit after Tax of £500,000

£20,000 issued 10p shares

Required

You are required to calculate the EPS for Gee company for the year ended at 31 December 20X3.

EPS =

$$\frac{\text{Earnings}}{\text{No of equity shares in issue}}$$

$$\frac{£500,000}{£20,000 \div £0.10}$$

$$\frac{£500,000}{200,000 \text{ shares}}$$

= £2.50 per share

EPS is the only ratio defined and set out in the IAS and differs from all the other standards governing financial reporting. In keeping with the format of the book, EPS will be covered in detail in our examination of accounting ratios (see Chapter 10).

6   Impairment of assets (IAS 36)

It has not been unknown for an entity to hold assets that are reported in their financial statements at a value greater than their recoverable value. Such positions often come to light during periods of economic downturns or financial crisis as witnessed at the start of this century. IAS 36 seeks to ensure that financial statements do not include assets at a value for which they cannot be recovered.

However, our traditional prudence concept should have prevented this practice. Prudence here is the accounting concept that requires the exercise of caution in the preparation of financial statements such that the assets and income of an entity are not overstated, and conversely liability and expenses are not understated. The underlying rationale of prudence is that an entity should not recognise an asset at a value that is higher than the amount which the entity expects to recover from its sale or use. The recoverable amount of an asset or a cash-generating unit is the higher of its fair value less costs of disposal and its value in use.

Fair value is the price that would be recovered on the disposal of an asset or paid to transfer a liability in an orderly transaction between market participants at the measurement date. Costs of disposal are the costs directly attributable to the disposal of an asset or cash-generating unit, excluding finance costs and income tax expense. Value in use is the present value of the future cash flows expected to be derived from an asset or cash-generating unit.

🖩 **WORKED EXAMPLE** **5.10**

A company acquired a new machine on 1 July 20X0 and has projected its cash flows for the next five accounting periods as follows:

Year ended	Cash inflows £	Cash outflows £
30 Jun X1	16,500	6,950
30 Jun X2	21,900	10,995
30 Jun X3	27,480	12,500
30 Jun X4	12,500	10,900
30 Jun X5	5,500	4,500

The machine is not expected to have any residual or resale value at the end of its five years. However, the cost to dispose of the machine environmentally is expected to be £2,500. The company applies a standard 10% discount rate.

Required
a Determine the value in use of the new machine for the company.
b Comment on the cash inflows and cash outflows supplied by the company.

Suggested solution
a The value in use of the new machine is shown below.

Year ended	Cash inflows £	Cash outflows £	Net cash flows £	Discount factor 10%	Present value £
30 Jun X1	16,500	6,950	9,550	0.9091	8,682
30 Jun X2	21,900	10,995	10,905	0.8264	9,012
30 Jun X3	27,480	12,500	14,980	0.7513	11,255
30 Jun X4	12,500	10,900	1,600	0.6830	1,093
30 Jun X5	5,500	7,000	(1,500)	0.6209	(931)
				Value in use	29,110

The value in use is based on the discounted net cash flows of the machine at a 10% discount factor.

The disposal cost of the machine at the end of the fifth year was added to the cash outflow, because this is borne by the company.

b The cash flows provided by the company must satisfy the requirements of IAS 36:
  ■ They should be based upon the machine in its current condition and exclude any cash flows that may arise from any enhancements to its performance.
  ■ The cash flows should exclude any obligations that have already been recognised.
  ■ Cash inflows and outflows arising from financing activities should be excluded from any tax payments or receipts.
  ■ The cash flows should have supportive, reliable and reasonable evidence, preferably obtained from an independent external source.

When an asset suffers an impairment loss, the carrying amount of the asset is reduced to its recoverable amount. The impairment loss is recognised as an expense. However, when an asset is revalued and an impairment loss arises, the resulting impairment loss is recognised initially as a reduction in the revaluation reserve. Therefore the revaluation is debited with the impairment loss and reflected in the statement of profit or loss and other comprehensive income as a negative amount.

WORKED EXAMPLE **5.11**

A company has five assets recorded in their non-current assets as follows.

Asset	Value in use £	Fair value less disposal costs £	Carrying amount £
A01	25,000	22,500	30,000
A02	16,000	17,950	14,000
A03	35,000	40,000	43,750
A04	18,500	18,500	18,500
A05	23,500	19,500	12,000

Required

a Advise the company whether they have any impairment loss in their non-current stock assets.

b Explain what is impairment loss.

Suggested solution

a The company has a total of £8,750 impairment loss arising from assets A01 and A03 as shown below.

Asset	Carrying amount £	Recoverable amount £	Impairment loss £
A01	**30,000**	25,000	5,000
A02	14,000	17,950	0
A03	**43,750**	40,000	3,750
A04	18,500	18,500	0
A05	12,000	19,500	0
			8,750

b Impairment loss is the loss that arises when an asset held by a company has a carrying amount greater than its recoverable amount (where the recoverable amount is the greater of the fair value less disposal costs and its value in use).

6.1 Cash-generating units

It may not always be possible to determine the recoverable amount of an individual asset. If this is the case, then the recoverable amount of the cash-generating unit (CGU) to which the asset belongs should be determined. In accordance with IAS 36, a cash-generating unit is 'the smallest identifiable group of assets that generates cash inflows that are largely independent of the cash inflows from other assets or groups of assets'.

When a CGU incurs an impairment loss, this loss should be allocated to reduce the carrying amount of the asset in the following order:

1 reduce the carrying amount of any goodwill allocated to the cash-generating unit (group of units); then

2 reduce the carrying amounts of the other assets of the CGU on a pro-rata basis.

The carrying amount of an asset should not be reduced below the highest of:

■ its fair value less costs of disposal (if measurable);
■ its value in use (if measurable); or
■ zero.

 **WORKED EXAMPLE 5.12**

On 1 July 20X6, a company had a cash-generating unit with the following assets:

	Carrying amount £,000
Goodwill	300
Property	750
Plant and machinery	500
	1,550

Following an impairment review the CGU had a recoverable amount of **£1,010,000 on 30 June 20x7.**

Required
Calculate the impairment loss as at 30 June 20X7, and show how it should be allocated across the items within the CGU.

Suggested solution

	Carrying amount 1 July 20X6 £,000	Carrying amount 30 June 20X7 £,000	Impairment loss £,000
Goodwill	300	0	300
Property	750	535	215
Plant and machinery	500	475	25
Total	1,550	1,010	540

The carrying amount on 30 June was £1,010,000 and generated an impairment loss of £540,000.
    The first £300,000 must be suffered by goodwill as per IAS 36.
    The remaining £240,000 should be shared between the two remaining assets on a pro-rata basis: £324,000 and £216,000 respectively.
    However, this would result in plant and machinery having a carrying amount of £284,000 and note (1) advises us that the carrying amount of plant and machinery at the year was £475,000.
    Therefore the residual impairment loss suffered by the property is £215,000: £540,000 less £(300,000 + 25,000).

7 Non-current assets held for sale and discontinued operations (IFRS 5)

Traditionally, non-current assets are not held for sale, as they are employed to generate revenue over their lifespan. However, there may be occasions when a single non-current asset or a group of them are held for sale. This may arise when a business operation is being discontinued. IFRS 5 classifies a non-current asset (or disposal group) as held for sale 'if its carrying amount will be recovered principally through a sale transaction rather than through continuing use'. It is imperative to note that to be treated as a disposal group, the whole group of assets must be subject to disposal in a single transaction, not in a series of piecemeal disposal transactions. In addition, the asset (or disposal group) must be available for immediate sale in its present condition subject only to the usual sale terms associated with such assets and the sale is highly probable.

A highly probable sale will be deemed to exist under the following conditions:

a   management is committed to a plan to sell the asset (or disposal group), and have taken action to locate a buyer and the disposal;

b   the asset (or disposal group) must be actively marketed for sale at a price that is reasonable in relation to its current fair value;

c   the sale should be expected to qualify for recognition as a completed sale within one year from the date of classification, unless there are conditions beyond the control of the entity; and

d   it is unlikely that decision to sell will be subject to changes or withdrawn.

Non-current assets cannot and should not be transferred to current assets or non-current assets for resale at the end of the reporting period if the conditions outlined above have not been satisfied. Only if these conditions are fulfilled can the assets be reclassified and a disclosure made in the financial statements. Non-current assets held for sale should be presented in the statement of financial position, but must be shown separately from other assets.

WORKED EXAMPLE 5.13

At the end of its accounting year on 30 June 20X7, a company has the following non-current assets in their portfolio:

- A01HQ – The company's head office in the city centre that the board of directors has agreed should be sold. The new head office on the outskirts of the city is still under construction and completion is not expected for at least another nine months. On completion, the relocation will commence as will the marketing of the building to prospective buyers.

- A02PP – The unused small processing plant is still occupied but is currently being viewed by prospective buyers following successful marketing by the selling agent. Vacation of the premises is not expected to take more than the customary four weeks following the agreement of the sale price by both parties.

- A03LV – A fleet of former leased vehicles that the board of directors has recently agreed to sell. This fleet will be marketed within the next month with an expectation of their disposal within three months.

Required

Advise the management whether the three assets listed above can be classified as non-current assets for sale.

Suggested solution

To be classified as non-current assets for sale in accordance with IFRS 5, the assets should be able to recover their carrying value through a sale and the fulfilment of all four conditions outlined in the previous section.

Asset A01HQ should not be classified as a non-asset held for sale, because it is not available for immediate sale as it has not been marketed and this cannot commence until the new building has been completed and relocation is underway. The completion of the new building may overrun the expected nine months and this may result in the sale not being possible within 12 months.

Assets A02PP and A03LV should be classified as non-current assets held for sale as they meet required conditions. Although A02PP is currently occupied, vacation will not extend beyond four weeks and hinder the sale.

It is important to recognise that a non-current asset held for sale should not be subject to depreciation as the non-current asset is no longer held for the purposes of generating revenue for the entity over its useful life. A non-current asset held for sale should be measured at the lower of its carrying amount and fair value less costs to sell.

If the carrying amount of an asset held for sale exceeds its fair value less costs to dispose of the asset, then an impairment loss should be recognised. In addition, any subsequent reduction in the fair value less disposal costs of an asset held for sale should also be recognised as an impairment loss. Conversely, any increase in the fair value less disposal costs of an asset held for sale should also be recognised as a gain. However, the gain cannot exceed the cumulative amount of any previously recognised loss of the asset.

Non-current assets held for sale may arise from the discontinuation of a business operation. Under IFRS 5, a discontinued operation is defined as:

'a component of an entity that either has been disposed of or is classified as held for sale and:

a) represents a separate major line of business or geographical area of operations;
b) is part of a single coordinated plan to dispose of a separate major line of business or geographical area of operations; or
c) is a **subsidiary** acquired exclusively with a view to resale.'

If there is any gain or loss from the sale of assets, this should be recognised in the statement of profit or loss and other comprehensive income.

Financial reporting regulations require that continuing operations are reported separately in the statement of profit or loss and other comprehensive income from discontinued operations, and that any gain or loss from the disposal of a segment (an entity whose activities represent a separate major line of business or market segment) be reported along with the operating results of the discontinued segment.

The results of operations of a component of a company that either has been disposed of, or is classified as being held for sale, are reported in discontinued operations only if *both* the following conditions are met:

- the operations and cash flows of the component have been (or will be) eliminated from the ongoing operations as a result of the disposal decision, and
- the company will not have any significant continuing involvement in the operations of the component after the disposal decision.

A component, as described under IFRS 5, consists of operations and cash flows that can be clearly distinguishable, operationally and for financial reporting purposes, from the rest of the entity. However, due to the subjectivity of the above definition, the International Accounting Standards Board (IASB) has aligned the definition with that used in IFRS 8 'Operating Segments'.

The importance of understanding changes over time in the various segments of activity that make up the whole of the company is illustrated in Table 5.1.

TABLE 5.1 Changing activities over time

Segment	20X6	20X7
1	Operational	Discontinued
2	Operational	Operational
3	Operational	Operational

This shows that in 20X6 the company had three main segments of activity – 1, 2 and 3 and in 20X1 segment 1 was discontinued. Any predictions made for 20X2 based on the results of 20X7 would be wrong to the extent that activity 1 no longer contributes towards the overall performance of the enterprise.

Similarly, comparisons between the actual results for 20X8 and those of the previous year should take account of the fact that the business has downsized. As the name indicates, IFRS 5 'Non-current Assets Held for Sale and Discontinued Operations' deals with a number of issues. Here we are concerned with the last-mentioned item.

7.1 Disclosure – statement of profit or loss and other comprehensive income

The impact of accounting for discontinued operations is that regulations require separate disclosure from continuing operations on the face of the statement of profit or loss and other comprehensive income. Business entities are required to show, as a minimum, the following items on the face of the statement of profit or loss and other comprehensive income:

- the post-tax profit or loss of discontinued operations;
- the post-tax gain or loss recognised on the measurement to fair value less cost of sale of the discontinued component(s).

Additionally, the quality of disclosure can be enhanced through further analysis of discontinued operations either in the statement of profit or loss and other comprehensive income or in the narratives to the financial reports:

- the revenue, expenses and pre-tax profit or loss of discontinued operations;
- the related income tax expense as required under IAS 12;
- the gain or loss recognised on the measurement to fair value less cost of sale of the discontinued component(s); and
- the related income tax expense, subject to IAS 12.

The disclosure for discontinued operations may be disclosed via two methods:

1   Method I on the face of the statement of profit or loss and other comprehensive income, using columnar format; or
2   Method II in a note to the accounts.

If the information is shown in a note to the accounts, the 'Profit for the period from discontinued operations' must appear as a single item on the face of the statement of profit or loss and other comprehensive income.

Method I
Statement of profit or loss and other comprehensive income for Crux plc for year ended 31 December 20X6 (comparatives omitted)

	Continuing operations £m	Discontinued operations £m	Total £m
Turnover	750	150	900
Cost of sales	(500)	(168)	(668)
Gross profit	250	(18)	232
Distribution costs	(72)	(5)	(77)
Administrative expenses	(63)	(9)	(72)
Finance costs	(8)	0	(8)
Profit for the period before tax	107	(32)	(75)
Taxation	31	0	31
Profit for the period	76	(32)	44

Method II
Statement of profit or loss and other comprehensive income for Crux plc for year ended 31 December 20X6

Continuing operations

	20X6 £m	20X5 £m
Turnover	750	720
Cost of sales	(500)	(481)
Gross profit	250	239
Distribution costs	(72)	(72)
Administrative expenses	(63)	(59)
Finance costs	(8)	(8)
Profit for the period before tax	107	100

Taxation	31	28
Profit for the period from continuing operations	76	72
Profit (loss) for the period from discontinued operations*	(32)	25
Profit for the period	44	97

* Required analysis (consisting of the information appearing on the face of the statement of profit or loss and other comprehensive income under Method I) given in the notes to the accounts.

We can see (Method II) that there has been a substantial reduction in the profit generated by Crux plc in 20X6 compared with the previous year. Profit has fallen by more than 50%, from £97m to £44m. The analysed statement of profit or loss and other comprehensive income shows that the decline in profit is entirely attributable to the discontinued operation, which suffered a loss of £32m in 20X6 compared with a profit of £25m in the previous year. Profits from continuing operations are in fact slightly up, at £76m compared with £72m in the previous year. The analysed statement of profit or loss and other comprehensive income therefore provides grounds for a deeper, and perhaps more optimistic, assessment of Crux plc's future prospects than would otherwise have been possible.

TEST YOUR KNOWLEDGE 5.3

a   What do you understand by the term 'discontinued operation'?
b   What constitutes a 'discontinued operation' under IFRS 5?

8   Operating segments (IFRS 8)

In the distant past the single-product firm dominated, but such specialisation gradually gave way to horizontal integration and vertical integration.

Horizontal integration is the process whereby an entity will acquire one or more other entities in the same sector engaged in the same stage of production/service. An example in the accounting software sector has been Sage's acquisition over the years of smaller accounting software companies. This may be undertaken to reduce competition and improve economies of scale. Vertical integration is the process where an entity acquires or merges with other entities at different stages in the production or supply chain, to either guarantee supply or access to the market. A notable example was when Boeing bought the supplier of its 787 airplane to overcome any problem of supply.

The move towards diversification (i.e. the increasing engagement in different types of business) gained pace during the 1960s with the growth of the multinational enterprise. The result is that companies today, or more usually groups of companies, engage in a wide range of activities, where:

■ there are significant variations in rates of profitability;
■ the activities involve different degrees of risk (e.g. different geographical areas raise problems of movements in exchange rate, political upheaval, expropriation of assets and high inflation rates); and
■ there are differential opportunities for growth.

These are, of course, often the very reasons for diversifying. However, the result is that aggregated performance data are of limited use for decision-making. Empirical research has shown that, for such companies, segmental data improves the shareholders' ability to make effective assessments of past results that can be used to predict future enterprise profits and developments. Disaggregated data is also of greater use to the government for planning purposes. It enables the accumulation of industry statistics that can be used for policy-making (e.g. to encourage inward investment to certain industries, or to provide financial assistance for depressed areas). Equally, more detailed information on the profitability of various parts of the business may be helpful to trade unions and employees for wage and salary bargaining purposes. The move towards **segmental reporting** in Britain started with the Companies Act 1967. This required the **directors' report** to provide turnover and profit by 'class' of activity. Today, the Companies Act 2006 requires this information to be given in the notes to the accounts so that it is specifically covered by the audit report. In addition, disclosure of turnover by geographical area is required.

Segmental reporting is the subject of IFRS 8 'Operating Segments'. The objective of this standard is to establish principles for reporting financial information. This helps users of financial statements to:

■ understand the enterprise's past performance better;
■ assess the enterprise's risks and returns better; and
■ make more informed judgments about the enterprise as a whole.

8.1 Identification of reportable segments

A business or geographical segment can be identified as reportable if a majority of its revenue is earned from sales to external customers and:

■ its revenue is 10% or more of total revenue, external and internal, of all segments; or
■ its result (either profit or loss) is 10% or more of the combined result of all segments in profit or the combined result of all segments in loss, whichever is the greater in absolute amount; or
■ its assets are 10% or more of the total assets of all segments.

8.2 Disclosures

The following must be disclosed for each primary reportable segment:

■ revenue (disclosing separately sales to external customers and inter-segment revenue);
■ the basis of inter-segment pricing;
■ results (before interest and taxes) from continuing operations and, separately, the result from discontinued operations;
■ carrying amount of segment assets;
■ carrying amount of segment liabilities; and
■ cost incurred in the period to acquire property, plant and equipment, and intangibles.

8.3 Nature of reportable segments

There are two types of reportable segments:

1 A business segment (one based on supply of products or services) is a distinguishable component of an enterprise that is engaged in providing an individual product or service or a group of related products or services and that is subject to risks and returns that are different from those of other business segments.
2 A geographical segment is a distinguishable component of an enterprise that is engaged in providing products or services within a particular economic environment and that is subject to risks and returns that are different from those of components operating in other economic environments.

Segmental information must be prepared for both business and geographical segments, with one treated as the primary segment and the other as the secondary segment. The primary segment is determined on the basis of whether particular products or services or particular geographical areas are more important in affecting the entity's risks and rates of return. Rather more information must be published in the primary segmental reports, but the differences are minor and are not considered further here.

Figure 5.1 sets out the treatment of inter-segment sales, which must be cancelled as they do not represent transactions with external parties.

The presentation of all the information from Figure 5.1 in a single statement may not work well in terms of improving the readability of annual reports. Sometimes companies will use a number of tables, each focusing on a different item to be reported.

Statement of profit or loss and other comprehensive income

	Paper products 20X1	Paper products 20X0	Office products 20X1	Office products 20X0	Publishing 20X1	Publishing 20X0	Other operations 20X1	Other operations 20X0	Eliminations 20X1	Eliminations 20X0	Consolidated 20X1	Consolidated 20X0
External sales	55	50	20	17	19	16	7	7				
Inter-segment sales	15	10	10	14	2	4	2	2	(29)	(30)		
Total revenue	70	60	30	31	21	20	9	9	(29)	(30)	101	90
Results												
Segment result	20	17	9	7	2	1	0	0	(1)	(1)	30	24
Unallocated corporate expenses											(7)	(9)
Operating profit											23	15
Interest expense											(4)	(4)
Interest income											2	3
Share of net profits of associates	6	5					2	2			8	7
Income taxes											(7)	(4)
Profit on ordinary activities											22	17
Uninsured earthquake damage to factory		(3)									0	(3)
Net profit										22	22	14

Statement of financial position

	Paper products 20X1	Paper products 20X0	Office products 20X1	Office products 20X0	Publishing 20X1	Publishing 20X0	Other operations 20X1	Other operations 20X0	Eliminations 20X1	Eliminations 20X0	Consolidated 20X1	Consolidated 20X0
Segment assets	54	50	34	30	10	10	10	9			108	99
Investment in equity methods associates	20	16					12	10			32	26
Unallocated corporate assets											35	30
Consolidated total assets											175	155
Segment liabilities	25	15	8	11	8	8	1	1			42	35
Unallocated corporate liabilities											40	55
Consolidated total liabilities											82	90
Capital expenditure	12	10	3	5	5		4	3				
Depreciation	9	7	9	7	5	3	3	4				
Non-cash expenses other than depreciation	8	2	7	3	2	2	2	1				

FIGURE 5.1 Pro-forma statements for business with multiple segments

8.4 Limitations of segmental reporting

A major problem associated with the preparation of segmental reports is the treatment of common costs relating to more than one segment. Entities often apportion some of their common costs for the purpose of internal reporting (perhaps based on sales). In such cases, it may be reasonable for these costs to be treated in the same way for external reporting purposes. If the apportionment would be misleading, however, common costs should not be apportioned to the segments, but should be deducted from the total segment result.

A similar situation arises in the case of assets and liabilities that cannot be directly linked with the activities of individual segments. The arbitrary allocations of such items would distort the financial information published, and undermine the usefulness of any accounting ratios that make use of figures for assets and/or liabilities (e.g. rate of return on capital employed). Common assets and liabilities must also, therefore, remain unallocated and be reported at the level of the group. At the same time, it must be realised that common costs, assets and liabilities do benefit the individual segments, so their true segmental values will inevitably be understated. This bias in reported data should be borne in mind when comparing segmental results with other companies, particularly those entities undertaking no other activities with the consequence that their reported results will take account of *all* costs, assets and liabilities.

One further factor affecting the reliability of segmental data arises where inter-segment sales take place. Here, there is the possibility of creative accounting if, for some reason, management wishes to inflate the reported results of one segment and deflate those of another. Even where best efforts are made to use realistic transfer prices, the possible error resulting from the subjective nature of this exercise should be borne in mind. Transfer prices should be fixed for this purpose.

TEST YOUR KNOWLEDGE 5.4

a   What is segmental accounting?
b   What are the two segmental bases for reporting segments?

END OF CHAPTER QUESTIONS

5.1   How should companies determine an entity's reportable segments?

5.2   Buffalo Ltd runs a chain of stationery stores providing three main products, namely copiers, paper and printing services, to its business customers. The current financial statements contain the following:

Statement of financial position of Buffalo Ltd as at 31 December 20X6:

Assets	£,000
Non-current assets at book value	2,443
Current assets	
Inventories	57
Receivables	44
Bank	225
Total assets	2,769
Equities and liabilities	
Equity	
Share capital	1,000
Retained earnings	1,449

? END OF CHAPTER QUESTIONS *continued*

Non-current liabilities

Long-term borrowing	210
Current liabilities	
Payables	78
Short-term borrowing	32
Total equities and liabilities	**2,769**

Statement of profit or loss and other comprehensive income of Buffalo Ltd as at 31 December 20X6:

	£,000	£,000
Revenue		1,110
Less: Cost of sales	574	
Administration expenses	96	
Distribution costs	142	
Finance costs	10	(822)
Net profit		288

The following table contains a breakdown of the company's financial results.

	Copiers £,000	Paper £,000	Printing £,000	HO £,000
Revenue	611	395	104	–
Cost of sales	384	146	44	–
Administration expenses	47	9	18	22
Distribution costs	101	17	24	–
Finance costs	6	1	1	2
Non-current assets at book value	1,012	767	432	232
Inventories	31	14	12	–
Bank	148	46	31	–
Payables	32	20	16	10
Short-term borrowing	13	7	4	8
Long-term borrowing	210	–	–	–

Required

Prepare a segmental statement of profit or loss and other comprehensive income for Buffalo Ltd complying, so far as information permits, with the provisions of IFRS 8 'Operating Segments' indicating revenues and expenses for each segment and the business as a whole:

a   revenue;

b   profit; and

c   net assets.

5.3   Identify the circumstances in which IAS 8 enables a company to change its accounting policy and indicate how the change must be treated in the accounts.

END OF CHAPTER QUESTIONS *continued*

5.4   The issued share capital of Hawkestone Ltd at 1 July 20X6 consisted of 20 million ordinary shares of £1 each issued at par. On 1 January 20X3, the directors made a rights issue of one share for every two shares held at £2.80 per share. The following further information is provided for Hawkestone Ltd for the year to 30 June 20X7:

	£,000
Turnover	74,400
Cost of sales (Note 1)	49,200
Loss on closure of manufacturing division (Note 2)	14,600
Distribution costs	7,200
Administrative expenses	12,400
Bad debts write off arising from prior period error (Note 3)	4,280
Retained profit at 1 July 20X6	25,200

Notes

1   The cost of sales figure includes closing inventories of finished goods valued at £4.74 million. The company's auditors have drawn attention to the fact that £1.04 million of these inventories is obsolete and should be written off.

2   In the past, the company's activities consisted of a manufacturing division and a service division. The service division has been making healthy profits in recent years, but the manufacturing division has been making losses. The manufacturing division was closed down during the year to 30 June 20X3.

3   It has been discovered that last year's accounts were wrongly prepared. Owing to a clerical error, a debt due to Hawkestone of £4,280,000 that was known to be bad was wrongly classified as cash at bank.

Required

a   Define a material item in accordance with the provisions of IAS 8.

b   Prepare the statement of profit or loss and other comprehensive income and statement of changes in equity of Hawkestone Ltd in accordance with good accounting practice and complying with standard accounting practice so far as the information permits.

Note: Ignore taxation.

5.5   Explain the nature of a non-recurring item and how it should be reported in the financial statements.

5.6   State and explain the conditions that must be met for an asset to be classified as being held for sale.

5.7   IFRS 5 explains the criteria for determining a discontinued operation. Explain the criteria.

5.8   What is an operating segment? Explain the criteria in identifying an operating segment.

Purpose of the statement of cash flows

■ CONTENTS

■ LEARNING OUTCOMES

Chapter 6 is the final chapter related to the syllabus section 'financial statements for single companies'. After reading and understanding the contents of the chapter, working through all the worked examples and practice questions, you should be able to:

■ appreciate the purpose of a statement of cash flows and its usefulness to users of financial information;
■ discuss and explain the concept of cash and cash equivalents in light of International Accounting Standard (IAS) 7 and the limitations of classifying items under cash and cash equivalents;
■ explain the components of a statement of cash flow statement under IAS 7;
■ understand and prepare a statement of cash flow statement under both the direct and indirect methods as guided by IAS 7;
■ be able to interpret a cash flow statement together with the other financial statements; and
■ understand the limitations of statements of cash flows and be able to recommend other useful information that would reduce the impact of these limitations.

1   Introduction

The statement of cash flows is one of the principal financial statements that must be disclosed together with the other principal statements, namely, a statement of profit or loss and other comprehensive income for the period and the statement of changes in equity. IAS 7 'Statement of Cash Flows' provides the basis under which the cash flow statement is to be prepared and the items to be disclosed.

The statement of cash flows reports the *cash* generated and used during the reporting period. While the statement of cash flows is referred to in this chapter over a 12-month reporting period, companies can and do prepare an interim statement of cash flows for quarterly and half-yearly reporting. IAS 7 requires the disclosure of cash flows under three main headings: operating, investing and financing activities, plus any supplemental information supporting the statement:

■ *Operating activities*: Converts the items reported on the statement of profit or loss and other comprehensive income from the accrual basis of accounting to cash.
■ *Investing activities*: Reports the cash flows relating to the purchase and sale of long-term investments and property, plant and equipment (PPE).
■ *Financing activities*: Reports the cash flows relating to the issuance and repurchase of the company's own bonds and shares and the payment of dividends.

The statement of cash flows explains the changes in cash and cash equivalents. Reporting entities can choose between the 'direct' or 'indirect' method of cash flows disclosure on the basis of IAS 7. The various terminologies used in preparing and presented the statement of cash flows will be discussed as they arise.

TEST YOUR KNOWLEDGE 6.1

Describe the four elements of a statement of cash flows and how they might be useful to users.

---

2 Purpose of the statement of cash flows

Financial statements are prepared under the accruals basis, rather than reflecting actual movements of cash. For example, some of the revenue reported in the statement of profit or loss and other comprehensive income may not have been collected at the reporting date. This uncollected revenue would contribute to the trade receivables figure reported in the statement of financial position. Similarly, although the expenses reported on the statement of profit or loss and other comprehensive income have been incurred, they are unlikely to have all been paid. These unpaid expenses would also be reflected in the statement of financial position.

The statement of cash flows facilitates an assessment of a company's liquidity as well as determining both the use of cash within a company and the ability of a company to generate cash. Movements in cash flows can impact the liquidity position of a company in various ways:

1   The cash from operating activities is compared to the company's net income. If the cash from operating activities is consistently greater than the net income, the company's net income or earnings are said to be of a 'high quality'. If the cash from operating activities is less than net income, this raises issues as to why the reported net income is greater than cash flows generated.

2   In business, 'cash is king'. Cash is the oxygen of any business because in its absence the business cannot meet its daily obligations. The cash flow statement identifies the cash that is flowing into and out of the company. If a company is consistently generating more cash than it is using, it will be able to increase its dividend, buy back some of its shares, reduce debt or acquire another company/asset/investment. All of these are perceived to be good for shareholder value.

3   Some financial models are based upon cash flow. In the short term, a company's performance may be measured on a profitability basis. However, in the long term, investors and stakeholders assess the financial health of a company on the present value of all future cash flows.

3 Cash and cash equivalents

IAS 7 states that:

> 'The objective of IAS 7 is to require the presentation of information about the historical changes in cash and cash equivalents of an entity by means of a statement of cash flows, which classifies cash flows during the period according to operating, investing, and financing activities.'

Cash equivalents are said to be highly liquid short-term assets that are readily convertible to known cash amounts (IAS 7 para. 7). Additionally, there must be little risk of change in value to cash equivalents. IAS 7 further suggests that, to qualify as cash equivalents, investments should normally have a maturity of three months or less.

Technically speaking, items that do not fall under the banner of operating, investing and financing activities do not get reported in the statement of cash flows. However, items that are deemed to be cash or cash equivalents are included in the statement of cash flows, as these items form part of the cash management of the business. Cash management includes the investment of excess cash in cash equivalents.

WORKED EXAMPLE 6.1

Exel Ltd's financial year end is 31 December 20X6. The company purchased some high-quality corporate bonds as a short-term investment. The bonds were purchased on 1 September 20X6 with a maturity date of 31 December 20X6.

Required
The CEO of Exel has included the corporate bonds in the cash and cash equivalent statement of financial position. Advise the CEO if this is correct.

Answer
At the date of purchase of the corporate bonds, 1 September 20X6, the bonds had a maturity date of four months. However, this does not comply with the three months or less rule in on the basis of IAS 7, so the bonds should not be classified as cash equivalent.

---

4 Components of the statement of cash flows

4.1 Cash flows from operating activities

Cash inflow and outflow generated by the normal course of business activity comes under operating activities. These include the revenues generated through production and the expenses incurred due to delivery of the company's product(s) resulting in cash transactions. Cash inflows are generated by sales, while cash outflows are incurred by expenses. The expenses may include production costs and distribution costs, as well as expenses for administration and taxes. Under IAS 7, operating cash flows include:

- operating profit;
- receipts from the sale of goods or services;
- receipts for the sale of loans, debt or equity instruments in a trading portfolio;
- interest received on loans;
- dividends received on equity securities;
- payments to suppliers for goods and services;
- payments to employees or on behalf of employees; and
- interest payments (alternatively, this can be reported under financing activities in IAS 7);
- income (corporation) tax paid.

Items that are added back to (or subtracted from, as appropriate) the net income figure (which is found on the statement of profit or loss and other comprehensive income) to arrive at cash flows from operations generally include:

- depreciation (loss of tangible asset value over time);
- deferred tax movements
- amortisation (loss of intangible asset value over time); and
- any gains or losses associated with the sale of a non-current asset, because associated cash flows do not belong in the operating section (unrealised gains/losses are also added back from the statement of profit or loss and other comprehensive income).

The above adjustments are only necessary if the indirect method is used, in which case the following adjustments will also be required:

- any increases/decreases in inventory; and
- any increase/decrease in receivables and payables.

These will also need to be added back. Having regard to the above items, the net cash flows generated account for the cash used in normal business activity.

4.2 Cash flows from investing activities

Non-current assets purchased and cash payments made are reported in the investing activities. Cash receipts on disposal of non-current assets are also disclosed in this section. Non-current assets may include, but are not limited to, such items as:

- purchase or sale of an asset (assets can be land, building, equipment, securities, etc.);
- financial investments (equities and loans); and
- acquisition of other businesses.

Loans made outside the company will generate cash inflow in the form of interest received. Investment in other companies will generate cash inflow in the form of dividends received. In both cases, the actual receipt of cash will be disclosed in the statement of cash flows.

4.3 Cash flows from financing activities

Financing activities typically include long-term bank loans and cash from investors such as new share issues, debentures and bonds. The company will also make cash payments to shareholders in the form of dividends representing an outflow of cash. IAS 7 gives some guidance on what can be included under financing activities:

- proceeds from issuing short-term or long-term debt;
- payments of dividends;
- payments for repurchase of company shares;
- repayment of debt principal, including leases; and
- for non-profit organisations, receipts of donor-restricted cash that is limited to long-term purposes.

The reason for segregating how cash flows arise in a business is to create a level of transparency for users. It is expected that the finances of companies should be generated through normal day-to-day activities (i.e. operating activities). This indicates how the business is performing and its long-term prospects.

TEST YOUR KNOWLEDGE 6.2

Explain why users of cash flow information would find it useful to have disclosure under the three headings of operating, investing and financing activities.

---

5 Methods for preparation of the statement of cash flows

IAS 7 provides clear guidance on how the operating cash flows should be prepared. Two alternative methods are provided: the 'direct' and 'indirect' methods. The two methods only differ in their reporting of cash generated from operating activities. However, IAS 7 clearly states that 'entities are encouraged to report cash flows from operating activities using the direct method'. Despite this statement, most companies elect to report their operating activities cash flows using the indirect method.

5.1 Direct method

When an entity uses the direct method for reporting cash generated from its operating activities, the disclosures address the major classes of gross cash receipts and gross cash payments. The disclosure under the direct method for reporting the cash generated from operations is shown in Table 6.1.

TABLE 6.1 Cash flows from operating activities

Cash flows from operating activities	£	£
Cash receipts from customers	xxxx	
Cash paid to suppliers of goods and services	(xxxx)	
Cash paid to employees	(xxxx)	
Cash generated from operations		xxxx

Under IAS 7, dividends received may be reported either under operating activities or investment activities. If taxes paid are directly linked to operating activities, they are reported under operating activities. If the taxes are directly linked to investment activities or financing activities, they are reported under investment or financing activities (see below).

 WORKED EXAMPLE 6.2

Louisa-Ann Plc – statement of profit or loss and other comprehensive income for the year ended 30 September 20X7:

	£
Sales	85,455
Cost of sales	(51,275)
Gross profit	34,180
Administrative and selling expenses	(27,380)
Interest payable	–
Profit before taxation	6,800
Taxation	(2,040)
Profit after tax	4,760

Louisa-Ann Plc – statement of financial position as at 30 September:

	20X7 £	20X6 £
Assets		
Non-current assets		
Land and buildings	22,400	14,000
Plant and machinery	14,800	7,000
	37,200	21,000
Current assets		
Inventories	11,200	6,400
Trade receivables	8,600	3,200
Bank	–	4,400
	19,800	14,000
Total assets	57,000	35,000
Equity		
Share capital	25,000	20,000
Retained earnings	8,760	4,000
	33,760	24,000

WORKED EXAMPLE 6.2 *continued*

Liabilities

Non-current

Long-term loans	–	4,000

Current

Trade payables	11,800	7,000
Taxation	2,040	–
Bank	9,400	–
	23,240	7,000
Total equity and liabilities	57,000	35,000

Notes

1 The administrative and selling expenses includes £17,600 employee-related expenses.
2 During the year, £8,600 was sent on additional plant and machinery and £8,400 was spent on the acquisition of land.
3 The annual depreciation charge of £800 is included in the administrative and selling expenses.

Requirement

Prepare a statement of cash flows for Louisa-Ann Plc using the IAS 7 direct method.

Suggested answer

Louisa-Ann Plc – statement of cash flows for the year ended 30 September 20X7:

Cash flows from operating activities

	£	£
Cash receipts from customers (W1)	80,055	
Cash paid to suppliers of goods and services (W2)	(60,255)	
Cash paid to employees (W3)	(17,600)	
Cash generated from operations		2,200

Interest paid	0	
Taxation paid	0	
Net cash generated from operating activities		2,200

Cash flows from investing activities £

Acquisition of subsidiary	0
Purchase of non-current asset (W4)	(17,000)
Proceeds from sale of non-current asset	0
Interest received	0
Dividends received	0
Net cash applied in investing activities	(17,000)

WORKED EXAMPLE **6.2** *continued*

Cash flows from financing activities	£	
Issued share capital (W5)	5,000	
Repayment of long-term borrowing (W6)	(4,000)	
Payment of finance lease	0	
Dividends paid		
Net cash applied in financing activities		1,000
Net cash increase/decrease in cash and cash equivalents		(13,800)

Cash and cash equivalents at 1 October 20X6	4,400
Cash and cash equivalents at 30 September 20X7	(9,400)

Workings

W1. Receipt from customers

	£
Sales	85,455
Plus opening trade receivables	3,200
Less closing trade receivables	(8,600)
	80,055

W2. Payment to suppliers

	£
Cost of sales	51,275
Less opening inventory	(6,400)
Plus closing inventory	11,200
Plus administrative and selling expenses	27,380
Plus opening payables	7,000
Less closing payables	(11,800)
Less depreciation	(800)
Employees expense	(17,600)
	60,255

W3. Cash paid to employees
Note 1 Administrative and selling expenses includes £17,600 employee-related expenses.

W4. Purchase of non-current assets

Note 2

Plant and machinery	8,600
Land	8,400
Total	17,000

W5. Issued share capital

As at 30 September 20X7	25,000
As at 1 October 20X6	20,000
Increase in share capital	5,000

W6. Long-term borrowing

As at 30 September 20X7	0
As at 1 October 20X6	4,000
Increase in long-term borrowing	(4,000)

5.2 Indirect method

The operating profit before taxation is the starting point when using the indirect method to determine the cash flows from operating activities. The profit has to be adjusted for all non-cash transactions that were included in its computation. These adjustments are usually as follows:

- Non-cash expenses, such as depreciation, and non-cash income, such as reduction in provisions for doubtful debt;
- Income or expenses that have arisen from investing or financing activities, such as dividends or interest that are payable or received. The income is always deducted as they have not arisen from trading activities and conversely the expenses are added.
- Changes in the working capital items, inventories, payables and receivables that have arisen during the accounting period. The adjustment to the operating profit before taxation for the respective working capital elements is set out below.

Working capital items	Increase	Decrease
Inventories	Deduction	Addition
Trade payables	Addition	Deduction
Trade receivables	Deduction	Addition

 WORKED EXAMPLE **6.3**

Louisa-Ann Inc – statement of profit or loss and other comprehensive income for the year ended 30 September 20X7:

	£
Sales	85,455
Cost of sales	(51,275)
Gross profit	34,180
Administrative and selling expenses	(27,380)
Interest payable	–
Profit before taxation	6,800
Taxation	(2,040)
Profit after tax	4,760

Louisa-Ann Plc – statement of financial position as at 30 September:

	20X7 £	20X6 £
Assets		
Non-current assets		
Land and buildings	22,400	14,000
Plant and machinery	14,800	7,000
	37,200	21,000
Current assets		
Inventories	11,200	6,400
Trade receivables	8,600	3,200
Bank	–	4,400
	19,800	14,000
Total assets	57,000	35,000

> 📷 **WORKED EXAMPLE** **6.3** *continued*

Equity

Share capital	25,000	20,000
Retained earnings	8,760	4,000
	33,760	24,000

Liabilities

Non-current

Long-term loans	–	4,000

Current

Trade payables	11,800	7,000
Taxation	2,040	–
Bank	9,400	–
	23,240	7,000
Total equity and liabilities	57,000	35,000

Notes

1 During the year, £8,600 was spent on additional plant and machinery and £8,400 was spent on the acquisition of land.

2 The annual depreciation charge of £800 is included in the administrative and selling expenses.

Requirement

Prepare a statement of cash flows for Louisa-Ann Plc using the IAS 7 indirect method.

Suggested answer

Cash flows from operating activities	£	£
Profit from operations	6,800	
Adjustments		
Depreciation	800	
	7,600	
Inventories increase	(4,800)	
Receivables increase	(5,400)	
Payables increase	4,800	
	(5,400)	
Cash generated from operations		2,200
Interest paid		
Tax paid		
Net cash generated from operating activities		2,200

Cash flows from investing activities	£	
Acquisition of subsidiary	0	
Purchase of non-current asset	(17,000)	
Proceeds from sale of non-current asset	0	
Interest received	0	
Dividends received	0	

WORKED EXAMPLE **6.3** *continued*

Net cash applied in investing activities	(17,000)

Cash flows from financing activities	£	
Issued share capital	5,000	
Repayment of long-term borrowing	(4,000)	
Payment of finance lease	0	
Dividends paid		
Net cash applied in financing activities		1,000
Net cash increase/decrease in cash and cash equivalents		(13,800)
Cash and cash equivalents at 1 October 20X6		4,400
Cash and cash equivalents at 30 September 20X7		(9,400)

Worked Examples 6.2 and 6.3 demonstrate that both methods produce identical net increase/decrease in cash and cash equivalents.

5.3 Rules for calculating cash flows under operating activities

The suggested answer in Worked Example 6.3 demonstrates how to derive cash flows from operating activities when a two-year comparative statement of financial position and the net income figures are given. Cash flows from operating activities can be calculated by adjusting net income relative to the change in start and end balances of cash at bank/overdraft, inventories/receivables and payables, and sometimes non-current assets. When comparing the change in non-current assets over a year, we must be certain that these changes were caused entirely by their depreciation/devaluation rather than purchases or sales (i.e. they must be operating items not providing or using cash, or they are non-operating items).

WORKED EXAMPLE **6.4**

Indirect method

Cash generated from operating activities	£
Profit from operations	6,800
Add: Depreciation	800
	7,600
Deduct: Increase in inventories	(4,800)
Deduct: Increase in receivables	(5,400)
Add: Decrease on payables	4,800
	(5,400)
Cash generated from operations	2,200

Rules for calculating the cash generated from operations under the indirect method are as follows:

- *Depreciation*: Since depreciation represents an accounting expense and is a non-cash item, it has to be added back to net profit.
- *Inventory*: An increase in inventory means the business has used cash and hence represents a cash outflow, to be deducted from net profit. A decrease in inventory represents a cash inflow, to be added to net profit.
- *Receivables*: Receivables represent goods and services sold to customers on credit. If receivables increase from one period to the next, this has an effect of decreasing cash to the business, which is deducted from net profit. If receivables decrease from one period to the next, this represents a cash inflow, which would be added to net profit.
- *Payables*: Payables represent payments outstanding to suppliers. If payables increase from one period to the next, this represents an inflow of cash to the business, which is added to the net profit. If payables decrease, we must deduct the difference from the net profit.

Other items:

- *Interest expense* is an accounting figure that should be added back to net profit; if this is a positive figure in the statement of profit or loss and other comprehensive income, it should be deducted. Interest actually paid in cash should be deducted from profits for the period.
- *Tax expenses* shown on the face of the statement of profit or loss and other comprehensive income must be must be added back to the net profit, as they represent an accounting tax estimate. However, taxes actually paid in cash must be deducted from the net profit figure.
- *Dividends paid* will be deducted from the net profit as these represent cash outflow from a business. However, dividends can be shown under 'cash from financing activities'.

WORKED EXAMPLE 6.5

The following information is relevant to Gamma Ltd for the year ended 31 December 20X6.

The financial statements of Gamma Ltd are as follows.

Statement of profit or loss and other comprehensive income for the year ended 31 December 20X6:

	£
Revenue	900,000
Cost of sales (Note 1)	(670,000)
Gross profit	230,000
Administration expenses (Note 2)	(87,800)
Distribution costs	(1,300)
Operating profit	140,900
Finance costs (Note 5)	(17,600)
Profit before taxation	123,300
Taxation	(34,000)
Profit for the period	89,300

Statement of financial position as at 31 December:

	20X6 £	20X5 £
Assets		
Non-current assets		
Property, plant and equipment at cost (Note 2)	350,000	334,000
Accumulated depreciation	(110,000)	(154,000)
	240,000	180,000

WORKED EXAMPLE 6.5 *continued*

Current assets

Inventory	82,000	83,900
Trade receivables	54,500	68,000
Cash	43,500	10,000
	180,000	161,900
Total assets	420,000	341,900

Equity and liabilities

Equity

Ordinary share capital (£1 ord. shares – Note 4)	120,000	100,000
Share premium (Note 4)	72,000	50,000
Revaluation reserve	20,000	10,000
Retained earnings	55,400	16,100
Total equity	267,400	176,100

Non-current liabilities

Long-term loans	90,000	100,000

Current liabilities

Trade payables	38,200	40,000
Taxation	24,400	7,000
Bank overdraft	0	18,800
Total liabilities	152,600	165,800
Total equity and liabilities	420,000	341,900

Notes

1 During the year, depreciation of £17,000 was charged to cost of sales and £23,000 to administrative expenses.
2 Plant and equipment disposed of during the year had an original cost of £90,000 and accumulated depreciation of £84,000. Cash received on disposal was £21,500. Additions to property, plant and equipment were purchased for cash.
3 The 20X5 dividend of £50,000 was paid during the year ended 31 December 20X6.
4 A cash issue of 20,000 £1 ordinary shares were made during the year for £2.10 per share.
5 All finance costs were paid in the year.

Required

Prepare a statement of cash flows for Gamma Ltd for the year ended 31 December 20X6, using the indirect method in accordance with IAS 7.

Answer

Gamma Ltd – statement of cash flows for the year ended 31 December 20X6:

Cash flows from operating activities	Item	£
Profit for the period		89,300
Add: depreciation	1	40,000
Gain on disposal of asset	2	(15,500)
Decrease in Inventory	5	1,900
Decrease in Trade receivables	6	13,500

WORKED EXAMPLE **6.5** *continued*

Tax expense	7	34,000
(Decrease) in Payables	8	(1,800)
Tax paid	7	(16,600)
Net cash flows from operating activities		144,800
Cash flows from investment activities		
Purchase of property, plant and equipment	4	(96,000)
Disposal of property, plant and equipment	Note 2	21,500
Net cash flows from investment activities		(74,500)
Cash flows from financing activities		
Share issue	Note 4	42,000
Dividends paid	Note 3	(50,000)
Repayment of long-term loan	9	(10,000)
Net cash flows from financing activities		(18,000)
Net increase/(decrease) in cash and cash equivalents		52,300
Opening cash and cash equivalents	10	(8,800)
Closing cash and cash equivalents	10	43,500

Notes 2, 3 and 4 are from the question.
Calculation of cash flow items:

Item 1: Depreciation write-back

Depreciation charge	**£**
Opening depreciation	154,000
Less: Depreciation on sale of asset	(84,000)
Adjusted opening depreciation	70,000
Closing depreciation	110,000
Less: Adjusted opening depreciation	70,000
To operating activities	40,000

Item 2: Gain/(Loss) on disposal of assets write-back

Gain/(loss) on disposal	**£**
Cost of disposed assets	90,000
Less: Accumulated depreciation	(84,000)
NBV of disposed assets	6,000
Cash received on disposal	21,500
Less: NBV of disposed assets	6,000
Gain on disposal of assets	15,500

Item 3: Gain/(Loss) on revaluation of assets write-back

Gain/(loss) on revaluation	**£**
Opening revaluation reserve	10,000
Gain on revaluation of assets	10,000
Closing revaluation reserve	20,000

WORKED EXAMPLE **6.5** *continued*

Item 4: Asset purchased for cash

Purchase of non-current assets	£
Opening PPE	334,000
Disposal of PPE	(90,000)
PPE cost before revaluation	244,000
Gain on revaluation of PPE	10,000
Cost of PPE after revaluation	254,000
Closing PPE	350,000
Less cost of assets after revaluation	254,000
To operating activities	96,000

Item 5: Inventory adjustment

Inventory	£
Closing inventory	82,000
Opening inventory	83,900
Change in inventory	(1,900)

Item 6: Trade receivables adjustment

Trade receivables	£
Closing trade receivables	54,500
Opening trade receivables	68,000
Change in trade receivables	(13,500)

Item 7: Tax expense and paid adjustments

Tax expense and tax paid	£
Opening tax balance	7,000
Tax charge for the year	34,000
	41,000
Closing tax balance	24,400
Tax paid in the year	16,600

Item 8: Payables adjustment

Payables	£
Closing payables	38,200
Opening payables	40,000
Change in payables	(1,800)

Item 9: Long-term loan adjustment

Long-term loan	£
Closing long-term loan	90,000
Opening long-term loan	100,000
Change in long-term loan	(10,000)

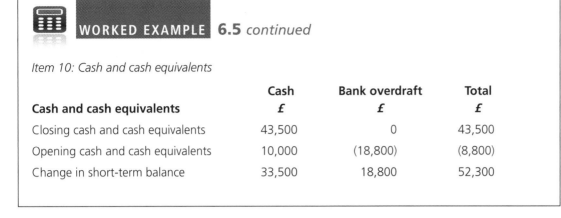

WORKED EXAMPLE **6.5** *continued*

Item 10: Cash and cash equivalents

Cash and cash equivalents	Cash £	Bank overdraft £	Total £
Closing cash and cash equivalents	43,500	0	43,500
Opening cash and cash equivalents	10,000	(18,800)	(8,800)
Change in short-term balance	33,500	18,800	52,300

6 Further guidance on statement cash flows

IAS 7 gives additional advice on the preparation of items disclosed on the face of the statement of cash flows. The additional guidance relates to specific treatment items and the way they should be presented:

'The exchange rate used for translation of transactions denominated in a foreign currency should be the rate in effect at the date of the cash flows (IAS 7.25).

Cash flows of foreign subsidiaries should be translated at the exchange rates prevailing when the cash flows took place (IAS 7.26).

Aggregate cash flows relating to acquisitions and disposals of subsidiaries and other business units should be presented separately and classified as investing activities, with specified additional disclosures (IAS 7.39). The aggregate cash paid or received as consideration should be reported net of cash and cash equivalents acquired or disposed of (IAS 7.42).

Cash flows from investing and financing activities should be reported gross by major class of cash receipts and major class of cash payments except for the following cases, which may be reported on a net basis: (IAS 7.22–24).

Cash receipts and payments on behalf of customers (e.g. receipt and repayment of demand deposits by banks, and receipts collected on behalf of and paid over to the owner of a property).

Cash receipts and payments for items in which the turnover is quick, the amounts are large and the maturities are short, generally less than three months (e.g. charges and collections from credit card customers, and purchase and sale of investments).

Cash receipts and payments relating to deposits by financial institutions.

Cash advances *and loans made to customers and repayments thereof.*

Investing and financing transactions which do not require the use of cash should be excluded from the statement of cash flows, but they should be separately disclosed elsewhere in the financial statements (IAS 7.43).

The components of cash and cash equivalents should be disclosed, and a reconciliation presented to amounts reported in the statement of financial position (IAS 7.45).

The amount of cash and cash equivalents held by the entity that is not available for use by the group should be disclosed, together with a commentary by management (IAS 7.48).'

Source: Deloitte IAS Plus

7 Interpretation of cash flow information and disclosures

A company's cash flow can provide useful information on its ability to meet current and future commitments. The cash flow of some companies move much faster than others, mainly due to the nature of their business and their business sector. Broadly speaking, companies whose customers are the general public (e.g. Tesco, Halfords, John Lewis) tend to deal primarily in cash transactions, hence they have a faster cash cycle. If we were to compare the cash flow statements of these companies, we would find trends in the cash cycle.

Analysis of cash flow trends and cycles allows managers to plan for difficult times and situations to ensure they can meet the company's short- and long-term commitments. Cash flow analysis can highlight when shortfalls in funding should be met with assistance from lenders and allow decision-makers to plan for either short-term or long-term borrowing.

Cash flow analysis can further help in cash flow management related to trade receivables and trade payables. In times of financial difficulty, management may need to review credit policy. When a company has a strong reputation, it can negotiate shorter credit terms with its suppliers. By the same token, a strong company can negotiate longer credit periods for payment of debt, enabling the company to hold on to cash for longer periods.

TEST YOUR KNOWLEDGE 6.3

Explain the potential information a user would be looking for in a statement of cash flows together with the other financial statements.

7.1 Cash flows from discontinued operations

Cash flows arising out of discontinued operations require separate disclosure in the financial statements. Additional information must be made similar to the requirement for the statement of profit or loss and other comprehensive income either on the cash flow statement or the narratives. An example taken from a discontinued operation by Vodafone is shown below.

Cash flows from discontinued operations:

	2017 £m	2016 £m
Net cash flows from operating activities	135	1,651
Net cash flows from investing activities	(266)	(939)
Net cash flows from financing activities	(29)	(536)
Net increase in cash and cash equivalents	(160)	176
Cash and cash equivalents at the beginning of the financial year	161	4
Exchange loss on cash and cash equivalents	(1)	(19)
Cash and cash equivalents at the end of the financial year	–	161

8 Limitations of the statement of cash flows

One problem often stated in relation to IAS 7 is that the classifications used are too broad. It could be argued that if a company's expenditure were explained in more detail, it would give users of financial information much greater insight in to the underlying economic reality. Items such as research and development, mining and exploration costs and marketing expenditure should be disclosed in the cash flow statement. However, the issue arises as to where such expenditure should be disclosed (i.e. under operating or investing activities).

The indirect method causes confusion for some users as it is based on the statement of financial position movements and reconciliation. For this reason it has been argued that IAS 7 should only permit the direct method. However, companies could counter-argue that new accounting procedures would need to be adopted to keep track of cash movements.

Another argument in favour of the indirect method is that a reconciliation of cash flows from operating activities from net profit allows users to see if profit figures are being manipulated; this would facilitate a greater degree of analysis and would allow users to make better informed economic decisions. Similarly, cash raised through financing instruments such as loans should not form part of cash flows from operating activities, but should be shown separately from cash flows generated through business activity.

TEST YOUR KNOWLEDGE 6.4

a Discuss the potential limitations of the statement of cash flows.
b What other information could usefully be included?

STOP AND THINK 6.1

Do you think we should simply revert to accounting on a cash basis?

9 Commenting on the statement of cash flows

When commenting on the liquidity of a business it is important to look at liquidity ratios, discussed in Chapters 9 and 10. Further value is gained if comparatives can be calculated with previous years' information if provided.

The most commonly used ratio is the Acid test or 'Quick' ratio, which measures the short-term liquidity of the business, if this is greater than 1 the business is deemed to be liquid i.e.: able to pay off current liabilities using current assets. The ratio is defined as: Current Assets, minus inventory, divided by current liabilities.

Further analysis can be made and conclusions drawn by examining other liquidity ratios and looking at the Statement of Cash flows to determine which areas of the business are contributing to this. Examining the cash generated from operations figure provides an immediate answer; a positive figure indicating the company is able to generate sufficient cash flows to maintain and grow the business.

END OF CHAPTER QUESTIONS

6.1 In a statement of cash flows, which of the following items will NOT appear in the cash flow from the investing activities section when using the indirect method?
    a   Purchase of non-current assets
    b   Taxation paid
    c   Purchase of investments
    d   Disposal proceeds of non-current assets
6.2 In accordance with IAS 7 'Statement of Cash Flows', which of the following categories is NOT used to classify cash flows in a statement of cash flows?
    a   Managing activities
    b   Financing activities
    c   Investing activities
    d   Operating activities
6.3 Why is reported profit different to a company's cash flow for a particular accounting period?
6.4 Explain how the following events will impact cash flow movements:
    a   Increase in inventory from one period to the next
    b   Decrease in payables
    c   Decrease in receivables
    d   Increase in the market value of a company's share price
    e   Gains made on disposal of a non-current asset
    f   Issue of new shares at market price

? END OF CHAPTER QUESTIONS *continued*

6.5 If credit sales for the year were £75 million, and trade receivables at the start of the year were £20 million and at the end of the year were £12 million, state how much cash was received from trade customers.

6.6 A company has made purchases of materials on credit totalling £36 million during the year. At the beginning of the year, the payables balance was £12 million. The closing payables balance was £18 million. State how much money was paid to suppliers during the year.

6.7 Give three examples of statement of profit or loss and other comprehensive income items that do not involve cash payment, and explain why.

6.8 The proceeds of cash sale of an item of plant amounted to £120,000. The item was originally purchased for £500,000 and had accumulated depreciation of £400,000. How will this information affect the cash flow statement?

6.9 Capri Ltd has net profits of £20 million, which includes a charge of £500,000 for depreciation. During the year, the inventory decreased by £800,000 and receivables increased by £200,000. Payables decreased by £400,000. Prepare a calculation of cash flows from operations.

6.10 Sarah Ltd is a manufacturer of a line of children's clothing with a 31 December financial year end. The results for last year are shown on the next page.

Statement of profit or loss and other comprehensive income for the year ended 31 December 20X6:

	£
Revenue	949,000
Cost of sales	(442,000)
Gross profit	507,000
Administration expenses	(47,000)
Distribution costs	(82,000)
Operating profit	378,000
Finance costs	(26,000)
Profit before taxation	352,000
Taxation	(36,000)
Profit for the period	316,000
Extract from statement of changes to equity	
Dividends	274,000

Statement of financial position as at 31 December 20X6:

	20X6 £	20X5 £
Assets		
Non-current assets		
Property, plant and equipment at cost	470,000	470,000
Accumulated depreciation	(230,000)	(180,000)
	240,000	290,000
Current assets		
Inventory	75,000	45,000
Trade receivables	144,000	120,000
	219,000	165,000
Total assets	459,000	455,000

END OF CHAPTER QUESTIONS *continued*

Equity and liabilities

Equity

Ordinary share capital (£1 ord. shares)	140,000	100,000
Share premium	8,000	–
Retained earnings	121,000	79,000
Total equity	269,000	179,000
Non-current liabilities		
Long-term loans	66,000	84,800
Current liabilities		
Trade payables	87,000	170,000
Taxation	30,000	18,000
Bank overdraft	7,000	3,200
	124,000	191,200
Total liabilities	190,000	276,000
Total equity and liabilities	459,000	455,000

Notes
1 Dividends relating to 20X6 £274,000 were paid in cash by the year end.
2 A total of 40,000 ordinary £1.00 shares were issued at the market price of £1.20.
3 There were no purchases of property, plant and equipment in the year.
4 Interest costs for 20X6 (£26,000) have not been paid.

Required
Prepare a statement of cash flows for Sarah Ltd for the year ending 31 December 20X6.

6.11 Plumbus Ltd is a small engineering firm that manufactures various types of piping for industrial clients. The information below relates to 30 September 20X7:

Statement of profit or loss and other comprehensive income for the year ended 30 September 20X7:

	£
Revenue	1,200,000
Cost of sales	(810,000)
Gross profit	390,000
Administration expenses	(105,000)
Distribution costs	(87,000)
Operating profit	198,000
Finance costs	(8,000)
Profit before taxation	190,000
Taxation	(54,000)
Profit for the period	136,000

Statement of financial position as at 30 September 20X7:

	20X7	20X6
	£	£
Assets		
Non-current assets		
Property, plant and equipment at cost	520,000	418,000
Accumulated depreciation	(260,000)	(188,000)
	260,000	230,000
Current assets		
Inventory	64,000	68,000
Trade receivables	38,000	45,000
Cash and cash equivalents	144,000	54,000
	246,000	167,000
Total assets	506,000	397,000
Equity and liabilities		
Equity		
Ordinary share capital (£1 ord. shares)	150,000	120,000
Share premium	24,000	–
Revaluation reserve	18,000	8,000
Retained earnings	56,000	33,000
Total equity	248,000	161,000
Non-current liabilities		
Long-term loans	224,000	165,000
Current liabilities		
Trade payables	12,000	60,000
Taxation	22,000	11,000
	34,000	71,000
Total liabilities	258,000	236,000
Total equity and liabilities	506,000	397,000

Notes

1   During the year a depreciation charge of £70,000 charge was made to cost of sales and £32,000 to administration expenses in the statement of profit or loss and other comprehensive income.
2   Property, plant and equipment (PPE) disposed of during the year had an original cost of £40,000 and accumulated depreciation of £30,000. Cash received on disposal was £8,000.
3   Additions to PPE were purchased for cash.
4   A cash issue of 30,000 ordinary £1 shares were made during the year for £1.80 per share.
5   Finance costs were not paid during the year.
6   All dividends were paid in cash during the year.

Required

a   Prepare a statement of cash flows for Plumbus Ltd for the year ending 30 September 20X7 using the indirect method under IAS 7.
b   Comment on your findings on the statement of cash flows and propose any remedial action that is required by the company.

6.12 Anderson Ltd is a small builders merchant sourcing and selling construction materials.
The most recent statement of profit and loss and other comprehensive income and statement of financial position (with comparatives for the previous year) of Anderson Ltd are set out below.

Anderson Ltd – Statement of profit or loss and OCI for the year ended 31 March 2017

	£000
Revenue	93,437
Cost of sales	(51,017)
Gross profit	42,420
Dividends received	6,264
Profit on disposal of property, plant and equipment	176
	48,860
Distribution costs	(12,359)
Administrative expenses	(26,718)
Profit from operations	9,783
Finance costs	(940)
Profit before tax	8,843
Tax	(2,420)
Profit for the period	6,423

Anderson Ltd – Statement of financial position as at 31 March 2017

	2017 £000	2016 £000
ASSETS		
Non-current assets		
Property, plant and equipment	82,864	63,832
	82,864	63,832
Current assets		
Inventories	10,348	9,480
Trade receivables	11,264	12,372
Cash and cash equivalents	12	348
	21,624	22,200
Total assets	104,488	86,032
EQUITY AND LIABILITIES		
Equity		
Share capital	34,500	28,000
Share premium	13,000	12,700
Retained earnings	25,095	18,672
Total equity	72,595	59,372

Non-current liabilities

Bank loans	23,000	19,600
	23,000	19,600

Current liabilities

Trade payables	5,976	5,140
Tax liabilities	2,760	1,920
Bank overdraft	157	–
	8,893	7,060
Total liabilities	31,893	26,660
Total equity and liabilities	104,488	86,032

Notes

1. The total depreciation charge for the year was £8,760,000.
2. Property, plant and equipment with a carrying amount of £394,000 was sold in the year.
3. All sales and purchases were on credit.
4. Other expenses were paid for in cash.

Required

a. Prepare the statement of cash flows for Anderson Ltd using the *indirect method* for the year ended 31 March 2017, including a reconciliation statement of cash and cash equivalents.

b. Comment on the liquidity of Anderson Limited; given the chance would you invest in them?

The preparation and presentation of financial statements for groups

■ **LIST OF CHAPTERS**

Part 3 covers the syllabus section entitled 'Group accounting'.

■ **OVERVIEW**

The dismantling of international trade barriers and the ability of large corporations to be cross-listed in other countries facilitated the need for reporting that conveyed the economic reality of a business as an economic unit, rather than just a legal entity within business combinations.

The ability of large corporations to unite several entities into one economic entity necessitated the need for changes to the way financial reports are prepared and presented in light of the relevant International Financial Reporting Standard (IFRS) and International Accounting Standard (IAS). Part Three addresses the issues specific to this process. It looks at the different ways in which companies combine and consolidate, and how this is reflected in accounts prepared for groups of companies.

The chapter ends with practice questions that require application of the knowledge gained.

7 Group accounting

■ **LEARNING OUTCOMES**

This chapter deals with the part of the syllabus section entitled 'The preparation and presentation of financial statements for groups in compliance with legal and regulatory requirements, including the relevant International Accounting Standards'. After reading and understanding the contents of the chapter, working through all the worked examples and practice questions, you should be able to:

■ understand the group and consolidation process;
■ identify the existence of a group of companies;
■ explain why parent companies are required to publish **consolidated accounts** and the circumstance in which this obligation does not apply;
■ prepare a consolidated statement of comprehensive income and a consolidated statement of financial position that takes account of adjustments required for: goodwill; post-acquisition profits and **non-controlling interest**;
■ demonstrate and apply an understanding of the nature and significance of other consolidation adjustments;
■ appreciate the value added to the accounting package available to external users by the existence of requirements to publish consolidated accounts;
■ identify and account for associated companies and joint ventures in accordance with standard accounting requirements;
■ show familiarity with the content of a consolidated cash flow statement; and
■ explain the purposes and limitations of group accounts.

1   Introduction

This chapter discusses issues related to group accounting and the provisions of the International Financial Reporting Standards (IFRS) and International Accounting Standards (IAS) that give guidance on how to disclose items in the financial statements. We start with a definition of a 'group' and explain the need for consolidated accounts and benefits to users of consolidated accounting information. The objective of IFRS 10 'Consolidated Financial Statements' is 'to establish principles for the presentation and preparation of consolidated financial statements when an entity controls one or more other entities'.

We will discuss various terminology used in a group accounting context and give an explanation as to their meaning and application. While IFRS 10 gives guidance on preparation and presentation of consolidated accounts, IFRS 12 'Disclosure of Interests in Other Entities' sets out disclosure requirements for reporting entities that have an interest in a subsidiary, joint arrangement, associate or unconsolidated structured entity.

The need to develop an IFRS to deal specifically with issues of consolidated accounts arose due to inherent weaknesses in IAS 27. While recognising that the basic model for consolidated accounts was fine in IAS 27, inconsistency in applying the provisions of IAS 27 necessitated the need for a single combined model that met the needs of both those preparing accounts and end users of financial information in a consistent manner.

TABLE 7.1 Summary of relevant IFRS

IFRS 10 (2011)	Consolidated financial statements
IAS 27 (2011)	Separate financial statements
IFRS 3 (2008)	Business combinations
IAS 28 (2011)	Investments in associates

1.1 Definition of key terms

The terms that underpin the consolidation of financial statements are set out in IFRS 10 and set out in Table 7.2.

TABLE 7.2 Terms relating to the consolidation of financial statements in IFRS 10

Consolidated financial statements	The financial statements of a group in which the assets, liabilities, equity, income, expenses and cash flows of the parent and its subsidiaries are presented as those of a single economic entity.
Control of an investee	An investor controls an investee when the investor is exposed, or has rights, to variable returns from its involvement with the investee and has the ability to affect those returns through its power over the investee.
Investment entity	An entity that: ■ obtains funds from one or more investors for the purpose of providing those investor(s) with investment management services; ■ commits to its investor(s) that its business purpose is to invest funds solely for returns from capital appreciation, investment income, or both; and ■ measures and evaluates the performance of substantially all of its investments on a fair value basis.
Parent	An entity that controls one or more entities.
Power	Existing rights that give the current ability to direct the relevant activities.
Protective rights	Rights designed to protect the interest of the party holding those rights without giving that party power over the entity to which those rights relate.
Relevant activities	Activities of the investee that significantly affect the investee's returns.

According to IFRS 10, an investor controls an investee if and only if the investor has all of the following elements (IFRS 10:7):

■ power over the investee (i.e. the investor has existing rights that gives it the ability to direct the relevant activities – the activities that significantly affect the investee's returns);
■ exposure, or rights, to variable returns from its involvement with the investee; and
■ the ability to use its power over the investee to affect the amount of the investor's returns.

1.2 Definition of a group

A business entity can exist in mutual relationship with other business entities in many ways. These relationships can be in the form of subsidiaries, associates and joint ventures.

In the context of a group, IFRS 3 'Business Combinations' describes a group as a:

'transaction or event in which an acquirer obtains control of one or more businesses. A business is defined as an integrated set of activities and assets that is capable of being conducted and managed for the purpose of providing a return directly to investors or other owners, members or participants.'

IFRS 10 gives a more definitive description of a group suggesting that a group exists where one enterprise (the parent) controls, either directly or indirectly, another enterprise (subsidiary). It follows that a group consists of a parent (owner) and subsidiary.

Additionally, an entity can have control over another entity or entities either directly or indirectly. Figures 7.1 and 7.2 demonstrate how direct or indirect control is achieved by a parent company:

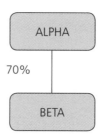

FIGURE 7.1 Direct control by a parent company

In Figure 7.1, the parent company (Alpha) has direct control of the subsidiary company (Beta) due to its controlling rights. This is manifested through a majority shareholding in the subsidiary company of 70% of the ordinary shares.

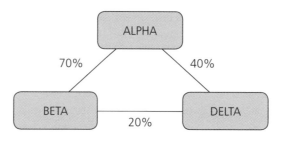

FIGURE 7.2 Indirect control by a parent company

In Figure 7.2, the parent company (Alpha) has an indirect control over Delta. Since Alpha has majority control over Beta (70%) and also has a 40% stake in Delta (due to the fact that Beta also has a 20% stake in Delta) Alpha has control over Delta (40% + 20%). Hence, both Beta and Delta will be regarded as subsidiaries of Alpha.

Linking together the various definitions, we can say that consolidated financial statements must be prepared where one company – the parent – controls the activities of another company – the subsidiary. So, how does one decide whether one entity is able to control another, giving rise to the obligation to prepare consolidated accounts? The basic rule, as we have seen above, is that a parent/subsidiary relationship exists where the first company owns a majority of the voting share capital of the latter company.

In a simple and straightforward world this would be enough, but the business world is neither simple nor straightforward. Over the years, various schemes were devised by managers, in conjunction with their professional advisers, with the objective of conducting a part of a company's business operations through another organisation that, although *in reality* a subsidiary, was not *in law* a subsidiary (e.g. the Special Purpose Entity or SPE). It therefore became necessary to define the parent/subsidiary relationship more closely in order to prevent these abuses.

Today, control is presumed to exist (and consolidated financial statements must, therefore, be prepared) when the parent acquires more than half the voting rights of the enterprise. In the absence of a majority of voting rights, a subsidiary should be consolidated where the parent has power:

- over more than one half of the voting rights by virtue of an agreement with other investors; or
- to govern the financial and operating policies of the other enterprise under a contractual agreement; or
- to appoint or remove the majority of the members of the board of directors; or
- to cast the majority of votes at a meeting of the board of directors.

Often two or more of these tests produce the same result. For example, it is usually necessary to acquire more than half the voting shares to control the composition of the board of directors. In certain circumstances, a parent company/subsidiary company relationship may exist by applying one test but not the other. Only one of the above points needs to apply for a subsidiary to exist.

WORKED EXAMPLE 7.1

Alpha Ltd purchased 102,000 ordinary shares in Beta Ltd on 1 January 20X6. The issued share capital of Beta Ltd consists of 200,000 ordinary shares of £1 each, which carry equal voting rights. Alpha Ltd is, therefore, the parent company of Beta Ltd, as from 1 January 20X6, because:

- it holds more than half the voting power and is therefore able to control the composition of the board of directors; and
- it owns more than half the equity share capital, and the relationship between the two companies can be presented as follows:
  - 51% Alpha Ltd (Parent) Beta Ltd (Subsidiary)

---

2 Combinations based on assets or shares

The combination of two or more businesses may be based on the purchase of assets or shares.

2.1 Combinations based on the purchase of assets

These occur where one company, A, acquires the assets of another company, B, and ownership of B's assets is transferred to A. B then goes into liquidation and A carries on the activities formerly undertaken by two companies. Alternatively, company C may be formed to acquire the assets of both A and B.

Companies A and B may then be wound up and a single legal entity, C, emerges to carry on the activities previously undertaken by the two companies. In both cases it is necessary to value the assets transferred for inclusion in the acquiring company's books. Once this has been done, the assets are accounted for in the normal way and the reporting problems that arise when the combination is based on shares (see below) are avoided.

2.2 Combinations based on the purchase of shares

This is achieved by one company acquiring enough shares of another to give it control (e.g. company A acquires the entire share capital of company B). You should note that agreement is reached between A and the *shareholders* of B. The transaction does not affect B directly and it remains in existence as a separate legal entity. A combination based on shares may alternatively involve the formation of a new company, C, to acquire the shares of A and B. Again, A and B remain in existence as separate legal entities.

The reasons for basing a combination on an acquisition of shares rather than assets are as follows:

- *Economy* – It is not necessary to purchase all the target company's shares; it is enough to ensure effective control over its activities.
- *Continuity* – Where the acquired company maintains a separate identity, its goodwill is more likely to survive unimpaired.
- *Decentralisation* – For both managerial and decision-making processes, decentralisation is facilitated where companies retain their own identity.

3   The group

3.1 Legal and economic forms

The external reporting requirements imposed by the Companies Acts, until 1948, applied only to separate legal entities. In Figure 7.1, for instance, Alpha and Beta each had to publish separate accounts, but these accounts were confined to the transactions directly affecting them as separate legal entities.

The accounts published by Alpha, therefore, included cash actually received from Beta in the form of dividends, but any profits earned and retained by the subsidiary were not reported by the parent company. This gave management an enormous amount of scope to publish misleading financial information if it was inclined to do so. For instance, when the parent company's profits were low, management was often able to conceal this by making large, undisclosed transfers of dividends from profitable subsidiaries.

In different circumstances, management allowed subsidiaries to retain all their profits and even made generous provisions for actual or potential losses of subsidiaries to depress a highly favourable profit figure that might otherwise have become the basis for unwelcome wage demands or dividend claims. Admittedly, these are extreme examples, but they indicate the scope for potential abuse where accounting reports are confined to the legal entity.

Where such abuses occurred, the parent company's accounts were of little use for assessment purposes or as a basis for resource allocation decisions. The legislature's response, in 1948, was to require parent companies to supplement their legal entity-based accounts with financial statements based on the affairs of the entire economic entity.

In Figure 7.3, Alpha (parent) and Beta (subsidiary) are separate legal entities which continue to publish legal entity-based accounts. In addition, Alpha is required to publish group accounts dealing with the affairs of the overall economic entity formed by Alpha and Beta.

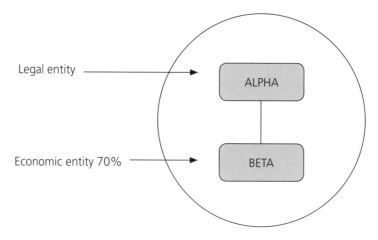

FIGURE 7.3 Separate legal entities

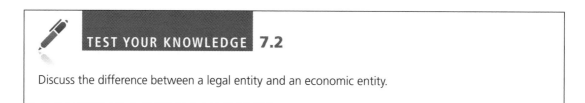

4   Consolidation

The concept underlying the preparation of **consolidated accounts** is extremely simple. The objective is to provide the shareholders and other stakeholders of the parent company with full information concerning the activities of the entire economic unit. This is achieved by combining all the assets and liabilities of the parent company and its subsidiary into a single statement of financial position to disclose the overall financial position of the group.

We will first consider the effect of a share purchase on the statement of financial position of the separate legal entities. Later, we turn our attention to the preparation of the consolidated statement of financial position.

4.1 General rule and exceptions

All parent entities are required to prepare consolidated financial statements (comprising the parent entity's accounts combined with the subsidiary). A parent is exempted from the requirement to prepare consolidated accounts if all the following conditions are met:

- it is a wholly or partially owned subsidiary of another entity whose owners have been informed about the decision not to consolidate and they do not have any objection to the decision;
- the intermediate parent entity that has decided not to consolidate does not have any debt or equity instruments that are publicly traded; and
- its ultimate or intermediate parent prepares consolidated financial statements for public use that comply with IFRS.

4.2 Determining the cost of a business combination

The consideration given by the parent entity to acquire control in the investee firm must be measured at fair value.

In general, the consideration given by the parent entity can be split in to four categories:

1   cash;
2   shares in the parent company;
3   deferred consideration; and
4   contingent consideration.

4.2.1 Components of the purchase consideration

Direct costs of the acquisition, such as legal and other consultancy fees, are *not* treated as part of the purchase consideration. They are expensed!

- *Cash*: This is the most straightforward form of acquisition. The parent company acquires the control of a subsidiary through a cash settlement.
- *Shares in the parent company*: The part of the purchase consideration settled in shares is valued at the market value of the parent entity's shares at the date of acquisition.
- *Deferred consideration*: This refers to the part of the purchase consideration that is payable at a future date. The present value of the amount payable should be recorded as part of the consideration transferred at the date of acquisition. At the end of the financial year, debit the consolidated retained earnings and credit the deferred consideration account with the interest that has accrued on the deferred consideration.
- *Contingent consideration*: This is payable in the future if, say, a target is met. Under revised IFRS 3, contingent consideration must be included at its fair value, even if it is deemed unlikely to be paid.

4.2.2 Parent company's statement of financial position

A parent company may acquire the shares of a subsidiary for cash or in exchange for its own shares or loan stock. You should note that where consideration is entirely in the form of cash, former shareholders of the subsidiary no longer retain any financial involvement with the group. Where consideration is entirely in the form of shares, the former shareholders of the subsidiary combine with the shareholders of the parent company and have a joint interest in the activities of the group.

In the parent company's statement of financial position, the investment in the subsidiary is shown at the 'fair value' of the purchase consideration. Where the purchase consideration is entirely in the form of cash, the investment is valued at the amount of cash paid. Where part of the consideration is shares or loan stock issued by the parent company, these securities are included at market price to arrive at the value of the investment. Worked example 7.2 demonstrates the parent company's statement of financial position on acquiring a subsidiary.

WORKED EXAMPLE 7.2

The summarised statements of financial position of Alpha Ltd and Beta Ltd as at 31 December 20X6 are as follows.

	Alpha Ltd £	Beta Ltd £
Assets		
Non-current assets at carrying value	36,000	27,000
Current assets		
Inventories	20,000	7,000
Trade receivables	18,000	8,000
Bank	37,000	1,000
Total assets	111,000	43,000
Equity and liabilities		
Share capital (£1 ordinary shares)	60,000	25,000
Retained profits	36,000	10,000
Equity	96,000	35,000
Liabilities	15,000	8,000
Total equity and liabilities	111,000	43,000

Alpha Ltd purchased the entire share capital of Beta Ltd for £35,000 on 31 December 20X6.

Required

Prepare revised statement of financial position for Alpha Ltd on the following alternative assumptions:

a The purchase consideration is paid entirely in cash.

b The purchase consideration consists of two elements: cash of £20,000; 10,000 shares in Alpha Ltd valued at £1.50 each.

Answer

	a) £	b) £
Assets		
Non-current assets at carrying value	36,000	36,000
Investment in Beta Ltd	35,000	35,000
Current assets		
Inventories	20,000	20,000
Trade receivables	18,000	18,000
Bank	2,000	17,000
Total assets	111,000	126,000

WORKED EXAMPLE **7.2** *continued*

Equity and liabilities

Share capital (£1 ordinary shares)	60,000	70,000
Share premium account		5,000
Retained profits	36,000	36,000
Equity	96,000	111,000
Liabilities	15,000	15,000
Total equity and liabilities	111,000	126,000

The investment in Beta Ltd is shown in each case at the fair value of the purchase consideration, namely £35,000. Under a), the only change is a redistribution of Alpha Ltd's assets; £35,000 is transferred from 'Bank' to 'Investment in Beta Ltd'. Under b), 'Bank' is reduced by £20,000; the remainder of the consideration is shares valued at £15,000. This gives rise to an increase in 'Share capital' of £10,000 and a balance on 'Share premium account' of £5,000. The statement of financial position of Beta remains unchanged in either case; the transaction is with shareholders of Beta Ltd and no resources transfer into or out of the subsidiary company as a result of the share purchase.

TEST YOUR KNOWLEDGE **7.3**

a Prepare a diagram showing the relationship between a parent company and a subsidiary company.

b Outline the conditions that must be met for one company to be considered, for financial reporting purposes, the subsidiary of another company.

---

5 Other consolidation adjustments

The preparation of consolidated accounts requires certain further adjustments to be made. On consolidation, there is a need to ensure that inter-company balances agree before they are eliminated. Differences in balances may be due to:

- inventory in transit;
- cash in transit; and
- management fees not recorded by subsidiary entity.

5.1 Inter-company loans and transfers of goods

Quite often, transfers of cash and goods are made between the members of a group of companies. Indeed, an important reason for takeovers and mergers is that they provide scope for achieving a more effective utilisation of available resources. Where, for instance, a public company with significant and readily available sources of finance acquires a controlling interest in a small family concern, which has good potential for expansion but finds it difficult to raise funds, a transfer of cash (via inter-company loan accounts) may follow almost immediately. The loan is, of course, reported respectively as an asset and liability in the separate accounts published for the parent company and subsidiary. Group accounts, however, regard these separate legal entities as a single undertaking and inter-company balances must be cancelled out on consolidation.

5.2 Inter-company unrealised earnings

The accounting convention that a transfer at arm's length must occur before profit is recognised must be applied on a group basis when preparing consolidated accounts. Intra-group transfers of inventories are quite common, particularly where the share purchase has resulted in an element of vertical integration designed to safeguard either sources of raw materials or consumer outlets. These transfers of inventories are often made at a figure that approximates market price, both to enable the performance of individual companies to be fairly assessed and to avoid unnecessary complications where minority shareholdings exist. Provided that the recipient company has resold the item transferred, either in its original form or incorporated in a different product, it is perfectly legitimate to recognise both elements of profit in the consolidated accounts (i.e. the profit arising on the intra-group transfer and the profit arising on the sale of the product to an external party). Where, however, the item transferred remains unsold by the transferee company at the end of the accounting period, consolidation adjustments must be made to reduce the value of the inventories to a figure which represents its original cost to the group and in order to eliminate the unrealised profit.

WORKED EXAMPLE 7.3

Small Ltd is a wholly owned subsidiary of Large Ltd. During 20X6, Small Ltd transferred inventories to Large Ltd, for £36,000. The transfer price was arrived at by adding 50% to the cost to Small Ltd of the inventories. At the year-end, 31 December 20X6, Large Ltd had resold three-quarters of the inventories for £31,000.

Required

Calculate the amount of unrealised profit and explain how it must be treated in the consolidated accounts.

Answer

The inventories which remain unsold by Large Ltd at the statement of financial position date have not left the economic entity and must be restated at cost to that entity.

Unsold inventories – £36,000 × 1/4 =	£9,000
Cost of unsold inventories = £9,000 × (100% / 150%) =	£6,000
Unrealised profit	£3,000

The unrealised profit must be deducted from both profit and the value of inventories

Journal entry to record the adjustment:	Debit	Credit
Statement of profit or loss and other comprehensive income	£3,000	
Inventories		£3,000

Note: Even if Large Ltd did not hold all the shares in Small Ltd, the entire unrealised profit should be removed as part of the consolidation exercise. The justification for this treatment is that the minority shareholders are outside the group and, so far as they are concerned, the profit has been realised and they should not therefore be affected by an adjustment designed to ensure that inventories are reported at cost.

5.3 Dividends out of pre-acquisition earnings

A controlling interest may be acquired after a new subsidiary has proposed a dividend payment but before it has been paid. The source of the dividend is therefore profits earned by the subsidiary before the combination took place. The dividend therefore represents a partial return of the capital cost and must be accounted for as a reduction in the value of the investment. The journal entry required to account for a dividend paid out of pre-acquisition profit is:

Journal entry to record the adjustment:	Debit	Credit
Cash	£xxxx	
Investment in subsidiary		£xxxx

Worked Example 7.4 illustrates the calculations needed to give effect to the three secondary adjustments discussed above as well as the three principal calculations already considered.

WORKED EXAMPLE 7.4

The summarised statement of financial position of Quick plc and Silver Ltd at 31 December 20X6 contained the following information.

	Quick £m	Silver £m
Non-current assets		
Property, plant and machinery at carrying value	172	27
30 million shares in Silver Ltd (Note 1)	43	
Loan to Silver	7	
	222	27
Current assets		
Inventories (Note 2)	20	17
Receivables	39	18
Cash and cash equivalents	30	10
	89	45
Total assets	311	72
Equity and liabilities		
Share capital (£1 ordinary shares)	200	40
Retained earnings	75	20
	275	60
Non-current liabilities		
Loan from Quick plc (Note 3)	0	5
	0	5
Current liabilities		
Trade and other payables	36	7
	36	7
Total equity and liabilities	311	72

Notes

1 The shares in Silver Ltd were purchased on 31 December 20X5, when the statement of financial position of that company included retained earnings amounting to £12 million. Silver Ltd paid a final dividend for 20X5 of £4 million on 31 March 20X6. Quick plc's share of the dividend is included in its retained earnings of £75 million in the above summarised statement of financial position.
2 At 31 December 20X6, the inventories of Silver Ltd include goods transferred from Quick plc, at cost plus a 50% mark-up, amounting to £3 million.
3 On 29 December 20X6, Silver despatched a cheque for £2 million to Quick plc, in part repayment of the loan, which was received by the latter company on 3 January 20X7.

Required

Set out the consolidated statement of financial position of Quick plc and its subsidiary company at 31 December 20X6.

Note: There were no differences between the carrying value and fair value of Silver's assets and liabilities at 31 December 20X5.

 **WORKED EXAMPLE** **7.4** *continued*

Answer

The following journal entries give the appropriate treatment, for consolidation purposes, of the items covered in section 5 above:

	Debit £m	Credit £m
Dividends out of pre-acquisition earnings		
Retained earnings	3	
Investment in Silver		3

	Debit £m	Credit £m
Inter-company unrealised profit (see calculation below)		
Reserves	1	
Inventories		1

	%
Cost	100
Mark-up	50
Selling price	150
Mark-up	50%
Selling price	150% × £3m = £1m

	Debit £m	Credit £m
Inter-company loan		
Cash-in-transit	2	
Loan to Silver		2

	Total equity £m	At acquisition £m	Since acquisition £m	Non-controlling interest (NCI) £m
Share capital (see calculations below)	40	30		10
Retained earnings:				
At acquisition	12	9		3
Since acquisition	8		6	2
	60	39	6	15
Price paid (£43m – £3m [pre-acquisition])		40		
Goodwill		1		
Retained earnings of parent company (£75m - £3m [pre-acquisition]) – £1m unrealised profit on inventories			71	
Gross retained earnings			77	

Percentage of shares purchased – calculation:

Total share capital in Silver Ltd: £40 million
Shares purchased by Quick plc: £30 million
% of shares purchased by Quick plc:
30 million /40 million × 100% = 75%
(Hence NCI = 25%)

WORKED EXAMPLE 7.4 *continued*

Statement of financial position as at 31 December 20X6:

Non-current assets	£m
Property, plant and equipment (172+27)	199
Goodwill (see working above)	1
(On consolidation inter-company loan is eliminated and does not appear on SOFP)	
	200
Current assets	
Inventories (£37m – £1m [unrealised profit on inventories])	36
Trade receivables (39+18)	57
Cash and cash equivalents (£40m + £2m [cash-in-transit])	42
Total assets	335
Equity and liabilities	
Parent company shareholders' equity	
Share capital	200
Retained earnings (see above)	77
	277
NCI (see above)	15
Total equity	292
Current liabilities	
Trade and other payables (36+7)	43
Total equity and liabilities	335

TEST YOUR KNOWLEDGE 7.4

What adjustments need to be made to take account of inter-company unrealised earnings?

5.4 Interpreting consolidated statement of financial position

We have already drawn attention to the fact that the basic objective of consolidated accounts is to provide the shareholders of the parent company with detailed information concerning the activities of the entire economic unit in which they have invested.

We have examined the various procedures followed when preparing a consolidated statement of financial position and it is now possible to consider more fully what this statement means.

The parent company's legal entity-based accounts deal with the results of a single organisation, whereas group accounts set out the combined results of at least two (and perhaps a much larger number of) legally separate businesses. Therefore, it is not surprising that there are often significant differences between the two sets of accounts. Some important differences may well be clearly visible from a simple comparison of the totals appearing in the statement of financial position. For instance, the parent company's statement of financial position may contain a large overdraft, whereas the consolidated statement of financial position shows a healthy cash surplus indicating that the subsidiaries are in possession of substantial amounts of cash.

A more searching comparison can be made of the information contained in economic entity-based and legal entity-based accounts by using techniques such as ratio analysis and cash flow analysis.

For illustrative purposes, a comparison is made below of the information contained in Clubs Ltd's own statement of financial position (see practice question 7.3) and the statement of financial position of the group given in the solution to that question. The main points of interest are as follows:

1 **Revenue reserves**

    Clubs Ltd   £43,000
    Group   £38,850

This shows that the two subsidiaries are not improving the overall profitability of the group; the post-acquisition profits of Diamonds Ltd are more than cancelled out by the post-acquisition losses of Hearts Ltd.

2 **Fixed assets**

    Clubs Ltd   £59,000
    Group   £488,200

This shows that most of the group's non-current assets are owned by the subsidiary companies. This information would be of particular interest to prospective creditors of the parent company, who might be keen to ensure that their advance is adequately secured. One option open to them would be to require subsidiaries to guarantee repayment of the loan.

3 **Solvency**
The working capital ratio relates to the ability of a company to meets its day-to-day cash requirements. The ratio gives an indication of the liquidity of a company to meet its short-term cash requirements and it will be discussed in Chapter 8. Therefore it may be useful to return to this section once you have read that chapter.

$$\text{Working capital ratio} \quad = \frac{\text{Current assets}}{\text{Current liabilities}}$$

For Clubs Ltd:

$$\text{Working capital ratio} \quad = \frac{£79,000}{£65,000} = 1.2 : 1$$

For the Group:

$$\text{Working capital ratio} \quad = \frac{(79,000 + 62,500 + 29,500)}{(65,000 + 37,400 + 75,600)} = 0.96 : 1$$

The working capital position of Clubs Ltd is significantly better than that of the group as a whole. This would suggest that there are underlying financial difficulties which are not evident from examining the content of Clubs Ltd's own statement of financial position. An examination of the subsidiary companies' statement of financial position shows that the problem is at Hearts Ltd, where current liabilities significantly exceed current assets, which shareholders of the group would not see.

4 **Gearing**
Gearing is a comparison between the amounts of borrowing a company has to its shareholders' funds. The gearing ratio indicates the proportion of capital available within the company in relation to that owed to sources outside the company and it will be discussed in Chapter 9. Therefore it may be useful to return to this section once you have read that chapter.

    Debt/equity ratio   Clubs Ltd   Zero (no loans)
                            Group   105%

Inter-company shareholdings cancel out on consolidation, whereas all the debentures held outside the group must be aggregated. Consequently, the consolidated statement reveals a much higher level of gearing than is evident from an examination of the individual statement of financial position of Clubs Ltd and the other companies within the group. The group pays annual interest to debenture holders totalling £37,500 (£250,000 × 15%). Annual profit figures are not given, but the interest charge is almost equal to the total retained profits. This would suggest that the group will find it difficult to meet its interest payments unless trading results improve.

The group accounts point to the existence of significant financial difficulties that are not evident from Clubs Ltd's own statement of financial position.

6 Consolidated statement of financial position

The reason for producing consolidated accounts is that the group of companies is in substance, though not in law, a single undertaking. It therefore follows that the essence of consolidation procedures is the cancellation of inter-company balances and the aggregation of any remaining balances. Following the acquisition, Red Ltd's revised statement of financial position contains an asset entitled 'Investment in Blue Ltd, £35,000', whereas Blue Ltd's statement of financial position shows a similar amount 'owing' to its shareholders (i.e. the total of share capital and reserves and equity (assets minus liabilities) of Red Ltd). When preparing a consolidated statement of financial position, these inter-company balances cancel out (signified by ¢) and the remaining assets and liabilities are combined to produce total figures for the group.

 WORKED EXAMPLE 7.5

Prepare the consolidated statement of financial position of Red Ltd and its subsidiary, Blue Ltd, for the year ended 31 December 20X6, from the summarised statements of financial position shown below.

	Red Ltd £	Blue Ltd £
Assets		
Non-current assets at carrying value	36,000	27,000
Current assets		
Inventories	20,000	7,000
Trade receivables	18,000	8,000
Bank	37,000	1,000
Total assets	111,000	43,000
Equity and liabilities		
Share capital (£1 ordinary shares)	60,000	25,000
Retained profits	36,000	10,000
Equity	96,000	35,000
Liabilities	15,000	8,000
Total equity and liabilities	111,000	43,000

Red Ltd purchased the entire share capital of Blue Ltd for £35,000 on 31 December 20X6. The purchase consideration was entirely in the form of cash.

WORKED EXAMPLE **7.5** *continued*

Answer

Consolidated statement of financial position and subsidiary workings:

	Red Ltd £	Blue Ltd £	Group £
Assets			
Non-current assets at carrying value	36,000	27,000	63,000
Investment in Blue Ltd	35,000		
Current assets			
Inventories	20,000	7,000	27,000
Trade receivables	18,000	8,000	26,000
Bank	2,000	1,000	3,000
Total assets	111,000	43,000	119,000
Equity and liabilities			
Share capital (£1 ordinary shares)	60,000	25,000	60,000
Retained profits	36,000	10,000	36,000
Equity	96,000	35,000	96,000
Liabilities	15,000	8,000	23,000
Total equity and liabilities	111,000	43,000	119,000

This illustrates the essence of consolidation procedures, but it is an oversimplification. It is very unlikely that the price paid on acquisition will exactly equal the figure for shareholders' equity in the subsidiary company's statement of financial position. Furthermore, a period of time usually elapses between the date when the shares are acquired and the consolidation date. Finally, the investing company may well take the opportunity, which this form of business combination permits, to achieve control while purchasing less than the entire share capital. Consequently, the preparation of consolidated accounts under the purchase method (the only method now allowed under IFRS, as the merger method is no longer used) involves the following three principal calculations:

1 goodwill;
2 post-acquisition profits;
3 non-controlling interest.

The calculation of these balances will now be examined.

6.1 Goodwill

Often, the price paid for the shares in a subsidiary significantly exceeds the carrying value of the underlying net assets. Part of this surplus is attributable to the favourable trading connections, or goodwill, built up by the subsidiary company over the years. The residual difference is a consequence of the fact that a disparity exists between the *carrying* value and the fair value of the assets and liabilities of the subsidiary at the takeover date. Standard accounting practice, therefore, requires goodwill to be computed in two stages:

1 Restate the subsidiary company's assets and liabilities at their 'fair value'. Fair value is intended to reflect conditions at the time of acquisition, which refers to the time of the company takeover and not the date of the acquisition of the assets by the subsidiary. They need not be written into the books of the subsidiary company and used for the purpose of its legal entity-based accounts, but they must be used for consolidation purposes. IAS 32,

'Financial Instruments: Disclosure and Presentation' and more recently, IFRS 13, provide guidance for the identification of fair value through the following definition: 'Fair value is the amount for which an asset can be exchanged, or a liability settled, between knowledgeable, willing parties in an arm's length transaction.'

2 Compute goodwill, in accordance with IFRS 3, as the excess of the price paid for the shares in the subsidiary over and above the net fair value of the identifiable assets, liabilities and contingent liabilities acquired. However, IFRS 3 prohibits the amortisation of goodwill. Instead, goodwill must be tested for impairment at least annually in accordance with IAS 36 'Impairment of assets'.

If the parent's interest in the fair value of the acquired identifiable net assets exceeds the cost of the business combination, that excess (sometimes referred to as negative goodwill) must be recognised immediately in the consolidated statement of profit or loss and other comprehensive income as a gain. Negative goodwill is, of course, a very unusual occurrence. It reveals that the business has been sold as a going concern for less than might have been produced by selling assets off individually at their fair value. Before concluding that 'negative goodwill' has in fact arisen, IFRS 3 requires that the parent *reassess* the identification and measurement of the subsidiary's identifiable assets, liabilities and contingent liabilities, and the measurement of the cost of the combination.

TEST YOUR KNOWLEDGE 7.5

Explain the effect on the legal entity-based statement of financial position of a holding company of acquiring the entire share capital of a new subsidiary for £350,000 in cash.

WORKED EXAMPLE 7.6

Tom Ltd purchased the entire share capital of Jones Ltd on 31 December 20X6.

The non-current assets of Jones Ltd are considered to possess a fair value of £54,000, but there are no material differences between the carrying values and fair values of the remaining assets.

The summarised statements of financial position of Tom Ltd and Jones Ltd at 31 December 20X6 are as follows.

	Tom Ltd £	Jones Ltd £
Assets		
Non-current assets at carrying value	60,000	46,000
Investment in Jones Ltd	75,000	
Current assets		
Inventories	32,000	13,000
Trade receivables	27,000	17,000
Bank	1,000	2,000
Total assets	195,000	78,000
Equity and liabilities		
Share capital (£1 ordinary shares)	100,000	50,000
Retained profits	70,000	12,000
Equity	170,000	62,000
Liabilities	25,000	16,000
Total equity and liabilities	195,000	78,000

WORKED EXAMPLE 7.6 *continued*

Required

a Calculate the goodwill arising on consolidation.

b Prepare the consolidated statement of financial position of Tom Ltd and its subsidiary at 31 December 20X6.

Answer

Calculation of goodwill arising on consolidation (net asset approach):

	£	£
Price paid		75,000
Less: value of business acquired:		
Non-current assets at fair value	54,000	
Inventories	13,000	
Trade receivables	17,000	
Bank	2,000	
Liabilities	(16,000)	70,000
Goodwill		5,000

Note

When solving examination questions, it is generally necessary to calculate the 'value of business acquired' using the equity components rather than the net asset approach above. The result is the same, but the former procedure is followed because, in most group accounting questions, a period of time will have elapsed between the dates of takeover and consolidation. Consequently, the figures for assets and liabilities may not be available, but sufficient information will be given to enable examinees to build up the figure for the shareholders' equity interest at that date. The calculation of goodwill applying the shareholders' equity approach is as follows.

a Calculation of goodwill arising on consolidation (shareholders' equity approach):

	£	£
Price paid		75,000
Less: value of business acquired:		
Share capital	50,000	
Fair Value adjustment (W1)	8,000	
Retained profits	12,000	(70,000)
Goodwill		5,000

Workings

W1 £54,000 (fair value of Jones' non-current assets) – £46,000 (book value)

b Consolidated statement of financial position of Tom Ltd at 31 December 20X6:

	£	£
Non-current assets		
Goodwill arising on consolidation	5,000	
Non-current assets (W2)	114,000	119,000
Current assets		

WORKED EXAMPLE 7.6 *continued*

Inventories (32+13)	45,000	
Trade receivables (27+17)	44,000	
Bank (1+2)	3,000	92,000
Total assets		211,000
Equity and liabilities		
Share capital (£1 ordinary shares)	100,000	
Retained profits	70,000	
Equity		170,000
Liabilities (25+16)		41,000
Total equity and liabilities		211,000

W2 balance includes the non-current assets of Jones Ltd at their fair value (60,000+54,000).

The consolidated profit figure consists only of the retained profits of the parent company and includes no part of the retained profits of the subsidiary at the takeover date. Profits earned prior to the date of acquisition (pre-acquisition profits) accrue to the former shareholders of Jones Ltd and are paid for in the purchase price. They are, therefore, unavailable for distribution to the shareholders of Tom Ltd and are instead treated as part of the capitalised value of the business at the takeover date.

This is clearly demonstrated in the calculation of goodwill that uses the shareholders' equity approach. The retained profits at acquisition and revaluation surplus, which are also pre-acquisition, are added to share capital to produce a figure of £70,000 for shareholders' equity. This is offset against the price paid (£75,000) and results in a balance of £5,000 that is described as 'goodwill arising on consolidation' in the consolidated statement of financial position. Profits earned after the date of acquisition accrue to the parent company's shareholders, and their accounting treatment will be examined in the next section.

6.2 Post-acquisition profits

A period of time usually elapses between the acquisition of a controlling interest in a subsidiary company and the date of the consolidated accounts. The subsidiary company may have generated profits during this period. These profits accrue to the shareholders of the parent company and, when transferred, are available for distribution. Their accounting treatment is dealt with in Worked Example 7.7.

WORKED EXAMPLE 7.7

The summarised statement of financial position of Tom Ltd and Jones Ltd at 31 December 20X6, Tom Ltd had purchased the entire share capital of Jones Ltd on 31 December 20X5, at which time the retained profits of Jones Ltd amounted to £9,500. The non-current assets of Jones Ltd were considered to possess a fair value of £8,000 above the carrying value at the date of acquisition. but there are no material differences between the carrying values and fair values of the remaining assets.

WORKED EXAMPLE **7.7** *continued*

	Tom Ltd £	Jones Ltd £
Assets		
Non-current assets at carrying value	60,000	46,000
Investment in Jones Ltd	75,000	
Current assets		
Inventories	32,000	13,000
Trade receivables	27,000	17,000
Bank	1,000	2,000
Total assets	195,000	78,000
Equity and liabilities		
Share capital (£1 ordinary shares)	100,000	50,000
Retained profits	70,000	12,000
Equity	170,000	62,000
Liabilities	25,000	16,000
Total equity and liabilities	195,000	78,000

Required

a Calculate:
  i   goodwill; and
  ii   post-acquisition profits of Jones Ltd.
b Prepare the consolidated statement of financial position of the group at 31 December 20X6.

Note

Goodwill arising on consolidation is to be included in the accounts at 31 December 20X6 at £6,000 based on an impairment at review date. Ignore depreciation of other non-current assets.

Answer

a Calculations
  i   Goodwill:

	£	£
Price paid		75,000
Less: value of business acquired:		
Share capital	50,000	
Fair value adjustment	8,000	
Retained profits	9,500	67,500
Goodwill		7,500

  ii   Post-acquisition profits:

	£
Retained profits at 31 December 20X1	12,000
Less: Retained profits at 31 December 20X0	9,500
	2,500

WORKED EXAMPLE **7.7** *continued*

The retained profit of the group therefore consists of the retained profit of Tom Ltd, £70,000, plus the post-acquisition profit of Jones Ltd, £2,500, *minus* goodwill impaired £1,500 (£7,500 − £6,000) = £71,000.

b Consolidated statement of financial position of Tom Ltd as at 31 December 20X6:

	£	£
Non-current assets		
Goodwill arising on consolidation (7500–1500 impairment)	6,000	
Non-current assets (W2)	114,000	120,000
Current assets		
Inventories (32+13)	45,000	
Trade receivables (27+17)	44,000	
Bank (1+2)	3,000	92,000
Total assets		212,000
Equity and liabilities		
Share capital (£1 ordinary shares)	100,000	
Retained profits (see above)	71,000	171,000
Equity		171,000
Liabilities (25+16)	41,000	41,000
Total equity and liabilities		212,000

W2 balance includes the non-current assets of Jones Ltd at their fair value. (60,000+46,000+8,000 fair value adjustment)

There are three further matters that require emphasis concerning the calculation of reported profits for inclusion in the consolidated statement of financial position:

1 Losses suffered by a subsidiary company since the acquisition date are attributable to the shareholders of the parent company in the same way as profit earned. Any post-acquisition losses must, therefore, be deducted from the parent company's balance of retained profits to compute the reported profit of the group.

2 We have seen that a subsidiary company's non-current assets must be stated at fair value in the consolidated accounts. Where the subsidiary chooses to retain non-current assets at historical cost for the purpose of its own accounts, a consolidation adjustment must be made equal to the difference between the historical cost-based charge for depreciation, already made, and an appropriate charge based on the re-valued amount.

3 To the extent that post-acquisition profits earned by a subsidiary are transferred to the parent company by way of dividends, the amount to be aggregated when consolidation takes place is correspondingly reduced. For instance, in Worked Example 7.5, assume Jones Ltd had paid an interim dividend of £800 during July 20X6. Tom Ltd's retained profits increase to £70,800, the retained profit of Jones Ltd falls to £11,200 and the post-acquisition retained profits of Jones Ltd become £1,700 (£11,200 − £9,500).

The consolidated balance of reported profit remains unchanged at £71,000 (£70,800 + £1,700 − £1,500 [goodwill impaired]).

TEST YOUR KNOWLEDGE 7.6

a   Explain the calculation of goodwill when shares are acquired in a subsidiary company.
b   Why is it that only the post-acquisition profits of a subsidiary are consolidated under the purchase method?

6.3 Non-controlling interest

In many cases, the parent company may choose a controlling interest of less than 100% either in the interests of economy, or because of the obstinacy of certain shareholders. In these circumstances, the investment confers an interest in the subsidiary company's net assets based on the proportion which the number of equity shares acquired bears to the total number of equity shares then in issue. This must be taken into account when preparing the consolidated statement of financial position. The appropriate procedure is to include the full amount of the subsidiary's assets and liabilities in the consolidated statement of financial position, with the proportion financed by outside investors represented by a credit balance described as a 'non-controlling interest' (also known as a **'non-controlling interest' (NCI)**). This is shown as a separate item, normally immediately following shareholders' equity. The NCI consists of an appropriate proportion of the share capital plus reserves and any other credit balances that accrue to the equity shareholders at the consolidation date.

WORKED EXAMPLE 7.8

The summarised statements of financial position of Zen Ltd and Duff Ltd at 31 December 20X6 are as follows:

	Zen Ltd	Duff Ltd
	£	£
Non-current assets at carrying value	94,000	58,000
Investment in Duff Ltd	90,000	–
	184,000	58,000
Current assets		
Inventories	103,000	52,000
Trade receivables	79,000	25,000
Cash and cash equivalents (West Bank)	35,000	–
	217,000	77,000
Total assets	401,000	135,000
Equity and liabilities		
Share capital (£1 ordinary shares)	200,000	80,000
Retained profits at 1 January 20X1	77,000	7,000
Add: Profit for 20X1	18,000	6,000
Equity	295,000	93,000
Current liabilities		
Trade payables	106,000	25,000
Cash and cash equivalents (East Bank)	–	17,000
Liabilities	106,000	42,000
Total equity and liabilities	401,000	135,000

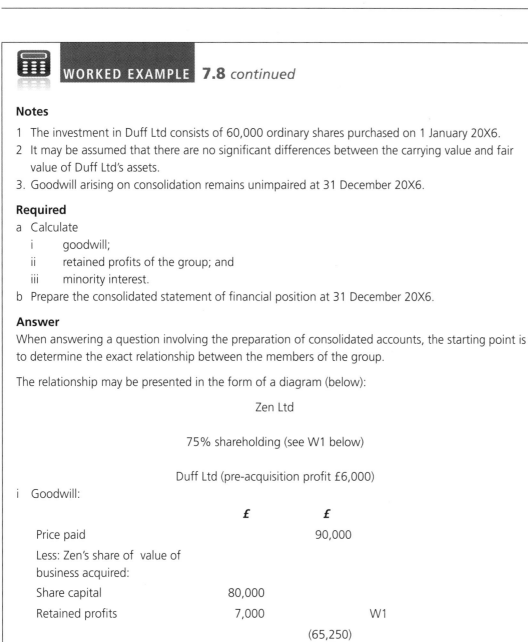

WORKED EXAMPLE **7.8** *continued*

Notes

1 The investment in Duff Ltd consists of 60,000 ordinary shares purchased on 1 January 20X6.
2 It may be assumed that there are no significant differences between the carrying value and fair value of Duff Ltd's assets.
3. Goodwill arising on consolidation remains unimpaired at 31 December 20X6.

Required

a Calculate
   i   goodwill;
   ii   retained profits of the group; and
   iii   minority interest.

b Prepare the consolidated statement of financial position at 31 December 20X6.

Answer

When answering a question involving the preparation of consolidated accounts, the starting point is to determine the exact relationship between the members of the group.

The relationship may be presented in the form of a diagram (below):

Zen Ltd

75% shareholding (see W1 below)

Duff Ltd (pre-acquisition profit £6,000)

i Goodwill:

	£	£
Price paid		90,000
Less: Zen's share of value of business acquired:		
Share capital	80,000	
Retained profits	7,000	W1
	(65,250)	
Goodwill		24,750

W1. Proportion of shares acquired 60,000/80,000 × 100% = 75% x 87,000= 65,250

ii Retained profits: Zen Ltd:

	£
Retained profits Zen Ltd	95,000
Duff Ltd, 6,000 (post-acquisition profit) × 75%	4,500
Group retained profits	99,500

iii NCI:

	£
Share capital	80,000
Retained profits	13,000
Total equity of Duff Ltd at the consolidation date	93,000

WORKED EXAMPLE **7.8** *continued*

Proportion attributable to NCI:

20,000/80,000 × 100% = 25%* × 93,000

                                    = 23,250

*Since Zen purchased 75% of the shares in Duff, the NCI will hold the other 25% of the shares.

Notes

The figures for goodwill, post-acquisition profit and NCI may be calculated in a convenient manner by constructing a table (see below), where:

1 the subsidiary's balance of total equity (including any revaluation reserve and consequential depreciation adjustment) is distributed between the parent company, distinguishing between the positions 'at' and 'since' acquisition, and the NCI;
2 goodwill is calculated by comparing the value of the subsidiary 'at acquisition' with the price paid;
3 the parent company's retained profits are added to the subsidiary's profits arising 'since acquisition' to arrive at group retained profits;
4 goodwill may be subject of impairment, though not so in this case; and
5 the balances for goodwill, if any, reported profit and NCI are transferred to the consolidated statement of financial position.

Duff Ltd

	Total equity £	At acquisition £	Since acquisition £	NCI £
Share capital (see calculations below)	80,000	60,000		20,000
Retained earnings:				
At acquisition	7,000	5,250		1,750
Since acquisition	6,000		4,500	1,500
	93,000	65,250	4,500	23,250
Price paid		90,000		
Goodwill on acquisition		24,750		
Retained earnings Zen Ltd			95,000	
Gross retained earnings		24,750	99,500	

An advantage of this presentation is that it is easy to check whether total equity has been fully allocated for the purpose of calculating goodwill, retained profits and NCI. Also, provided the additions and cross-casts are checked, the possibility of arithmetical error is reduced.

	£	£
Non-current assets		
Goodwill at carrying value	24,750	
Non-current assets at carrying value	152,000	176,750
Current assets		
Inventories	155,000	
Trade receivables	104,000	
Cash and cash equivalents (E1)	35,000	294,000
Total assets		470,750
Equity and liabilities		

WORKED EXAMPLE **7.8** *continued*

Share capital (£1 ordinary shares)	200,000	
Retained earnings	99,500	299,500
NCI		23,250
Total equity		
Current liabilities		
Trade and other payables		131,000
Cash and cash equivalents (E1)		17,000
Total equity and liabilities		470,750

E1. The bank overdraft and bank balance are at different banks. Best accounting practice, therefore, requires these items to be shown separately and not offset against one another. If they were offset, current assets and current liabilities would both be understated. In large companies holding many bank accounts, a practical step might be to amalgamate and show all bank balances which are overdrawn and show as **one** overdrawn figure and amalgamate all bank balances that are not overdrawn, to overcome the difficulty of reporting each individual bank balance(s).

7 Consolidated statement of profit or loss and other comprehensive income

We have seen above that, for the purpose of preparing the consolidated statement of financial position, the investment in a subsidiary is replaced by the subsidiary's underlying net assets (and the non-controlling interest, if any). The same logic applies for the purpose of preparing the consolidated statement of profit or loss and other comprehensive income where the dividend income from the subsidiary, if any, is replaced by the underlying income and expenditure of the subsidiary (less the non-controlling interest, if any). This method of consolidation is often described as line-by-line consolidation, or sometimes full consolidation. This name is derived from the fact that, on each line of the statement of financial position and the consolidated statement of profit or loss and other comprehensive income, the figures of the subsidiary are aggregated with those of the parent. We have seen above that inter-company transactions must be eliminated on consolidation. Most of the possibilities relevant to financial reporting and analysis examination have already been considered. We only need to draw attention here to the need to eliminate inter-company sales when preparing the consolidated statement of profit or loss and other comprehensive income.

WORKED EXAMPLE **7.9**

The individual statements of profit or loss and other comprehensive income of Fast plc and Loose plc contain the following information for the year ended 31 December 20X6.

	Fast plc £,000	Loose plc £,000
Revenue	6,000	5,000
Cost of sales	(4,100)	(3,200)
Gross profit	1,900	1,800
Dividends received	75	

WORKED EXAMPLE 7.9 *continued*

Distribution expenses	(250)	(500)
Administration expenses	(900)	(700)
Profit before taxation	825	600
Taxation	(200)	(160)
Profit for the year	625	440
Note		
Dividends paid	0	(100)
Retained earnings 20X1	625	340

The retained earnings of Fast and Loose at 1 January 20X6 amounted to £500,000 and £1.1 million, respectively.

Fast acquired 150,000 shares (out of a total of 200,000 shares) of £1 each in Loose on 1 January 20X6. During the year, goods that cost Fast £50,000 were sold to Loose for £68,000; however, none of these were in inventory at the end of the year. An interim dividend of £100,000 for 20X6 was paid by Loose on 31 July 20X6.

Required

Provide:

a the consolidated statement of profit or loss and other comprehensive income of Fast plc and its subsidiary Loose plc for the year ended 31 December 20X6; and

b an explanation of how the retained earnings of Loose plc at 1 January 20X6 would be treated in the consolidated accounts.

Answer

a Consolidated statement of profit or loss and other comprehensive income for the year ended 31 December 20X6:

	Fast plc £,000	Loose plc £,000	Adj £,000	Group £,000
Revenue	6,000	5,000	(68)	10,932
Cost of sales	(4,100)	(3,200)	68	(7,232)
Gross profit	1,900	1,800	(18)	3,700
Dividends received	75	0	(75)	0
Distribution expenses	(250)	(500)		(750)
Administration expenses	(900)	(700)		(1,600)
Profit before taxation		600		1,350
Taxation	(200)	(160)		(360)
Profit for the year		440		990
Attributable				
Equity holders of the parent				880
NCI (440 × 25%)				110
				990

b The retained earnings of Loose plc at 1 January 20X6 have accrued during the period prior to acquisition and are treated as part of the shareholders' equity in the subsidiary for the purpose of computing goodwill arising on consolidation.

7.1 Summary of consolidation procedures

Consolidated statement of profit or loss and other comprehensive income.
Adjustment to profits to consider:

■ Eliminate intra-group sales on consolidation.
■ Eliminate unrealised profit on intra-group sales of unsold goods still in closing inventory.
■ Aggregate the adjusted sales and cost of sales figures.
■ Aggregate expenses.
■ Deduct impairment loss.
■ Adjustment to intra-group dividends and interest:
  – eliminate dividends paid to parent by subsidiary; and
  – eliminate intra-group interest paid.
■ Aggregate the taxation figures (parent and subsidiary).
■ Allocate net profit to parent's shareholders and NCI.

 **TEST YOUR KNOWLEDGE 7.7**

Discuss the accounting treatment of dividends and interest on consolidation.

8   Investment in associates

During the 1960s, companies increasingly began to conduct part of their activities through other companies in which they had acquired a less than 50% equity interest and which, consequently, escaped the group accounting provisions introduced in the Companies Act 1948 (now incorporated in the Companies Act 2006). Significant influence was exercised, however, either through the existence of some form of partnership agreement, or because of a wide dispersal of shares. Consequently, the directors of the investing company were able to influence both the commercial and financial policies of the company in which shares were held.

The growing demand for fuller disclosure was therefore fully justified:

a to remove obvious opportunities for the managers of investing companies to manipulate their company's reported results, for instance, by building up undisclosed profits in the accounts of the investee company which could, when required, be transferred to the investing company in the form of a dividend; and
b to provide more meaningful performance data concerning the activities of the entire economic unit over which some influence was exercised. In this context, the growing popularity of the price/earnings ratio emphasised the increasing significance attached to reported earnings as a performance indicator. It was therefore important to take steps to ensure that the investing company's published earnings fairly represented their actual performance.

The matter was referred to the Accounting Standards Committee (as it then was), which concluded that where management assumes a measure of direct responsibility for the performance of its investment by actively participating in the commercial and policy-making decisions of an associated company, it must present a full account to its members.

Accordingly, it was decided that group accounts, prepared in accordance with the Companies Act, should be extended to incorporate additional information concerning the activities of these associated companies.

This decision obliged the regulators to draft requirements covering:

■ the identification of an associated company; and
■ the additional information to be published.

8.1 Definition of an associate

IAS 28 defines an associate as 'an entity over which the investor has significant influence and that is neither a subsidiary nor an interest in a joint venture'. Significant influence is defined as 'the power to participate in the financial and operating policy decisions of the investee but is not control or joint control over those policies'. Holding 20% or more of the voting power leads to the presumption of significant influence. (Note, however, that the carrying amount of the investment in the associate is tested for impairment.)

8.2 Indicators of significant influence

On the basis of IAS 28, and for the purposes of financial reporting, the following items will be indicators of significant influence by the investor company which may give rise to reporting for associates:

- representation on the board;
- participation in decisions about profit distribution and retention;
- material transactions between the investor and investee; and
- exchange of managerial staff.

8.3 Accounting for associates

IFRS 12 'Disclosure of Interests in Other Entities' gives guidance on reporting in relation to associate entities. The standard suggests that interests in unconsolidated structured entities shall be disclosed taking into account the following. IFRS 12:24 states that an entity shall disclose information that enables users of its financial statements to:

- understand the nature and extent of its interests in unconsolidated structured entities; and
- evaluate the nature of, and changes in, the risks associated with its interests in unconsolidated structured entities.

Associates are accounted for using the equity method-single line consolidation. The amount reported in the statement of financial position is arrived at as follows:

- Initial investment in associate	x
+/- share of associates post	x
- Impairment of goodwill	x
Acquisition profits	
+/- Share of post-acquisition	x
Reserves, e.g. revaluation reserves	x
Carrying amount of investment in associate	x

The accounting treatment for associates is not the same as for subsidiaries. Consideration must be given to the following issues:

- Transactions between investor and associate – the investor's share of any unrealised profit must be adjusted against the share of associates profit for the period.
- How do we account for unrealised profit on goods sold by associate to the parent company?
- How do we account for unrealised profit on goods sold by parent to the associate company?
- Intercompany balances are not eliminated.

8.4 Applying the equity method of accounting

The following are the key issues that require attention where an investment is accounted for in accordance with the equity method.

1   The investment must be recorded initially at cost of acquisition. Any difference (whether positive or negative) between cost and the investor's share of the fair values of the net identifiable assets of the associate is attributed to goodwill and accounted for in accordance with IFRS 3 'Business Combinations'.

2   At subsequent accounting dates, the investing company's share of the post-tax profits less losses of associated companies must be computed. This amount is then brought into the investing company's accounts as an addition:

   a   to profit in the consolidated statement of profit or loss and other comprehensive income (credit entry); and

   b   to the value of the investment in the associated company reported in the statement of financial position (debit entry). The carrying value of the investment must of course be reduced to the extent that the profits of the associate have been transferred to the investor in the form of dividends.

3   Any goodwill shown as part of the carrying amount of the investment in an associate must be checked annually as normal for impairment, in accordance with the provisions of IFRS 3.

4   Unrealised profits and losses resulting from upstream (associate to investor) and downstream (investor to associate) transactions should be eliminated to the extent of the investor's interest in the associate.

5   If the associate uses accounting policies that differ from those of the investor, the associate's financial statements should be adjusted to reflect the investor's accounting policies for the purpose of applying the equity method.

Investments accounted for in accordance with the equity method must be classified as non-current assets in the statement of financial position.

 **WORKED EXAMPLE** **7.10**

On 31 December 20X5, Investment plc purchased 25% of the equity share capital of Associated plc for £1 million. At the acquisition date, Associated plc possessed identifiable assets, net of liabilities, with a fair value of £3.6 million.

In 20X6, Associated plc earns a profit of £300,000, of which £140,000 is paid out as a dividend during 20X6 (ignore taxation).

Required

a   Allocate the price paid for the shares in Associated plc between fair value and goodwill.

b   For 20X6, show the amounts which must be recognised in the accounts of Investment plc in respect of its shares in Associate plc.

Answer

a	£,000
Price paid	1,000
Fair value of net assets acquired £3.6m x 25%	900
Goodwill	100

b Statement of financial position – non-current assets	£,000
Investment in associate	1,000
Share of undistributed profits ([300,000 -140,000]x25%)	40
	1,040
Consolidated statement of profit or loss and other comprehensive income £300,000 x 25%	75

WORKED EXAMPLE 7.11

The results of L plc and its subsidiaries for 20X6 have already been consolidated. The results of K plc, an associated company, must now be incorporated by applying the requirements contained in IAS 28. The following information is provided.

Consolidated statement of profit or loss and other comprehensive income for year ended 31 December 20X6:

	L Group £m	K plc £m
Revenue	51	290
All operating costs	(36)	(170)
Profit before tax	15	120
Taxation	(4)	(20)
Profit for the year	11	100

Statement of financial position at 31 December 20X6:

	L Group £m	K plc £m
Non-current assets		
Property, plant and equipment	54	178
Investment in K plc at cost	80	
	134	178
Current assets	95	364
Total assets	229	542
Equity and liabilities		
Share capital	137	170
Retained earnings	21	192
	158	362
NCI	16	
	174	362
Current liabilities	55	180
Total equity and liabilities	229	542

L plc acquired 25% of the share capital of K plc on 31 December 20X5 at which date the retained earnings of K plc stood at £40 million. At 31 December 20X5, the statement of financial position of K plc contained net assets whose fair value and carrying value were identical at £260 million.

The goodwill attributable to the shareholding of the L Group in K plc was the subject of an impairment review after the above accounts were prepared. The impairment review revealed that a write-off of £6 million was required. The amount of tax payable remains unaffected.

Required

Provide the consolidated statement of profit or loss and other comprehensive income of the L group of companies for 20X6 and the consolidated statement of financial position as at 31 December 20X6 incorporating the results of the associated company K plc.

Answer

Consolidated statement of profit or loss and other comprehensive income for the year ended 31 December 20X6:

> **WORKED EXAMPLE** **7.11** *continued*
>
> | | £m | L Group £m |
> |---|---|---|
> | Revenue | | 51 |
> | All operating costs | | (36) |
> | Profit for the period | | 15 |
> | Share of profit of associate (120 × 25%) – 6 (impairment review) | | 24 |
> | Profit before taxation | | 39 |
> | Taxation – L Group | (4) | |
> | Associate (20m x 25%) | (5) | (9) |
> | Profit for the year | | 30 |
>
> Consolidated statement of financial position at 31 December 20X6:
>
> | | £m | L Group £m |
> |---|---|---|
> | Non-current assets | | |
> | Property, plant and equipment | | 54 |
> | Investment in K plc at cost | 80 | |
> | Add: post acquisition retained profit | | |
> | ([192 – 40] ×25%) – 6 | 32 | 112 |
> | Current assets | | 95 |
> | Total assets | | 261 |
> | | | |
> | Equity and liabilities | | |
> | Share capital | | 137 |
> | Retained earnings (21 + 32) | | 53 |
> | | | 190 |
> | NCI | | 16 |
> | Total equity | | 206 |
> | Current liabilities | | 55 |
> | Total equity and liabilities | | 261 |

Table 7.3 indicates the likely categorisation of an equity investment, based on the level of shareholding, as an investment, an associate or a subsidiary. Remember that the level of shareholding is not the definitive test.

TABLE 7.3 Accounting for equity investments

Accounting for equity investment		
% of shares held	**Classification**	**Accounting method**
< 20%	Investment	Cash basis
> 20% < 50%	Associate	Equity method
> 50%	Subsidiary	Purchase method

9   Interest in joint ventures

A joint venture involves the pooling of resources and expertise by two or more businesses to achieve a particular goal. The risks and rewards of the enterprise are also shared. The reasons behind the formation of a joint venture often include business expansion, development of new products or moving into new markets, particularly overseas. Collaborating with another company for this purpose may be useful because, for example, it provides access to:

- more resources;
- greater capacity;
- increased technical expertise;
- established distribution channels.

Joint ventures are particularly popular where cooperation between businesses in different countries is an advantage (e.g. in the areas of transport, tourism and hotels).

9.1 Relevant IFRS and IAS to joint ventures

IAS 28 'Investments in Associates and Joint Ventures' describes a joint venture as 'A joint arrangement whereby the parties that have joint control of the arrangement have rights to the net assets of the arrangement'. The objective of IAS 28 is to prescribe the accounting treatment for joint ventures. Where a joint venture clearly exists, management shall report on the same conditions under IAS 28.

IFRS 11 'Joint Arrangement' requires parties to a joint arrangement to determine the type of joint arrangement in which they are involved by assessing its rights and obligations, and account for those rights and obligations in accordance with that type of joint arrangement.

IFRS 12 'Disclosure of Interests in Other Entities' prescribes the disclosure of information that enables users of financial statements to evaluate:

- the nature of, and risks associated with, its interests in other entities; and
- the effects of those interests on its financial position, financial performance and cash flows.

9.2 Disclosure requirements

There are no disclosures specified in IAS 28. Instead, IFRS 12 'Disclosure of Interests in Other Entities' outlines the disclosures required for entities with joint control of, or significant influence over, an investee.

9.3 Identifying a joint venture

IAS 28 describes three types of joint ventures:

1 *Joint arrangement* – An arrangement of which two or more parties have joint control.
2 *Joint control* – The contractually agreed sharing of control of an arrangement, which exists only when decisions about the relevant activities require the unanimous consent of the parties sharing control.
3 *Joint venture* – A joint arrangement whereby the parties that have joint control of the arrangement have rights to the net assets of the arrangement.

9.4 Accounting for a joint venture

IAS 28 only allows accounting for joint ventures under the equity method and defines various aspects of accounting treatment as follows.

1 *Basic principle*: Under the equity method, on initial recognition the investment in an associate, investment is above 20% but less than 50%, or a joint venture, a contractually agreed sharing of control, is recognised at cost and the carrying amount is increased or decreased to recognise the investor's share of the profit or loss of the investee after the date of acquisition.
2 *Distributions and other adjustments to carrying amount*: The investor's share of the investee's profit or loss is recognised in the investor's profit or loss. Distributions received from an investee reduce the carrying amount of the investment. Adjustments to the carrying

amount may also be necessary for changes in the investor's proportionate interest in the investee arising from changes in the investee's other comprehensive income (e.g. to account for changes arising from revaluations of property, plant and equipment and foreign currency translations).

3   *Potential voting rights*: An entity's interest in an associate or a joint venture is determined solely on the basis of existing ownership interests, and generally does not reflect the possible exercise or conversion of potential voting rights and other derivative instruments.

4   *Interaction with IFRS 9*: IFRS 9 'Financial Instruments' does not apply to interests in associates and joint ventures that are accounted for using the equity method. Instruments containing potential voting rights in an associate or a joint venture are accounted for in accordance with IFRS 9, unless they currently give access to the returns associated with an ownership interest in an associate or a joint venture.

5   *Classification as non-current asset*: An investment in an associate or a joint venture is generally classified as a non-current asset, unless it is classified as held for sale in accordance with IFRS 5 'Non-current Assets Held for Sale and Discontinued Operations'.

10 8-step method to consolidate

1   Identify the group structure: consider the element of control per IFRS 10 a potential combination of subsidiary, associate or joint venture.

2   Determine the consideration transferred: as previously discussed this maybe a straight cash payment, share exchange, deferred consideration or deferred contingent consideration or a combination of elements.

3   Calculate the fair value of net assets of the subsidiary at acquisition and reporting date: consider further information regarding adjustments to fair values and subsequent depreciation, exclusion of any assets not deemed recognisable under IAS 38 and consider any unrealised profit on inter-company sale of goods.

4   Apportion the post-acquisition profit between parent and NCI.

5   Calculate goodwill as detailed previously.

6   Calculate the NCI element.

7   Calculate the consolidated retained earnings.

8   Prepare the consolidated statement of financial position for the group: applying the general rule for assets and liabilities: parent + subsidiary +/– adjustments and including parents equity only, in the equity section.

WORKED EXAMPLE 7.12

Grumpy plc and Sleepy plc jointly established Dopey Ltd to operate a holiday business. Grumpy and Sleepy have equal shares in Dopey and share profits equally. The results of Grumpy plc and Dopey Ltd are set out below.

Statement of profit or loss and other comprehensive income for the year ended 31 December 20X6:

	Grumpy plc £m	Dopey Ltd £m
Revenue	300	170
All operating costs	(229)	(86)
Profit before tax	71	84
Taxation	(15)	(18)
Profit for the year	56	66

WORKED EXAMPLE **7.12** *continued*

Statement of financial position at 31 December 20X6:

	Grumpy plc £m	Dopey Ltd £m
Non-current assets		
Property, plant and equipment	111	100
Investment in Dopey Ltd at cost	60	
	171	100
Current assets	49	134
Total assets	220	234
Equity and liabilities		
Share capital	50	120
Retained earnings	140	90
	190	210
Current liabilities	30	24
Total equity and liabilities	220	234

Required

Provide the consolidated statement of profit or loss and other comprehensive income and consolidated statement of financial position and notes showing movement on reserves of Grumpy plc for 20X6 incorporating the results of Dopey on the equity method on the basis of IAS 28.

Answer

Consolidated statement of profit or loss and other comprehensive income for the year ended 31 December 20X6:

	Grumpy plc £m
Revenue	300
All operating costs	(229)
Profit before tax	71
Share of profit of joint venture (84 x50%)	42
	113
Taxation	
Grumpy plc	(15)
Joint venture (18 x 50%)	(9)
Profit for the year	89

Consolidated statement of financial position at 31 December 20X6:

	Grumpy plc £m
Non-current assets	
Property, plant and equipment	111
Investment in Dopey Ltd at cost	60

WORKED EXAMPLE **7.12** *continued*

ADD: Post acquisition retained profit (90 × 50%)	45	
	216	
Current assets	49	
Total assets	265	
Equity and liabilities		
Share capital	50	
Retained earnings	185	
	235	
Current liabilities	30	
Total equity and liabilities	265	

Statement of change in equity:

	Grumpy plc
	£m
Balance at 1 January 20X6: 140 − 56 = 84 + 50% of (90 − 66)	96
Earnings for the period	89
Balance at 31 December 20X6	185

TEST YOUR KNOWLEDGE **7.8**

Why do companies enter into joint ventures?

END OF CHAPTER QUESTIONS

7.1 The summarised statements of financial position of Halesworth Ltd and Haverhill Ltd as at 31 October 20X6 were as follows:

	Halesworth	Haverhill
	£,000	*£,000*
Assets		
Investment in Haverhill	6,000	
Other net assets at book value	7,200	3,700
	13,200	3,700
Financed by:		
Ordinary share capital (£1 shares)	10,000	1,000
Retained profit at 1 October 20X5	2,940	1,720
Net profit for 20X5–X6	260	980
	13,200	3,700

? END OF CHAPTER QUESTIONS *continued*

Halesworth purchased the entire share capital of Haverhill on 1 November 20X5 for £6 million. The fair value of the net assets of Haverhill at that date was £1.2 million in excess of book value.

Required

Prepare the consolidated statement of financial position of Halesworth and its subsidiary, as at 31 October 20X6, based on the information provided. You should use the purchase method and comply, as far as the information permits, with standard accounting practice.

7.2 The following summarised statement of financial position is provided for Twickenham Ltd as at 30 September 20X6.

	£,000
Non-current assets at carrying value	2,000
Net current assets	1,600
Total assets	3,600
Share capital (£1 ordinary shares)	2,700
Retained profit at 1 October 20X5	600
Profit for year to 30 September 20X6	300
Total equity and liabilities	3,600

Wembley Ltd purchased 1.8 million shares in Twickenham Ltd on 1 October 20X5 for £2.5 million. There were no differences between the carrying values and fair values of the Twickenham's assets and liabilities at that date, and the company has paid no dividends for some years.

Required

Based on the above information, calculate the balances to be included in the accounts of the Wembley Ltd group of companies for the year to 30 September 20X6 in respect of:
1 goodwill
2 NCI
3 post-acquisition profits.

7.3 The summarised statement of financial position of Clubs Ltd and its subsidiary companies Diamonds Ltd and Hearts Ltd at 31 December 20X6 were as follows:

	Clubs Ltd £	Diamonds Ltd £	Hearts Ltd £
Non-current assets at carrying value	59,000	299,500	129,700
80,000 shares in Diamonds Ltd	126,000	–	–
30,000 shares in Hearts Ltd	44,000	–	–
	229,000	299,500	129,700
Current assets	79,000	62,500	29,500
Total assets	308,000	362,000	159,200
Equity and liabilities			
Share capital (£1 shares)	200,000	80,000	40,000
Retained earnings at 31 December 20X5	36,000	33,200	7,200
Profit/(loss) for 20X6	7,000	11,400	(13,600)
	243,000	124,600	33,600

Non-current liabilities

15% debentures		200,000	50,000
	243,000	324,600	83,600
Current liabilities	65,000	37,400	75,600
Total equity and liabilities	308,000	362,000	159,200

Clubs Ltd acquired the shares in both subsidiaries on 31 December 20X5. Neither subsidiary paid a dividend during the year.

Required

Prepare the consolidated statement of financial position for the Clubs group at 31 December 20X6 presented in vertical format so as to disclose the balance for net current assets.

Notes

1   Ignore taxation.
2   Assume no differences between the carrying values and fair values of the assets and liabilities of Diamonds Ltd and Hearts Ltd.
3   You should assume that any goodwill arising on consolidation suffers impairment equal to one-quarter of its initial value at the end of 20X6.
4   Interest on debentures has been charged in arriving at the profit or loss for the year.

7.4   During the year ended 30 September 20X6, Company A (the parent company) sells inventory to Company B (the subsidiary) at cost plus a mark-up of 25%.

Explain the appropriate accounting treatment, for consolidation purposes, of the profit arising in the books of Company A on transfers of inventory to Company B.

7.5   Smith Ltd acquired 70% of the voting share capital of Jerry Ltd on 1 January 20X7. The extracts below are taken from the Income statements for the year ended 31 December 20X7 of Smith Ltd and Jerry Ltd respectively:

	Smith Ltd	Jerry Ltd
	£	£
Revenue	123,400	16,750
Cost of Sales	(62,830)	(2,960)
Gross Profit	60,570	13,790

The following Information Is also available:

Smith Ltd made £7,000 worth of sales to Jerry Ltd during the year. Smith Ltd originally purchased the goods at a cost of £5,000. Half these goods were included within the closing inventory figure of Jerry Ltd at the year end.

Required

Calculate the consolidated revenue of the Smith Group for the year ended 31 December 20X7.

7.6   Robins plc acquired 60% of the issued share capital and voting rights of Knight Ltd on 1 April 20X6 for £1,700,000. At that date Knight Ltd had issued share capital of £1,300,000, share premium of £410,000 and retained earnings of £180,000.

END OF CHAPTER QUESTIONS *continued*

Extracts of the statements of financial position for the two companies one year later at 31 March 20X7 are as follows:

	Robins plc £000	Knight Ltd £000
ASSETS		
Non-current assets		
Investment in Knight Ltd	1,700	
Property, plant and equipment	3,982	2,139
	5,682	2,139
Current assets		
Total current assets	3,400	1,486
	3,400	1,486
Total assets	9,082	3,625
EQUITY AND LIABILITIES		
Equity		
Share capital	4,400	1,300
Share premium	365	410
Retained earnings	580	220
Total equity	5,345	1,930
Non-current liabilities		
Long term loans	1,380	1,200
	1,380	1,200
Current liabilities		
Total current liabilities	2,357	495
	2,357	495
Total liabilities	3,737	1,695
Total equity and liabilities	9,082	3,625

Additional data

■ At 1 April 2016 the fair value of the non-current assets of Knight Ltd was £500,000 more than the carrying amount. This revaluation has not been recorded in the books of Knight Ltd (ignore any effect on the depreciation for the year).

■ Included in the current assets of Robins plc and in the current liabilities of Knight Ltd is an inter-company balance of £184,000.

■ The directors of Robins plc have concluded that goodwill has been impaired by £34,000 during the year.

■ The non-controlling interest of Knight Ltd had a fair value of £1,100,000 as at the date of acquisition.

Required

Draft the consolidated statement of financial position for Robins plc and its subsidiary undertaking as at 31 March 2017.

7.7 Alpha paid £265,000 to acquire 70% of the equity shares of Beta on 1 January 20X6. Beta's retained earnings at the date of acquisition were £50,000. The market price of Alpha's shares on 1 January 20X6 was £4 each. The market price of Beta's shares was £2.50 each. The statements of financial position for the two companies at the close of business on 31 December 20X6 were as follows.

	Alpha £	Beta £
Non-current assets		
Intangible non-current assets	–	30,000
Tangible non-current assets	500,000	70,000
Investments	290,000	60,000
	790,000	160,000
Current assets		
Inventory	100,000	50,000
Trade receivables	150,000	100,000
Cash and cash equivalents	30,000	20,000
	280,000	170,000
Total assets	1,070,000	330,000
Equity and liabilities		
Ordinary shares of £1 each	700,000	100,000
Share premium	140,000	50,000
Retained earnings	100,000	100,000
	940,000	250,000
Current liabilities		
Trade payable	90,000	60,000
Accruals	40,000	20,000
	130,000	80,000
Total equity and liabilities	1,070,000	330,000

Additional information

1 At the date of acquisition, 1 January 20X6, Beta owned a piece of land that had a fair value of £20,000 in excess of its book value. The fair value adjustments have not been reflected in the individual financial statements of Beta.

2 One-half of goodwill arising on acquisition of Beta is impaired.

3 During the year to 31 December 20X6, Alpha sold goods to Beta for £20,000 (at a mark-up on cost of 20%). Beta had one-half of these goods in its inventory at 31 December 20X6.

4 Intangible assets of Beta are all of a type whose recognition would not be permitted under IAS 38. This is to be followed in preparing the consolidated financial statements. When Alpha made its investment in Beta on 1 January 20X6, the intangible assets of Beta included £10,000 that would not qualify for recognition under IAS 38.

5 Creditors reported by Beta include £10,000 owed to Alpha, whereas the corresponding amount in Alpha books is £15,000. The difference in inter-company balances is due to cash in transit.

6 It is group policy to value the non-controlling interest at the date of acquisition based upon number of shares held at market price at acquisition date. The non-controlling interest in Beta is to be valued at its (full) fair value. For this purpose, Beta's share price at that date of acquisition can be taken to be indicative of the fair value of the shareholding of the non-controlling interest at the date of acquisition.

Required

Prepare a consolidated statement of financial position for Alpha at 31 December 20X6.

7.8 Explain what is meant by the parent entity concept and how the choice of this concept affects the preparation of consolidated financial statements.

7.9 House plc paid £450,000 to acquire 75% of the equity shares of Martin Ltd on 1 January 2017. Martin's retained earnings at the date of acquisition were £68,000. The draft statements of financial position for the two companies at the close of business on 31 December 2017 were as follows:

Extracts of the statements of financial position for the two companies one year later at 31 December 2017 are as follows:

	House plc £	Martin Ltd £
ASSETS		
Non-current assets		
Intangible non-current assets	–	80,000
Property, plant and equipment	400,000	70,000
Investments	490,000	10,000
	890,000	160,000
Current assets		
Inventory	150,000	50,000
Trade Receivables	110,000	100,000
Bank	40,000	20,000
Total assets	1,190,000	330,000
EQUITY AND LIABILITIES		
Ordinary shares of £1 each	800,000	120,000
Share premium	140,000	40,000
Retained earnings	100,000	120,000
Total equity	1,040,000	280,000
Current Liabilities		
Trade Payables	90,000	20,000
Accruals	60,000	30,000
Total equity and liabilities	1,190,000	330,000

Additional information

1   Martin owned a piece of land that had a fair value of £10,000 below its carrying value on 1 January 2017. The fair value adjustment has not recorded in the individual financial statements of Martin.

2   During the year to 31 December 2017, House sold goods to Martin for £40,000 (at a mark up on cost of 25%). Martin had one half of these goods in its inventory at 31 December 2017.

3   Intangible assets of Martin are all of a type whose recognition would not be permitted under IAS 38. All of Martin's intangible assets were acquired before 1 January 2017. IAS 38 is to be followed in preparing the consolidated financial statements.

4   Trade receivables reported by Martin include £12,000 due from House; whereas the corresponding amount in House books is £10,000. The difference in inter-company balances is due to cash in transit.

5   The non-controlling interest in Martin is to be valued at its fair value. For this purpose, Martin's share price at that date of acquisition can be taken to be indicative of the fair value of the shareholding of the NCI at the date of acquisition. The market price of Martin's shares was £3 each on 1 January 2017.

6   House's non-current assets include an asset that is carried in the books at £20,000 above its recoverable amount.

7   Goodwill arising on the acquisition of Martin was not impaired.

Required

a   Prepare a consolidated statement of financial position for House at 31 December 2017.

b   In the context of IFRS 10, Consolidation, define the term control and explain the three main elements of control.

Analysis and interpretation of accounts

Part Four covers the syllabus section entitled 'Analysis and interpretation of accounts'.

■ **OVERVIEW**

Part Four looks at and discusses, with relevant examples, the analysis and interpretation of financial reports. This allows users to make informed economic decisions and to evaluate emerging trends.

8 Trend analysis and introduction to ratio analysis

■ CONTENTS

■ LEARNING OUTCOMES

This chapter deals with the part of the syllabus section entitled 'Analysis and interpretation of accounts'. After reading and understanding the contents of the chapter, working through all the worked examples and practice questions, you should be able to:

- undertake horizontal analysis of accounts between two periods based on percentage changes;
- take account of the effect of exceptional items on comparability;
- apply trend analysis to the results of a series of accounting periods;
- undertake vertical analysis based on common size statements; and
- understand the nature of accounting ratios and the use that can be made of them.

1   Introduction

Stakeholders, current and potential investors, creditors, customers and employees all have a vested interest in the financial performance and other aspects of a company. Financiers and credit providers need to gauge the creditworthiness of a company prior to any commitment of finances. This need for stakeholder servicing by companies is mostly enshrined in law, as well as in national and international guidelines.

Published financial reports provide stakeholders with financial information. Each stakeholder having a different vested interest in a business entity requires access to financial information that serves their purposes. The information may be accessible in different forms, allowing users of financial information to determine the current state of affairs of a company and to anticipate its future prospects.

Increased importance is placed on the impact of non-financial information, provided in the form of an integrated report that details sustainability measures on an economic, ecological and social level, when assessing the risk of a business. Integrated reporting (IR) is not yet a legal requirement and currently a tool deployed by larger companies in a bid for increased transparency in an environment of uncertainty and market volatility.

Changes to company and related law and the development of, and considerable amendments to, International Financial Reporting Standards (IFRS) has placed a greater burden on companies to deliver additional and more detailed information, thereby facilitating a greater depth and quality of transparency, particularly after the 'credit crunch' that began in 2007–08.

This chapter will primarily evaluate company financial performance on the basis of published financial reports of listed companies. The nature of the modern corporation, being a limited liability entity, gives it a legal personality distinct from its owners. However, the nature of limited liability ensures that the liability of owners is limited to the extent of their ownership stake.

2 Stewardship and the role of managers

Stewardship refers to a situation under which one party is responsible for taking good care of resources entrusted to them. The owners of a business (for example, the shareholders) trust others to manage the business on their behalf. Shareholders entrust the board of directors of a company with the responsibility for managing the affairs of the company by giving it direction, providing control and strategy, and ensuring continuance.

The board of directors consists of non-executive and executive directors. Executive directors are 'hands-on'; they are involved in the day-to-day operations and management of the company. Non-executive directors are not involved in the day-to-day operation of the business. These directors provide a wider perspective.

The board employs managers to implement their strategic vision and to help ensure the investments of owners are maximised. To ensure this happens effectively, owners put mechanisms in place to monitor managerial behaviour. The UK Code on Corporate Governance (2010) provides guidelines for board conduct, behaviour, duties and obligations. The UK Code is principle-based and requires directors to conduct business with integrity, responsibility and accountability. Corporate governance and ethical issues are covered in Chapter 12. The remainder of this chapter discusses and analyses financial reports using various analysis techniques.

TEST YOUR KNOWLEDGE 8.1

What is meant by stewardship?

3 Horizontal and vertical analysis of accounts

3.1 Performing a horizontal analysis

The main point of performing a horizontal analysis on the financial statements is to see how things have changed from one period to the next. A horizontal analysis of the accounts is a comparison of two or more years' financial data. Horizontal analysis is facilitated by showing changes between years in both pound and percentage form (see Worked Example 8.1). Showing changes in pound form helps the analyst to focus on key factors that have affected profitability or financial position.

A horizontal analysis allows the user to compare the financial numbers from one period to the next, using financial statements from at least two distinct periods. Each line item has an entry in a current period column and a prior period column. Those two entries are compared to show both the pound difference and the percentage change between the two periods.

For example, in Worked Example 8.1, although sales increased in 20X1 by £4 million, the comparative increase in the cost of sales of £4.5 million contributed to a decrease in gross profit in 20X1.

The expression of the comparative annual changes in absolute monetary terms does not provide the analyst with a true scale of the periodic change. An increase in sales of £4 million may seem very significant or material, but the significance cannot be determined by relying simply on the monetary value of the change. To ascertain the scale of periodic changes between two or more accounting periods, the annual changes are expressed in percentage terms. The expression in percentage terms provides the analyst and readers of financial statements with information relating to the scale of the change, as the expression of the percentage is based upon the movement in the item from the original position. Analysts and readers are able to see that the £4 million increase in sales during the period represented an increase of 8.3%. The proportionate change of 8.3% is more useful than knowing the sales increased by £4 million.

WORKED EXAMPLE 8.1

The comparative financial statements of Jane plc as at 31 December 20X1 and 20X0 are shown below.

Statement of financial position as 31 December:

	20X1 £,000	20X0 £,000
Non-current assets		
Property, plant and equipment:		
Land	4,000	4,000
Building	12,000	8,500
Total non-current assets	16,000	12,500
Current assets		
Cash	1,200	2,350
Accounts receivable	6,000	4,000
Inventory	8,000	10,000
Prepaid expenses	300	120
Total current assets	15,500	16,470
Total assets	31,500	28,970
Equity and liabilities		
Share capital (£12 shares)	6,000	6,000
Share premium	1,000	1,000
6% preferred shares (£100 nominal value)	2,000	2,000
Retained earnings	8,000	6,970
	17,000	15,970
Long-term liabilities:		
Bonds payable 8%	7,500	8,000
Total long-term liabilities	7,500	8,000
Current liabilities		
Accounts payables	5,800	4,000
Accrued payables	900	400
Other payables	300	600
Total current liabilities	7,000	5,000
Total liabilities	14,500	13,000
Total equity and liabilities	31,500	28,970

Consolidated statement of profit or loss and other comprehensive income for the year ended 31 December:

	20X1 £,000	20X0 £,000
Sales	52,000	48,000
Cost of goods sold	(36,000)	(31,500)
Gross profit	16,000	16,500

| | | WORKED EXAMPLE **8.1** *continued* |

Operating expenses

Selling expenses	(7,000)	(6,500)
Administrative expense	(5,860)	(6,100)
Total operating expenses	12,860	12,600
Operating profit before interest and taxation (PBIT)	3,140	3,900
Interest expense	(640)	(700)
Profit before tax	2,500	3,200
Income taxes (30%)	(750)	(960)
Profit for the period	1,750	2,240

Required

Provide a horizontal analysis for Jane plc for the two years.

Answer

Horizontal analysis of the statement of financial position for the financial years ended 31 December 20X1 and 20X0:

	20X1 £,000	20X0 £,000	Increase/ (decrease) £,000	Change %
Non-current assets				
Property, plant and equipment:				
Land	4,000	4,000	0	0.00%
Building	12,000	8,500	3,500	41.18%
Total non-current assets	16,000	12,500	3,500	28.00%
Current assets				
Cash	1,200	2,350	(1,150)	−48.94%
Accounts receivable	6,000	4,000	2,000	50.00%
Inventory	8,000	10,000	(2,000)	−20.00%
Prepaid expenses	300	120	180	150.00%
Total current assets	15,500	16,470	(970)	−5.89%
Total assets	31,500	28,970	2,530	8.73%
Equity and liabilities				
Share capital (£12 shares)	6,000	6,000	0	0.00%
Share premium	1,000	1,000	0	0.00%
6% preferred shares				
(£100 nominal value)	2,000	2,000	0	0.00%
Retained earnings	8,000	6,970	1,030	14.78%
	17,000	15,970	1,030	6.45%
Long-term liabilities				
Bonds payable 8%	7,500	8,000	(500)	−6.25%
Total long-term liabilities	7,500	8,000	(500)	−6.25%

WORKED EXAMPLE 8.1 *continued*

Current liabilities

Accounts payables	5,800	4,000	1,800	45.00%
Accrued payables	900	400	500	125.00%
Notes payables	300	600	(300)	–50.00%
Total current liabilities	7,000	5,000	2,000	40.00%
Total liabilities	14,500	13,000	1,500	11.54%
Total equity and liabilities	31,500	28,970	2,530	8.73%

Horizontal analysis of the consolidated statement of profit or loss and other comprehensive income for the financial years ended 31 December 20X1 and 20X0:

	20X1	20X0	Increase/ (decrease)	Change
	£,000	£,000	£,000	%
Sales	52,000	48,000	4,000	8.33%
Cost of goods sold	36,000	31,500	4,500	14.29%
Gross profit	16,000	16,500	(500)	–3.03%
Operating expenses				
Selling expenses	7,000	6,500	500	7.69%
Administrative expense	5,860	6,100	(240)	–3.93%
Total operating expenses	12,860	12,600	260	2.06%
Operating profit before interest and taxation	3,140	3,900	(760)	–19.49%
Interest expense	640	700	(60)	–8.57%
Profit before tax	2,500	3,200	(700)	–21.88%
Income taxes (30%)	750	960	(210)	–21.88%
Profit for the period	1,750	2,240	(490)	–21.88%

TEST YOUR KNOWLEDGE 8.2

a   What is horizontal analysis is and how is it carried out?
b   What useful information can the user extract by performing horizontal analysis?

3.2 Performing a vertical analysis

Vertical analysis is often referred to by financial analysts as 'common size' analysis. Vertical analysis provides a business with a greater understanding of how its sales revenue is being consumed within the business. A vertical analysis of the statement of profit or loss and other comprehensive income restates every expenditure item as a proportion of the sales revenue. Knowledge of where the sales revenue is being consumed or applied enables management to undertake further investigation and/or any necessary action if the level of activity is deemed to be adverse for the business.

Similarly, a vertical analysis of the statement of financial position restates each asset as a percentage of the total assets, and each liability is restated as a percentage of total equity and liabilities. This provides the analyst with an understanding of the significance of each asset and liability within the business.

Worked Example 8.2 demonstrates what a vertical analysis looks like for both a statement of profit and loss and a statement of financial position.

WORKED EXAMPLE 8.2

Comparative vertical analysis of the consolidated statement of profit or loss and other comprehensive income for Jane plc for the years ended 31 December:

	20X1 £,000	20X1 %	20X0 £,000	20X0 %
Sales	52,000	100.00	48,000	100.00
Cost of goods sold	36,000	69.23	31,500	65.63
Gross profit	16,000	30.77	16,500	34.38
Operating expenses				
Selling expenses	7,000	13.46	6,500	13.54
Administrative expenses	5,860	11.27	6,100	12.71
Total operating expenses	12,860	24.73	12,600	26.25
Operating profit before interest and taxation	3,140	6.04	3,900	8.13
Interest expenses	640	1.23	700	1.46
Profit before income tax	2,500	4.81	3,200	6.67
Less income taxes (30%)	750	1.44	960	2.00
Post tax profit	1,750	3.37	2,240	4.67

It can readily be seen that, although actual sales increased in 20X1, the gross profit had fallen by 3.61% due to the increased cost of goods sold in 20X1. This needs to be investigated and reasons sought as to why this has happened. It could be that material was more expensive in 20X1 than in 20X0. Even though the rest of the expenses were comparatively higher in 20X0 to sales, net profits were lower in 20X1 due to the increased cost of sales.

Comparative vertical analysis of the statement of financial position for Jane plc for the comparative the years ended 31 December:

	20X1 £,000	20X1 %	20X0 £,000	20X0 %
Non-current assets				
Property and equipment:				
Land	4,000	12.70	4,000	13.81
Building	12,000	38.10	8,500	29.34
Total non-current assets	16,000	50.79	12,500	43.15
Current assets				
Cash	1,200	3.81	2,350	8.11
Accounts receivable	6,000	19.05	4,000	13.81
Inventory	8,000	25.40	10,000	34.52
Prepaid expenses	300	0.95	120	0.41

🖩 **WORKED EXAMPLE** **8.2** *continued*

Total current assets	15,500	49.21	16,470	56.85
Total assets	31,500	100.00	28,970	100.00
Equity and liabilities				
Share capital (£12 shares)	6,000	19.05	6,000	20.71
Share premium	1,000	3.17	1,000	3.45
6% preferred shares				
(£100 nominal value)	2,000	6.35	2,000	6.90
Retained earnings	8,000	25.40	6,970	24.06
	17,000	53.97	15,970	55.13
Long-term liabilities:				
Bonds payable 8%	7,500	23.81	8,000	27.61
Total long-term liabilities	7,500	23.81	8,000	27.61
Current liabilities				
Accounts payables	5,800	18.41	4,000	13.81
Accrued payables	900	2.86	400	1.38
Notes payables	300	0.95	600	2.07
Total current liabilities	7,000	22.22	5,000	17.26
Total liabilities	14,500	46.03	13,000	44.87
Total equity and liabilities	31,500	100.00	28,970	100.00

The vertical analysis of the statement of financial position reveals that during the year, the company has increased its non-current assets as a proportion of its total assets. In addition, the liabilities share of the equity and liabilities has increased. The expression of the changes in proportionate terms are more useful to analysts and other readers of the financial statements.

✒ **TEST YOUR KNOWLEDGE** **8.3**

a Explain vertical analysis. How is it carried out?
b What useful information can the user extract by performing a vertical analysis?

3.2.1 Dealing with exceptional items

Exceptional items are those items that occur during the ordinary course of the business but need to be disclosed due to their size or incidence. A customer may go bankrupt and this may materially increase the bad debt of an entity for the period. The actual size of the debt owing to the entity, not the bankruptcy, is what gives rise to the item being exceptional.

An operational definition of exceptional items is used by ITV plc in their Annual Report and Accounts for the year ended 31 December 2015:

'Exceptional items are material and non-recurring items excluded from management's assessment of profit because by their nature they could distort the Group's underlying quality of earnings. These are excluded to reflect performance in a consistent manner and are in line with how the business is managed and measured on a day-to-day basis.'

These exceptional items should be identified and isolated for consideration before any analysis is undertaken. Readers of financial statements are concerned about the financial performance arising from the ordinary trading activities; hence, any exceptional items should be isolated prior to any analysis. The separation of exceptional items from any analysis allows the analyst to determine any trends or patterns in the company performance arising from its ordinary trading activities. Examples of exceptional items may include abnormally high losses specifically relating to an event during the year or abnormally high revenue figure following an exceptionally large sales order.

4 Trend analysis to a time series

Horizontal analysis of financial statements can also be carried out by computing trend percentages. Trend percentage restates multiple years' financial performance results in terms of a base year. The base year equals 100%, with all other years expressed relative to this to this base.

WORKED EXAMPLE 8.3

Consider a corporation that runs a multinational chain of fast-food outlets and restaurants, with thousands of outlets and restaurants worldwide. The corporation enjoyed tremendous growth in the years 20X0–20Y0, as evidenced by the following data.

£,000	201Y0	20X9	20X8	20X7	20X6	20X5	20X4	20X3	20X2	20X1	20X0
Sales	14,200	13,300	12,400	11,400	10,700	9,800	8,300	7,400	7,100	6,700	6,380
Operating income	1,980	1,950	1,550	1,640	1,570	1,430	1,220	1,080	960	860	796

An observation of the data reveals an annual increase in sales every year, and an increase in operating income every year except 20X8. It is difficult to determine the rate of annual change from the data presented. It is also difficult to determine whether the sales and operating profit have exhibited any direct or indirect relationship over the ten-year period.

It is easier to judge the significance of annual changes in the sales and operating income when they are restated in terms of the first year (the base year). The restatement is as follows.

£,000	201Y0	20X9	20X8	20X7	20X6	20X5	20X4	20X3	20X2	20X1	20X0
Sales	223%	208%	194%	179%	168%	154%	130%	116%	111%	105%	100%
Operating income	249%	245%	195%	206%	197%	180%	153%	136%	121%	108%	100%

This trend analysis, if plotted on a graph, would reveal almost parallel growth in both sales, apart from a dip in operating income in 20X8. A review of the company's statement of profit or loss and other comprehensive income and the statement of financial position would be required to ascertain the contributory factors to the decline in operating income growth in 20X8. One possible explanation may be a temporary increase in costs – for example, due to a food scare affecting the price of beef or supplier raising prices over uncertainty in the financial climate related to the 'credit crunch'. If the expenditure in 20X8 was found to be exceptional, it would be prudent for the purposes of analysis to write-back the expense to profits in determining the trend over the ten-year period.

---

5 Principles of ratio analysis

Ratios, as a tool of financial analysis, provide evidence that enables judgments to be made concerning the financial health of a business. As previously mentioned, different groups of people are interested in different aspects of a business. The significance of ratio analysis differs for different groups. This will be explained below.

5.1 Usefulness of ratios to management

5.1.1 Decision making

The management of a company will generally have quicker and easier access to financial information than other stakeholder groups. However, they may suffer from 'information overload' as the mass of information contained in internal reports and financial statements may be unintelligible and confusing. Ratios help to highlight areas requiring attention and any corrective action needed, facilitating rapid decision-making.

5.1.2 Financial forecasting and planning

Ratios collated over a period of time help management to understand the history of the business. They also provide useful data on the existing strengths and weaknesses of the business. This knowledge is vital, as it allows management to plan and forecast for the future.

5.1.3 Communication

Ratios can help to communicate information to interested parties in a way that makes the significance of figures easier to understand. This enables groups to make better-informed economic decisions – for example, by enabling the current situation to be understood better and enabling judgments to be made about prospects for the future.

5.1.4 Facilitate co-ordination

By being precise, brief and highlighting specific areas, ratios are likely to improve co-ordination between internal management: for example, the management teams responsible for different business functions and business units.

5.1.5 Control is more effective

Planning and forecasting systems establish budgets, develop forecast statements and lay down standards. The use of rations enables meaningful comparison to be made between forecasts, standards and actual results. Variances can be computed and analysed by managers, thereby administering an effective system of control.

5.1.6 Owners/shareholders

Existing, as well as prospective owners or shareholders, are fundamentally interested in the long-term solvency and profitability of the business. Ratio analysis enables these key indicators to be understood better and enables judgments to be made about prospects for the future.

5.1.7 Creditors

Creditors are owed money by the business. Their primary interest is ensuring the business is able to pay them. Short-term, trade creditors are interested in the immediate and short-term liquidity of the business.

Long-term creditors, such as financial institutions (mortgage holders) and debenture holders are interested in the capacity of the business to repay its loans and interest over the term of the loan.

Ratio analysis enables both types of creditors to judge better the financial position of the business and the risk attached to the repayment of what they are owed.

5.1.8 Employees

Employees are interested in fair wages and salaries, acceptable fringe benefits and bonuses linked with productivity and profitability. Ratio analysis can provide them with information regarding the efficiency and profitability of the business. This allows them to bargain more effectively for improved wages, bonuses and other aspects of their employment contracts.

5.1.9 The government

The government is interested in obtaining financial information from businesses for a variety of reasons and uses. Financial information from businesses regarding production, sales and profit provides central government with useful information to assess their prospective taxation revenue. However, on a wider level, government requires such information both to assess current policy and to assist in the determination of future policies. In addition, the financial information provides a valuable source of information for statistical analysis of the business sector as a whole and/or subsectors.

Group information from industry is required to formulate national policies and planning. In the absence of dependable information, government plans and policies may not achieve their desired results.

The accounts published annually by companies constitute an important source of information for external users, and their form and content are regulated with the intention of ensuring that they are a helpful and reliable guide to corporate progress. The amount of useful information that can be obtained from the statement of profit or loss and other comprehensive income for the period and statement of financial position may be severely limited, even when a detailed breakdown of trading results is provided. For example, the consolidated statement of profit or loss and other comprehensive income might show sales amounting to £500 million and the statement of financial position might disclose trade receivables totalling £21 million (sales to trade receivables ratio), but, taken in isolation, it is impossible to assess whether these amounts are satisfactory or unreasonable, comparative figures from previous year's results or cross-industry competitors would add further depth to the analysis and confidence in the figures here.

5.2 Nature of ratio analysis

Ratios, by themselves, are one of the means of understanding the financial health of a business entity. Ratio analysis is a technique for establishing and identifying relationships between items within the financial statements and interpreting the relationships to form a judgment regarding the financial affairs of a business.

Ratio analysis has been developed to help translate the information contained in the accounts into a form more helpful and readily understandable to users of financial reports. The ratios do not appear in the accounts, however, and users must calculate and interpret them themselves or employ someone with the necessary skills to do the job.

Accounting ratios are calculated by expressing one or more items in the financial statements as a ratio or percentage of another item or items. The objective is to identify and disclose relationships and trends that may not be immediately evident from the examination of the individual financial statements. The ratio that results from a comparison of two figures possesses real significance only if an identifiable commercial relationship exists between the numerator and the denominator. For example, one may expect there to be a positive relationship between operating profit and the level of sales. Assuming that each item sold produces a profit, one would expect a higher sales figure to produce more profit. So, mere observation of the fact that profit is £5 million is not particularly illuminating. What may be of greater interest is operating profit expressed as a percentage of sales.

The significance of an accounting ratio is enhanced by comparison with some yardstick of corporate performance. There are three main options available, namely comparison with:

■ results achieved during previous accounting periods by the same company (trend analysis);
■ results achieved by other companies (inter-firm comparisons); and
■ predetermined standards or budgets.

The advantage of making comparisons is that it enables users to judge a company's performance in context. For example, by comparing a ratio against other similar businesses or against past performance of the same business, a judgment may be made that classifies performance as good, average or poor. Sifting through the large volume of information contained in annual reports is cumbersome; reducing such information to a handful of important and very useful ratios enables the user to answer key questions on the economic reality of a company:

1   Does the profit being earned reflect good progress?
2   Is the company sufficiently cash-enabled?
3   Is there sufficient amount of capital on a long-term basis?

4   Are the resources of the company being used efficiently?
5   Are trade receivables and payables being managed efficiently?

Ratios are regarded as a highly efficient way of determining the answers to the above questions, particularly if they are used on a time-series basis.

6   Primary ratios

The primary ratios are a combination of profitability and liquidity ratios to allow analysts (and users of financial statements) to ascertain an initial assessment of the financial strength of an entity.

6.1 Primary operative ratios (GPM and OPM)

Two primary operative ratios exist to enable the analyst and reader gain a better understanding of the financial performance of a business. These ratios are the gross profit margin (GPM) and the operating profit margin (OPM). These ratios are calculated as follows:

$$\text{Gross profit margin} = \frac{\text{Gross profit}}{\text{Sales}} \times 100$$

$$\text{Operating profit margin} = \frac{\text{Operating profit}}{\text{Sales}} \times 100$$

The GPM and OPM are measures of the returns generated from each monetary unit of sales revenue.

WORKED EXAMPLE 8.4

Jane plc has provided you with their consolidated statement of profit or loss and other comprehensive income below for the years ended 31 December in 20X0 and 20X1.

	20X1 £,000	20X0 £,000
Sales	52,000	48,000
Cost of goods sold	(36,000)	(31,500)
Gross profit	16,000	16,500
Operating expenses:		
Selling expenses	(7,000)	(6,500)
Administrative expense	(5,860)	(6,100)
Total operating expenses	12,860	12,600
Operating profit before interest and taxation	3,140	3,900
Interest expense	(640)	(700)
Profit before tax	2,500	3,200
Income taxes (30%)	(750)	(960)
Profit for the period	1,750	2,240

WORKED EXAMPLE 8.4 *continued*

Required

Calculate the primary operative ratios for 20X0 and 20X1.

Answer

The comparative primary operative ratios are as follows.

		Gross profit margin	Operating profit margin
	=	$\dfrac{\text{Gross profit}}{\text{Sales}} \times 100$	$\dfrac{\text{Operating profit}}{\text{Sales}} \times 100$
20X1	=	$\dfrac{16{,}000}{52{,}000} \times 100$	$\dfrac{3{,}140}{52{,}000} \times 100$
	=	30.77%	6.04%
20X0	=	$\dfrac{16{,}500}{48{,}000} \times 100$	$\dfrac{3{,}900}{48{,}000} \times 100$
	=	34.38%	8.13%

The GPM shows the profit generated per monetary unit of sales. In 20X0, Jane plc generated £34 gross profit per £100 of sales revenue, whereas in 20X1, the company generated a lower return per £100 of sales revenue. This decline in GPM would need to be investigated. However, from the consolidated statement of profit or loss and other comprehensive income and our previous horizontal analysis, the decline in the GPM can be attributed to an increase in cost of sales greater than the increase in sales revenue. The rate of increase in the cost of sales is often outside the control of the company, and perhaps a solution may be to source alternative and lower-priced cost of sales. However, the management should be mindful that lower cost of inputs may have an adverse impact on the quality of output.

The OPM shows the operating profit generated per monetary unit of sales. In 20X0, Jane plc generated £8 operating profit per £100 sales revenue, whereas in 20X1, the company generated a lower return: £6, per £100 of sales revenue. This decline in OPM would need investigation. However from the consolidated statement of profit or loss and other comprehensive income and our previous horizontal analysis, the decline in the OPM can be attributed to an increase in cost of sales.

Despite the decline in both the GPM and OPM in 20X1, it is not all bad news. The company exercised greater control over its operating expenses in 20X1, as the GPM less OPM declined from 26.25% to 24.73% between 20X0 and 20X1. The difference between the GPM and OPM is a general measure on the operating expenses consumption of the sales revenue.

TEST YOUR KNOWLEDGE 8.4

a   Why would you expect the operating profit margin to increase when sales increase?

b   Outline three possible reasons for an increase in the gross profit margin.

6.2 Primary liquidity ratio

Businesses require working capital to function in their day-to-day operations. Any pressure on working capital could lead to a business either defaulting on its current obligations (e.g. to trade payables and employees) or, in the worst-case scenario, lead to total business failure. Liquidity ratios measure the working capital employed in a business and changes in the working capital over time provide an indication of the financial strains the business is experiencing in the short term.

There are two standard ratios that are used for the purpose of assessing and measuring the primary liquidity of a business. These ratios are the current ratio and the acid test, and are examined below.

6.2.1 Working capital (current) ratio

The working capital (current ratio) is defined as the excess of current assets over current liabilities, and a surplus is normally interpreted as a reliable indication of the fact that a company is solvent. The current ratio is calculated as follows:

$$\text{Current ratio} = \text{Working capital ratio} = \frac{\text{Current assets}}{\text{Current liabilities}} : 1$$

The purpose of the current ratio is to assess and measure the ability of a company to pay its current debts as they fall due. A question often asked by readers of financial statements is: 'What is a correct working capital ratio?' A general benchmark for the current ratio is 2:1. However, this should not be interpreted as a set standard for all companies. Any deviation from 2:1 should not be interpreted as indicating a better or worse company.

Analysts must familiarise themselves with the rate at which current assets are converted into cash and how quickly current liabilities must be paid. This very much depends on what the generally accepted or agreed practice is within the particular sector. For example, a retailer who sells goods for cash would generally operate with a much lower current ratio than a manufacturer who sells goods on credit. In the retail industry, resources are converted directly from inventories into cash, whereas in manufacturing, goods sold are probably tied up as debts outstanding for six to eight weeks before cash becomes available. The period for which inventories are held varies from one industry to another. A manufacturer of small metal products is likely to convert raw materials into finished goods and sell them much more quickly than a construction company where inventories are likely to comprise a much higher proportion of current assets to reflect the relatively slow rate of turnover.

For these and other reasons, one should guard against always accepting accounting ratios at face value, and should assess their significance after carefully considering the economic facts that lie behind them.

The current ratio as a measure of solvency suffers from one limitation, namely its inclusion of inventory. To be solvent, a company needs to be able to convert its current assets into cash at short notice and minimal cost. Unfortunately, inventories are not readily convertible into cash. This renders the current ratio as an ineffective and unreliable measure of solvency.

6.2.2 Acid test (quick ratio)

The acid test or quick ratio is used to examine solvency to overcome the limitation of the current ratio. It is calculated in a similar manner to the working capital ratio, but with one important difference: the exclusion of inventory from the current assets and the liquidity ratio concentrates attention more on a company's prospect of paying its debts as they fall due. It is for this reason that the calculation is often described as the 'quick ratio' or 'acid test of solvency'. The acid test is derived as follows:

$$\text{Acid test} = \frac{\text{Current assets} - \text{inventory}}{\text{Current liabilities}} : 1$$

A liquidity ratio of 1:1 is desirable as it affords a company the comfort of knowing it can meet its short-term debts. However, 1:1 is not a good or bad ratio in isolation from other non-financial factors, such as the operating sector, the company, its reputation, the economy etc.

WORKED EXAMPLE **8.5**

Jane plc has provided you with its statement of financial position for the years ended 31 December in 20X0 and 20X1.

	20X1 £,000	20X0 £,000
Non-current assets		
Property and equipment:		
Land	4,000	4,000
Building	12,000	8,500
Total non-current assets	16,000	12,500
Current assets		
Cash	1,200	2,350
Accounts receivable	6,000	4,000
Inventory	8,000	10,000
Prepaid expenses	300	120
Total current assets	15,500	16,470
Total assets	31,500	28,970
Equity and liabilities		
Share capital (£12 shares)	6,000	6,000
Share premium	1,000	1,000
6% preferred shares		
(£100 nominal value)	2,000	2,000
Retained earnings	8,000	6,970
	17,000	15,970
Long-term liabilities:		
Bonds payable 8%	7,500	8,000
Total long-term liabilities	7,500	8,000
Current liabilities		
Accounts payables	5,800	4,000
Accrued payables	900	400
Notes payables	300	600
Total current liabilities	7,000	5,000
Total liabilities	14,500	13,000
Total equity and liabilities	31,500	28,970

Required
Calculate the primary liquidity ratios for the years ended 31 December 20X0 and 20X1.

WORKED EXAMPLE **8.5** *continued*

Answer

The primary liquidity ratios for Jane plc for the years ended 31 December 20X0 and 20X1 are as follows.

		Current ratio	Quick ratio
		$\dfrac{\text{Current assets}}{\text{Current liabilities}}:1$	$\dfrac{\text{Current assets} - \text{Inventories}}{\text{Current liabilities}}:1$
20X1	=	$\dfrac{15{,}500}{7{,}000}:1$	$\dfrac{15{,}500 - 8{,}000}{7{,}000}:1$
	=	$2.21:1$	$1.07:1$
20X0	=	$\dfrac{16{,}470}{5{,}000}:1$	$\dfrac{16{,}470 - 10{,}000}{5{,}000}:1$
	=	$3.29:1$	$1.29:1$

TEST YOUR KNOWLEDGE **8.5**

a   Why is it important to have an adequate level of working capital?

b   Explain how the liquidity ratio is calculated.

6.3 Return on capital employed (ROCE)

The return on capital employed (ROCE) ratio is a measure of efficiency and profitability. It measures how well capital has been utilised. The ratio is derived from the earnings (profit) before interest and taxation (from the statement of profit or loss and other comprehensive income for the period) expressed over the total capital employed in the business. The total capital employed is the total assets less the current liabilities. It is important to state at this point that, in practice, there are multiple variations on both the denominator and numerator used for the ROCE and other ratios that seek to measure a return. It is therefore important, when conducting financial analysis or reviewing financial analysis, to ensure one knows the basis for the computations before advancing to conclusions or any comments on performance. ROCE is calculated as follows:

$$\frac{\text{Profit before interest and taxation}}{\text{Total assets} - \text{Current liabilities}} \times 100$$

The earnings before interest and taxation are used because this figure represents the actual returns before any distortion by interest rates or taxation, especially when conducting comparative analysis. Purists within the business and financial analyst community may go further and use EBITDA (earnings before interest, taxation, depreciation and amortisation) as the numerator, because EBITDA is regarded as the pure return unaffected by distorters such as depreciation, interest charges and taxation.

ROCE is used to indicate the value the business has obtained from its capital (expressed as assets less liabilities). The ratio is used to show how efficiently a business is using its resources. However, the main drawback of ROCE is that it measures return against the book value of assets in the business. As these depreciate, the ROCE will increase even if the cash generated remained the same. Thus older businesses, with depreciated assets, will tend to have higher ROCE than newer, possibly more profitable businesses. In addition, while cash flow is affected by inflation, the book value of assets is not. Consequently, revenue increases with inflation, while capital employed generally does not (as the book value of assets is not affected by inflation).

6.4 Return on equity (ROE)

Return on equity (ROE), also known as return on shareholders equity (ROSE), is a primary investment ratio used in financial analysis. The ratio measures the profitability of the business and how effective management have been in generating a return for shareholders. In general terms, investors are seeking a high ROE. Therefore, when conducting comparative analysis, a higher ROE would be preferable to a lower ROE. The ratio is expressed as follows:

$$\frac{\text{Profit before interest and taxation}}{\text{Total equity}} \times 100$$

The earnings (profit) before interest and taxation (from the statement of profit or loss and other comprehensive income for the period) and after dividends to preference shareholders, is expressed over the total equity of the company. The total equity is extracted from the statement of financial position. There are a number of variations on this ratio depending upon information available, for example; ROE may also be calculated more precisely using the 'average shareholders equity' as a denominator as you will see in the next chapter. Average shareholders equity is calculated by adding shareholders equity at the beginning and end of the given period and dividing by two.

Because the ratio is based upon the operating profit from the business activity of the company before deductions for interest charges and taxation, ROE provides an insight to the income generating ability of an entity.

Despite the merits of ROE, as with all ratios it should be interpreted with caution and assessed in the context of other indicators. A company with a low equity base – for example, a knowledge-driven business – is likely to have a much lower equity base than a business that requires significant investment in production machinery. As a result, the knowledge-based business will exhibit a higher ROE. Conversely, companies that require larger amounts of investment may be prone to a lower ROE.

WORKED EXAMPLE 8.6

The comparative financial statements for Jane plc for the years ended 31 December 20X0 and 20X1 are as follows.

Statement of financial position as 31 December:

	20X1 £,000	20X0 £,000
Non-current assets		
Property and equipment:		
Land	4,000	4,000
Building	12,000	8,500
Total non-current assets	16,000	12,500
Current assets		
Cash	1,200	2,350
Accounts receivable	6,000	4,000
Inventory	8,000	10,000
Prepaid expenses	300	120
Total current assets	15,500	16,470
Total assets	31,500	28,970

WORKED EXAMPLE **8.6** *continued*

Equity and liabilities

Share capital (£12 shares)	6,000	6,000
Share premium	1,000	1,000
6% preferred shares		
(£100 nominal value)	2,000	2,000
Retained earnings	8,000	6,970
	17,000	15,970
Long-term liabilities:		
Bonds payable 8%	7,500	8,000
Total long-term liabilities	7,500	8,000
Current liabilities		
Accounts payables	5,800	4,000
Accrued payables	900	400
Notes payables	300	600
Total current liabilities	7,000	5,000
Total liabilities	14,500	13,000
Total equity and liabilities	31,500	28,970

Consolidated statement of profit or loss and other comprehensive income for the year ended 31 December:

	20X1 £,000	20X0 £,000
Sales	52,000	48,000
Cost of goods sold	(36,000)	(31,500)
Gross profit	16,000	16,500
Operating expenses:		
Selling expenses	(7,000)	(6,500)
Administrative expense	(5,860)	(6,100)
Total operating expenses	12,860	12,600
Operating profit before interest and taxation (PBIT)	3,140	3,900
Interest expense	(640)	(700)
Profit before tax	2,500	3,200
Income taxes (30%)	(750)	(960)
Profit for the period	1,750	2,240

Required
Calculate the ROCE and ROE for Jane plc for each of the two years.

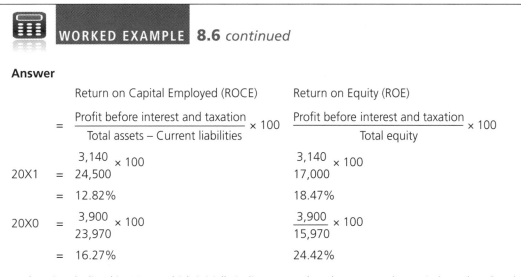

WORKED EXAMPLE **8.6** *continued*

Answer

	Return on Capital Employed (ROCE)	Return on Equity (ROE)
	$= \dfrac{\text{Profit before interest and taxation}}{\text{Total assets} - \text{Current liabilities}} \times 100$	$\dfrac{\text{Profit before interest and taxation}}{\text{Total equity}} \times 100$
20X1	$= \dfrac{3{,}140}{24{,}500} \times 100$	$\dfrac{3{,}140}{17{,}000} \times 100$
	$= 12.82\%$	18.47%
20X0	$= \dfrac{3{,}900}{23{,}970} \times 100$	$\dfrac{3{,}900}{15{,}970} \times 100$
	$= 16.27\%$	24.42%

Both ratios declined in 20X1, which initially indicates a reduced return on the capital employed and return for shareholders. However, closer examination reveals the decline can be further explained as result of the decline in PBIT and increases in the capital employed and total equity. The increases in capital employed and equity did not generate a greater level of profitability. This may give rise to further investigation by the management of Jane plc.

STOP AND THINK **8.1**

The real value in **financial ratios** lies in cash-flow-based ratios – accounting ratios do not show much. Do you agree or disagree with this?

END OF CHAPTER QUESTIONS

8.1 Explain the role of stewardship in managing a company's financial affairs.

8.2 Explain the principal features of ratio analysis.

8.3 State the primary accounting ratios and explain their purpose and usefulness in assessing a firm's performance.

8.4 An extract of balances for current assets and liabilities in respect of Roadster Ltd are presented below:

	20X2	20X1
	£,000	*£,000*
Current assets		
Inventory	180	240
Trade receivables	520	400
Cash and cash equivalents	60	55
	760	695
Current liabilities		
Account payables	320	425
Accrued expenses	40	80
	360	505

? END OF CHAPTER QUESTIONS *continued*

Required

a   Calculate the liquidity ratios for the two years 20X1 and 20X2 respectively.

b   Comment on the movements of the liquidity ratios and any issues of concern arising.

8.5   The following information relates to Brent Limited for the two years to 31 December 20X1 and 20X2.

Brent Ltd – statement of profit or loss and other comprehensive income for the years to 31 December:

	20X2		20X1	
	£,000	£,000	£,000	£,000
Sales (all credit)		1,900		1,500
Opening inventory	100		80	
Purchases	1,400		995	
	1,500		1,075	
Closing inventory	200		100	
Cost of goods sold		(1,300)		(975)
Gross profit		600		525
Less: Expenses		(350)		(250)
		250		275

Brent Ltd – Statement of financial position at 31 December

	20X2		20X1	
	£,000	£,000	£,000	£,000
Non-current assets (NBV)		460		580
Current assets				
Inventory	200		100	
Trade receivables	800		375	
Cash and cash equivalents	0		25	
		1,000		500
Total assets		1,460		1,080
Equity and liabilities				
Ordinary shareholders fund		500		500
Retained earnings		550		300
Total equity		1,050		800
Non-current liabilities				
Debentures		200		200
Current liabilities				
Bank overdraft	10		0	
Trade payables	200	210	80	80
Total liabilities		410		280
Total equity and liabilities		1,460		1,080

Note: Ignore taxation.

⁇ END OF CHAPTER QUESTIONS *continued*

Required

a   Calculate the following accounting ratios for 20X1 and 20X2 respectively:

      i   gross profit margin;

      ii   current ratio;

      iii operating profit margin;

      iv acid test;

      v   return on capital employed;

      vi return on equity.

b   Comment on the company's performance for the year to 31 December 20X2.

8.6 Using the information from Brent Ltd in Question 8.5, carry out vertical and horizontal analysis for the company, and comment on your findings.

9 Analysis and interpretation of accounts 1

■ LEARNING OUTCOMES

This chapter continues with the part of the syllabus section entitled 'Analysis and interpretation of accounts'. After reading and understanding the contents of the chapter, working through all the worked examples and practice questions, you should understand:

- the purpose of and explanations for gearing ratios;
- the purpose of and explanations for company performance ratios;
- the impact of debt on company profitability;
- the link between gearing and profitability;
- the impact of gearing on shareholders return;
- the impact of working capital on cash flow and company profit;
- company efficiency and asset usage ratios; and
- the pyramid of ratios.

1   Introduction

This chapter delves more deeply into ratio analysis, examining company performance from the perspectives of profitability, asset usage and efficiency. We discuss the specific ratios used to evaluate company financial performance and those that measure levels of financial commitment in relation to resources employed.

2   Subsidiary ratios

2.1 Gearing ratio

The capital employed in a company comes from two sources: equity or debt. Gearing is the term used to explain the proportion of debt a company has in its capital structure. One way of measuring gearing is through ratios. The debt : equity ratio is the most common ratio used to measure the level of gearing. A number of different approaches are used to measure gearing. However, for our purposes, gearing refers to the relationship between long-term debt and total equity. As such, the gearing ratio is as follows:

$$\frac{\text{Long-term debt}}{\text{Total equity}} \times 100$$

The gearing ratio is a key ratio in financial analysis. The ratio measures the proportion of long-term debt carried by a company, which can be a key indicator of financial health. In general terms, an entity is deemed to be highly geared if the gearing ratio exceeds 50%. However, the determination of high or low gearing will be dependent upon the industry and sector. A company with a ratio of over 50% has more debt than equity in its capital structure. This renders the company vulnerable to external takeover and adverse changes in interest charges. Increasing levels of gearing increases a company's exposure to interest rate movements. This can have a critical impact on the survival of the company, especially in periods of declining sales and profitability. Despite this concern about gearing, in some circumstances it may be argued that increasing gearing is the correct course of action.

Gearing may be measured in either of two ways:

a   Debt defined as long-term loans:

$$\text{Debt : Equity ratio} = \frac{\text{Long-term loans}^\star}{\text{Shareholders' equity}} : 1 \text{ Shareholders' equity}$$

* This could include any preference shares outstanding.

b   Debt defined as total borrowing:
Lenders, when assessing risk, want to examine a business's full financial exposure. For this reason, they often find it useful to extend the definition of debt, used for the purpose of calculating the debt : equity ratio, in the following manner:

$$\text{Total debt : Equity ratio} \times \frac{\text{Total financial debt}^\star}{\text{Shareholders' equity}} : 1$$

* Includes loans from directors and bank overdrafts that, although technically for the short term, are a permanent source of financing for many businesses.

The use of debt capital has direct implications for the profit accruing to the ordinary shareholders, and expansion is often financed in this manner with the objective of increasing, or 'gearing up', the shareholders' rate of return. This objective is achieved, however, only if the rate of return earned on the additional funds raised exceeds that payable to the providers of the loan.

WORKED EXAMPLE 9.1

Ludlow plc has presented its statement of financial position for the year ended 31 December as follows.

	20X1		20X0	
	£	£	£	£
Non-current assets				
Cost		900,000		700,000
Accumulated depreciation		(185,000)		(150,000)
		715,000		550,000
Current assets				
Inventories	1,500,000		1,360,000	
Trade receivables	1,560,000		960,000	
Cash and cash equivalents	120,000		20,000	
	3,180,000		2,340,000	
Less: Current liabilities				
Trade payables	567,500		467,500	
Taxation	177,500		172,500	
	745,000		640,000	

WORKED EXAMPLE 9.1 *continued*

Working capital	2,435,000	1,700,000
	3,150,000	2,250,000
Non-current liabilities:		
10% debenture loan	(800,000)	
Net assets	2,350,000	2,250,000
Equity		
Share capital	1,500,000	1,500,000
Reserves	850,000	750,000
Shareholders' funds	2,350,000	2,250,000

Required

a Calculate the gearing for Ludlow plc for both years.

b Comment on your findings.

Answer

a The comparative years gearing is as follows:

Gearing	20X1	20X0
$\dfrac{\text{Long-term debt}}{\text{Total equity}} \times 100$	$\dfrac{800,000}{2,350,000} \times 100$	$\dfrac{0}{2,250,000} \times 100$
	34.04%	0.00%

b In 20X0, the company did not have any long-term debt, therefore its gearing was 0%. In 20X1, the company raised £800,000 via a 10% debenture, which led to the company having a gearing level of 34%. As the gearing level is less than 50%, this may be regarded as a low level of gearing. However, this 34% level of gearing must be viewed within the context of the industry and sector before one can be satisfied that Ludlow plc is lowly geared. Furthermore, the company should be mindful of further increases in gearing, as this can begin to put pressure on the operating profit, especially if sales and operating profit begin to decline.

WORKED EXAMPLE 9.2

Ponty Ltd and Pop Ltd are established companies engaged in similar lines of business. Trading conditions change significantly from year to year. An analysis of past results achieved by companies in the same line of business as Ponty and Pop shows that operating profit before deducting interest charges can fluctuate by up to 50% up or down from year to year. The forecast results for the next financial year are shown below.

	Ponty £,000	Pop £,000
Ordinary share capital (£1 shares) at 1 June 2016	1,500	3,200
Revaluation surplus at 1 June 2016	500	1,000
Capital redemption reserve at 1 June 2016	0	800
14% debentures at 1 June 2016	4,000	1,000
Operating profit before interest 2016–17	840	840

📟 **WORKED EXAMPLE** **9.2** *continued*

It is the policy of each company to pay out its entire profits in the form of dividends.

Required

a For each company, calculate:
  i   the estimated rate of return on shareholders' equity;
  ii   the gearing (debt: equity) ratio.
b Set out a discussion of the relative merits of the capital structures of each of the two companies from the shareholders' point of view. The discussion should include calculations of *maximum* possible variations in the return on shareholders' equity.

Note: Ignore taxation.

a)

	Ponty £,000	Pop £,000
$\dfrac{\text{Operating profit before interest}}{\text{Total equity}} \times 100$	$\dfrac{840}{1,500} \times 100$	$\dfrac{0}{1,500} \times 100$
	56.00%	0.00%
$\dfrac{\text{Long-term debt}}{\text{Total equity}} \times 100$	$\dfrac{4,000}{2,000} \times 100$	$\dfrac{1,000}{5,000} \times 100$
	200.00%	20.00%
Answer:	2:1 or 200%	1:5 or 20%

b

	Ponty Up 50% £,000	Ponty −50% £,000	Pop Up 50% £,000	Pop −50% £,000
Operating profit	1,260	420	1,260	420
Interest	560	560	140	140
Profit/(Loss)	700	(140)	1,120	280
Ordinary share capital	1,500		3,200	
Revaluation surplus	500		1,000	
Capital redemption reserve	0		800	
Equity	2,000	2,000	5,000	5,000
Return on shareholders' equity	(1,260/2,000)	(420/2,000)	(1,260/5,000)	(420/5,000)
	63%	21%	25.20%	8.40%

The following relevant comments might be made:
1 The capital structure of Ponty Ltd is highly geared, which means that there is a high ratio of debt to equity finance.
2 The main advantage of gearing is that any return in excess of the cost of borrowing is returned to shareholders.
3 This can be seen above, with an increase in profits of 50% resulting in the return on shareholders' equity increasing from 42% to 63%.
4 Conversely, when profits decline, the return on equity falls quickly due to the fact that the fixed interest charges, in the case of Ponty £560,000, must still be paid.

⌨ **WORKED EXAMPLE 9.2** *continued*

---

5 A fall in operating profit of 50% would result in a level of operating profit that is insufficient to cover interest charges.
6 The capital structure of Pop, in contrast, has a relatively low level of gearing with a debt:equity ratio of 1:5 or 20%.
7 A 50% rise in profits results in an increase in the return on shareholders' equity, but the rise is more modest, to 25.2%.
8 Conversely, a fall in profits is not so detrimental to the equity shareholders, who continue to receive a return of 8.4% on their investment.
9 A further drawback of a high level of gearing is that the company may face acute financial difficulties if there is a significant fall in profits. Whereas dividends can be reduced when profits are low (if necessary, to zero), interest charges are a legal obligation, and must be paid irrespective of profit levels.

✎ **TEST YOUR KNOWLEDGE 9.1**

Explain the purpose of calculating the gearing ratio in the analysis of financial statements.

2.2 Proprietorship ratio – a brief discussion

Before discussing other ratios related to liquidity, it may be helpful to touch upon a longer-term financial ratio related to how a company is financed.

The total assets belonging to a company are financed by a combination of resources provided by shareholders and lenders. The proportion of business assets financed by the shareholders is measured by the proprietorship ratio, which is conventionally calculated by expressing the shareholders' investment, or equity, in the company as a percentage of total sources of finance.

$$\text{Proprietorship ratio} = \frac{\text{Shareholder's equity}}{\text{Total sources of finance}^*} \times 100$$

* Total *sources of finance* include both non-current and current liabilities.

This ratio is a measure of financial stability, since the larger the proportion of business activity financed by shareholders, the smaller the creditors' claims against the company. This produces two advantages:

1. Equity finance is normally repaid only when the company is wound up. Even then, repayment occurs only if sufficient cash remains after all other providers of finance have been refunded the amounts due to them. Where an excessive proportion of total finance is provided by short-term creditors, management is likely to be under continuous pressure to finance repayments falling due. In these circumstances, any withdrawal/reduction of a source of finance causes the company acute financial embarrassment.
2. Dividends are payable at the discretion of management, whereas interest payable on loan capital is a legally enforceable debt. A company with a large proportion of equity finance is therefore more able to survive a lean period of trading than a highly geared company that is legally obliged to make interest payments irrespective of profit levels.

It is difficult to specify an appropriate percentage, as this depends a great deal upon trading conditions within the industry. In general, a higher percentage is expected in those industries where there are large fluctuations in profitability, because reliance on overdraft and loan finance gives rise to heavy interest charges that a company may find it difficult to pay when results are poor. In any event, one normally expects shareholders to provide at least half the finance, and the implications of significant changes from one year to the next should receive careful investigation.

The proprietorship ratio, viewed from the creditor's standpoint, provides a useful indication of the extent to which a company can stand a fall in the value of its assets before the creditor's position is prejudiced. Carrying values are not the same as current values, of course, but a proprietorship ratio of, say, 75% would indicate that a significant cushion for creditors exists, and the resale value of assets would have to fall to less than one-quarter of their carrying value before the creditors' position on liquidation would be jeopardised.

Total assets	950,000
Intangible assets	150,000
Shareholders' equity	240,000

From the above information we can compute proprietary ratio as follows:

$$\text{Proprietorship ratio} = \frac{\text{Shareholder's equity}}{\text{Total sources of finance}} \times 100$$

$$\frac{240,000}{800,000} \times 100$$

$$55\%$$

The proprietary ratio is 55% meaning shareholder' have contributed 55% of the total tangible assets. The remaining 45% have been contributed by creditors.

3 Liquidity ratios

The primary liquidity ratios, current and quick ratios, were demonstrated in Chapter 8, section 6.2. We will now discuss subsidiary ratios related to working capital.

3.1 Interest cover

The fact that a company is legally obliged to meet its interest charges was referred to when examining the proprietorship ratio (see section 2 above). There is no legal restriction on sources of cash that may be employed by management to meet its interest payments; management may even make an additional share issue with the intention that part of the proceeds should be used for that purpose. Nevertheless, interest payments are a business expense and, in the long run, all such costs must be met out of operating profit if the company is to remain viable. Interest cover stresses the importance of a company meeting its interest charges out of revenue, and it does this by expressing net profit before interest charges (operating profits) as a multiple of the interest charged.

$$\text{Interest cover} = \frac{\text{Profit before interest}}{\text{Interest charges}} \times 100$$

The interest cover ratio measures the ability of a company to meet its fixed interest obligations out of profit. The lower the level of interest cover, the greater the burden of the interest charges on the company and the greater is its likelihood of financial failure. For example, debentures may be raised with two to three years' capital requirements in mind, but a full utilisation of the additional resources made available is unlikely to be achieved straight away. In this situation, current earnings have to bear the full weight of the additional charges, but the extra revenue, which is expected to result from an expansion programme, takes longer to materialise.

Interest cover is a ratio that receives a significant amount of attention from analysts in general and lenders in particular. Traditional measures of asset utilisation and asset cover for advances are of little relevance in service-based industries where tangible assets are at a low level. In these circumstances, it is particularly important to measure a company's ability to generate enough operating profit to cover finance charges and leave a sufficient balance for dividends and to finance eventual loan repayments. The ratio of earnings to finance charges helps a great deal in this situation.

4 Asset turnover ratios

The ratios examined in this section are designed to measure management's effective utilisation of its resources. These ratios help to explain the upward and downward movement in the solvency of a business. They also provide clues to underlying changes in profitability.

4.1 Rate of inventory turnover

The rate of inventory turnover measures the number of times per year that a company turns over its inventory. The calculation is made as follows.

Inventory turnover = Cost of goods sold/Average inventory held

Two typical queries asked about the above formula are:

1 Why use the cost of goods sold rather than sales?
2 Why use the average inventory level rather than closing inventory?

The reason is the same in both cases – to ensure that both the numerator and the denominator are computed on a comparable basis. However, it must be emphasised that in practice, the cost of sales is not used. Inventory, which makes up the denominator, is valued at cost for accounting purposes and the numerator must be computed on a similar basis. The sales figure *can* be used to produce a ratio that enables users to make helpful inter-period comparisons, when cost-of-sales figures are not available. However, there is a risk that incorrect conclusions may be drawn if there are changes in the gross profit margin from one accounting period to another.

Turning to the reason for using average inventory levels, the numerator measures the cost of goods dispatched to customers *during* an accounting period, and the denominator must therefore represent the investment in inventory *during* the same time period. In practice, inventory levels are likely to fluctuate a great deal; they are often built up during relatively quiet times and subsequently run down when the level of activity increases.

For this reason, it is important to calculate the average investment in inventory rather than use the inventory level at a particular point in time. The average is usually based on the opening and closing figures. A more precise calculation makes use of inventory levels at various dates during the year, perhaps at the end of each month (for similar reasons, average figures are used in the calculation of a number of other ratios considered below).

Many analysts prefer to present this ratio in terms of the number of days that have elapsed between the date that goods are delivered by suppliers and the date they are dispatched to customers (i.e. the stockholding period). This is done by modifying the formula so as to achieve the desired result in the following single step.

$$\text{Inventory days} = \frac{\text{Average inventory held}}{\text{Cost of goods sold}} \times 365$$

Companies strive to keep the stockholding period as low as possible to minimise associated costs. An increase in the stockholding period from, say, 30 to 60 days causes the investment in inventory to double. Extra finance then has to be raised, handling and finance costs increase, and the potential loss from damage to inventory and obsolescence is much greater. But although management aims to keep inventory to a minimum, it must at the same time ensure that there are sufficient raw materials available to meet production requirements (in the case of a manufacturer) and enough finished goods available to meet consumer demand. It is, therefore, management's job to maintain a balance between conflicting objectives.

For example, a company with an average inventory level of £120,500 and cost of goods sold of £900,000 will have an inventory turnover of 7.47 times per year, and hold its inventory for 48.87 days.

The calculations are as follows.

$$\text{Inventory turnover} = \frac{\text{Cost of goods sold}}{\text{Average inventory held}}$$

$$\frac{900,000}{120,500}$$

$$= 7.47 \text{ times, commonly expressed as } 7.47\text{x}$$

$$\text{Inventory days} = \frac{\text{Average inventory held}}{\text{Cost of goods sold}} \times 365$$

$$\frac{120,500}{900,000} \times 365$$

$$= 48.87 \text{ days}$$

There is a clear relationship between both ratios. If the inventory turnover is divided into 365, the number of inventory days is found.

TEST YOUR KNOWLEDGE 9.3

Why is it usual to use cost of goods sold rather than sales for the purpose of computing the rate of inventory turnover?

4.2 Rate of collection of trade receivables

The period of credit taken by customers varies between industries, but as a general rule, companies extract the maximum amount of credit from suppliers, since (in the absence of discounts for prompt payment) accounts unpaid represent a free source of finance. At the same time, undue delays should be avoided, as these have a harmful long-term effect on the company's credit rating. In practice, it is quite usual for customers to take six to eight weeks to pay their bills. The rate of collection of trade receivables is calculated in days, as follows:

$$\text{Trade receivable days} = \frac{\text{Average trade receivables}}{\text{Sales}} \times 365$$

It should be noted that the denominator is sales and not credit sales, because credit sales are never extractable from published financial statements.

The ability of a company to collect its trade receivables on time has a direct impact upon its solvency and its solvency and liquidity ratios. As a benchmark, the trade receivables of a company should be less than its average length of credit days. Changes in the collection of trade receivables may arise from changes in general economic conditions, changes in credit management policies, changes in discounts granted and taken, or from the fear of penalties for late payment. These changes may be responsible for an improvement or deterioration in the collection of trade receivables.

4.3 Rate of payment of trade payables

The rate of payment of trade payables measures the time taken by companies to pay their suppliers. The result must be interpreted with particular care, as not all suppliers grant similar terms of credit, but provided there are no significant changes in the mix of trade creditors, the average payments period should remain stable.

$$\text{Trade payable days} = \frac{\text{Average trade payables}}{\text{Cost of sales}} \times 365$$

A change in the rate of payment of suppliers may well reflect an improvement or decline in the solvency position of a company. For instance, if a company is short of cash, it is likely that suppliers will have to wait longer for the payment of amounts due to them. This may be an acceptable short-term strategy.

Changes in payment of trade payables is similar to collection of trade receivables, and has a direct relationship with the solvency of a company. A delay in the payment to creditors may be a policy to improve cash holdings or result from a worsening in cash balances. Conversely, early payment of creditors may arise from surplus cash balances or a desire to maintain a good credit rating.

TEST YOUR KNOWLEDGE 9.4

a   What are the possible reasons for an increase in the rate of collection of trade receivables?
b   Is an increase in the rate of payment of trade payables a good or a bad thing?

---

5   The cash operating cycle

A period of time elapses between the payment for goods or raw materials received into inventory and the collection of cash from customers in respect of their sale. The gap is known as the cash operating cycle. During this period of time, the goods acquired, together with the value added in the case of a manufacturer, must be financed by the company. The shorter the length of time between the initial outlay and ultimate collection of cash, the smaller the amount of working capital that needs to be financed.

To estimate the length of the cash operating cycle, it is necessary to:

1   calculate the time that the product spends in each stage of its progression from acquisition to sale and subsequent cash receipt; and
2   deduct, from the length of time found in step 1, the period of credit received from suppliers.

The combination of the previously identified asset turnover ratios are the elements of the cash operating cycle.

$$\text{Inventory days} = \frac{\text{Average inventory held}}{\text{Cost of goods sold}} \times 365$$

Plus

$$\text{Trade receivable days} = \frac{\text{Average trade receivables}}{\text{Sales}} \times 365$$

Less

$$\text{Trade payable days} = \frac{\text{Average trade payables}}{\text{Cost of sales}} \times 365$$

However, in a manufacturing sector that involves the holding of raw materials, semi-finished and finished goods, a more detailed examination of the cash operating cycle will be involved. This will be illustrated in the upcoming Worked Example 9.3, which shows that Wing Ltd's cash operating cycle has 145 days in 2010 and 192 days in 2011.

5.1 Inventory

Items are purchased or produced, held for a period of time and then used or sold. We have previously seen that estimates of the length of time for which various categories of inventory that are held must be based on a comparison of the average inventory levels with the issues of inventory during the period under consideration. In the case of a manufacturing company, separate calculations must be made for each of the following three categories of inventory.

1   *Raw materials* – These are acquired, held in stock and then transferred to production. Stocks of raw materials are related to raw materials consumed to find the average length of time for which they are held.

2   *Work in progress* – Raw materials are taken from stock and processed, which involves additional manufacturing costs. The average production time is found by relating the value of work in progress to the cost of goods manufactured.

3   *Finished goods* – When production is complete, the finished goods are transferred from the factory to the warehouse. (In the case of a trader, finished goods, stored in the warehouse, are purchased from outside.) The average length of time for which items are held can be found by relating the stock of finished goods to the cost of goods sold during the accounting period.

5.2 Trade receivables

The average age of debts is found from the values of trade receivables and sales (see section 4.2).

5.3 Trade payables

Trade payables finance the production and selling cycle from the time raw materials or goods are received into stock until they are paid for. The period of credit is found from the values of trade payables and purchases (see section 4.3).

The length of the cash operating cycle is obtained by aggregating the periods of time calculated for each of the above items.

 WORKED EXAMPLE 9.3

The cash balance of Wing Ltd has declined significantly over the last 12 months. The following financial information is provided.

Year to 31 March	20X7 £	20X6 £
Sales	573,000	643,000
Purchases of raw materials	215,000	264,000
Raw materials consumed	210,000	256,400
Cost of goods manufactured	435,000	515,000
Cost of goods sold	420,000	460,000
Balances at 31 March	**20X7**	**20X6**
Trade receivables	97,100	121,500
Trade payables	23,900	32,500
Inventory:		
Raw materials	22,400	30,000
Work in progress	29,000	34,300
Finished goods	70,000	125,000

All purchases and sales were made on credit.

Required

a   Provide an analysis of the above information which should include calculations of the cash operating cycle (i.e. the time lag between making payment to suppliers and collecting cash from customers) for 20X6 and 20X7.

b   Create a brief report on the implications of the changes that have occurred between 20X6 and 20X7.

WORKED EXAMPLE **9.3** *continued*

Notes

1 Assume a 365-day year for the purpose of your calculations and that all transactions take place at an even rate.
2 All calculations are to be made to the nearest day.

Answer

a

		20X2		20X1
		days		*days*
Raw materials	$\frac{22,400}{210,000} \times 365$	39	$\frac{30,000}{256,400} \times 365$	43
Less				
Credit from suppliers	$\frac{23,900}{215,000} \times 365$	41	$\frac{32,500}{264,000} \times 365$	45
Plus				
Production period	$\frac{29,000}{435,000} \times 365$	24	$\frac{34,300}{515,000} \times 365$	24
Plus				
Finished goods	$\frac{70,000}{420,000} \times 365$	61	$\frac{125,000}{460,000} \times 365$	99
Plus				
Credit to customers	$\frac{97,100}{573,000} \times 365$	62	$\frac{121,500}{643,000} \times 365$	69
Cash operating cycle		145		190

b The cash operating cycle has decreased by 45 days or 31%. The decreased investment in working capital may be calculated as follows.

	£	£
Inventory	121,400	189,300
Receivables	97,100	121,500
	218,500	310,800
Less		
Payables	23,900	32,500
	194,600	278,300

The decreased period for which raw materials are held has been balanced by an equivalent decrease in the period of credit taken from suppliers. Furthermore, the production period has remained constant at 24 days, suggesting no change in the efficiency with which resources are moved through the factory. There are no areas of concern, as there are significant decreases in the period of credit taken by customers and decreases in the holding of finished goods – the latter has fallen from the equivalent of three months' sales at the end of 20X6 to two months' sales at the end of 20X7.

The company has experienced a significant decline in its gross profit percentage. More information is needed to assess the likely consequences of decrease in profit on the business.

5.4 Non-current asset turnover ratio

The non-current asset (NCA) turnover ratio measures the effectiveness of NCAs in generating sales. This is particularly pertinent to manufacturing companies where there is a concern to assess whether the investment in NCAs has generated the desired impact on sales.

$$\text{NCA turnover ratio} = \frac{\text{Sales}}{\text{Average NCAs}} : 1$$

The ratio is likely to reveal excess capacity from time to time during the life of a business, and it may be unavoidable. Possible reasons include:

■ temporary inconveniences, such as a strike or a fire that destroys essential equipment;
■ the collapse in demand for a product line, unless steps are promptly taken to dispose of the equipment or transfer it to an alternative use;
■ the acquisition of additional NCAs. The point is eventually reached where existing NCAs are used to their full capacity and any further increase in business activity first requires the acquisition of additional plant. It is some while before demand increases sufficiently to absorb the extra capacity, however, and meanwhile NCA turnover declines.

Note: As NCAs depreciate and sales are constant, NCA turnover rises. Also, when sales increase with inflation and NCAs do not, NCA turnover rises.

WORKED EXAMPLE 9.4

During 20X4, Rhyl Ltd operated at full capacity and 1,000 units of output were produced and sold for £50 each using plant that cost £20,000. On 1 January 20X5, management purchased additional plant for £20,000, with a capacity to produce a further 1,000 units. Output for the years 20X5–X7 is as follows.

20X5	1,200 units
20X6	1,500 units
20X7	2,000 units

The selling price remained unchanged at £50 per unit.

Required
Calculate the NCA turnover ratio for each year, ignoring depreciation.

Answer

$$20X4 \ \frac{50,000}{20,000} \ : \ = 2.5{:}1$$

$$20X5 \ \frac{60,000}{40,000} \ : \ = 1.5{:}1$$

$$20X6 \ \frac{75,000}{40,000} \ : \ = 1.9{:}1$$

$$20X7 \ \frac{100,000}{40,000} \ : \ = 2.5{:}1$$

The new plant is working at only one-fifth of its capacity during 20X5, and the result is that NCA turnover declines to 1.5:1. Only when both new and old plant are working at full capacity in 20X7 is the ratio restored to 2.5:1.

5.5 Total asset turnover ratio

Management is responsible for making the most effective use of a company's available resources to achieve their corporate goals, whether these are maximisation of profit, shareholder value or any other agreed goal. The total asset turnover ratio seeks to measure management's ability to make effective use of its asset base to generate sales. This is important, as the ability to generate sales is key to business survival and success. The total asset turnover ratio is derived as follows.

$$\text{Total asset turnover} = \frac{\text{Sales}}{\text{Average total assets}} : 1$$

The ratio indicates the monetary unit of sales generated per monetary unit of average total assets. Generally, a higher ratio is preferred, as the higher the ratio, the better the return on total assets. A decline in the ratio suggests that assets are under-utilised and may indicate they should either be used more effectively or sold. One drawback of the calculation is that it produces a more favourable ratio for companies using older assets. Older assets are likely to have a relatively low book or carrying value, as they will have been depreciated over time.

Consider the following results that were extracted from Louisa plc for the year ended 30 June.

	20X7	20X6
	£,000	£,000
Sales	7,000	6,000
Assets	3,895	2,890

On 1 July 20X5, Louisa plc's total assets were £2,710,000.

The comparative total asset turnover ratios would be as follows.

20X2	20X1
$\dfrac{7,000}{(3,895+2,890) \times 0.5}$	$\dfrac{6,000}{(2,890+2,710) \times 0.5}$
2.06 : 1	2.14 : 1

The ratio may be expressed either in the above form or as an amount of sales per £1 invested (i.e. sales were £2.14 per £1 invested in 20X1 and £2.06 per £1 invested in 20X2). It is therefore apparent that a 3.7% reduction in asset utilisation has occurred from 20X6 to 20X7.

5.6 Profit ratios

The profit ratios were introduced in Chapter 8, section 6.1. As a reminder, the primary profit ratios are as follows.

$$\text{Gross profit margin} = \frac{\text{Gross profit}}{\text{Sales}} \times 100$$

$$\text{Operating profit margin} = \frac{\text{Operating profit}}{\text{Sales}} \times 100$$

The expectation that the gross profit margin should remain relatively stable, irrespective of the level of production and sales, is based on the assumption that all costs deducted when computing gross profit are directly variable with sales. This is explored further in Worked Example 9.5 and throughout the rest of this section.

> **WORKED EXAMPLE 9.5**
>
> Chester is a trader who purchases frame tents for £40 each and sells them, through a mail order catalogue, at a price of £50 each. During 20X6 and 20X7, sales amounted to 1,000 tents and 2,000 tents, respectively. There is no opening or closing stock.
>
> **Required**
> Prepare Chester's trading account for 20X6 and 20X7, and calculate the gross profit margin for each year.
>
> **Answer**
>
> | Trading account | 20X7 £ | 20X6 £ |
> |---|---|---|
> | Sales | 100,000 | 50,000 |
> | Less: Cost of goods sold | (80,000) | (40,000) |
> | Gross profit | 20,000 | 10,000 |
> | Gross profit margin | 20% | 20% |
>
> Sales have doubled in 20X7. Because the cost of goods sold are directly variable with sales, they have also doubled. This has resulted in gross profit twice the 20X6 level. Although the actual gross profit has doubled, the gross profit margin remains unchanged at 20%.

A stable gross profit margin may be usual for a retail trader like Chester, but is less likely for a manufacturer. This is because the cost of goods sold figure for a manufacturing company is likely to fluctuate, due to the impact of variable costs on the profit margin. However, any large variation in the gross profit margin would require careful investigation. Possible causes include the following.

5.6.1 Price cuts (selling price)

A company may need to reduce its selling price to achieve the desired increase in sales. For example, let's assume that Chester had to reduce the selling price from £50 to £48 to sell 4,000 tents in 20X8. The revised trading account would be as follows.

Trading account	20X7 £
Sales	192,000
Less: Cost of goods sold	(160,000)
Gross profit	32,000
Gross profit margin	16.67%

5.6.2 Cost increases

The cost of goods purchased from suppliers, during a period of inflation, is likely to rise. If these costs rise but the selling price remains the same, a company will experience a reduction in its gross profit margin. Let's assume Chester had to pay an additional £4 for each of its tents in 20X7 such that the unit price rose to £44 per tent and the original selling price of £50 remains unchanged.

Trading account	20X7 £
Sales	100,000
Less: Cost of goods sold	(88,000)
Gross profit	12,000
Gross profit margin	12%

5.6.3 Changes in mix

A change in the range or mix of products sold results in an overall change in the gross profit margin, assuming individual product lines earn different gross profit percentages.

5.6.4 Undervaluation or overvaluation of inventory

If closing inventory is undervalued, this results in the cost of goods sold being overstated and profit understated. An incorrect valuation might be the result of an error during the stocktaking process, or the result of a more serious misdemeanour, such as fraud. For example, a business might intentionally undervalue inventory to reduce the amount of tax payable (lower profit means lower tax). It must, of course, be remembered that the closing inventory of one period is the opening inventory of the next, so the effect of errors may be reversed in the following period.

5.6.5 Rate of return on gross assets (ROA)

The rate of return on gross assets (ROA) is often alternatively described as the rate of return on capital employed.

The problem with the latter description is that the term 'capital employed' is used, in accounting, to signify at least two different financial totals:

- shareholders' equity;
- gross or net assets.

The rate of ROA, which is calculated as follows.

$$\text{Rate of ROA} = \frac{\text{Profit before interest}}{\text{Average gross assets}} \times 100$$

6   Pyramid of ratios

6.1 Relationship between accounting ratios

A common weakness when analysing company reports with ratios is the failure to examine the relationship between the various ratios that have been calculated. One particularly important relationship is expressed in what is known as the DuPont formula, a three part method used to assess a company's return on equity (ROE). The DuPont analysis is based on the assumption that ROE is effected by three key elements: operating efficiency, asset use efficiency and financial leverage. Linking these three ratios provides the investor with a clearer picture of which component has the greatest effect on the ROE. This is separated into primary and secondary ratios below.

Secondary ratios   *Primary ratios*

Total asset turnover × Operating profit margin = Rate of ROA

Management endeavours to maximise the return earned on gross assets, and it can accomplish this objective in two ways. Firstly, management can aim to increase the net profit percentage. Secondly, management can endeavour to achieve a higher rate of asset utilisation. It may be the case that that greater asset utilisation – for instance, more sales – can only be achieved by lowering prices. Management has to decide whether the increased volume of activity is sufficient to justify the lower gross and net margins that result from implementing a policy of price reduction.

WORKED EXAMPLE 9.6

Holly and Head run separate businesses in different geographical areas, marketing a similar product for which there exists a ready market. They meet at a conference and are interested to discover that, whereas Holly keeps prices low in order to keep the business operating at full capacity, Head supplies goods only at 'normal prices for the industry'. They decide to compare their results and extract the following information from recently published accounts.

	Holly	Head
	£	£
Operating profit	50,000	100,000
Sales	600,000	750,000
Average total assets	200,000	500,000
Profit before interest (i.e. operating profit)	50,000	100,000

Required
Calculate the 'primary' and 'secondary' ratios (per the DuPont formula) of Holly and Head.

Answer
Applying the formula:

	Secondary ratios					**Primary ratios**	
	Total asset turnover	×	Operating profit margin	× 100	=	ROA	
Holly =	$\dfrac{\text{Sales}}{\text{Average total assets}}$	×	$\dfrac{\text{Profit before interest}}{\text{Sales}}$	× 100	=	$\dfrac{\text{Profit before interest}}{\text{Average total assets}}$	
	$\dfrac{600{,}000}{200{,}000}$	×	$\dfrac{50{,}000}{600{,}000}$	× 100	=	$\dfrac{50{,}000}{200{,}000}$	× 100
	3	×	8.33%		=	25.00%	
Head =	$\dfrac{750{,}000}{500{,}000}$	×	$\dfrac{100{,}000}{750{,}000}$	× 100	=	$\dfrac{100{,}000}{500{,}000}$	× 100
	1.5	×	13.33%		=	20.00%	

The above calculations show that Holly achieves a greater asset utilisation (£3 of sales per £1 invested, as compared with the £1.50 achieved by Head), but its operating profit percentage is lower (8.3% compared with Head's 13.3%). Overall, Holly's policies seem to be more successful (i.e. the greater asset utilisation more than compensates for the lower margins, and achieves a rate of return on gross assets of 25%).

 **TEST YOUR KNOWLEDGE 9.6**

Explain the nature and purpose of the DuPont formula.

STOP AND THINK 9.1

Do you think companies should publish financial ratios rather than leaving the user to calculate them?

? END OF CHAPTER QUESTIONS

9.1 The minority-shareholding in Merino Ltd is 20%. The company manufactures kitchen implements that are sold to retail chains and through a cash sales outlet from the company's factory premises. The minority shareholders are unsure whether this company is being well managed and have asked for your help in studying the accounts.

The minority shareholders tell you that the mark-up is usually 100% on cost in this type of business, of which about two-thirds of costs are allocated to overheads. The minority shareholders have also discovered that external liabilities are normally about one-quarter of equity and that interest normally comprises about 20% of operating profit. The following financial information is available for Merino Ltd.

Consolidated statement of profit or loss and other comprehensive income for the year to 31 December 20X6:

	£,000
Sales	5,500
Cost of sales	(2,700)
Gross profit	2,800
Administration expenses	(375)
Distribution costs	(1,175)
Operating profit	1,250
Interest costs	(300)
Profit before tax	950
Tax	(220)
Profit for the year	730

Statement of financial position at 31 December 20X6:

	£,000	£,000
NCAs		6,000
Current assets		
Inventory	235	
Trade receivables	235	
Cash and cash equivalents	230	700
Total assets		6,700
Equity and liabilities		
Share capital		1,835
Retained earnings		1,230
		3,065

Non-current liabilities

Debentures		3,000
Current liabilities		
Trade payables	405	
Taxation	230	635
Total liabilities		3,635
Total equity and liabilities		6,700

Required

a Calculate:
   i three ratios based on the above accounts which examine the management of working capital;
   ii three ratios based on the above accounts which examine the profitability of the company; and
   iii two ratios based on the above accounts which examine the capital structure of the company.
   Wherever possible, the ratios calculated should be those in respect of which comparative data is available.

b Set out a discussion of the financial position and performance of Merino Ltd based on the results of your calculations under a) and the information provided in the question.

9.2 The following information is provided for Tanner Ltd and Spanner Ltd, which supply a similar range of products but are located in different geographical areas and are not in competition with one another.

	Tanner £,000	Spanner £,000
Operating profit	1,000	1,200
Turnover	7,200	9,000
Average investment in total assets	2,400	6,000

The following accounting ratios are provided by the trade association to which they each belong. The ratios are averages for members of the association.

Gross asset turnover	2
Operating profit percentage	14%
Operating profit on total assets	21%

❔ END OF CHAPTER QUESTIONS *continued*

Required

a   Provide separate calculations for Tanner Ltd and Spanner Ltd of the accounting ratios equivalent to those provided by the trade association.

b   An explanation of the relationship between the three ratios and advice about how the relationship might be explored in greater depth.

c   An analysis of the performance of Tanner Ltd and Spanner Ltd by comparison with members of the trade association and with each other.

Note

Calculations should be to one decimal place.

9.3   You are given the following financial information for XYZ Ltd in the following table.

£,000	20X7	20X6	20X5	20X4
Sales	290	190	160	90
Net assets	420	340	280	190
Total assets	1140	950	880	680

Required

Using the net asset turnover ratio and the total asset turnover ratio, calculate the ratios and comment on the efficiency of asset usage of the company.

9.4   A company has 90 days' inventory outstanding, 60 days' receivables outstanding and 70 days' payables outstanding.

Required

Calculate the cash operating cycle of the business.

10 Analysis and interpretation of accounts 2

■ CONTENTS

■ LEARNING OUTCOMES

This chapter discusses further topics related to the analysis and interpretation of accounts. After reading and understanding the contents of the chapter, working through all the worked examples and practice questions, you should be able to:

■ understand the purpose and explanations for segmental and cash flow ratios;
■ understand how to analyse and interpret cash flow ratios;
■ analyse using various investor ratios;
■ carry out inter-company comparison; and
■ discuss and calculate various measures of earnings per share (EPS).

1   Introduction

As discussed in Chapters 8 and 9, accounting ratios enable users and analysts to assess company financial performance. In this chapter we discuss further uses of ratios by looking at segmental analysis of ratios, and investor ratios that cast light on shareholder returns and the efficiency of company finances by looking at various measures of cash flow ratios.

2   Segmental accounting and analysis

The primary purpose of all profit-making businesses is to make profit. The continued success of a business is dependent upon sustained and satisfactory levels of income. This requires good decision-making and performance evaluation. The statement of profit or loss and other comprehensive income, while serving many purposes, is primarily a tool for performance evaluation by the varied stakeholders.

Businesses make financial disclosures on a number of items in the financial reports. While financial results can be reported in a number of ways, International Financial Reporting Standard (IFRS) 8 and International Accounting Standard (IAS) 14 provide the basis for financial disclosure of activities of different business segments (segmental activity). IFRS 8 defines reportable and operating segments, while IAS 14 defines the requirements for financial disclosure.

The purpose of segmental accounting and segmental analysis is to account for, and analyse, the performance of an identifiable part or segment of a business. IAS 14 defines reportable segments on the basis of geographical segments and product segments.

Two primary ways of analysing segments are the full cost approach and marginal contribution approach. These two management accounting techniques are used to help analyse the performance of a business segment.

2.1 Full cost approach

From a segmental perspective, there are two types of expenses incurred by a business: direct and indirect.

Direct expenses are those expenses of a segment that are directly traceable to a business segment. The closure of a segment would mean those costs would then not be incurred. Indirect expenses are expenses common to the overall business entity. These expenses are not directly caused by any one particular segment, but arise due to the overall functioning of a business entity.

The key characteristic of indirect expenses from a segmental viewpoint is that they must be allocated in order to measure the net income of a segment. Examples of indirect expenses include:

- salaries of senior management (e.g. the chief executive officer (CEO));
- head office operating expenses;
- insurance on head office and head office equipment; and
- salaries of head office staff.

The underlying theoretical consideration for the full cost approach is that all expenses, regardless of where and why they have been incurred, must be charged to the segments that benefit directly and indirectly. As such, these types of expenses must be allocated using some basis. Because various methods of allocation are available and because different methods result in different allocation percentages, the allocated cost may be perceived to be somewhat arbitrary. Some of the methods used to allocate indirect expenses include:

- sales by value;
- number of employees;
- assets employed;
- floor space occupied.

The method(s) used should be based on a logical apportionment on an equitable basis. Inappropriate use of methods would tend to give the wrong impression of financial performance of segments of a business.

The basic principles of the full cost approach are summarised as follows:

a   The objective is to measure net income of each operating segment.
b   Overall net income of the business is the sum of the segmental net income.
c   All indirect expenses must be allocated across each segment.
d   Allocation of indirect expenses involves selecting bases of allocation.

The segmental net income approach may be defined mathematically as follows:

Segmental net income = segmental sales – direct expenses – allocated indirect expenses
Or:
SNI = S – DE – AIE

Direct expenses are those expenses that can be traced directly to the business segment. Variable expenses are activity-based expenses and are directly traceable to a segment. Fixed expenses may be direct or indirect, and can also be allocated or not to a segment depending on their nature. This is examined in the next section. The contractual nature of fixed expenses must be examined carefully to determine whether or not the expense is direct.

2.2 Segmental contribution approach

A problem with the full cost approach when applied to a segment is that it is technically possible for a segment to show an operating loss, yet at the same time be making a positive contribution to net income. In other words, if the seemingly unprofitable segment is closed, it is possible that the overall net income of the business will decrease. To avoid this shortcoming of the full cost approach, many businesses prefer to use the contribution approach to measuring segmental profitability.

The segmental contribution approach, as indicated by its name, measures segmental contribution. This contribution may simply be defined as sales less direct expenses. Note that segmental contribution differs from contribution margin, which is sales less variable expenses. As some fixed expenses can be direct expenses, segmental contribution and contribution margin are not the same.

The principles of the segmental contribution approach are as follows.

a   Only the contribution of each segment is computed. No attempt is made to compute the net income of the segment.
b   Indirect expenses of each segment are not allocated.
c   Indirect expenses, however, are usually deducted from total segmental contribution in order to arrive at overall business net income.
d   A segment is considered profitable if sales of the segment exceed the direct expenses of the segment.

The segmental contribution approach may be presented mathematically as follows:

Segmental contribution (SC) = Segmental sales (SS) – Direct expenses (DE)

This may be expressed as:

1   $SC = SS - DE$
2   $DE = V(Q) + FD$
3   $SS = P(Q)$

Where:

- DE = direct expenses
- P = price of the product in the segment
- V = variable cost rate for the segment
- Q = units of sales in a specific segment
- FD = direct fixed expenses of the segment.

Therefore, the equation above may be restated as follows:

$SC = P(Q) - V(Q) - FD$

It is apparent from this second equation that the principles of cost–volume–profit analysis apply to segmental decision-making. Variable costs are always direct costs. When activity ceases, variable costs cease. When activity increases, variable costs by definition increase. Indirect expenses are almost always fixed expenses.

The indirect expenses allocated to a segment will continue to be incurred, regardless of whether the segment is continued or discontinued. Therefore, as long as the segment is making a contribution towards indirect fixed expenses, continuing operations at least in the short run makes the business better off.

WORKED EXAMPLE 10.1

The following example illustrates the basic principles of the full cost and segmental contribution approaches.

Full cost approach

	Alpha	Beta	Total
	£	£	£
Sales	40,000	30,000	70,000
Expenses			
Cost of goods sold	24,000	18,000	42,000
Sales salaries	6,000	9,000	15,000
Executive salaries	6,000	5,000	11,000
Total expenses	36,000	32,000	68,000
Net income/(loss)	4,000	(2,000)	2,000

![calc] WORKED EXAMPLE	**10.1** *continued*

Segmental contribution approach

	Alpha	Beta	Total
	£	£	£
Sales	40,000	30,000	70,000
Direct expenses			
Cost of goods sold	24,000	18,000	42,000
Sales salaries	6,000	9,000	15,000
Total direct expenses	30,000	27,000	57,000
Segmental contribution	10,000	3,000	13,000
Indirect expenses			
Executive salaries			11,000
Net income/loss			2,000

In the above example, cost of goods sold and sales salaries are direct expenses of each segment. Executive salaries are an indirect expense. This expense needs to be charged to the segments by being allocated on some (ideally logical) basis. However, under the segmental contribution approach, indirect expenses are not allocated.

Let's consider, from the above example, how allocations were made under the full cost approach. Under this approach, segment Alpha was allocated £6,000 of the executive salaries cost and segment Beta £5,000. As a consequence, segment Beta is operating at a net loss of £2,000. It may seem logical to close down segment B, as the business would be better off by £2,000. However, the segmental contribution approach shows that segment B is making a contribution of £3,000. Secondly, it can be seen that executive salaries were allocated in the ratio of 57:43. The allocation percentages were determined by dividing segmental sales by total sales.

Segmental analysis provides management with the tools to isolate and analyse the performance of each sector (whether the sector is based on a geographical basis or product basis). By examining trends and results carefully in each segment, management is able to understand the value of each sector better, and make better-informed decisions.

3 Rate of return on shareholders' equity

The factor that motivates shareholders to invest in a company is the expectation of an adequate return on their funds. Shareholders will periodically assess the rate of return earned in order to decide whether to continue with their investment. The rate of return on shareholders' equity is generally referred to as ROSE (return on shareholders' equity), and is derived as follows:

$$\text{ROSE} = \frac{{}^{*}\text{Earnings for equity shareholders}}{\text{Average shareholders' equity}} \times 100$$

*The ROSE ratio may be based on a pre- or post-tax basis but, whichever basis is used, any preference dividends payable must be deducted, since they reduce profits available for ordinary shareholders. An argument for using the pre-tax basis is that the resulting ratio can be related more meaningfully to the other calculations demonstrated in this chapter. On the other hand, corporation tax must be deducted to arrive at the balance available for distribution to shareholders and the post-tax basis implies full recognition of this fact.

WORKED EXAMPLE 10.2

The following information was extracted from the financial statements of Ludlow plc for the year ended 31 December:

	20X2 £,000	20X1 £,000
Pre-tax earnings	355	345
Post-tax earnings	177	173
Shareholders' equity	2,350	2,250

The shareholders' equity on 1 January 20X1 was £2,155,000.

Required

Calculate the ROSE equity for each year (for both pre-tax and post-tax earnings).

Answer

ROSE – Pre-tax earnings basis

$$20X1 \quad \frac{345}{(2,155 + 2,250)\, 0.5} \times 100 \quad 15.66\%$$

$$20X2 \quad \frac{355}{(2,250 + 2,350)\, 0.5} \times 100 \quad 15.43\%$$

ROSE – Post-tax earnings basis

$$20X1 \quad \frac{173}{(2,155 + 2,250)\, 0.5} \times 100 \quad 7.85\%$$

$$20X2 \quad \frac{177}{(2,250 + 2,350)\, 0.5} \times 100 \quad 7.70\%$$

There has been a modest decline in the return earned for shareholders. The return earned for shareholders is dependent on three key factors:

1 profit margins;
2 asset utilisation;
3 capital structure.

In the previous chapter, we explained that the rate of return on gross assets is a function of profit margins and asset utilisation. However, this measure takes no account of the company's capital structure (this can be confirmed by observing the fact that the numerator comprises net profit *before* deducting any interest charges). We explain the significance for the equity shareholders of financing a part of a company's activities with loan capital later, in the section covering gearing.

4 Inter-company comparison

Ratio analysis facilitates inter-company comparison by providing data from different companies that enables differences and similarities between firms and between sectors to be measured. An inter-company comparison provides the relevant data for the comparison of the performance of different firms and/or sectors. The comparison enables judgments to be made using relative performance.

Inter-firm comparisons enable variances and trends to be identified and tracked over time. If a company's performance ratios are inferior to other companies in the same sector, the comparison will show this, and enable management to investigate and take action to remedy the situation.

The analysis of ratios from different companies enables relative comparison of overall financial health, profitability and operational efficiency, depending upon the ratios included in the comparison. This helps ensure management has the information required to manage the company effectively, including optimum utilisation of a company's assets.

Table 10.1 offers some comparisons of the food retail sector and indicates the top retailers with their respective results in the form of return on assets (ROA) and after-tax profit margins.

TABLE 10.1 Ratios for Tesco and Sainsbury's – 2011

Company	Business sector	ROA	Profit margin	EPS	ROCE
Tesco	Retailer clothing, food and financial services	4.00%	5.72%	33.3p	12.90%
J Sainsbury	Retailer clothing, food and financial services	5.90%	3.61%	34.4p	8.00%

Note:

- ROA = Return on assets
- EPS = Earnings per share
- ROCE = Return on capital employed

Table 10.1 provides some level of inter-company comparison for two UK retail giants. The two companies have similar ratios but overall, based on these ratios, Tesco has performed better than J Sainsbury.

The ROA is lower for Tesco than J Sainsbury. Investigation of this may reveal that the ROA reflects a higher level of investment in fixed assets made by Tesco.

Tesco's higher profit margin could be interpreted to mean that Tesco has been more efficient with costs and has negotiated lower prices with suppliers than J Sainsbury.

J Sainsbury has achieved a higher EPS (discussed later in this chapter), and Tesco achieved a higher ROCE.

This snapshot of ratios would require more detailed analysis and investigation before any definite conclusions could be drawn. Management could use the comparison as a starting point for investigation. For example, J Sainsbury management may want to investigate why their profit margin is lower than Tesco and take remedial action. Similarly, J Sainsbury's ROCE is also much lower than Tesco's and this will also warrant further examination.

5   Cash flow-based accounting ratios

The usefulness of financial statements is enhanced by an examination of the relationship between them, and also by comparison with previous time periods, other entities and expected performance. We have seen that value can be further added through the calculation and interpretation of accounting ratios. An examination of accounting textbooks and the pages of accounting periodicals reveals an enthusiasm for rehearsing the potential of 'accounting ratios', demonstrated through calculations of the net profit margin, return on capital employed, current ratio and a host of other 'traditional' measures based on the contents of the consolidated statement of profit or loss and other comprehensive income and statement of financial position. None of these focuses on cash flow.

Traditional ratios suffer from the same defect as the financial statements (the statement of profit or loss and other comprehensive income and statement of financial position) on which they are based. Such ratios are the result of comparing figures that have been computed using accounting conventions which include the use of estimates and judgment. Given the difficulty of deciding the length of the period over which non-current assets (NCAs) should be written off, whether the tests which justify the capitalisation of development expenditure have been satisfied or the amount of the provision to be made for claims under a manufacturer's 12-month guarantee (to give just a few examples), ratios based on such figures won't always provide an accurate picture.

This is not to suggest that the traditional ratios are irrelevant. Clearly this is not so, as they reveal important relationships and trends that are not apparent from the examination of individual figures appearing in the accounts. However, given the fact that cash flow ratios contain at least one element that is factual (the numerator, the denominator or both), their historic lack of prominence in accounting literature and their limited use in the business world is puzzling.

The principal focus for informed investment decisions is cash flows, whether the capital project appraisal method is 'pay-back' or one of the more sophisticated discounted cash flow-based techniques, namely 'net present value' and 'internal rate of return'. Turning to performance evaluation, however, the emphasis usually shifts to techniques such as return on capital employed.

Below are presented:

1   ratios that link the cash flow statement with the consolidated statement of profit or loss and other comprehensive income and statement of financial position; and
2   ratios based entirely on the contents of the cash flow statement.

To illustrate these calculations, the results of XYZ plc for 20X1 and 20X2 are shown in Figure 10.1. For each ratio, both the calculation and a discussion of its significance are presented. Inevitably, there will be some overlap in the messages conveyed by the various ratios presented. This may be due to similarities in the nature of the calculations or to the fact that the results of just one company are used for illustration purposes. The application of the same ratios to different financial facts might well yield additional valuable insights.

The following information is provided as at 31 December 20X0:

- property, plant and equipment at cost, £2,700,000;
- current assets, £1,802,000;
- payables and taxation, £838,000; and
- Called-up share capital, £1,400,000.

Note: XYZ raised a loan of £1 million during 20X2. This, together with the already existing loan, is repayable by ten equal annual instalments commencing in 20X3.

5.1 Ratios linking the cash flow statement with the two other principal financial statements

Cash generated from operations to current liabilities:

$$\text{Cash generated from operations to current liabilities} = \frac{\text{Cash generated from operations}}{\text{Average current liabilities}} \times 100$$

Where:

- cash generated from operations is taken directly from the cash flow statement published to comply with IAS 7; and
- average current liabilities are computed from the opening and closing statement of financial position.

This ratio examines the liquidity of the company by providing a measure of the extent to which current liabilities are covered by cash flowing into the business from normal operating activities. The ratio is thought by some to be superior to the statement of financial position-based ratios, such as the liquidity ratio, as a measure of short-term solvency. This is because statement of financial position ratios are based on a static positional statement (the 'instantaneous financial photograph') and are therefore subject to manipulation by, for example, running down inventory immediately prior to the year-end and not replacing them until the next accounting period. Ratios based on statements of financial position may alternatively be affected by unusual events that cause particular items to be abnormally large or small. In either case, the resulting ratios will not reflect normal conditions.

Cash flow statement (using indirect method)

	20X2 £,000	20X1 £,000
Cash flows from operating activities		
Operating profit	501	420
Depreciation charges	660	600
Increase/decrease in inventory	(305)	250
Increase/decrease in receivables	(184)	220
Increase in payables	420	120
Cash generated from operations	1,092	1,610
Interest paid	(150)	(50)
Dividends paid	(160)	(60)
Taxation paid	(130)	(210)
Net cash generated from operating activities	652	1,290
Cash flows from investing activities		
Purchase of property, plant and equipment	(1,620)	(900)
Cash flows from financing activities		
Proceeds from issue of loan	1,000	100
Net increase in cash	32	490

Statement of profit or loss and other comprehensive income extracts

	20X2	20X1
Operating profit	501	420
Interest paid	(150)	(50)
Profit before tax	351	370
Taxation	(125)	(115)
Profit for the year	226	225
Extracts from statements of changes to equity		
Dividends paid	(175)	(145)
Retained profit for the year	51	80

Statement of financial position at 31 December

	20X2 £,000	20X1 £,000
Assets		
Property, plant and equipment at cost	5,220	3,600
Less: accumulated depreciation	(2,360)	(1,700)
	2,860	1,900
Current assets (including cash)	1,893	1,372
Total assets	4,753	3,272
Equity and liabilities		
Called up share capital (£1 ordinary shares)	1,400	1,400
Share premium account	250	250
Retained earnings	333	282
	1,983	1,932
Non-current liabilities		
10% loan repayable 20X3–Y2	1,350	500
Current liabilities		
Loan repayment due	150	–
Tax	125	115
Payables	1,145	725
Total current liabilities	1,420	840
Total equities and liabilities	4,753	3,272

FIGURE 10.1 Draft accounts of XYZ plc for 20X2 and 20X1

Calculations for XYZ plc

Cash generated from operations to average current liabilities:

20X2

$$\frac{1{,}092}{(1{,}420 + 840)\,0.5} \times 100$$

$$96.64\%$$

20X1

$$\frac{1{,}610}{(840 + 838)\,0.5} \times 100$$

$$191.90\%$$

There has been a significant decrease in this ratio between 20X1 and 20X2, falling to half of the previous level. The decrease reflects a reduction in the operating cash flow plus a rise in the average current liabilities. Nevertheless, the current liabilities (which include taxation which may not be payable until the next financial year) remain adequately covered by cash flow on the assumption that this aspect of XYZ's financial affairs is repeated in the year 20X3.

5.2 Cash recovery rate

The cash recovery rate (CRR) is a measure of the rate at which a company recovers its investment in non-current assets (NCAs). The quicker the recovery period, the lower the risk. The CRR is effectively the reciprocal of the pay-back period used for capital project appraisal purposes, assuming projects have equal (or roughly equal) annual cash flows. The CRR is derived as follows:

$$\text{Cash recovery rate} = \frac{\text{Cash flow from operations}}{\text{Average gross assets}} \times 100$$

Where:

- cash flow from operations is made up of 'cash generated from operations' together with any proceeds from the disposal of NCAs; and
- gross assets (current and NCAs) is the average gross value (before deducting accumulated depreciation) of the entity's assets over an accounting period.

However, the statement of financial position usually shows the carrying value of NCAs. A search of the notes is needed to find the gross value. Assets are required to generate a return that is ultimately, if not immediately, in the form of cash.

The CRR for XYZ plc is as follows:

20X2	**20X1**
$\dfrac{1{,}092}{(7{,}113 + 4{,}972)\,0.5} \times 100$	$\dfrac{1{,}610}{(4{,}972 + 4{,}502)\,0.5} \times 100$
18.07%	33.99%

The CRR has also fallen by almost half over the period. The implication is that the company is now taking almost twice as long in 20X2 to recover its investment in business assets than in 20X1.

5.3 Cash flow per share

Cash flow per share represents the net operating cash a company generates per share. As it is the actual cash generated it is deemed less likely to be manipulated as the earnings in the EPS ratio. Consequently, some analysts find it to be a more reliable measure of a company's financial situation than the EPS metric.

$$\text{Cash flow per share} = \frac{\text{Net cash flow from operating activities}}{\text{Weighted average number of shares}}$$

This ratio provides a general indication of a company's ability to fund long-term investment out of resources generated internally. A higher cash flow per share is preferred, as it is often deemed to be a measure of good performance. However, this may not always accurately reflect a company's overall financial position or strength.

The number of shares used as the denominator should be the weighted average of the number in issue during the year. However, the average needs to be weighted only if there is an issue of shares involving an inflow of resources; in the case of a bonus issue (where no extra resources are generated), the number of shares post-bonus issue should be used without weighting and the number in issue the previous year made comparable.

The comparative cash flow per share for XYZ plc is as follows.

20X2	20X1
£652	£1,290
1,400 shares	1,400 shares
0.47	0.92
47p	92p

The significant decline in the cash flow per share reflects the significant disinvestment in working capital that occurred in 20X1.

5.4 Capital expenditure per share

The capital expenditure per share measures the amount of capital expenditure which the company incurs in order to maintain its operating assets. Capital expenditure is the cash flows from investing activities.

This ratio, in conjunction with cash flow per share, can be used in order to provide a general indication of whether a business is a net generator of cash or whether it is cash-hungry. The ratio is derived as follows.

$$\text{Cash expenditure per share} = \frac{\text{Cash flow from investing activities}}{\text{Weighted average number of shares}}$$

The comparative capital expenditure per share for XYZ plc is as follows:

20X2	20X1
£1,620	£900
1,400 shares	1,400 shares
1.16	0.64
116p	64p

The capital expenditure per share has risen dramatically, by 80%, and indicates the cash hunger and consumption of the business has caused a need to seek alternative sources to fund investments made during 20X2.

5.5 Debt service coverage ratio

The debt service coverage ratio (DSCR) seeks to measure the ability of a company to meet its debt and interest commitments from pure earnings. EBITDA (earnings before interest, tax, depreciation and amortisation) is taken as a pure non distorted measure of earnings. The DSCR is determined as follows.

$$\frac{\text{EBITDA}}{\text{Annual debt repayment and interest charges}}$$

The greater the DSCR, the less exposed a company is likely to be to external changes in interest rate changes and other external risks. One limitation of DSCR, particularly when comparing different years, is that it does not take into account variations in the level of capital repayments – these can vary considerably, depending on the period of the loan repayment and the capital project.

The comparative DSCR for XYZ plc is as follows.

20X2	20X1
$\dfrac{501 + 660}{150 + 150}$	$\dfrac{420 + 600}{50 + 150}$
3.87 times	5.1 times

The DSCR for 20X1 is strong, with EBITDA providing 5.1x coverage of the prospective interest charges. For 20X2, the ratio declines to 3.9x, but still shows debt commitments to be comfortably covered out of internally generated cash flow. The multiple also suggests that there is surplus cash available to meet working capital requirements and for tax and dividend payments and capital expenditure. Note that repayment of the capital of the loan does not start until 2013.

5.6 Ratios based entirely on the contents of the cash flow statement

It is possible to add to the interpretative value of the cash flow statement by expressing some of the financial totals contained in the cash flow statement as ratios of one another. As is always the case with ratio analysis, the usefulness of a ratio depends on the existence of an expected relationship between the financial magnitudes being compared. A number of valid ratios could be computed, and two are presented below to illustrate the possibilities available. We will now calculate some key ratios from the cash flow statement of XYZ plc presented in Figure 10.1.

5.7 The internal : external finance ratio

The relationship between internal finance and external debt finance may be examined by expressing net cash generated from operations as a ratio of external financing (cash flows from financing activities). A low ratio indicates the company is reliant on external funding. A ratio that falls indicates increased reliance on external finance, perhaps for the purpose of further investment.

The comparative internal : external finance ratio for XYZ plc is as follows.

	20X2	20X1
internal : external finance ratio	652 : 1,000	1,290 : 100
	0.65 : 1	12.9 : 1

It is evident that the sources of finance XYZ plc used changed significantly. XYZ plc increased their dependence upon external finance in 20X2. This is reflected in the statement of financial position by a revision of the long-term capital structure of the company, which could be further examined by computing leverage ratios.

5.8 The shareholder funding ratio

The shareholder funding ratio measures the extent to which capital investment has been funded internally by the shareholders. This ratio is determined as follows:

Shareholder funding ratio = Net cash generated from operating activities : expenditure on NCAs

The comparative results for XYZ plc are as follows:

20X2	**20X1**
652 : 1,620	1,290 : 900
0.40 : 1	1.4 : 1

The shareholders of XYZ plc comfortably funded the entire business investment in 20X1, leaving a significant surplus to improve the company's liquidity position. However, in 20X2, only 40% of expenditure on non-current assets was funded internally. XYZ plc relied primarily upon debt to fund the investment programme undertaken during 20X2.

5.9 Review

The purpose of the cash flow statement is to improve the informative value of published financial reports. The sections above have demonstrated the contribution of two types of calculation:

a   ratios that link the cash flow statement with key related items appearing in the statement of financial position; and

b   ratios that explore the inter-relationship between items within the cash flow statement.

As usual, it should be noted that different ratios are expressed in different ways, as percentages, as multiples or in pence, as well as in the classic form. The interpretative value of individual ratios will depend upon the nature of the financial developments at a particular business. It is also the case that the messages conveyed by certain ratios may be similar for a particular company covering a particular year, but in a different time and place the same ratios may yield different insights.

Finally, one must remember the importance of not attaching too much weight to any single ratio but to use a representative range of ratios that combine cash flow ratios with traditional ratios to build up a meaningful business profile.

TEST YOUR KNOWLEDGE 10.2

Explain how ratios can be used to improve the informational value of the cash flow statement.

---

6   Earnings per share

The EPS calculation reveals the amount of profit accruing to the holder of one share in a company.

EPS is widely used as a measure of company performance, due to:

■ the belief that earnings are an important determinant of share price. They may set an upper limit for dividends, and, by comparing earnings with dividends, a measure of likely future growth from retained earnings can be obtained;

■ the popularity of the price/earnings ratio as an indicator of financial performance and also a method of business valuation; and

■ the determination of financial commentators to reduce the complexities of corporate activity to a single figure.

6.1 Definition of EPS

The nature, purpose and calculation of EPS are dealt with in IAS 33 'Earnings Per Share'. EPS may be defined as the earnings, in pence (for UK companies), attributable to each equity share, and is calculated using the following formula:

$$EPS = \frac{\text{Earnings}}{\text{No of equity shares in issue}}$$

Where:

- earnings = the profit (or in the case of a group the consolidated profit) of the period after tax, minority interests after deducting preference dividends and other appropriations in respect of preference shares; and
- shares = the number of equity shares in issue and ranking for dividend in respect of the period.

Further points to note:

- IAS 33 applies only to listed companies.
- When a loss is suffered, the EPS is a negative figure.
- The importance attached to EPS is reflected by the requirement for the current year's figure, together with the comparative for the previous year, to be displayed *on the face of the consolidated statement of profit or loss and other comprehensive income*. It cannot be 'tucked away' in the notes.

A company is permitted to disclose, in addition to basic earnings per share, a second calculation, the diluted EPS, based on a different figure for earnings and/or number of shares. An alternative disclosure is likely to occur where the directors consider that earnings have been affected by a non-recurrent transaction, so that exclusion of its effect produces a more useful indication of the projected performance of the enterprise. The revised figure is often referred to as the underlying earnings per share. The accounts should disclose how the revised earnings figure has been computed and the 'underlying' EPS must be given no greater prominence than the basic EPS.

An illustration of how the two figures might be reported is given in Figure 10.2 and is taken from the accounts of Tesco plc.

Full year 26 Feb	20X1 52 weeks	20X0 52 weeks
Revenue	67,573	62,537
Underlying profit from operations	3,754	3,424
Underlying operating margin	6.00%	5.90%
Joint ventures and associates	57	33
Profit from operations	3,811	3,457
Underlying profit before tax*	3,813	3,395
Profit before tax	3,535	3,176
Underlying EPS*	27.10p	29.31p
Basic EPS	27.14p	29.33p

FIGURE 10.2 Extract from financial statement of Tesco plc 20X0–X1

* Underlying profit excludes the impact of non-cash elements of IAS 17, 19, 32 and 39 (principally the impact of annual uplifts in rents and rent free period, pension cost, and the mark-to-market of financial instruments), the amortisation charge on intangible assets arising on acquisition, acquisition costs and the non-cash impact of International Financial Reporting Standards Interpretation Committee (IFRIC) 13. It also excludes costs relating to restructuring (US and Japan), closure costs (Vin Plus) and the impairment of goodwill in Japan.

Source: www.tescoplc.com/investors/financials/five-year-summary; http://ar2011.tescoplc.com/pdfs/tesco_annual_report_2011.pdf.

6.2 Calculation of EPS

We start with the basic calculation where no shares have been issued during the year.

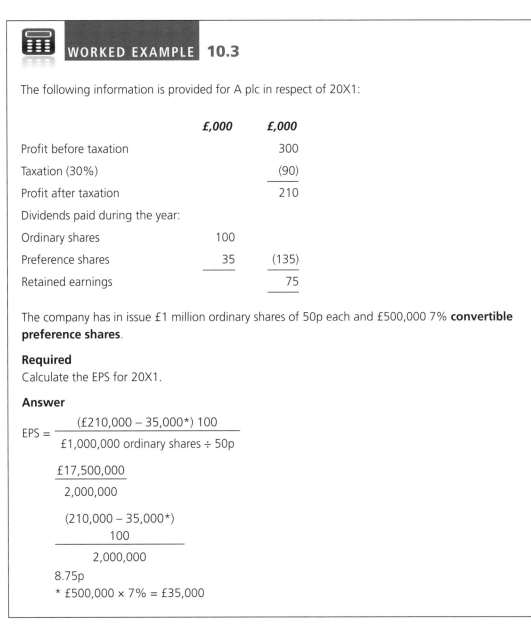

WORKED EXAMPLE **10.3**

The following information is provided for A plc in respect of 20X1:

	£,000	£,000
Profit before taxation		300
Taxation (30%)		(90)
Profit after taxation		210
Dividends paid during the year:		
Ordinary shares	100	
Preference shares	35	(135)
Retained earnings		75

The company has in issue £1 million ordinary shares of 50p each and £500,000 7% **convertible preference shares**.

Required
Calculate the EPS for 20X1.

Answer

$$EPS = \frac{(£210,000 - 35,000^*)\ 100}{£1,000,000\ \text{ordinary shares} \div 50p}$$

$$\frac{£17,500,000}{2,000,000}$$

$$\frac{(210,000 - 35,000^*)\ 100}{2,000,000}$$

8.75p
* £500,000 × 7% = £35,000

6.3 Share issues during the year

We now introduce the complication of a share issue being made during the current year. There are three possibilities:

1   an issue at full market price;
2   a bonus issue during the year; and
3   a rights issue during the year.

6.3.1 Issue at full market price

This increases both the number of shares in issue *and* the earnings capacity of the company. The earnings for the period must, therefore, be spread over the increased number of shares in issue. However, where the issue takes place partway through the year, it is necessary to calculate the average number of shares in issue during the year, on a weighted time basis, as the extra shares only increase earnings capacity *after* they have been issued.

 **WORKED EXAMPLE 10.4**

A plc (see Worked Example 10.3) issues a further 600,000 ordinary shares on 1 May 20X2. The profit for the year for the year ended 31 December 20X2 is £280,000.

Required
Calculate the EPS for 20X2.

Answer

$$EPS = \frac{(£280,000 - 35,000)\ 100}{(2,000,000 \times 4/12ths) + (2,600,000 \times 8/12ths)}$$

$$\frac{£24,500,000}{2,400,000\ shares}$$

$$10.21p$$

6.3.2 Bonus issue

A bonus issue of shares to current shareholders of a company produces no cash and so will not increase the available resources nor affect earnings capacity. The effect of the issue, therefore, is to spread the earnings over a greater number of shares. Because the bonus issue does not increase earnings capacity, there is no need to calculate a weighted average for the shares in issue during the year. Therefore, the date of the bonus issue, if given in a question, is irrelevant and can be ignored. However, it is necessary to restate the comparative EPS figure, for the previous year, in order to place it on a 'like for like' basis.

 **WORKED EXAMPLE 10.5**

The results of A plc for 20X1 are shown below. During 20X2, A plc makes a bonus issue of one additional ordinary share for every two shares presently held. Profits after tax for the year for 20X2 are £280,000.

	£,000	£,000
Profit before taxation		300
Taxation (30%)		(90)
Profit for the year		210
Dividends paid during the year:		
Ordinary shares	100	
Preference shares	35	(135)
Retained earnings		75

Required
a Calculate the EPS for 20X2.
b Calculate the revised EPS for 20X1.

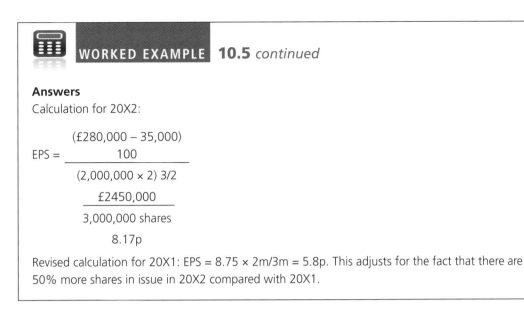

WORKED EXAMPLE **10.5** *continued*

Answers

Calculation for 20X2:

$$EPS = \frac{\dfrac{(£280,000 - 35,000)}{100}}{(2,000,000 \times 2)\ 3/2}$$

$$\frac{£2450,000}{3,000,000\ \text{shares}}$$

$$8.17p$$

Revised calculation for 20X1: EPS = 8.75 × 2m/3m = 5.8p. This adjusts for the fact that there are 50% more shares in issue in 20X2 compared with 20X1.

6.3.3 Rights issue

A rights issue occurs when new shares are issued to existing shareholders, usually at below the existing market price. This increases the number of shares in issue, but does not increase the earning capacity of the company proportionally. After a rights issue, the market price should therefore fall. The dilution in the value of pre-rights issue share capital, in such circumstances, can be demonstrated as follows.

WORKED EXAMPLE **10.6**

	£
Four shares in circulation before rights issue at a market price of say £2 each:	8.00
Rights issue of, say, one for two at an artificially low price of 50p each for illustrative purposes:	1.00
Six shares then in issue will have theoretical post-rights issue worth of:	9.00
Theoretical ex-rights price will be £9 ÷ 6 shares	1.50

Diluted post-rights equivalent of pre-rights issue shares:

Four shares worth £2 each (pre-issue) = 4 × (£2 ÷ £1.5) = 5.3 shares post issue

Proof:

	£
Four shares at pre-issue market price of £2:	8.00
5.3 shares at theoretical ex-rights price of £1.5:	8.00

The above adjustments are incorporated in the calculation of EPS in the following manner:

1 Calculate total value of equity before rights issue: market price × number of shares.
2 Calculate proceeds of new issue.
3 Calculate *theoretical* price after issue:

$$\frac{1 + 2}{\text{Number of shares after rights issue}}$$

WORKED EXAMPLE **10.6** *continued*

4 Calculate the post-issue equivalent of the number of shares outstanding pre-issue:

$$\text{Number of shares} \times \frac{\text{Actual pre-issue price}}{\text{Theoretical post-issue price}}$$

5 Calculate the number of shares in issue during the year on the weighted average basis.
6 Compute EPS.
7 Obtain corresponding comparative figure for previous year:

$$\text{Last year's EPS} \times \frac{\text{Theoretical post-issue price}}{\text{Actual pre-issue price}}$$

The following information is provided for B Ltd:
- B plc has earnings of £16,640 for 20X2.
- There were 120,000 ordinary shares in issue at the start of the year.
- A total of 40,000 further shares were issued on 31 August 20X2 at £1.50 each.
- The market price of each share immediately before the rights issue was £2.

Required
Calculate the EPS for 20X2.

Answer
Procedure to calculate EPS:
1 Calculate total value of equity before issue: market price × number of shares:
  £2 × 120,000 = £240,000
2 Calculate proceeds of new issue:
  £1.50 × 40,000 = £60,000
3 Calculate *theoretical* price after issue:

$$\frac{(£240,000 + 60,000)}{£120,000 + 40,000}$$

$$\frac{300,000}{160,000 \text{ shares}}$$

$$£1.875$$

4 Calculate the post-issue equivalent of the number of shares outstanding pre-issue:

$$120,000 \times \frac{2}{1.875} = 128,000$$

5 Calculate the number of shares in issue during the year on the weighted average basis:
  (128,000 × 8/12ths) + (160,000 × 4/12ths) = 138,667 shares
6 Compute EPS:

$$\frac{£16,640}{138,667} \times 100 = 12\text{p}$$

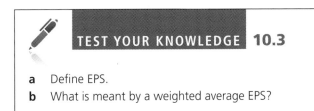

TEST YOUR KNOWLEDGE 10.3

a Define EPS.
b What is meant by a weighted average EPS?

6.3.4 Diluted earnings per share (DEPS)

IAS 33 describes diluted earnings per share as follows:

'Dilution: A reduction in earnings per share or an increase in loss per share resulting from the assumption that convertible instruments are converted, that options or warrants are exercised, or that ordinary shares are issued upon the satisfaction of specified conditions.'

On occasions, a company, whose shares are traded on a stock exchange, can issue shares that in effect are below the market price of those shares had they been available to interested parties ordinarily. The impact of offering shares at less than market price is the same as offering all or a portion of shares for free. Consequently this has a diluting effect on EPS.

WORKED EXAMPLE 10.7

The results of A Ltd for 20X1 are as in Worked Example 10.3. During 20X2, the entire 7% convertible preference shares of £1 each totalling £500,000 are converted at four ordinary shares for one convertible preference share. Profits for the year for 20X2 are £280,000.

Required
Calculate the diluted EPS for 20X2.

Answer

	No of shares £,000	Earnings £,000	Price p
Basic EPS (W1)	2,000	280–35	12.25
Convertible preference shares (W2)	2,000	35	
Diluted EPS	4,000	280	7.00
Diluted EPS	7.00p per share		

The net effect of the preference shares converting to ordinary shares is that basic EPS has reduced from 12.25 pence per share to 7.00 pence per share.

(W1)
For basic EPS purposes, profits available would have been:
(£280,000 – £35,000) / 2,000 shares = 12.25p per share

(W2)
Preference share conversion:
2 ordinary shares × 1 (£1 preference share)
2 × 500,000 = 2 million ordinary shares.

TEST YOUR KNOWLEDGE 10.4

Explain the difference between basic and diluted EPS.

10.1 The following information is provided in respect of Roxon plc:

a   Statement of profit or loss and other comprehensive income extracts, year to 31 December

	20X2	20X1
	£m	£m
Operating profit	132	108
Interest payable (note iii)	36	36
Profit before tax	96	72
Taxation (33%)	32	24
Profit for the period	64	48

Extract from statement of changes in equity

Dividends: ordinary shares (note i)	(32)	(16)
8% preference shares (note ii)	(8)	(8)

i   The ordinary share capital consisted of 30 million shares of £1 each in 20X1 and through to 30 April 20X2, when a bonus issue was made of one new ordinary share for every five shares presently held.

ii   The 8% preference share capital amounted to £100 million throughout 20X1 and 20X2.

iii   The interest payable is in respect of 12% debenture stock. The debenture holders have the right to convert their stock into ordinary shares at any time after 1 January 20X2. The terms of the conversion are 20 ordinary shares of £1 each for every £300 of debenture stock.

Required

a   Define EPS in accordance with standard accounting practice.

b   Explain what is meant by a *bonus issue* of shares, and indicate its likely effect on the market price of the shares.

c   Compute the figures for EPS, including re-stated EPS for 20X1, to be disclosed in the accounts of Roxon for 20X2.

d   Outline the circumstances in which the obligation to compute the diluted earnings per share arises.

e   Compute the figures for diluted earnings per share to be disclosed in the accounts of Roxon for 20X2.

10.2 The DuPont Analysis is a technique for analysing the three components of return on equity (ROE):

a   Net margin = Net income / Sales. How much profit a company makes for every £1 it generates in revenue. The higher a company's profit margin, the better.

b   Asset turnover = Sales / Total assets. The amount of sales generated for every pound of assets. This measures the firm's efficiency at using assets. The higher the number, the better.

c   Leverage factor = Net income / Shareholders' equity. The higher the number, the more debt the company has.

The DuPont analysis uses the following formula:

$$\frac{\text{Net income}}{\text{Sales}} \times \frac{\text{Sales}}{\text{Assets}} \times \frac{\text{Assets}}{\text{Equity}} = \frac{\text{Net income}}{\text{Equity}}$$

Given the following information, in £,000, calculate firm efficiency for Alpha plc:

- Net income = 3,300
- Sales = 19,600
- Assets = 135,000
- Equity = 9,500

? **END OF CHAPTER QUESTIONS** *continued*

10.3 The following information appeared under equity in the statement of financial position of Anfield Ltd at 31 December 20X4:

Equity

	20X4 £,000	20X3 £,000
Issued share capital (£1 ordinary shares)	45,000	25,000
Share premium account	13,500	6,000
Retained earnings	16,200	19,000
	74,700	50,000

You discover that the directors of Anfield arranged a bonus issue of one new ordinary share of £1 each for every five shares held on 31 March 20X4. This was followed by a rights issue at £1.50 per share on 1 May 20X4. The directors of Anfield paid an interim dividend for 20X4 of 15p per share on 31 July 20X4.

Required

Compute the following items for inclusion in the cash flow statement and related notes of Anfield for 20X4, so far as the information permits:

a   proceeds from rights issue; and

b   profit for the period (20X4).

Notes

1   Ignore taxation.

2   Anfield neither received nor paid any interest during 20X4.

11 Limitations of published accounts

■ CONTENTS

■ LEARNING OUTCOMES

Chapter 11 covers the syllabus section entitled 'Limitations of Published Accounts'. After reading and understanding the contents of the chapter, working through all the worked examples and practice questions, you should be able to:

- understand and explain subjectivity and **earnings management** and how managers can take opportunity to meet their own aims;
- appreciate and demonstrate how creative accounting occurs and the various means by which managers manipulate accounting numbers such as debt factoring, consignments, sale and repurchase agreements;
- discuss and apply the principle of substance over form; and
- discuss the role of the external audit and the implications of audit and non-audit services for corporate governance.

1 Introduction

The International Financial Reporting Standards (IFRS) provide guidance to those who prepare financial statements; they also provide discussion and reflection on the presentation of financial statements. IFRS and International Accounting Standards (IAS) cover the general format of financial reporting. When an accounting issue arises, those involved in the preparation of accounts can consult the framework for guidance on how to report. The general aim is to ensure matters are reported in a manner that is transparent and useful to users.

However, financial reporting standards cannot ensure financial statements always provide a completely accurate and full picture to all users of accounting information. Some of the main limitations of financial statements are discussed below:

1 The financial position of a business is affected by several factors: economic, social and financial, but only financial factors are presented in the financial statements. Economic and social factors are excluded. Thus, the financial position disclosed by these statements is incomplete. However, a trend towards reporting on social and environmental impact by businesses is becoming common practice, particularly with large listed UK companies. This wider approach is known as 'integrated reporting'.
2 The financial statements only cover a specific period of time. They are essentially interim reports presented on an annual basis. Past performance may not be an accurate indicator of future performance.
3 Facts that have not been recorded in the accounts are not depicted in the financial statement. Only quantitative factors are taken into account. Qualitative factors, such as reputation and the prestige of the business with the public, the efficiency and loyalty of its employees, and the integrity and skill-set of management do not appear in the financial statements.

4   The past 'buying power' of a national currency may not reflect current buying power. Historic cost accounting is based on the assumption that the value of the monetary unit remains constant. Assets are recorded by the business at the price at which they are acquired, and liabilities are recorded at the amounts at which they are contracted. However, a monetary unit is never completely stable, especially under inflationary conditions. In times of inflation, this results in significant distortions in financial statements.

5   Many items included in financial statements have a significant impact on reported profit, but depend on the personal judgment of management (e.g. provision for depreciation, inventory valuation, bad debts provision).

6   The convention of accounting conservatism: the consolidated statement of profit or loss and other comprehensive income may not disclose the true income of a business entity as probable losses are considered, while probable income is not reported.

7   The non-current (fixed) assets are shown at cost less depreciation. But the market value of non-current assets may not be the same on disposal. The disposal of a non-current asset may give rise to a significant loss or gain that distorts the financial statements.

8   Management's judgment is always involved in the preparation of financial statements, leaving the statements open to manipulation. Financial data must be analysed and evaluated in some way to give some sort of indication of the future prospects of a business. It is the analyst or user who gives meaning to financial information.

2   Limitations of accounting ratios

The various calculations illustrated in this and the last two chapters suffer from a number of limitations that should be borne in mind by anyone attempting to interpret their significance. The main limitations are as follows.

Accounting ratios can be used to assess whether performance is satisfactory, by means of inter-company comparison, and also whether results have improved, worsened or remained stable, by comparing this year's results with those achieved last year. The ratios do not provide *explanations* for observed changes, however, and the external user's ability to obtain further information varies considerably. The shareholder may ask questions at the annual general meeting, while a financial institution may demand extra information when an advance is requested, but only management has direct access to the information needed to provide the right answer.

Deterioration in an accounting ratio cannot necessarily be interpreted as poor management. For example, a decline in the rate of inventory turnover initially appears undesirable, but further investigation might reveal the accumulation of scarce raw materials that enable the plant to continue working when competitors are forced to suspend production.

Too much significance should not be attached to individual ratios (e.g. a rate of return on gross assets of 30% might indicate that all is well, but this conclusion might be unjustified if further analysis revealed a liquidity ratio of 0.4:1).

Changes in many ratios are closely associated with one another and produce similar conclusions (e.g. the ratio of total debt to total assets (not illustrated in this chapter) and the debt : equity ratio). Care should therefore be taken when selecting ratios to be used as the basis for the analysis; a representative selection should be made and duplication avoided.

Company financial statements are usually based on historical cost and, therefore, accounting ratios based on these figures would be expected to improve, irrespective of efficiency during a period of rising prices (e.g. total asset turnover of £3 per £1 invested might be computed from historical cost accounts, whereas a figure of £1.80 per £1 invested might be obtained if assets were restated at current values).

Differences in accounting policies may detract from the value of inter-company comparisons (e.g. the valuation of inventory on the LIFO (last in, first out) basis (now banned) rather than the FIFO (first in, first out) basis would probably produce a much lower working capital ratio).

Financial statements and accounting ratios can be distorted as the result of one-off large transactions such as the credit purchase of plant, which will significantly increase current liabilities until payment is made, or a profit on the sale of a non-current asset. Analysts should similarly be on their guard for evidence of window-dressing, perhaps designed to conceal a deteriorating financial position.

Where a company undertakes a mix of activities, it is important to calculate separate ratios for each section wherever possible.

Particular care must be taken when interpreting accounting ratios calculated for a seasonal business. Where sales are high at a particular time during the year (e.g. at Christmas), stock might be expected to increase and cash to decline in the months leading up to the busy period. In these circumstances, deteriorations in both the liquidity ratio and the rate of inventory turnover, compared with the previous month, are not necessarily causes for concern.

Consideration must be given to variations in commercial trading patterns when assessing the significance of accounting ratios computed for particular companies. For example, a retail chain of supermarkets would be expected to have a much lower liquidity ratio and a much higher rate of inventory turnover than a constructional engineering firm. In this context, accepted 'norms' such as a working capital ratio of 2:1 must be used with care.

TEST YOUR KNOWLEDGE 11.1

Outline three limitations of accounting ratios.

---

3 Subjectivity and earnings management – impact on reported figures

Modern accounting methods are based on the accruals (or matching) concept in which revenues and expenses are reported in the period they are incurred, irrespective of when physical cash transactions take place. IAS 1 requires business entities to prepare accounts on an accruals basis.

There are many reasons why those preparing financial information may not present a completely accurate picture. This was discussed earlier with regard to agency theory. Managers, typically, use accounting techniques that either enhance actual earnings or defer earnings to future periods. One reason why managers may enhance earnings figures is self-interest (e.g. meeting bonus and remuneration targets).

Earnings have two components: cash and accruals. In an accruals-based accounting system, revenues and expenses are matched in the period they are incurred. Accruals, however, are a *subjective* measure of revenue and expenses. Nevertheless, the non-discretionary accruals (NDAC) element of total 'accruals' can be shown to be accurate – for instance, sales at the end of the year. In certain cases, managers will use their judgment to accrue revenues and expenses that are not clearly definable. They use their inside knowledge to communicate this information to the outside world. For example, a contract for services straddles more than one financial year. The value of the contract is £10 million and the contract runs for five years. Management may decide that the bulk of the contractual income (say 60%) will be in the first two years. Guidance on deciding which period to recognize this revenue, per recently revised IFRS 15 'Revenue from Contracts' (effective 1 January 2018), relates to the identification of a performance obligation as the promise to transfer a good or service to a customer in a contact.

They will thus reflect 60% of the contractual income in the first two years in reported financial figures. This is acceptable if managers follow the relevant accounting standards and can explain their reasoning to the external auditors.

Conversely, managers may sometimes manage earnings for their own purposes to meet certain targets. This is known as managerial opportunism. As mentioned earlier, the main mechanism for managing reported earnings is through accruals manipulation. The nature of accruals is such that they reverse in the next accounting period. This has repercussions on reported figures. Any unassigned accruals will not be matched by the eventual receipt or payment of cash. This has an impact on current and future reported earnings.

Apart from meeting earnings expectations to achieve bonus targets, managers may increase (by various means) reported earnings to meet market expectations (e.g. by reducing gearing levels or increasing earnings per share (EPS)), hence strengthening the statement of financial position.

WORKED EXAMPLE 11.1

The following are the financial figures of Raymond Ltd. In exercising judgment, management has been over-optimistic about the amount of revenue it believes should be reported.

The pre-accruals column shows the actual figures as they should be reported. The post-accruals column shows the figure after managers have accrued an extra £8 million revenue. The impact of this is demonstrated below:

	Pre-accruals £,000 20X1	Post-accruals £,000 20X1
Sales	52,000	60,000
Cost of goods sold	(36,000)	(36,000)
Gross profit	16,000	24,000
Operating expenses		
Selling expenses	(7,000)	(7,000)
Administrative expenses	(5,860)	(5,860)
Total operating expenses	12,860	12,860
Net operating income	3,140	11,140
Interest expenses	(800)	(800)
Profit before tax	2,340	10,340
Income taxes (30%)	(1,638)	(3,102)
Profit after tax	1,638	7,238

	Pre-accruals £,000 20X1	Post-accruals £,000 20X1
Non-current assets		
Property, plant and equipment	16,000	16,000
Current assets		
Inventory	8,000	8,000
Receivables	6,000	14,000
Prepaid expenses	300	300
Cash and cash equivalents	3,700	3,700
Total current assets	18,000	26,000
Total assets	34,000	42,000
Equity and liabilities		
Share capital (£1 shares)	6,000	6,000
Share premium	1,000	1,000
6% Preferred shares	2,000	2,000
Retained earnings	8,000	15,400
	17,000	24,400

WORKED EXAMPLE **11.1** *continued*

Non-current liabilities

8% loan	10,000	10,000

Current liabilities

Accounts payable	5,800	5,800
Accrued payable	900	900
Taxation	300	900
Total current liabilities	7,000	7,600
Total liabilities	17,000	17,600
Total equity and liabilities	34,000	42,000

Raymond Ltd is a manufacturer of machine parts. To assist in the cash management and expansion of the business, Raymond secured a £10 million long-term loan from its bankers. The terms and conditions of the loan stipulated that Raymond should not exceed a 50% debt : equity ratio (see formula given above). However, at the end of 20X1, the debt covenant with the lender appears to have been breached. Managers at Raymond Ltd decided to increase revenue sales figures by an extra £8 million. The premise for this increase is based on over-optimistic expectation of revenues from contracts with certain customers.

Required

Calculate the gearing ratio pre- and post-accruals for Raymond Ltd, and make relevant comments on the change in gearing.

Answer

	Pre-accruals	Post-accruals
	£,000	*£,000*
	20X1	**20X1**
Sales	52,000	60,000
Earnings	1,638	7,238
Long-term finance	10,000	10,000
Shareholders' funds	17,000	24,400
Gearing ratio	$\dfrac{10,000}{17,000}$	$\dfrac{10,000}{24,400}$
=	59%	41%

WORKED EXAMPLE **11.2**

Given the above information, the consequence of actions taken by Raymond Ltd would have repercussions on other aspects of the company's financial figures.

Required

Calculate the change in earnings per share and any expectations by shareholders and potential investors.

 **WORKED EXAMPLE** **11.2** *continued*

Answer

	Pre-accruals	Post-accruals
	£,000	£,000
	20X1	20X1
Sales	52,000	60,000
Earnings	1,638	7,238
Shares in issue	6 million	6 million
	1,638	7,238
EPS	6,000	6,000
	= 27.3p	120.6p

It would appear that based on pre-accruals figures, Raymond Ltd would have defaulted on the debt covenant agreed with the lender. The pre-accruals gearing ratio is 59%, above the agreed level. Managers at Raymond Ltd have accrued an extra £8 million in revenue, which has increased total shareholders' funds by about 44%. This appears to indicate that drastic action has been taken by Raymond's managers to ensure they remain within the terms of the debt covenant in the current year. However, the impact of this £8 million extra accrual will have consequences for the following financial year, as revenue will be reduced by £8 million in 20X1. Unless Raymond Ltd increases its actual revenue by an equal amount in 20X1, the company will face the same difficulties (i.e. default on the debt covenant).

The action taken by Raymond Ltd has meant an increase in earnings from the pre-accruals position to the post-accruals position of 320%. Similarly, the EPS has also risen by over 320% from pre-accrual EPS of 27p per share to £1.20 per share. This may cause difficulties for the company, as shareholders are likely to expect a dramatic rise in dividends to be announced. When this does not materialise, this may give cause for concern, not just to the shareholders and lenders of Raymond, but also to other stakeholders.

Taking the example from Raymond Ltd (above), discuss any further impact the action of management will have on the statement of financial position for Raymond.

WORKED EXAMPLE **11.3**

The table below indicates the impact of change in ratio measuring company performance.

	Pre-accruals	Post-accruals	% change
	£,000	£,000	post-accruals
	20X1	20X1	20X1
Current ratio	2.57	3.42	33.07%
Acid test	1.43	2.37	65.73%
Total asset turnover	1.53	1.43	−6.54%
Return on equity (ROE) (W1)	10%	32%	220.00%
Return on capital employed (ROCE) (W2)	6%	21%	250.00%

WORKED EXAMPLE 11.3 *continued*

	Pre-accruals	Post-accruals
	£,000	£,000
W1	20X1	20X1
ROE		
Equity (excluding preference shares)		
Share capital	6,000	6,000
Share premium	1,000	1,000
Retained earnings	8,000	15,400
	15,000	22,400
Net income	1,638	7,238
Dividends to preferred shareholders	(120)	(120)
Income attributable to shareholders	1,518	7,118
ROE	1,518	7,118
	15,000	22,400
ROE	10.12%	31.77%
W2		
ROCE		
Capital employed	27,000	35,000
ROCE	1,638	7,238
	27,000	35,000
ROCE	6.07%	20.68%

As would be expected, as a result of accruing significant additional income, the post-accruals figures indicate substantial strengthening of the statement of financial position for Raymond Ltd.

- *Current ratio*: This suggests that the liquidity position of the company has improved substantially. However, this is mainly due to the increase in receivables following the increase in revenue brought about through inappropriate accruals management.
- *Acid test*: The acid test ratio, a more stringent version of the current ratio that excludes inventory in its calculation, again suggests that the liquidity of the company has strengthened. Again, though, this is due to the increase in revenue brought about through inappropriate accruals management.
- *Total asset turnover ratio*: This suggests that company efficiency has fallen, even though revenues have increased substantially. This is due to the corresponding increase in total asset increase, since the accruals effect has also increased receivables.
- *Return on equity*: The figures indicate that an increase of 220% has taken place due to the effects of increase in revenues and hence earnings. The increase in earnings is not, however, matched by any level of increase in shareholders' equity. Hence, a sharp rise in the ROE ratio is indicated.
- *Return on capital employed*: This ratio takes into account the total shareholders' fund that includes reserves and retained earnings. The figures suggest an increase in ROCE by 250% due to increased earnings and increased total shareholders' fund.

It would be interesting to see how the company manages its revenues in 20X2. An actual rise in revenue, without accruals management, would cancel out the effects of the use of accruals in 20X1. However, if no action is taken and no accruals management occurs in 20X2, we would expect a sharp and substantial fall in the ratios indicated. This would have repercussions for stakeholders, and confidence in company performance may fall.

TEST YOUR KNOWLEDGE 11.2

Outline the reasons why managers may engage in earnings management.

4 Creative accounting or earnings management

Creative accounting can be defined in a number of ways. However, a working definition is: 'A process by which managers use their knowledge of accounting choices available to them to manipulate the figures reported in the accounts of a business.'

Creative accounting, or (to use the more modern phraseology) earnings management, can occur in a number of ways, both intentional and unintentional. Some basic reasons why creative accounting occurs and the role of audit in mitigating such practices are as follows:

- *Accounting system* – The weaknesses inherent in the accepted accounting methods render the system susceptible to manipulation by opportunistic managers.
- *Accounting choices* – Accounting rules allow companies to choose between relevant accounting methods. In many countries, a company can choose between a policy of writing off development expenditure as it occurs, or amortising it over the life of the related project. A company can, therefore, choose the accounting policy that suits its purpose.
- *Accounting judgment* – By and large, the manner in which accounting rules and regulations are drafted demand management to deliver some level of estimates. Currently, the IFRS require management to provide some level of estimate where exact or accurate figures are either unavailable or inaccessible (e.g. pension costs). The defined benefits (DB) scheme is notorious for estimating pension costs to companies. In some circumstances, relevant experts are engaged to make estimates; for instance, an actuary would normally be employed to assess the prospective pension liability. In this case, the creative accountant can manipulate the valuation both by the way in which the expert is briefed and by engaging an expert known to take either a pessimistic or an optimistic view. In either case, management may select the most favourable expert.
- *Accounting transactions* – Certain entries in the accounts involve an unavoidable degree of estimation, judgment and prediction. In some cases, such as the estimation of an asset's useful life made to calculate depreciation, these estimates are normally made inside the business and the creative accountant has the opportunity to err on the side of caution or optimism in making the estimate.

Artificial transactions can be entered into both to manipulate the statement of financial position balances and to move profits between accounting periods. This is achieved by entering into two or more related transactions with an obliging third party, normally a bank. Suppose an arrangement is made to sell an asset to a bank, then lease that asset back for the rest of its useful life. The sale price under such a 'sale and leaseback' can be pitched above or below the current value of the asset, because the difference can be compensated for by increased or reduced rentals.

Genuine transactions can also be timed so as to give the desired impression in the accounts. As an example, suppose a business has an investment of £1 million at historic cost which can easily be sold for £3 million, being the current value. The managers of the business are free to choose in which year they sell the investment and so increase the profit in the accounts at a desired time.

5 Substance over form

The principle of 'substance over form' allows a company to ensure that its financial reports offer a true and fair view of the economic realities of the business. In this way, the economic substance rather than the legal form is reported. The IASB (International Accounting Standards Board) has, in recent years, diverted its attention on the statement of financial position approach. Standards have been developed and either enhanced or amended to allow the substance of a transaction, rather than its legal form, to convey economic reality.

Some transactions present a window of opportunistic behaviour for managers. The 'substance over form' concept has addressed some of the mechanisms that were used (or in some cases that may still be used, perhaps in smaller companies) to hide the true nature of a transaction. Some of these mechanisms are discussed below.

5.1 Sale and leaseback arrangement

A company that needs cash can enter into a financial arrangement with a willing third party, such as a bank. The company sells its machinery to the bank and gets it back via a lease. This is called a 'sale and leaseback' arrangement, as mentioned above. Under this arrangement, although the legal ownership has transferred, the underlying economics remain the same. Under the 'substance over form' principle, the sale and subsequent leaseback are considered to be one transaction. If two companies swap their inventories, they will not be allowed to record a sale, because no sale has occurred, even if they have entered into a valid enforceable contract.

5.2 Consignment stock

Consignment sales are arrangement between two parties: the principal and the agent. In this arrangement, the agent holds the goods on behalf of the principal with a view to selling on the good on behalf of the principal, thereby earning a fee or a commission.

In a *consignment* arrangement, the consignor (seller) ships goods to the consignee (buyer), which acts as the agent of the consignor in trying to sell the goods. There are many forms of consignment arrangements; however, the two main methods are:

- where the consignee receives a commission; or
- where the consignee 'purchases' the goods simultaneously with the sale of goods to the final customer.

Goods out on consignment are properly included in the inventory of the consignor and *excluded* from the inventory of the consignee. Disclosure may be required of the consignee, however, since common financial analytical inferences (such as days' sales in inventory or inventory turnover) may appear distorted unless the financial statement users are informed. However, the IFRS do not explicitly address this.

5.3 Debt factoring

A factoring arrangement involves the factor, which is usually a financial institution or specialist factoring company, buying some or all of an entity's accounts receivable or debt outright. The factor then administers the sales ledger, taking responsibility for sending out statements to customers and chasing up outstanding payments. The specific arrangements made (e.g. the amount advanced and responsibility for bad debts) can vary significantly. For example, the arrangement may involve an advance of 90% of the value of receivables with the remaining amount paid over, when collected, less a commission plus interest on the advance. The Scottish Enterprise website states that factoring is particularly attractive to businesses whose growth is sales-based and who need regular injections of working capital to buy materials, to increase production and to fund inventories purchase as sales rise. They continue:

> Late payment is the bane of most small businesses. Factoring substantially reduces the average payment period on invoices, something that can do wonders for the financial performance of a rapidly growing business. In particular, factoring can help avoid 'over-trading' and with a more predictable cash flow, your business can plan more effectively.

According to statistics released by the Factors & Discounters Association, factoring or invoice discounting in the UK was, as of 2012, being used by almost 42,000 companies, generating a combined turnover in excess of £212 billion.

The accounting treatment of a factoring arrangement naturally depends on who has the risks and rewards of ownership. If the total receivables are the subject of an outright sale, risks and rewards are transferred to the factor, and the asset should be derecognised in the vendor's statement of financial position. If, at the other extreme, there are full rights of recourse in respect of bad debts, then the risks and rewards are not transferred, and the receivables should continue to be reported in the entity's statement of financial position.

TEST YOUR KNOWLEDGE 11.3

a Explain debt factoring.
b Describe how debt factoring can be useful for small companies.

5.4 Sale and repurchase arrangement

In effect, a sale and repurchase agreement is a loan. In this arrangement, the sale of an asset takes place between two parties with a view to the asset's subsequent repurchase at a higher price. The difference between the sale price and the repurchase price represents interest, which is at times referred to as the 'repo' rate. The party that originally buys the securities effectively acts as a lender. The original seller is effectively acting as a borrower, using their security as collateral for a secured cash loan at a fixed rate of interest.

A sale and repurchase agreement is another arrangement that can be exploited to produce off-statement of financial position finance. Its essential feature is that the company purports to have sold an asset, but has not relinquished all the risks and rewards associated with that asset in a manner which one would expect in the case of a normal sale. Fundamentally, therefore, it is a form of secured borrowing.

WORKED EXAMPLE 11.4

A whisky blending company contracts to sell part of its stock of whisky to a bank for £10 million on 1 January 20X5. The agreement makes provision for the whisky company to buy back the whisky two years later, for £12.1 million. The whisky remains at the blending company's premises.

The market rate of interest for an advance to a whisky blending company is known to be 10%.

Required
Explain the substance of this transaction and how it should be accounted for in the books and accounts of the whisky company in 20X5–X6.

Answer
If the transaction were accounted for as a normal sale, inventory would be reduced by £10 million and cash would be increased by £10 million in the company's statement of financial position. In such a case, the financing arrangement would remain off-statement of financial position and the assets of the company would also be understated.

However, this is a financing arrangement rather than a normal sale. The company has transferred no risks and rewards of ownership to the bank, and has merely borrowed money on the security of an appreciating asset.

The inventories should remain in the statement of financial position of the whisky blending company, at the date of the initial advance (1 January 20X5), at £10 million, with the cash received from the bank shown as a liability.

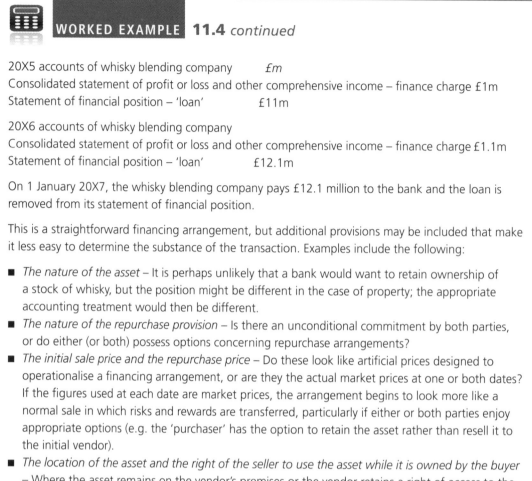

WORKED EXAMPLE 11.4 *continued*

20X5 accounts of whisky blending company   *£m*
Consolidated statement of profit or loss and other comprehensive income – finance charge £1m
Statement of financial position – 'loan'   £11m

20X6 accounts of whisky blending company
Consolidated statement of profit or loss and other comprehensive income – finance charge £1.1m
Statement of financial position – 'loan'   £12.1m

On 1 January 20X7, the whisky blending company pays £12.1 million to the bank and the loan is removed from its statement of financial position.

This is a straightforward financing arrangement, but additional provisions may be included that make it less easy to determine the substance of the transaction. Examples include the following:

- *The nature of the asset* – It is perhaps unlikely that a bank would want to retain ownership of a stock of whisky, but the position might be different in the case of property; the appropriate accounting treatment would then be different.
- *The nature of the repurchase provision* – Is there an unconditional commitment by both parties, or do either (or both) possess options concerning repurchase arrangements?
- *The initial sale price and the repurchase price* – Do these look like artificial prices designed to operationalise a financing arrangement, or are they the actual market prices at one or both dates? If the figures used at each date are market prices, the arrangement begins to look more like a normal sale in which risks and rewards are transferred, particularly if either or both parties enjoy appropriate options (e.g. the 'purchaser' has the option to retain the asset rather than resell it to the initial vendor).
- *The location of the asset and the right of the seller to use the asset while it is owned by the buyer* – Where the asset remains on the vendor's premises or the vendor retains a right of access to the asset, the transaction would appear not to possess the characteristics of a normal sale.

A sale and repurchase agreement, sometimes referred to as a 'repo' often involves securities rather than tangible goods and involves an arrangement disclosure.

6   The role of audit in mitigating creative accounting

The external auditor is increasingly viewed as a way to hold managers to account through an appropriate application of accounting policies and sound judgment when preparing financial reports. To this end, an external auditor could help in mitigating creative accounting practices. This requires two fundamental perspectives:

1   expertise in determining errors and misstatements in reported financial figures; and
2   the independence to report such errors or misstatements.

These are discussed below.

The audit process, being a mechanism of corporate governance, is supposed to provide a measure of reassurance to users of accounts. In providing such assurance, the auditor must convey two primary characteristics:

- *Auditor expertise* – In being able to mitigate errors or misstatements (creative accounting), the auditor must have expertise both in their profession and, in some cases, in the industry in which they specialise. Faced with a new customer, or perhaps a new industry, smaller auditors may not have the acumen to conduct effective audits, and therefore offer reassurance to end users who may rely on their opinion.
- *Auditor independence* – Auditors depend on audit fees, in large part, to sustain their business. If an auditor has a small client base that makes up the bulk of their income, this

may compromise auditor independence. However, in the UK, no more than 10–15% of fees income can arise from one client. Auditor independence is measured by the auditor's ability to demand correction to errors or misstatements made by management in financial accounts.

Auditor expertise and independence together constitute what is called *audit quality*. This is the joint probability that an auditor will detect and report an error or a misstatement. The detection of an error or misstatement relates to auditor expertise. The auditor's ability to report this relates to their independence.

6.1 External auditor – principles and practices

The external audit is a mechanism of corporate governance. Corporate governance has risen to prominence, particularly in the last 25 years, due mainly to high-profile corporate failures, some of which are listed below.

The company Enron, as an example, became synonymous with all that is bad in accounting and managerial opportunism. Lawsuits and criminal proceedings were instituted against the top management of the company, with losses running into billions of dollars.

At the time, Arthur Andersen (once one of the 'big four') was Enron's auditor and was paid audit fees indicated to be around $23 million. The scandal led to the dissolution of Arthur Andersen and the company had to surrender its licence to practice.

The Powers Committee (appointed by Enron's board to look into the firm's accounting in October 2001) made the following assessment:

'The evidence available to us suggests that Andersen did not fulfil its professional responsibilities in connection with its audits of Enron's financial statements, or its obligation to bring to the attention of Enron's Board (or the Audit and Compliance Committee) concerns about Enron's internal contracts over the related-party transactions.'

Some of the principal qualities expected of auditors are as follows.

1 *Independence* from related parties who have an interest in the financial affairs of a company. In this respect, auditors must not be swayed from their principal duty of being independent. Independence of mind is an additional pre-requisite. It is essential that the auditor not only acts independently, but also appears to be independent. If an auditor is in fact independent, but one or more factors suggest otherwise, this could lead to stakeholders concluding that the audit report does not give a 'true and fair view'. The two types of independence threat can be summarised as:
   a *independence of mind:* freedom from the effects of threats to auditor independence that would be sufficient to compromise an auditor's objectivity; and
   b *independence in appearance:* no activities, relationships, or other circumstances that could lead well-informed investors and other users reasonably to conclude that there is an unacceptably high risk that an auditor lacks independence of mind (source: *The CPA Journal*).
2 *Client–auditor relationship* – This refers to the level of professionalism in an audit engagement. The client is a source of income for the auditor. This could lead to a compromise on standards if the client puts pressure on the auditor to act in a specific manner.
3 *The size of the audit fee* – This can be a mitigating factor on independence and professionalism in practice. The larger the fee, the greater the probability that an auditor will relinquish their responsibilities and perform the audit without due diligence. If auditor fees are concentrated around a limited number of clients, this could have an impact on auditor professionalism and independence.
4 *Repeat business* – An auditor needs to secure regular income and foster long-term client relationships. This may lead to lower fee quotations, so the auditor may reduce their level of substantive and due diligence work to cover costs.
5 *Familiarity* – Auditors are required to be sceptical of information and representations made by their clients. Over-reliance on the client's word can compromise both independence and professionalism. For example, an auditor may become overly familiar with a client if they have a particularly close or long-standing personal or professional relationship with them.
6 *Non-audit services* – The long-standing debate on non-audit services has particular repercussions on auditor professionalism and independence. Many studies have suggested that

to secure the more lucrative non-audit services contracts, auditors have tended to low-ball or undercut the audit price. Again, this practice may entice auditors to perform to a low standard by cutting corners in audit work.

The role of the auditor and corporate governance were introduced in Chapter 1.

7   Auditors and non-audit services

Non-audit services provided by auditors to client companies have been a contentious issue in recent years. The issue mainly relates to auditors auditing their own work and the compromise to the quality of audit this presents. The Code on Audit Committee and Auditors provides a basis for the auditor–audit committee relationship:

> 'The board should establish formal and transparent arrangements for considering how they should apply the corporate reporting and risk management and internal control principles and for maintaining an appropriate relationship with the company's auditor.'

In implanting the above principal of corporate governance practice, the code further suggests that the task of the audit committee is:

> 'to review and monitor the external auditor's independence and objectivity and the effectiveness of the audit process, taking into consideration relevant UK professional and regulatory requirements.'

There is currently no bar on auditors providing non-audit services for the same client; however, the code suggests that audit committees need:

> 'to develop and implement policy on the engagement of the external auditor to supply non-audit services, taking into account relevant ethical guidance regarding the provision of non-audit services by the external audit firm, and to report to the board, identifying any matters in respect of which it considers that action or improvement is needed and making recommendations as to the steps to be taken.'

In this regard, the code requires the audit committee to explain to shareholders, in the annual report, how auditor objectivity and independence is maintained if the auditor provides audit and non-audit services, and the amount of payment for the non-audit services has to be disclosed in the published accounts.

The audit committee deliberates on auditor remit in relation to audit and non-audit services, to ensure these do not impair the auditor's independence and that they comply with legislation. Under the code's guiding principles, the auditor's independence will be deemed to be impaired if the auditor provides a service where they:

- have a management role in the company; or
- audit their own work; or
- serve in an advocacy role for the company.

The three compromising actions above are not exhaustive, but are the main reasons for auditor compromise in due diligence. There needs to be a balance between the level of auditor involvement in a company's affairs and their independence and professionalism.

END OF CHAPTER QUESTIONS

11.1 Explain the term 'creative accounting'.

11.2 How does creative accounting arise in financial reporting systems?

11.3 Luboil Ltd supplies a special type of machine oils to the manufacturing industry. On 1 January 20X6, Luboil entered in to a contract with Seeder Ltd to supply £10 million worth of oil over five-year period. The contract stipulated price variation subject to market forces agreed in advance between the two parties.

As part of the contract, Seeder agreed to pay Luboil £10 million in advance subject to the price review. The supply of oil would be in equal instalments.

At 31 December 20X6, Luboil's financial statements included the total £10 million in revenue invoiced to Seeder. However, only £1 million of inventory was disclosed in the cost of sales.

Required

a   As auditor of Luboil Ltd, explain to the management the accounting treatment that should have been disclosed.

b   Discuss the impact on the ratios for Luboil after the necessary accounting changes.

12

Financial reporting within the business environment

■ CONTENTS

1 Introduction
2 Subscription databases and company accounts
3 XBRL – business reporting language and business application
4 CSR reports and the triple bottom line (TBL)
5 Nature of business ethics
6 The role of ethics in modern business
7 Ethics and accountants in practice
8 Professional ethics – regulations

■ LEARNING OUTCOMES

Chapter 12 addresses the developing role of financial reporting and the accountant within organisations. After reading and understanding the contents of the chapter, working through all the worked examples and practice questions, you should be able to:

- explain the nature and purpose of subscription-based databases and their relationship to company accounts;
- discuss and demonstrate how XBRL business language fits in with, and applies to, accounting and financial reporting;
- understand and appreciate the role of the accountant in a capitalist society and the implications of the role for reporting;
- understand and explain what stand-alone environmental reports are;
- demonstrate the purpose and application of the Eco-Management and Audit Scheme, and its importance for business strategy;
- understand and explain the main features of social accounting in Britain;
- understand the purpose of corporate social responsibility reporting and the triple bottom line;
- relate to the positivist and normative approaches to business ethics;
- understand the relevance and importance of emerging role of ethics in business; and
- understand the implications for accountants and the ethical dimension.

1 Introduction

This chapter discusses current issues relevant to the role of chartered secretaries in the modern business environment. The role of the chartered secretary is very demanding and requires a person to be knowledgeable generally, but particularly in the changing and diverse business setting.

Companies regularly share information with a number of organisations such as the stock markets on which they are listed. Companies also need to provide financial and related information to government agencies. The cost of information distribution can be high and, in some cases, is enormous. Developments such as the IT platform **eXtensible Business Reporting Language (XBRL)** facilitate business efficiency, allowing companies to develop cost-effective data storage and retrieval systems that allow flexibility in data analysis and data transformation.

Environmental concerns have become more prominent in recent years, and companies are now expected to operate responsibly and proactively in relation to environmental and social issues. Many organisations such as Greenpeace lobby governments to pass legislation that makes companies responsible for their actions.

Companies are now expected to report social aspects of their business activities, the impact their activities have on the environment, and how they contribute to the environment and society in which they operate. Reporting on corporate social responsibility is increasingly becoming common in the annual reports of listed companies, and is part of a movement towards 'integrated reporting'.

2   Subscription databases and company accounts

The ever-increasing demand for information efficiency and cost-effective information systems has led to the widespread development and use of database systems. Databases are software systems designed to store and retrieve data in the format an entity requires in the most cost-effective manner. As with any system, in order to be cost-effective and add value, the benefits that the system brings (such as better informed decision-making) must outweigh the costs of development and implementation. Several subscription databases exist that process and present financial information in a standardised format. These databases take financial data and information from companies, and process this data into a standardised form that facilitates comparability, analysis and usage. Some of these databases are described below.

2.1 Amadeus

Amadeus contains financial information on over 400,000 European public and private companies (the Amadeus website states it holds information on over 19 million companies, but the information held on the majority of these companies would be relatively basic). For some companies, Amadeus holds up to ten years of detailed information in a standardised financial format comprising 22 statements of financial position items, 24 statement of comprehensive income account items and 25 ratios.

The database provides descriptive information that includes:

- official national identification number, address, telephone, email address, fax, website and legal form;
- year of incorporation;
- senior managers;
- auditors' details;
- number of employees;
- quoted/unquoted indicator;
- industry and activity codes; and
- a trade description in the local language and English.

It offers company peer group analysis and ranked and formatted output.

2.2 Bloomberg

Bloomberg's database covers international companies and markets. The database system provides real time and historical financial market data and economic data, covering all sectors worldwide. It also features analytics, company financials, news and customisable charting. Bloomberg provides company descriptions, five to ten years of financials, interest rates, time series of statistics, and company and industrial news.

2.3 Datastream

Datastream is a Thomson Reuters database that stores financial information on international companies, markets and economic statistics. It includes company accounts and ratios, equity and capital market data, interest and exchange rates, economic and industrial statistics, long time series for all data and downloads easily.

2.4 FAME

FAME (Financial Analysis Made Easy) covers companies registered in the UK and Ireland. It offers up to ten years of detailed information for 1.6 million companies, plus summarised information for a further 1 million companies, including those that have recently formed and have yet to file their first set of accounts. The detailed information includes:

- company profile;
- consolidated statement of profit or loss and other comprehensive income;
- statement of financial position;
- statement of cash flows; ratios and trends;
- County Court Judgments and mortgage data;
- credit score and rating;
- complete lists of holding companies, subsidiaries, directors and shareholders (including enhanced shareholders' option); and
- all 'site/trading' addresses and activity information, including brand names and miscellaneous information.

The demand from the user community to have access to web-based applications such as XBRL and Inline XBRL or iXBRL-based databases is increasing at an alarming rate. XBRL and iXBRL is explained in section 3. Developers are constantly trying to keep pace with this ever-increasing demand. With the advancement of computer and wireless technology, users can access information on the go.

The world of accounting practice is undergoing a transformation in terms of integration and online software as cloud operation increases. With the evolution of data storage on the cloud accounting software has also moved online with cloud-based accounting packages particularly attractive to small medium sized enterprises (SME) enabling them to access their accounting records from any mobile device, paying on a monthly basis for reporting as they require, however this does throw up certain other issues such as online security and access authorisation. The referral to the cloud is really the use of remote hosted servers that are accessible via the internet to enable access from any desktop computer or mobile device. Despite the explosion of the use of hosted remote networks, it may be regarded as a return to desktops being 'dumb terminals'.

'Our results suggest that accountants are increasingly looking for added integration with their day-to-day mobile applications to maximise efficiency', said Andrew Flanagan, managing director, Digita for the Tax & Accounting business of Thomson Reuters. 'It is crucial to understand the changing needs of the profession and this survey is just part of an ongoing dialogue to ensure that Digita applications deliver the innovative functionality the profession demands.'

Business entities that wish to integrate their business processes are increasingly under pressure to formalise web-based applications both in-house (i.e. within the company to integrate sharing of information on work practices and financial information) and externally, to integrate with other applications such as subscription-based databases such as Bloomberg, or government departments such as HM Revenue and Customs (HMRC) for tax and related matters. Increasingly XML (eXtensible Markup Language) based web languages are used to accommodate the switch to common web-based platforms for cost-effective data transfer and migration. The following is an example of a common data transfer requirement:

WORKED EXAMPLE 12.1

An individual who is preparing financial reports has the following query:

'As a practice we only produce one set of accounts in Excel spreadsheet format, so we are looking for a way of converting them into iXBRL without having to spend a fortune on software and without having to spend hours tagging everything ourselves. Some kind of Excel spreadsheet add-on would be the perfect solution. I'm sure there must be other practices facing the same problem, so I would appreciate any recommendations you could pass on to us.'

WORKED EXAMPLE **12.1** *continued*

Answer

Scenario 1 – by respondent 1

You can indeed buy a 'tagging tool', which can be used to convert files from Word or Excel into XBRL. These are cheaper than a full software package, but, as I understand it, are inevitably slightly more limited, so some manual tagging is necessary. Software developer, IRIS plc, provides such a tagging tool. I'm sure all of the big software companies do, as there are undoubtedly numerous firms that still use Excel and Word for preparing accounts. Alternatively, you could consider outsourcing the tagging function to a third party – which again is a solution offered by IRIS – but this can be fairly costly.

Scenario 2 – by respondent 2

You can use the VT[3] add-in to produce an iXBRL file from any set of accounts or tax computation in any Excel workbook. Views differ on how easy it is to self-tag a set of accounts. If you have to select tags from the full list (called *taxonomy*), then it is not easy at all. However, VT includes a special tagging dialog in which all the tags for a small company are laid out in the form of a sample set of accounts. It's easy to find the tag you want. It is possible, with experience, to self-tag a small set of accounts in 15 minutes. All the tagging data is saved in your own workbook (but is only accessible via the VT add-in).

Once your workbook is tagged, you just have to click on the Generate iXBRL File button on the toolbar created by the add-in. VT will check your tagging and tell you if there are any problems. If there are critical problems, it will not generate an iXBRL file. In theory, it is not possible to generate an iXBRL file using VT that will be rejected by HMRC, but things can go wrong further down the line.

Since April 2011, HMRC has required company accounts to be submitted in the form of an iXBRL file. Paper and pdf files are no longer accepted. An iXBRL file has the same format as a page on a website and the accounts it contains can be viewed in any web browser simply by opening the file. In addition, much of the data is specially tagged so that it can also be machine read.

TEST YOUR KNOWLEDGE **12.1**

a   Explain the purpose and use of a subscription database.
b   How can subscription databases help in communicating with relevant company stakeholders?

---

3   XBRL – business reporting language and business application

The common language of the internet is Hypertext Markup Language (HTML), which enables users to disseminate and share data and information on the internet in various ways and formats. Soon after the advent of the internet, many types of hypertext languages were developed specialising in the facilitation of various applications such as moving pictures, interactivity and sound, and real-time communication.

The business world, too, made headway in the development of hypertext languages that enabled users of financial information to exchange and store data in a reusable format at minimal cost.

The development of XBRL enabled the business community electronically to communicate economic and financial information in a manner that cut down costs, provides a greater level of efficiency of use and improved reliability to users and suppliers of information.

XBRL uses the XML syntax and related XML technologies, which are the standard tools used to communicate information between businesses and the internet. Data can be converted to XBRL by appropriate mapping tools designed to convert electronic data to XBRL format, or data can be written directly in XBRL by suitable software.

XBRL works on a system of tags. Instead of treating financial information as a block of text, as in a standard internet page or a printed document, XBRL provides an identifying tag for each individual item of data. This is computer readable. For example, company revenues and items of expenses and net profit have their own unique tag. This enables manipulation by users, through query forms, to generate data and information in the required format.

The introduction of XBRL tags enables automated processing of business information by computer software, facilitating efficient re-use of data for comparison. Computers can treat XBRL data 'intelligently', enabling the following:

- *Storage* of data and information in XBRL enables selection, analysis, exchange and presentation in a variety of ways, dependent on the end-users' requirements.
- *Speed* – XBRL greatly increases the speed of handling of financial data, reduces the chance of error and permits automatic checking of information.
- *Costs* – Companies can use XBRL to save costs and streamline their processes for collecting and reporting financial information.
- *Retrieval* – Consumers of financial data, including investors, analysts, financial institutions and regulators, and researchers, can locate, manipulate, compare and analyse data much more rapidly and efficiently in XBRL than by other online facilities.
- *Data handling* – XBRL can handle data in different languages and accounting standards. It can easily be adapted to meet different requirements and uses.

WORKED EXAMPLE 12.2

What file format is used by iXBRL files?

Answer

iXBRL files are written in HTML, the language used by web pages. An iXBRL file can be displayed in your web browser by double clicking on it. XBRL tags are also buried within the HTML, but are not visible in a standard web browser. These tags can only be seen in specialist software such as *VT Fact Viewer* or Corefiling's *Magnify* (Corefiling are HMRC's consultants).

HMRC's computer system only 'sees' the tagged items that are shown with a yellow background in VT Fact Viewer. However, if your accounts or tax computation are ever reviewed by a human being at HMRC, they will see all the text that you normally expect to see in a set of accounts or computation (as shown on the *Document* tab of VT Fact Viewer or in a web browser).

TEST YOUR KNOWLEDGE 12.2

a   What is XBRL?
b   How can companies make use of XBRL in financial reporting and information sharing within the company and with outsiders?

3.1 XBRL metadata

Metadata terminology is fundamental to understanding the way in which XBRL works. Put simply, metadata is data about data. In XBRL, financial data is tagged so that it can be understood and processed by computers.

For example, the word Asset together with brackets < and > would be called a tag: <Asset>. If XBRL included <Asset>900</Asset>, the computer would use the tags and the value to ascertain there is an Asset with a value of 900.

Elsewhere, other tags would help ensure assets are categorised and treated appropriately, in line with accounting rules.

Any aspect of the business process can be transferred to XBRL using the system of tags in the taxonomy dictionary. As is indicated from the answer in scenario 2 in Worked Example 12.1, many UK governmental returns are now submitted using XBRL formula-based technology.

3.2 XBRL taxonomy

XBRL taxonomies are the repositories that act as dictionaries containing assigned tags for specific individual items of financial data (e.g. profit). This enables the development of country- or company-specific taxonomies facilitating the application of accounting rules, regulations, standards and laws. From a user's perspective, there is no need to understand the technicalities of the language. It is a user-defined spectrum allowing for data migration, transferability, use and analysis.

XBRL supports an open standard of financial reporting. This means that it is flexible enough to support all the current ways of reporting in different countries and industries. The XBRL system is free; there are no licence fees either to supply or to access the information. It is a non-profit venture primarily supported by XBRL International, which is a collaboration of around 550 major international companies, organisations and government agencies. XBRL has already been implemented and is regularly used in a growing number of countries and industries around the world.

The IFRS Foundation now publishes an annual taxonomy that is in effect a translation of IFRS (International Financial Reporting Standards) into XBRL.

3.3 IFRS and XBRL developments

The purpose of IFRS in the business community are to pave the way for global reporting processes that are common across countries. To facilitate and strengthen this process, the International Accounting Standards Board (IASB) and XBRL entities are working together to develop a set of XBRL taxonomies that will enable the creation and use of common set of internet-enabled reporting formats throughout the world.

The IFRS Foundation now publishes an annual taxonomy that is in effect a translation of IFRS into XBRL.

The following passages are from the IASB website:

Both IFRS and XBRL are intended to standardise financial reporting in order to promote transparency and to improve the quality and comparability of business information, therefore, the two entities form a perfect partnership.

The **IASB XBRL Team** is responsible for developing and maintaining the XBRL representation of the IFRS, known as the **IFRS Taxonomy**. The IFRS Taxonomy is used around the world to facilitate the electronic use and exchange of financial data prepared in accordance with IFRS.

The IASB's XBRL activities include:
- *Taxonomy development* – for companies reporting in IFRS, the Foundation publishes tags for each IFRS disclosure. These tags are organised and contained within the IFRS Taxonomy.
- *Support materials* – the Foundation produces support materials to facilitate use and understanding of the IFRS Taxonomy.
- *Translations* – translations of the IFRS Taxonomy into key languages are provided to support users of both IFRS and the IFRS Taxonomy whose primary language is not English.
- *Global outreach* – the Foundation makes a concerted effort to promote the use of XBRL in conjunction with IFRS around the world. The Foundation also encourages co-operation and communication with users of the IFRS Taxonomy.

The collaboration between IASB and XBRL is an important move towards harmonisation of financial reporting processes. This will have tremendous implication for the capital markets around the world enabling information capture, analysis and decision-making at greater speed than at any other time in history.

The accountant is no longer the isolated bean-counter in the back room. The role and practice of the accountant is now very much at the forefront, driving and steering the business through unchartered waters, some of which are shark infested!

The accountant is now a key player in the strategy development of an entity and no longer reports solely on financial performance to a narrow audience. Accountants today play a central, direct role in the process of business. They communicate a wide range of accounting and financial information to internal and external stakeholders.

4   CSR reports and the triple bottom line (TBL)

Sustainability and corporate social responsibility (CSR) and integrated reporting (IR) is concerned with being a 'good corporate citizen'. While CSR reporting includes social accounting, it is a broader aspect of corporate reporting, integrating financial reporting with social and environmental perspectives.

Powerful multinational corporations touch people's lives in more ways now than at any time in the past. This necessitated a change in corporate attitude towards the environment and society in which they operate. CSR reporting is a corporate tool that engages companies' self-assessment and self-regulation by integrating business functions with social needs, thereby taking account of ethical considerations as well as various stakeholder interests. Guiding principles and practices have developed from a number of perspectives, including the three we discuss below.

4.1 ISO 26000

ISO 26000 (International Organization for Standardization – an independent, non-governmental international organisation) is an international standard, principle-based guidance, rather than requirement, on CSR practices and is designed to assist companies in implementing and integrating business practices with social awareness. This is not a certifiable standard and hence cannot be used as part of a social audit. The ISO website presents the following components of ISO 26000:

ISO 26000 will help all types of organisations – regardless of their size, activity or location – to operate in a socially responsible manner by providing guidance on:
- concepts, terms and definitions related to social responsibility;
- background, trends and characteristics of social responsibility;
- principles and practices relating to social responsibility;
- core subjects and issues related to social responsibility;
- integrating, implementing and promoting socially responsible behaviour throughout the organisation and, through its policies and practices, within its sphere of influence;
- identifying and engaging with stakeholders; and
- communicating commitments, performance and other information related to social responsibility.

ISO 26000 is developed on the basis of best practice from around the world for multi-national enterprises and is seen as an important initiative in helping and guiding companies to integrate best practices in their business activity. Indeed, January 2016 saw the 2030 Agenda for Sustainable Development come into effect which includes a set of 17 Sustainable Development Goals to end poverty, fight inequality and injustice and tackle climate change by 2030, ISO 26000 provides a 'visible, influential and pragmatic way to impulse change'.

4.2 Triple bottom line framework

Initially developed for the public sector, this approach has become a dominant feature in providing the basis for reporting beyond profit figures. There are three components to the triple bottom line (TBL) framework approach:

1 economic;
2 ecological;
3 social.

However, TBL has not taken off significantly, although CSR has become an important issue in modern business practices. Freer Spreckley (1981) argued for an extended version of the 'bottom' line in company financial reports. His idea of the TBL was developed in *'Social audit: a management tool for co-operative working'*.

The concept of the TBL encapsulates all stakeholders who are impacted by corporate behaviour, and advocates an integrated approach to business activity that takes account of environmental, ecological and sustainability issues.

As an example, the Kjaer group (Denmark) deals in automotive parts in North Africa. In its 2015 Annual Report, the group made the following statement:

'The Kjaer Group Way of Management
The Kjaer Group Way of Management consists of the Group's mission, vision, key processes, policies and adoption of the '**Triple Bottom Line**' principle, which ensures that decisions are made with equal balance between financial results as well as social and environmental responsibility.'

As the bulk of the group's business is with North African countries, it maintains the highest of standards in dealing fairly with its customer base and links economic progress with social progress in a number of ways (e.g. it is involved in and contributes to non-governmental organisation's (NGOs) work with people living in poverty in North Africa).

4.3 Global Reporting Initiative (GRI)

This is a not-for-profit organisation that promotes both economic and sustainability issues. The GRI initiative is an important development and encompasses a number of issues for corporations and entities to take into account in both their business and non-business activities. These include ecological footprint reporting, TBL reporting, environmental social governance (ESG) reporting and corporate governance reporting. The idea behind GRI is to promote equal importance to social, environmental and governance matters with regard to economics.

4.4 Social, ethical and environment issues – a summary

All the initiatives discussed above demonstrate the relevance and global need for a greater quality of reporting above and beyond simple economic performance. The continuing integration of national processes within the greater global community now demands fairness for all. The developed world has to work hand-in-hand with the developing world, with a fair return for all. The Fair Trade initiative seeks to promote a better quality of life for workers in developing economies. Increasingly, retailers of consumer goods are disclosing how they source their raw material and finished and semi-finished goods from countries such as India, Pakistan and some African states.

 **TEST YOUR KNOWLEDGE 12.3**

Explain the purpose of the TBL concept and its usefulness to companies' corporate reporting.

5 Nature of business ethics

Ethics is concerned with the concept of right and wrong. Ethics can mean different things to different people. At its core, ethics subscribes to human behaviour that provides a basis for fairness and socially acceptable conduct that does not allow one group of people to infringe on the rights of another. Some definitions of ethics are provided below:

- Ethics is fundamental to human behaviour and is related to good or bad practices in society.
- Moral conduct can be described as either being right or wrong, acceptable or unacceptable.
- Business ethics substantially relates to good or bad behaviour.

Business ethics examine the ethical principles and moral or ethical problems that arise in a business environment. It is a field of ethics that deals with moral and ethical dilemmas in many areas of human endeavour such as medicine, technology and the law.

In an ever-changing corporate landscape, business ethics has gained ground. Capitalism can no longer be seen as a simple case of making a profit. However, since capitalism requires people to make it work, societies and individuals demand fairness in their lives. Business ethics can provide benefits for companies through the efficient adoption of ethical practices that impact upon:

- the common good of society;
- a sense of ethical motivation and sustainability;
- a balanced approach to the needs of stakeholder groups;
- social and economic reputation;
- security from legal implications; and
- enhanced employee commitment and retention.

Ethical implications relate to all areas of a business including finance, marketing and operational, and management activity. By giving due regard to business ethics, companies can enhance their reputational capital and thus retain customer loyalty.

5.1 Ethical motivation

This protects a company's reputation by creating an efficient and productive working environment. In the current economic climate, promoting ethical principles gives employees greater sense of security.

5.2 Needs of stakeholders

This is a primary issue in business ethics. Stakeholder interest has a greater connotation in terms of societal pressures placed upon companies to be seen to be ethical. Company values and reputation are built not only on adopting ethical behaviour but also by applying, demonstrating and communicating that behaviour and its measurable impact on the environment and society.

5.3 Employee commitment and retention

Even in constrained times, businesses lose employees due to changes that are perceived as being unfair. This could prove to be a costly exercise when employees with good skills lose confidence in their employment. An ethical programme of employee engagement could prove to be a worthwhile exercise in which making the right decisions provides perceived benefits and rewards.

5.4 Legal implications of unethical behaviour

Legal implications can arise both from within a company and from external litigation. Employees who feel aggrieved by their company's policies should have an avenue open to them, within the business, that enables them to air their concerns without fear. Employee concerns should be dealt with systematically and fairly.

Additionally, legal implications may arise if companies do not have robust detection and prevention measures in place to check and deal with legal issues that may cause reputational risk. For instance, if a company is fully compliant with legal requirements for health and safety, the possibility of legal liability would be greatly reduced.

Selected issues have been discussed above to demonstrate the nature of business ethics. Prior research has shown that unethical practices cost industry many millions in lost revenue. For example, work-related stress means employees are off work for many days or weeks, resulting in lost revenue and production and the higher costs of employing temporary replacements.

TEST YOUR KNOWLEDGE 12.4

Explain business ethics and the role it plays in modern corporations.

STOP AND THINK 12.1

Consider the policies a petrochemical company based in North Scotland should consider in its ethical approach to business.

6 The role of ethics in modern business

Much of what comprises business ethics has already been discussed. Increasingly the business community can no longer function efficiently unless it can demonstrate a commitment to ethical practices. To understand this concept further, let's look at some comments made by Charles Harrington of Parsons Inc (US), a mid-size company employing 11,200 workers:

> Our strong commitment to our six Core Values – Safety, Quality, Integrity, Diversity, Innovation and Sustainability – governs everything we do at Parsons. Our Core Values are the very beliefs that form the culture of our organization, that make us who we are, that form the basis for all of our decisions. We strive hard to create an atmosphere where the question of deviating from those Core Values, from doing what is right, whether for perceived individual or corporate gain, never even gets raised.

In the above commentary, important words and phrases used are:

■ core values;
■ commitment;
■ safety;
■ quality;
■ integrity;
■ diversity;
■ innovation;
■ sustainability;
■ beliefs;
■ organisational culture;
■ doing what is right.

Some very important terminologies are used here, demonstrating that CSR and ethics are embedded in the business management processes of Parsons Inc. Similarly, in the UK, Tesco plc has embedded the ethical approach to its business processes as part of its business strategy, thereby enhancing company image, value and reputation. It is critical that the values, mission, and identity of the company come from the leaders and are implemented throughout the organisation so that it becomes second nature to the employees of the company.

In formulating participatory business ethics, applied ethics can assist companies to determine policies and processes that are developed from a shared perspective, offering stakeholders the opportunity to participate in the decision-making process.

Companies that attempt to create a balance between value maximisation and non-financial issues generally are trying to manage their businesses on a sustainable basis. The fact is that national and international accounting standards exist to regulate financial reporting, yet huge corporate collapses still occur (e.g. Satyam in India in 2009). This demonstrates that ethical malpractices abound in both developed and developing countries. However, many corporate collapses are simply down to economic factors or fail due to business strategy (e.g. Woolworths, Peacocks and Game).

Hotly contested and much debated are intellectual property rights (IPR). An intellectual property right is the ownership of an idea, thought, code or information. For instance, protection of a particular drug developed over years of research ensures that the developing company has the right to any revenues that transpire. However, recent events indicate that patents are a company's way of monopolising a certain market. This suggests the stifling of competition in a capitalist market where competition is seen as good for the economy and protection for consumers. Competition forces companies to develop their business strategy to meet and manage competing forces.

Companies view IPR from a utilitarian perspective. However, a moral perspective has a counter-argument in that utility is developed from societal needs and that a product that has universal application and provides relief for vast numbers of human beings cannot, by nature, be protected from value-maximising economic constraints; hence it must be shared universally. Some 39 pharmaceutical companies filed a lawsuit against South Africa's 1997 Medicines and Related Substances Control Amendment Act, as its provisions aimed to provide affordable HIV medicines. This has been cited as a harmful effect of patents-based monopolisation by a handful of corporations.

British companies are seen as very proactive in ethical matters. Larger corporations have an integrated and embedded ethical approach to managing their business processes. Some companies have appointed ethics officers to manage the company's ethical affairs. Much ethical concern developed between 1980 and 2010, due to highly publicised corporate collapses mainly in the US. With the enactment of the Sarbanes-Oxley Act 2002, ethics-related development formed a backdrop to unethical American business practices. Ethics is about setting boundaries beyond which it would be considered wrong to engage in activity that would damage a company's reputation.

7 Ethics and accountants in practice

Accountants have a fiduciary duty towards their employers as well as to their investors and to the larger world. This duty is based on both legal and ethical considerations. The past two decades have seen some remarkable corporate collapses, mainly in the US, with Enron, Worldcom, Tyco, etc. Methods of accounting, such as off-statement of financial position finance and special purposes entities, were one of the main causes of financial irregularities coupled with (in some cases) unprofessional conduct by management and external auditors. These events have drawn attention to the professionalism of practising accountants and levels of ethical standards.

The 'crisis' in the accounting profession that followed and the criticism it faced led to a stream of regulations emanating from both accounting bodies and governments to prevent further damage to the profession and bring a sense of stability and confidence to stakeholders.

In an article published in 2007 in the *Managerial Auditing Journal*, mitigating factors were identified that contributed to ethical weaknesses for accountants. The article surveyed 66 members of the International Federation of Accountants (IFAC). The main factors that were identified included:

- self-interest;
- failure to maintain objectivity and independence;
- inappropriate professional judgment;
- lack of ethical sensitivity;
- improper leadership and ill-culture;
- failure to withstand advocacy threats;
- lack of competence;
- lack of organisational and peer support; and
- lack of professional body support.

Above all, the main threat to an accountant's ethical behaviour is the self-interest that places personal consideration above ethical and professional judgment. For example, if an auditor questions the appropriateness of a particular accounting entry in an audit, the financial consideration in terms of fees being charged to the client may allow the auditor to act unethically and ignore the issue. In such circumstances, the accountant is faced with making professional decisions that include:

- reporting a particular matter or set of issues to an immediate superior both formally and informally; such issues could be related to lack of clarity on cash flows in and out of a company;
- whistle-blowing to an external and relevant agency as seen in the recent Panama Papers leak from one of the largest off shore law firms Mossack Fonseca – this would require careful consideration on the part of the accountant as it may involve exposure to possible litigation (e.g. illegal sourcing of products or trading with banned organisations or even countries);
- ignoring the issue and letting the system catch up with it (an unethical alternative and not recommended). However, there may be legal implications for 'not doing nothing', and in certain circumstances the law may require an individual to have deemed to have known certain facts and thereby taken some sort of an action to disclose a relevant issue; and
- considering resigning from their post on ethical grounds.

8 Professional ethics – regulations

After the notoriety of corporate scandals since the 1980s, new and enhanced regulations have emerged, putting the onus on accountants to take ethical actions in circumstances that demand it.

8.1 Money laundering regulations

Money laundering has become a sophisticated venture for some organisations and persons. HMRC provides some guidance on this issue:

> The Money Laundering Regulations 2007 came into force in December 2007. All businesses that are covered by the regulations have to put suitable anti-money laundering controls in place. If the regulations apply to your business you must put these controls in place as soon as possible.
>
> As part of the anti-money laundering controls that you have to put in place, you need to appoint a nominated officer (sometimes called the money laundering reporting officer).

Changes to the Money Laundering Regulations in 2007 recognised the same client–accountant privilege as exists with lawyers. This means that, since 2007, accountants are no longer required to report suspicious transactions to the National Criminal Intelligence Service. However, professional accounting bodies still retain an ethical dimension in their guidelines.

All UK professional accounting bodies publish a code of conduct for their members, in both industry and practice, based upon the IFAC's ethical standards. The ethical standards that shape the codes of the professional accountancy bodies are:

- *Integrity* – members must be honest, trustworthy and forthright in all business and professional relationships.
- *Objectivity* – members must not allow conflict of interest, bias or external pressures to influence professional judgment.
- *Professional competence and due care* – members must provide advice based upon current knowledge and relevant skills, acting diligently and in accordance with applicable technical standards.
- *Confidentiality* – members must not disclose confidential information acquired from business and professional relationships to third parties or for personal advantage.
- *Professional behaviour* – members must comply with relevant laws and regulations and uphold a professional demeanour in all business and professional relationships

TEST YOUR KNOWLEDGE 12.5

Identify and explain the implications for the accountant with regard to business ethics.

Accountants, both in practice and in business, are seeing emerging trends for accountability and the requirement for ethical behaviour. The accountant in business comes under the scrutiny of the auditor. A conflict of loyalty may arise between the requirement to be transparent and management pressure to comply with its agenda. In such situations, ethical judgment needs to be exercised by accountants that may have professional and career implications.

END OF CHAPTER QUESTIONS

12.1 Abbey Group plc is a manufacturer of specialised machine parts and has a presence in most major growing economies such as China, India, Pakistan and Brazil, as well as the European Union. Abbey maintains a divisionalised group structure where each country is a division. The group maintains a decentralised structure with divisions able to make decisions on a local basis; however, strategy is developed by Abbey HQ.

Each division maintains its own IT policy with heterogeneous systems employed across the various divisions. Up to now, the data sharing between divisions has been minimal as each division specialises in its own area of expertise and manufactures totally different machine parts. However, collecting the financial data is a laborious exercise and the annual group financial reports are badly affected. Financial and accounting data is collected in different formats and, in some cases, this information reaches the HQ in the form of e-mail attachments.

The chief finance officer (CFO) of Abbey plc is unhappy about the length of time taken to collect and process financial and accounting data into a usable format for group purposes. The group is listed on the London and New York stock markets and has been previously warned by the listing regulators about the delay in submitting the group financial report.

The CFO calls a meeting of a working group to investigate the solutions to Abbey's IT problems. The chief systems officer (CSO) suggests that the group could develop a common information sharing platform based on XBRL technology.

Required

a   From the information the case of Abbey plc, explain XBRL.

b   How can Abbey plc use XBRL to share financial information?

c   What would be the level of cost involved in setting up the new technology without going into the amounts in detail?

d   What platform would XBRL require?

e   Comment on the benefits of using XBRL to Abbey plc.

12.2 James is the environmental compliance officer for a medium-sized car parts manufacturing company. James has to decide whether or not the company should invest in new technology that would reduce toxic emissions from current technology being released into the atmosphere. The company's emission levels are within legal guidelines; however, James knows that environmental regulations for this particular toxin are lagging behind scientific evidence. A recent academic research paper suggests that if toxins of this type are not legislated for, it would impact on the health of people living near the company.

Required

a   Consider the ethical concerns that James is dealing with.

b   What action should the company take in assessing its environmental impact?

c   How should the company report such an impact?

12.3 Stakeholders are increasingly looking to the quality and quantity of corporate social reporting. In assisting users of corporate social reports, disclosures in the annual financial reports play an important role.

Required

a   Apart from a company's business performance, how can users of annual financial reports assess corporate social behaviour and a company's attitude towards its environment?

b   What other sources of information are available to ascertain corporate social behaviour?

Answers to end of chapter questions

Chapter 1 – The regulatory framework for the preparation and presentation of financial statements

1.1
- To develop, in the public interest, a single set of high-quality, understandable and enforceable global accounting standards that require high-quality, transparent and comparable information in financial statements and other financial reporting to help participants in the world's capital markets and other users make economic decisions.
- To promote the use and rigorous application of those standards.
- To bring about convergence of national accounting standards and International Financial Reporting Standards (IFRS).

1.2 Accounting standards:
- oblige companies to disclose the accounting policies they have used to prepare their published financial reports. This should make the financial information easier to understand and allow both shareholders and investors to make informed economic decisions;
- require companies to disclose information in the financial statements that they might not disclose if the standards did not exist;
- reduce the risk of creative accounting. This means that financial statements can be used to compare either the financial performance of different entities or the same entity over time; and
- provide a focal point for discussion about accounting practice. They should increase the credibility of financial statements by improving the uniformity of accounting treatment between companies.

1.3 The external audit provides an independent opinion on the true and fair representation of financial statements that a company has produced. The audit provides the users of the financial statements with an assurance of increased confidence and reduced risks in the use of the financial statements for their own economic decisions. In addition, the external audit serves as a part of the corporate governance process in that the auditor is reporting on the effectiveness and reliability of the systems installed by management as part of the financial reporting process.

1.4 Corporate governance concerns the systems by which a company is directed and serves as the overall framework within which financial reports are generated. The effectiveness and reliability of the internal controls put in place by management are the operational framework that enable the production of financial statements for the multiple user groups. Corporate governance is designed to ensure that the output of the financial reporting system, the financial statements, are reliable and may be used by the various user groups.

1.5 Social accounting is the formal process by which an entity reports on the wider social impact of its economic activity to stakeholders. The range of social reporting may include:

- recycling of waste;
- education;
- environment/pollution emission/chemicals;
- regeneration, social inclusion and community investment;
- workforce issues;
- responsible behaviour in developing countries;
- agriculture;
- pharmaceuticals/animal testing/drug development; and
- regeneration issues.

Chapter 2 – The conceptual framework for the preparation and presentation of financial statements

2.1 The general purpose of financial reports is to provide information about the financial position of a reporting entity, which is information about the entity's economic resources and the claims against the reporting entity. Financial reports also provide information about the effects of transactions and other events that change a reporting entity's economic resources and claims. Both types of information provide useful input for decisions about providing resources to an entity.

2.2 a False
   b False
   c True
   d False
   e True
   f False

2.3 The four enhanced characteristics that make financial reporting information useful for its readers are as follows.

Comparability
Comparability is the qualitative characteristic that enables users to identify and understand the similarities in, and differences among, items in their comparative analysis. Comparability does not relate to a single item. Consistency, although related to comparability, is not the same. Comparability is not uniformity.

Verifiability
Verifiability is the quality that helps to assure users that the reported financial information faithfully represents the economic phenomena it purports to represent. Verifiability would permit two or more different knowledgeable and independent observers to reach consensus that a particular depiction is a faithful representation. Verification can be direct or indirect. Direct verification may arise from the process of direct observation, such as the end-of-year stock count. Indirect verification is the process of checking using a calculation model or technique to verify the financial information.

Timeliness
Timeliness is the provision of the information to decision-makers with sufficient time to allow the information to influence their decisions.

Understandability
Information should be classified, characterised and presented clearly and concisely to facilitate understanding by users. The users of financial information are deemed to have a reasonable knowledge of business and economic activities such that the exclusion of a complex phenomenon should not occur to ease understanding.

2.4 The going concern concept is the underlying assumption identified in the conceptual framework. 'Going concern' means that the financial statements of an entity are normally prepared on the assumption that the entity will continue in operation for the foreseeable future. Hence, it is assumed that the entity has neither the intention nor the need to liquidate or curtail materially the scale of its operations; if such an intention or need exists, the financial statements may have to be prepared on a different basis and, if so, the basis used should be disclosed.

2.5 Own answers.

2.6 The two concepts of capital maintenance are as follows.

Financial capital maintenance
Profit is earned only if the financial (or monetary) amount of the net assets at the end of the period exceeds the financial (or monetary) amount of net assets at the beginning of the period, after excluding any distributions to, and contributions from, owners during the

period. Financial capital maintenance can be measured in either nominal monetary units or units of constant purchasing power.

Physical capital maintenance

Profit is earned only if the physical productive capacity (or operating capability) of the entity (or the resources or funds needed to achieve that capacity) at the end of the period exceeds the physical productive capacity at the beginning of the period, after excluding any distributions to, and contributions from, owners during the period.

Chapter 3 – Financial accounting and the preparation of financial reports

3.1 The four principal statements that a company is required to publish and include are:

- a statement of financial position (balance sheet) at the end of the period;
- a statement of profit or loss and other comprehensive income for the period (presented as a single statement, or by presenting the profit or loss section in a separate statement of profit or loss, immediately followed by a statement presenting comprehensive income beginning with profit or loss);
- a statement of changes in equity for the period; and
- a statement of cash flows for the period.

The statement of financial position demonstrates to the user the assets and liabilities and equity of a company at any particular moment in time, usually the year end.

The purpose of the statement of profit or loss and other comprehensive income for the period is to show the financial performance of the company based on inputs and outputs and the profits that transpire.

The statement of changes in equity for the period shows all changes in an owner's equity for a period of time.

The statement of cash flows for the period shows the cash flow in and out of the company through three main headings: cash flow from operating activities; cash flow from investing activities; and cash flow from financing activities.

3.2 Answer: c best reflects the statement of changes in equity.

3.3 Sigma plc

Statement of financial position as at 31 December 20X6

Assets	£,000
Non-current assets	
Property, plant and equipment	900
Brand	100
Capitalised development expenditure	200
Investments in subsidiaries	200
Other receivables (due to be received 20X7)	300
Goodwill	400
	2,100
Current assets	
Inventory	300
Trade and other receivables	950
Derivative financial assets (short-term)	100
Cash and cash equivalents	200
	1,550

Total assets	3,650
Equity and liabilities	
Equity	
Ordinary share capital (£1 ordinary shares) (see W1)	2,390
Capital redemption reserve	80
Revaluation reserve	150
Retained earnings	300
Total equity	2,920
Non-current liabilities	
10% bonds – 20X8	60
Deferred tax	100
Provision for decommissioning of nuclear plant in 20X5	50
Retirement benefit obligations	120
	330
Current liabilities	
Trade payables	300
Taxation	100
	400
Total equity and liabilities	3,650
(W1)	
Total assets	3,650
Non-current liabilities	330
Current liabilities	400
Total liabilities	730
Equity items:	
Capital redemption reserve	80
Revaluation reserve	150
Retained earnings	300
Total equities	530
Total equity and liabilities (excluding share capital)	1,260
Share capital – £1 ordinary shares: £3,650 – £1,260	2,390

3.4 **1. Opal Ltd**

Statement of profit or loss and other comprehensive income for the year ended 31 December 20X6

	£,000	
Revenue	5,100	
Cost of sales	(2,480)	
Gross profit	2,620	
Distribution costs	545	
Administrative expenses	971	W1 = 924 + 60 – 13
Profit from operations	1,104	
Interest payable	12	W2 = 200 × 6%
Profit before tax	1,092	
Tax	300	Note 9

Profit for the year	792

2. Opal Ltd
Statement of changes in equity for the year ended 31 December 20X6

	Share capital	Share premium	Retained earnings	Total
	£,000	*£,000*	*£,000*	*£,000*
Balance 01/01/20X2	1,750	250	850	2,850
SOCI			792	792
Dividends			(35)	(35)
New issue of shares	250	200		450
	2,000	450	1,607	4,057

3. Opal Ltd
Statement of financial position at 31 December 20X6

	£,000	*£,000*	
Non-current assets			
Equipment		4,490	W2 = 3,890+600
Current assets			
Inventory	270		Note 6
Trade receivables	208		
Prepayments	13	491	Note 3 (W4 = 26,000 / 2 = 13,000)
		4,981	
Equity and liabilities			
Share capital	2,000		Notes 7 and 8 (W5 = 2,200 − 200)
Share premium	450		
Retained earnings	1,607	4,057	
Non-current liabilities			
6% debenture loan	200	200	
Current liabilities			
Trade and other payables	229		W8 = 212 + 12 + 5
Income tax	300	544	Note 9
		4,801	

4. a   IFRS 3 defines fair value as 'the amount for which an asset could be exchanged, or a liability settled, between knowledgeable, willing parties in an arm's length agreement'.

b   Measurement and recognition of revenues – IFRS 15 prescribes the measure and recognition of revenue. The measurement of revenue is provided in IAS 18 as follows:

Revenue should be measured at the fair value of the consideration received or receivable. An exchange for goods or services of a similar nature and value is not regarded as a transaction that generates revenue. However, exchanges for dissimilar items are regarded as generating revenue.

Recognition of revenues – IFRS 15 provides an explanation of revenue as follows:

Recognition, as defined in the IASB Framework, means incorporating an item that meets the definition of revenue (above) in the income statement when it meets the following criteria:

- it is probable that any future economic benefit associated with the item of revenue will flow to the entity, and
- the amount of revenue can be measured with reliability.

c   Other comprehensive income is defined as gains or losses on non-current assets that have yet to be realised. These items may include:

- gains or losses on foreign currency translations;
- changes in the fair value of available-for-sale financial assets;
- actuarial gains and losses arising on a defined benefit pension plan;
- revaluations of property, plant and equipment; and
- changes in the fair value of a financial instrument in a cash-flow hedge.

d   Reporting entities: An entity that carries on business and conducts financial transaction is classified as a reporting entity and is required to file accounts with at least the tax authority (HMRC). These include: sole traders, partnerships, clubs and societies, and limited companies. In the latter case there may be other requirements, such as publication of annual reports (for listed companies) and the submission of accounts to Companies House.

Chapter 4 – Accounting policies 1

4.1 c   Recognise the reduction as an impairment indicator and carry out an impairment test.

4.2 Lease Payments

Year	Loan	Repay	Capital	Interest	Loan O/S
	£	£	£	£	£
0	38,211	0	38,211	0	765,789
1	765,789	230,010	168,747	61,263	597,042
2	597,042	230,010	182,247	47,763	414,795
3	414,795	230,010	196,826	33,184	217,969

Depreciation charge

Year	Opening value	Depn charge	Closing value
	£	£	£
1	804,000	201,000	603,000
2	603,000	201,000	402,000
3	402,000	201,000	201,000
4	201,000	201,000	0

The opening balance of lease charges are: £800,000 – £38,211 = £761,789.

In each year of the lease, the company will make a depreciation charge of £201,000; however, in the first year, the procurement cost of £4,000 will be capitalised, hence the total cost of purchase of the lease will show a balance of £761,789.

4.3 a   The initial cost of tangible non-current assets should be measured according to the provisions of IAS 16:

An item of property, plant and equipment should initially be recorded at cost. Cost includes all costs necessary to bring the asset to working condition for its intended use. This would include not only its original purchase price, but also costs of site preparation, delivery and handling, installation, related professional fees for architects and engineers.

b   The circumstances in which subsequent expenditure on those assets should be capitalised are:

- that expenditure provides an enhancement of the economic benefits of the tangible non-current asset in excess of its previously assessed standard of performance;
- a component of an asset that has been treated separately for depreciation purposes is replaced or restored; or
- subsequent expenditure relates to a major inspection or overhaul that restores the economic benefits that have already been consumed and reflected in depreciation.

IAS 16's requirements regarding the revaluation of non-current assets and the accounting treatment of surpluses and deficits on revaluation and gains and losses on disposal provide the following:

- Depreciation should be on a systematic basis over the useful economic life of the asset. However, a periodic review of the fair value of an asset must be carried out by the directors and disclosed in the financial reports.
- If on fair value inspection an asset appreciates in value, the difference between the fair value and the carrying value must be credited to reserve and debited to property, plant and equipment or another class of non-current assets.
- Any subsequent loss in value should first debit against the revaluation reserve. If the whole amount can be charged to the revaluation reserve, no entry is needed in the statement of income.
- If the revaluation reserve is less than the impaired value, the revaluation reserve is depleted first, then any difference is charged to the income statement.
- On disposal of an asset, any gains or losses on disposal are charged to the income statement.

4.4 Year	Loan	Repay	Capital	Interest	Loan O/S
1	1,500,000	160,000	85,000	75,000	1,415,000
2	1,415,000	160,000	89,250	70,750	1,325,750
3	1,325,750	160,000	93,712	66,288	1,232,038
4	1,232,038	160,000	98,398	61,602	1,133,640
5	1,133,639	160,000	103,318	56,682	1,030,321
6	1,030,321	160,000	108,484	51,516	921,837
7	921,837	160,000	113,908	46,092	807,929
8	807,929	160,000	119,604	40,396	688,326
9	688,326	160,000	125,584	34,416	562,742
10	562,742	160,000	131,863	28,137	430,879
11	430,879	160,000	138,456	21,544	292,423
12	292,423	160,000	145,379	14,621	147,044
13	147,044	154,396	147,044	7,352	0

The final instalment payment is reduced to £154,396 as per the question.

4.5 An adjusting event is an event that arises after the reporting period but its condition was known to exist at the end of the reporting period. This includes any event that may render the going concern assumption to be breached. The discovery that the inventories had been overstated or understated during the end-of-period stock-checking process would be an example of an adjusting event.

A non-adjusting event is any event that arises after the reporting period and its condition was not in existence at the end of the reporting period. Although such an event does not give rise to an adjustment in the financial statements, a disclosure is made in the financial statements if the event is material. The damage to inventory through a fire or flood following after the reporting period is an example of a non-adjusting event as the damage occurred after the reporting period. The materiality of the damage would determine whether a disclosure was required in the notes to the financial statements.

In conclusion, the determining factor in the classification of adjusting or non-adjusting is whether the condition was known to exist at the reporting date.

4.6 a

	20X3	Restated 20X2
	£,000	£,000
Turnover	850	600
Cost of goods sold	410	255
Gross profit	440	345
Operating expenses	460	335
Profit/(Loss) before taxation	(20)	10
Taxation at 20%	0	2
Post tax profit/(Loss)	(20)	8

b

Retained earnings

	£,000
31 Dec 20X1	85
31 Dec 20X2 (Revised)	8
	169
31 Dec 20X3 (Revised) Loss	(20)
31 Dec 20X3	225

Chapter 5 – Accounting policies 2

5.1 Due to quantity or value, not all operating segments need to be separately reported. Operating segments only need to be reported if they exceed quantitative thresholds.

Quantitative thresholds (IFRS 8 para 13)
Information on an operating segment should be reported separately if:

- reported revenue (external and inter-segment) is 10% or more of the combined revenue of all operating segments;
- the absolute amount of the segment's reported profit or loss is 10% or more of the greater of: the combined reported profit of all operating segments that did not report a loss; and the combined loss of all operating segments that reported a loss; or
- the segment's assets are 10% or more of the combined assets of all operating segments.

Two or more operating segments may be combined (aggregated) and reported as one if certain conditions are satisfied. The objective of this standard is to establish principles for reporting financial information by segment to help users of financial statements:

- better understand the enterprise's past performance;
- better assess the enterprise's risks and returns; and
- make more informed judgments about the enterprise as a whole.

5.2 **Statement of profit or loss and other comprehensive income of Buffalo Ltd as at 31 December 20X6**

	Copiers	Paper	Printing	HO	Total
	£,000	£,000	£,000	£,000	£,000
Revenue	611	395	104	0	1,110
Less: Cost of sales	384	146	44	0	574
Administration expenses	47	9	18	22	96
Distribution	101	17	24	0	142
Finance costs	6	1	1	2	10
Net profit	73	222	17	(24)	288

Statement of financial position of Buffalo Ltd as at 31 December 20X6

Assets	Copiers	Paper	Printing	HO	Total
	£,000	£,000	£,000	£,000	£,000
Non-current assets at book value	1,012	767	432	232	2,443
Current assets					
Inventories	31	14	12	–	57
Receivables	23	12	9	–	44
Bank	148	46	31	–	225
Total assets	1,214	839	484	232	2,769
Equity and liabilities					
Share capital				1,000	1,000
Retained earnings				1,449	1,449
Non-current liabilities					
Long-term borrowing	210	–	–	–	210
Current liabilities					
Payables	32	20	16	10	78
Short-term borrowing	13	7	4	8	32
Total equity and liabilities	255	27	20	2,467	2,769

5.3 An entity must change its accounting policy only if the change is:

- required by standard accounting practice; or
- results in the financial statements providing more relevant and reliable information about the entity's financial position, financial performance or cash flows.

Usually, a change in accounting policy is applied *retrospectively* to all periods presented in the financial statements, as if the new accounting policy has always been applied. This means that the brought-forward carrying value of the asset or liability and retained profits must both be appropriately adjusted.

5.4 a IAS 8 defines an item as material in the following circumstances. Omissions or mis-statements of items are material if they could, by their size or nature, individually or collectively influence the economic decisions of users taken on the basis of the financial statements. Materiality depends on the size and nature of the omission or misstatement judged in the surrounding circumstances. The size or nature of the item, or a combination of both, could be a determining factor.

b **Statement of profit or loss and other comprehensive income of Hawkestone Ltd as at 31 December 20X6**

	£,000
Revenue	74,400
Cost of sales (Note 1)	(50,240)
Gross profit	24,160
Distribution costs	(7,200)
Administrative expenses	(12,400)
Profit from continuing operations	4,560
Closure of manufacturing division (Note2)	(14,600)
Loss for period	(10,040)

	£,000
Cost of Sales	49,200
Adjustment: obsolete inventories	1,040
	50,240

Statement of changes in equity of Hawkestone Ltd for year to 30 June 20X6

	Share capital	Share premium account	Retained earnings	Total
	£,000	*£,000*	*£,000*	*£,000*
Balance at 1 July 20X1	20,000		25,200	45,200
Prior period error (note 3)			(4,280)	(4,280)
Restated balance at 1 July 20x1			20,920	
Changes in equity during the ye				
Loss for the period			(10,040)	(10,040)
Issue of share capital	10,000	18,000		28,000
Balance 30 June 20X2	30,000	18,000	10,880	58,880

5.5 A non-recurring item is a gain or loss found on a company's income statement that is not expected to occur regularly (e.g. litigation costs, write-offs of bad debt or worthless assets, employee litigation costs, and repair costs for damage caused by natural disasters).

Analysts seeking to measure the sustainable profitability of a company typically disregard non-recurring items, as these items are not expected to affect the company's future net income. If non-recurring items have a significant effect on the company's finances, they should be listed, net of tax, on a separate line below operating profit from continuing operations. Additionally, narratives to the accounts should provide further analysis and explanation as to the nature of the non-recurring items.

5.6 IFRS 5 determines the basis for classification for an asset held for sale and suggests that, in general, the following conditions must be met for an asset (or 'disposal group') to be classified as held for sale:

- management is committed to a plan to sell;
- the asset is available for immediate sale;
- an active programme to locate a buyer is initiated;
- the sale is highly probable, within 12 months of classification as held for sale (subject to limited exceptions);
- the asset is being actively marketed for sale at a sales price reasonable in relation to its fair value; and
- actions required to complete the plan indicate that it is unlikely that plan will be significantly changed or withdrawn.

In essence, once an asset has been declared as held for sale, it must be transferred to current assets and disposed of during the next 12 months.

5.7 Discontinued operations represent divisions within a business that have either ceased operations due to a lack of profitability or have been sold. This may be due to the fact that the operation is unprofitable, or a change of business direction. IFRS 5 requires listed companies to report earnings per share of all divisions in its business, including discontinued operations.

IFRS 5 indicates the definition of discontinued operations as:

A discontinued operation is a component of an entity that either has been disposed of or is classified as held for sale, and:

- represents either a separate major line of business or a geographical area of operations, and is part of a single co-ordinated plan to dispose of a separate major line of business or geographical area of operations, or
- is a subsidiary acquired exclusively with a view to resale and the disposal involves loss of control.

5.8 IFRS 8 defines an operating segment as a component of an entity:

- that engages in business activities from which it may earn revenues and incur expenses (including revenues and expenses relating to transactions with other components of the same entity);
- whose operating results are reviewed regularly by the entity's chief operating decision-maker to make decisions about resources to be allocated to the segment and assess its performance; and
- for which discrete financial information is available.

Chapter 6 – Purpose of the statement of cash flows

6.1 b   Taxation paid.

6.2 a   Managing activities.

6.3 Cash flows are not a measure of a company's profit, but represent the cash flow in and out of a company due to its revenues and expenses and cash flow from investing and financing activities. Company profit takes into account all goods and services received but not paid for. These are recorded under the accruals concept thus facilitating a profit.

Cash flow indicates a company's ability to meet its financial obligations. Positive cash flow enables a company to meet payroll, pay suppliers, meet debt repayments and make distributions to owners. Cash can be generated by operations, or provided by lenders or owners.

Profits provide the basis for a company to measure firm performance against set criteria and expectation and plan investment activity or rationalise operations to meet economic environment.

6.4 a   Increase in inventory leads to a cash outflow since payment has been made for the increase in inventory.

b   Decrease in payables also leads to a cash outflow since the creditors have been paid.

c   Decrease in receivables means an inflow of cash, as debtors have been reduced.

d   The increase in market value of a company's shares directly does not have any effect on in/outflow of cash unless new shares are issued by the company.

e   A gain is an accounting entry and does not have an impact on the cash flow per se; however, cash inflow will be realised on disposal of assets.

f   When shares are issued, these represent financing activity; hence cash inflow will be recorded under this activity.

6.5

	£m	
Opening receivables	20	
Credit sales for the year	75	
	95	
Cash received from debtors	83	Balancing figure
Closing receivables	12	

Cash received from trade receivables is: £83 million during the year.

6.6

	£m	
Opening payables	12	
Credit purchases for the year	36	
	48	
Cash paid to Payables	30	Balancing figure
Closing Payables	18	

Cash paid to creditors: £30 million during the year.

6.7 a   Depreciation – this is a calculated charge over the useful life of an asset.
  b   Impairment charge – this is a non-cash charge to the income statement and does not have a cash flow impact.
  c   Gains and losses – these are also non-cash movements as they are computed profit or loss on disposal of an asset.

6.8 Irrespective of the gains or losses incurred on disposal of the asset, the only item that will be recorded in the cash flow statement under investing activity is the £120,000 received on disposal of the asset.

However, the statement of comprehensive income will record the following profit or loss:

	£,000
Cost of purchase	500
Accumulated depreciation	400
	100
Cash on disposal	120
Profit made on disposal	20

The profit made on disposal of the asset is £20,000. This will also be shown as an adjustment in calculating operating cash flows.

6.9

	£,000
Profit	20,000
Add: depreciation	500
	20,500
Decrease in inventory	800
Increase in receivables	(200)
Decrease in payables	(400)
Cash from operating activities	20,700

6.10 Sarah Ltd – statement of cash flow to 31 December 20X6

Operating activities	Item	*£*	*£*
Profit before taxation		352,000	
Adjustments			
Depreciation	1	50,000	
		402,000	
Changes in working capital			
Inventories	2	(30,000)	
Receivables	3	(24,000)	
Payables	4	(83,000)	
		(137,000)	
Cash generated from operations		265,000	
Tax paid	5	(24,000)	
Net cash from operations			241,000
Financing activities		*£*	

Issued share capital		6	48,000	
Repayment of long-term borrowing		7	(18,800)	
Payment of finance lease			0	
Dividends paid			(274,000)	
Net cash applied in financing activities				(244,800)
Net cash increase/decrease in cash and cash equivalents				(3,800)
Cash and cash equivalents at the start of period				(3,200)
Cash and cash equivalents at the end of period				(7,000)
Check				(3,800)

Calculations:

Item		£
1	Depreciation:	
	Opening depreciation	180,000
	Balancing charge	50,000
	Closing depreciation	230,000
2	Inventory:	
	Opening inventory	45,000
	Balancing movement	30,000
	Closing inventory	75,000
3	Trade receivables:	
	Opening trade receivables	120,000
	Balancing movement	24,000
	Closing trade receivables	144,000
4	Payables:	
	Opening payables	170,000
	Balancing movement	(83,000)
	Closing payables	87,000
5	Tax paid:	
	Opening tax	18,000
	Tax charge to income statement	36,000
		54,000
	Less closing tax	30,000
	Tax paid in the year	24,000
6	Share issue:	
	Shares issue: £1.20 × 40,000	48,000
7	Loan:	
	Closing loan balance	66,000
	Opening loan balance	84,800
	Loan movement during the year	(18,800)

6.11 a   **Plumbus Ltd – statement of cash flow to 30 September 20X7**

Operating activities	Item	£	£
Profit before tax		190,000	
Adjustments			
Depreciation	1	102,000	
			292,000
Changes in working capital			
Inventories		4,000	
Receivables		7,000	
Payables		(48,000)	
Loss on disposal	2	2,000	
			(35,000)
Cash generated from operations			257,000
Tax paid	3	)	(43,000)
Net cash from operations			214,000
Investing activities			
Purchase of NCA	4	(132,000)	
Proceeds from sale of NCA		8,000	
Net cash applied in investing activities			(124,000)
Financing activities			
Issued share capital		54,000	
Long-term borrowing		59,000	
Dividends paid	5	(113,000)	
Net cash applied in financing activities			0
Net cash increase/decrease in cash and cash equivalents			90,000
Cash and cash equivalents at the start of period			54,000
Cash and cash equivalents at the end of period			144,000
Check			90,000

1 Depreciation

Opening	188,000
Disposal	(30,000)
Depreciation for the year	102,000
	260,000

2 PPE disposal

Book value	40,000
Depreciation	(30,000)
Net Book Value	10,000
Sold	8,000
Loss on disposal	2,000

3 Taxation

Opening	11,000
Taxation for the year	54,000
	65,000
Closing tax balance	22,000
Paid	43,000

4 Property, plant and equipment (PPE)

Opening PPE	418,000
Additions	132,000
Disposal	(40,000)
Revaluation reserves	10,000
Closing PPE	520,000

5 Dividends

Opening retained profit	33,000
Profit for the year	136,000
Dividends paid in cash	113,000
Closing retained profit	56,000

b   The company appears to be in a stable financial condition.

The company appears to be managing its payables and receivables well. However, it seems this company may be an SME in its growth stage, so it should review its supplier and customer policy on credit received and allowed, to increase working capital and liquidity in the company.

The company could also consider raising both its shareholding and further long-term capital through a new share issue to private investors. Plumbus is a small limited company and may not be able to offer its shares to the general investor.

6.12 a   Anderson Ltd – Statement of cash flows for the year ended 31 March 2017   £000

Profit from operations		9,783
Adjustments for:		
Dividends received		(6,264)
Profit on disposal of property, plant and equipment		(176)
Depreciation		8,760
Decrease/(increase) in inventories		(868)
Decrease/(increase) in trade receivables		1,108
(Decrease)/increase in trade payables		836
Cash generated by operations		13,179
Tax paid		(1,580)
Interest paid		(940)
Net cash from operating activities		10,659
Investing activities		
Dividends received		6,264
Proceeds on disposal of property, plant and equipment	w1	570
Purchases of property, plant and equipment	w2	(28,186)
Net cash used in investing activities		(21,352)
Financing activities		
New bank loans		3,400
Proceeds of share issue		6,800
Net cash from financing activities		10,200
Decrease in cash and cash equivalents		(493)
Opening cash and cash equivalents		348
Closing cash and cash equivalents		(145)

Statement of Reconciliation of Cash and Cash Equivalents:

	2017	2016	Movement
	£	£	£
Cash and cash equivalents	12	348	336
Overdraft	(157)	–	(157)
	(145)	348	(493)

Workings

1

Carrying amount of assets sold	394
Profit on disposal	176
	570

2

PPE at start	63,832
Less depreciation	(8,760)
Less carrying amount of assets sold	(394)
PPE at end	(82,864)
Additions	(28,186)

3

Cash and cash equivalents	12
Bank overdraft	(157)
	(145)

b   When commenting on the liquidity of a business it is important to look at liquidity ratios, discussed in Chapters 9 and 10. Further value is gained if comparatives can be calculated with previous years' information if provided.

   The most commonly used ratio is the Acid test or 'Quick' ratio, which measures the short-term liquidity of the business if this is greater than 1 the business is deemed to be liquid ie: able to pay off current liabilities using current The ration is defined as: Current Assets, minus inventory, divided by current liabilities. Anderson ltd Acid Test Ratio:

2017	**2016**
$\dfrac{(21,624 - 10,348)}{8,893} = 1.27$	$\dfrac{(22,200 - 9,480)}{7,060} = 1.8$

The liquidity of Anderson ltd is clearly reduced from 2016, 1.8 to 1.27 in 2017 although still over 1 and thus still liquid. Further analysis can be made and conclusions drawn by examining other liquidity ratios and looking at the Statement of Cash flows to determine which areas of the business are contributing to this.

   Cash generated from operations is positive indicating the company is able to generate sufficient cash flows to maintain and grow the business.

Chapter 7 – Group accounting

7.1   **£,000**

Goodwill on acquisition	6,000 – [1,000 + 1,720 + 1,200]	2,080
Other net assets at book value	7,200 + 3,700 + 1,200	12,100
		14,180

Financed by:

Ordinary share capital (£1 shares)	10,000
Retained profit at 31 October 20X0	2,940
Net profit for 20X8–9 260 + 980	1,240

7.2

	£,000	£,000
Consideration		2,500
Share capital	1,800	
Pre-acquisition profits 1 Oct 20X0: 600 × 2/3	400	
Goodwill		300
NCI: 3,600 × 1/3		1,200
Post-acquisition profits: 300 × 2/3		200

7.3

	Total equity	At acquisition	Since acquisition	NCI
	£	£	£	£
Diamonds				
Share capital	80,000	80,000		
Retained profits:				
At acquisition date	33,200	33,200		
Since acquisition	11,400		11,400	
	124,600	113,200	11,400	

	Total equity	At acquisition	Since acquisition	NCI
	£	£	£	£
Hearts				
Share capital	40,000	30,000		10,000
At acquisition date	7,200	5,400		1,800
Since acquisition	(13,600)		(10,200)	(3,400)
	33,600	35,400	(10,200)	8,400

	Total equity	At acquisition	Since acquisition	NCI
	£	£	£	£
Totals (Diamond and Hearts)	158,200	148,600	1,200	8,400
Total price paid, £126,000 + £44,000		170,000		
Goodwill on acquisition		21,400		
Retained profits, Clubs Ltd (36000+7000)			43,000	
Goodwill impairment (21,400/4)		(5,350)	(5,350)	
	158,200	16,050	38,850	8,400

Consolidated statement of financial position for Clubs Ltd and Subsidiaries at 31 December 20X6

		£
Goodwill		16,050
Non-current assets at carrying value (59,000+299,500+129,700)		488,200
Current assets (79,000+62,500+29,500)	171,000	
Less: Current liabilities (65,000+37,400+75,600)	178,000	
Net current assets		(7,000)
Total assets less current liabilities		497,250
Less: 15% debentures (200,000+50,000)		250,000
		247,250
Financed by:		
Share capital (£1 shares)		200,000
Retained profits		38,850
Non-controlling interest		8,400
		247,250

7.4 In the process of preparing consolidated financial statements, it is necessary to eliminate intra-group balances and transactions such as plant and machinery, purchase and sales of inventories and other assets between parent and subsidiary. In many cases, the separate financial statements of a parent company and a subsidiary include amounts of inter-company items that should be offset or eliminated. Before preparing the consolidated financial statements, accounting entries should be prepared to bring the balances up to date and to eliminate the inter-company balances.

Company A will have to adjust its profits figure by following the accounting treatment for unrealised profits:

- Reduce the retained earnings of Company A by 25% (the mark-up) or 20% of the selling price.
- Reduce the inventory of Company B by 25% (the mark-up) or 20% of the price.

The above adjustments **only** apply to unsold inventory.

The gross amount of the sale will have to be deducted from Group Revenue and Group Cost of Sales.

7.5

	A	B	C	D
	Parent	**Subsidiary**	**Elimination**	**Aggregate**
	(Smith)	(Jerry)		
	£	£	£	£
Revenue	123,400	16,750	−7,000	133,150

7.6 Robins Group

Step 1: Group Structure

Parent = 60%, NCI 40%

Step 2: Purchase consideration transferred

Consideration = £1,700,000.

Step 3: Fair Value (FV) of net assets at acquisition and reporting date

	FV of Net Assets 01/04/ 20X6	FV of Net Assets 31/03/ 20X7
	£	£
Share capital	1,300,000	1,300,000
Share premium	410,000	410,000
Retained earnings	180,000	220,000
Fair value adjustment for PPE	500,000	500,000
	2,390,000	2,430,000

		£
Calculate the post acquisition profit of Jade		
Fair value of Knight assets at the reporting date		2,430,000
Fair value of Knight assets at the date of acquisition		2,390,000
Post acquisition profit		40,000

Step 4

		£
This will be shared between the group and the NCI as follows:		
Group	60%	24,000
NCI	40%	16,000
		40,000

Step 5: Goodwill

	£
Consideration transferred	1,700,000
Fair value of NCI	1,100,000
	2,800,000
Fair value of net assets at acquisition date	−2,390,000
Goodwill arising on acquisition	410,000
Less impairment loss	−34,000
	376,000

	£
Allocation of impairment loss	
Parent	20,400
NCI	13,600
	34,000

Step 6: Calculate the NCI at the reporting date

	£
Fair value of NCI at the date of acquisition	1,100,000
Goodwill impairment loss	−13,600
Add NCI share of the post-acquisition profit of Knight	16,000
NCI at the reporting date	1,102,400

Step 7: Calculate the consolidated retained earnings

	£
Robins retained earnings	580,000
Add group's share of the post-acquisition profit of Knight	24,000
Goodwill impairment loss	−20,400
	583,600

Step 8: Consolidated statement of financial position for Robins Plc as at 31 March 2017

	£
ASSETS	
Non-current assets	
Goodwill	376,000
Property, plant and equipment (3,982 + 2,139 + 500)	6,621,000
	6,997,000
Current assets	
Total current assets (3,400 + 1,486 – 184)	4,702,000
Total assets	11,699,000
EQUITY AND LIABILITIES	
Equity	
Share capital	4,400,000
Share premium	365,000
Retained earnings	583,600
Non-controlling interest	1,102,400
Total equity	6,451,000
Non-current liabilities	
Long term loans	2,580,000
Current liabilities	
Total current liabilities (2,357 + 495 – 184)	2,668,000
Total liabilities	5,248,000
Total equity and liabilities	11,699,000

7.7   **Step 1: Group structure: 70% Parent, 30% NCI**

Step 2: Calculate the consideration transferred

Given in the question	265,000

Step 3: Calculate fair value of net assets at the date of acquisition and at the reporting date

	Fair value of net assets	
	£	£
	01/01/20X7	31/12/20X7
Share capital	100,000	100,000
Share premium	50,000	50,000
Retained earnings	50,000	100,000
Fair value adjustment	20,000	20,000
Intangible non-current assets written off	(10,000)	(30,000)
	210,000	240,000

Step 4: Calculate the post-acquisition profit of Beta

Fair value of NCI assets at the reporting date	240,000
Less fair value of NCI assets at the date of acquisition	210,000
Post-acquisition profit	30,000
Group (70% × 30,000)	21,000
NCI (30% × 30,000)	9,000

Step 5: Calculate the goodwill at the date of acquisition and at the reporting date

Consideration transferred	265,000
Fair value of NCI (30% × 100,000 × 2.5)	75,000
	340,000
Less fair value of net assets at acquisition date (from step 3)	210,000
Goodwill arising on acquisition	130,000
Less goodwill impairment (50% x 130,000)	65,000
Goodwill at 31 December 2006	65,000
Goodwill impairment will be split between the group and the NCI as follows:	
Group (70% × 65,000)	45,500
NCI (30% × 65,000)	19,500

Step 6: Calculate the NCI at the reporting date

Fair value of NCI at the date of acquisition	75,000
Add NCI's share of the post-acquisition profit of Beta (step 4)	9,000
Less NCI's share of goodwill impairment	(19,500)
NCI at the reporting date	64,500

Step 7: Calculate the consolidated retained earnings

Alpha's retained earnings	100,000
Add group's share of the post-acquisition profit of Beta (step 4)	21,000
Less unrealised profit on inventory (20/120 × 20,000 × 1/2)	(1,667)
Less group's share of goodwill impairment (step 5)	(45,500)

Alpha Group
Consolidated statement of financial position at 31 December 20X7

	£	£
		73,833
Non-current assets		
Goodwill		65,000
Property plant and equipment (500,000 + 70,000 + 20,000)		590,000
Investments (290,000 + 60,000 – 265,000)		85,000
		740,000
Current assets		
Inventory (100,000 + 50,000 - 1,667)	148,333	
Trade receivable (150,000 + 100,000 - 15,000)	235,000	
Bank (30,000 + 20,000 + 5,000)	55,000	
	438,333	
Total assets		1,178,333
Equity and liabilities		
Share capital		700,000
Share premium		140,000
Consolidated retained earnings		73,833
		913,833
Non-controlling interest		64,500
		978,333

Current liabilities		
Trade payables (90,000 + 60,000 – 10,000)	140,000	
Accruals	60,000	200,000
		1,178,333

7.8 The parent entity concept considers the group to consist of the net assets of the parent and all its subsidiaries with the non-controlling interest being a liability of the group.

The effects of the preparation of consolidated financial statements are:

a   the non-controlling is classified as liability; and

b   the effects of intra-group transactions are proportionally adjusted.

According to IFRS 10: 'Control of an investee arises when an investor is exposed, or has rights, to variable returns from its involvement with the investee and has the ability to affect those returns through its power over the investee.'

An investor controls an investee if, and only if, the investor has *all of* the following elements (IFRS 10:7):

- power over the investee (i.e. the investor has existing rights that gives it the ability to direct the relevant activities – those that significantly affect the investee's returns);
- exposure or rights to variable returns from its involvement with the investee; and
- the ability to use its power over the investee to affect the amount of the investor's returns.

7.9 a   **House Plc Group suggested solution**

Step 1: Group Structure

Parent = 75%, NCI = 25%

Step 2: Purchase Consideration Transferred

£450,000

Step 3: Calculate Fair value of net assets at the date of acquisition and at the reporting date.

	FV of Net Assets £	FV of Net Assets £
	01/01/2017	31/12/2017
Share capital	120,000	120,000
Share premium	40,000	40,000
Retained earnings	68,000	120,000
Intangible non-current assets written off	(80,000)	(80,000)
Fair value adjustment for land	(10,000)	(10,000)
	138,000	190,000

Step 4: Calculate the post acquisition profit of House plc	£000
Fair value of Pool assets at the reporting date	190,000
Fair value of Pool assets at the date of acquisition	138,000
Post acquisition profit	52,000

This will be shared between the group and the NCI as follows:		**£000**
Group	75%	39,000
NCI	25%	13,000
		52,000

Step 5: Calculate the goodwill at the date of acquisition and at the reporting date

	£000
Consideration transferred	450,000
Fair value of NCI (25% x 120000 x 3)	90,000

	540,000
Fair value of net assets at acquisition date	(138,000)
Goodwill arising on acquisition	402,000

Step 6: Calculate the consolidated retained earnings	**£000**
House plc retained earnings	100,000
Unrealised profit on goods (50% x 40,000 x 0.2)	(4,000)
Impairment	(20,000)
Add group's share of the post acquisition profit of Martin	39,000
	115,000

Step 7: Calculate the NCI at the reporting date	£000
Fair value of NCI at the date of acquisition	90,000
Add NCI' share of the post acquisition profit of House Ltd	13,000
NCI at the reporting date	103,000

Step 8:

Martin Plc Group

Consolidated Statement of Financial Position at 31 December 2017	**£000**	**£000**
Non-current assets		
Goodwill		402,000
Property plant and equipment (400,000 + 70,000 – 10,000 – 20,000)		440,000
Investments (490,000 + 10,000 – 450,000)		50,000
		892,000
Current assets		
Inventories (150,000 + 50,000 – 4,000)	196,000	
Trade receivable (110,000 + 100,000 – 12,000)	198,000	
Cash and cash equivalents (40,000 + 20,000 + 2,000)	62,000	
		456,000
		1,348,000
Equity and liabilities		
Share capital		800,000
Share premium		140,000
Consolidated retained earnings		115,000
		1,055,000
Non-controlling interest		103,000
		1,158,000
Current liabilities		
Trade payables (90,000 + 20,000 – 10,000)	100,000	
Accruals (60,000 + 30,000)	90,000	
		190,000
		1,348,000

b   Consolidated financial statements are prepared when an entity controls another entity or entities. According to IFRS 10 'control of an investee' arises when an investor 'is exposed, or has rights, to variable returns from its involvement with the investee and has the ability to affect those returns through its power over the investee'. According to IFRS 10, an investor controls an investee if and only if the investor has all of the following elements: [IFRS 10:7]

- Power over the investee, i.e. the investor has existing rights that give it the ability to direct the relevant activities (the activities that significantly affect the investee's returns)
- Exposure, or rights, to variable returns from its involvement with the investee
- The ability to use its power over the investee to affect the amount of the investor's returns.

Chapter 8 – Trend analysis and introduction to ratio analysis

8.1 Alternative theories exist that attempt to explain the nature and characteristics of the modern corporation. However, in contrast to the agency theory, stewardship theory suggests that, left to their own devices, managers will act responsibly to maximise shareholder wealth.

Stewardship, therefore, has a pivotal role in managing the affairs of a company. Management will select the best strategies given the limited resources of the firm and, within the context of those limited resources, managers will attempt to increase the value of the firm. This basically means managers have custody of the firm's assets and in the presence of competing demands will select the options that maximise returns.

8.2 Ratio analysis is a form of financial statement analysis that is used to obtain a quick indication of a firm's financial performance in several key areas. The ratios are categorised as short-term solvency, debt management, asset management, profitability and market value.

As a tool, ratio analysis possesses several important features. The data, provided by financial statements, is readily available. The computation of ratios facilitates the comparison of firms that differ in size. Ratios can be used to compare a firm's financial performance with the industry average. They can also be used as a form of trend analysis to identify areas where performance has improved or deteriorated over time.

Because ratio analysis is based on accounting information, its effectiveness is limited by the distortions that arise in financial statements (e.g. historical cost accounting and inflation). Therefore, it should only be used as a first step in financial analysis, to obtain a quick indication of a firm's performance and to identify areas which need to be investigated further.

8.3 There are three main ratios that can be used to measure the profitability of a business:
1. gross profit margin
2. net profit margin
3. return on capital employed (ROCE).

The gross profit margin
This measures the gross profit of the business as a proportion of the sales revenue.

The net profit margin
This measures the net profit of the business as a proportion of the sales revenue.

Return on Capital Employed (ROCE)
This is often referred to as the 'primary accounting ratio' and it expresses the annual percentage return that an investor would receive on their capital.

8.4 The liquidity ratios are measured using the current ratio and the quick ratio. The current ratio is current assets divided by current liabilities. The quick ratio measures liquidity in a company by excluding inventory (stock) from the current ratio:

a		**20X2**	**20X1**
		760	695
Current ratio		360	505
Current ratio		2.1	1.4
Quick ratio		$\dfrac{760-180}{360}$	$\dfrac{695-240}{505}$
Quick ratio		1.6	0.9

b The two ratios suggest that Roadster Ltd has improved its liquidity position over the two-year period from 20X1 to 20X2. The current ratio has gone up from 1.4 to 2.1 suggesting the company has been efficient in its use of current assets.
The quick ratio has also gone up from 0.9 to 1.6, an increase of 78%, suggesting that the company has been highly efficient in current asset management.

8.5 a

	20X2		20X1	
Gross profit margin	(600/1,900)	31.6%	(525/1,500)	35.0%
Operating profit margin	(250/1,900)	13.2%	(275/1,500)	18.3%
Current ratio	(1,000/210)	4.8	(500/80)	6.3
Acid test	((1,000-200)/210)	3.8	((500-100)/80)	5.0

Two ratios outstanding

b Comments on company performance – Brent Ltd:
The highlights from the profit margins and liquidity ratio analysis suggest the company has not performed as well in 20X2 as it did in 20X1.

The gross profit and operating profit ratios indicate a decline in profitability. This argument is strengthened by the fact that ROCE has declined from 34% in 20X1 to 24% in 20X2.

The liquidity ratios have also deteriorated during the year, though the general liquidity levels do not suggest the company is at risk of corporate failure. However, the cash position of Brent Ltd has moved from positive cash and cash equivalents balance in 20X1 to a £10,000 overdraft at the end of 20X2.

The cash movement may warrant closer monitoring by the management, even if it is linked to a strategic development plan.

Comments on two ratios outstanding

8.6 Vertical analysis – Brent Ltd

Brent Ltd – income statement for the years to 31 December

	20X2		20X1	
	£,000	%	£,000	%
Sales (all credit)	1,500	100	1,900	100
Opening inventory	80		100	
Purchases	995	66%	1,400	74%
Closing inventory	100		200	
Cost of goods sold	975	65%	1,300	68%
Gross profit	525	35%	600	32%
Less: Expenses	250	17%	350	18%
	275	18%	250	13%

The company appears to be making reasonable operating profits in both years. However, profitability has declined in 20X2. This appears to be due to purchases and expenses.

Horizontal analysis – Brent Ltd

Year	Sales	CoGS	Gross profit	Expenses	Op profit
20X1	1,500	975	525	250	275
20X2	1,900	1,300	600	350	250

	Sales	CoGS	Gross profit	Expenses	Op. profit
20X1	100%	100%	100%	100%	100%
20X2	127%	133%	114%	140%	91%

CoGS = Cost of goods sold

The horizontal analysis clearly shows where problems have occurred during 20X2. The CoGS and expenses during 20X2 have contributed to the decline in 20X2 profits. Management may wish to consider the above analysis and investigate why this has happened.

Chapter 9 – Analysis and interpretation of accounts 1

9.1 a **Working capital management**

Current ratio $= \dfrac{CA}{CL}$ $\dfrac{700}{635}$ $= 1.1:1$

Acid test ratio $= \dfrac{CA - Inventory}{CL}$ $\dfrac{700 - 235}{635}$ $= 0.73:1$

Asset turnover ratio $= \dfrac{Turnover}{Total\ assets}$ $\dfrac{5,500}{6,700}$ $= 0.8\ times$

Inventory turnover ratio $= \dfrac{Inventory}{Cost\ of\ sales} \times 365$ $\dfrac{235}{2,700} \times 365 = 32\ days$

Profitability

Gross profit margin $= \dfrac{Gross\ profit}{Turnover} = \dfrac{2,800}{5,500} = 51\%$

Operating profit margin $= \dfrac{Operating\ profit}{Turnover} = \dfrac{1,250}{5,500} = 23\%$

Return on assets $= \dfrac{Operating\ profit}{Total\ assets} = \dfrac{1,250}{6,700} = 19\%$

Capital structure

Gearing 1 $= \dfrac{Long\text{-}term\ liabilities}{Total\ equity\ fund} = \dfrac{3,000}{3,065} = 98\%$

Interest cover $= \dfrac{Operating\ profit}{Interest\ expense} = \dfrac{1,250}{300} = 4.2\ times$

b **Working Capital Management**

This ratio shows that the company is its working capital reasonably well. With the current ratio at 1.1 and the acid test ratio at 0.73, and the nature of the business being in retail, the level of liquidity is acceptable. However, this situation can change quickly and management must have sound plans to keep the current and acid test ratios at the same or higher levels.

Profitability

All three profitability ratios show a healthy return to the investor. The gross margin ratio shows a 51% turnover which is due to the usual sector return (100% mark up = 50% margin). The net profit margin and return on asset ratios also seem to be in line with expectation. Nevertheless, the kitchen appliance business is very susceptible to economic downturn; people will delay home improvements in austere times, so, while returns appear to be acceptable, there could be severe impact on the business in tough economic conditions.

Capital structure

The gearing ratios can be estimated in two ways: debt/equity or debt/(equity + debt). Lenders will usually set a debt covenant based on gearing levels. Some lenders may stipulate that a company's gearing may not go over, say, 50% based on debt/debt + equity estimation. However, the interest cover ratio (4:1) suggests the company can meet its interest payments.

The ratio suggests the company is highly geared and any further increase in debt will risk a default on the debt covenant. The company needs to lower its debt and/or increase its profits and profitability to stay within agreed bounds.

9.2 a

	Tanner	Spanner
	£,000	£,000
Operating profit	1,000	1,200
Turnover	7,200	9,000
Average investment in gross assets	2,400	2,600
Gross asset turnover	3 times	1.5 times
Operating profit percentage	(1,000/7,200)13.89%	(1,200/9,000)13.33%
Operating profit to gross assets	(1,000/2,400)41.67%	(1,200/2,600)20.00%

b   The three ratios are intrinsically linked to each other, as they are all a different measure of company performance. The gross asset turnover and the operating profit ratios compare company performance in relation to sales. As gross asset turnover moves up or down, this is reflected in the movement respectively in the operating profit percentage ratio. Again, the rate of return on gross assets is linked to gross asset turnover. As the gross asset turnover moves up or down, the rate of return on gross assets moves likewise.

c   Both Tanner and Spanner seem to be in line with the trade association performance. However, Tanner has gross asset turnover of three times as compared with the trade association and Spanner, who have two times and 1.5 times gross asset turnover respectively. Tanner seems to be more efficient in its costs and expenses, and has superior operating profits and operating profit to gross assets. This suggests Tanner is more profitable than Spanner.

9.3   Net asset turnover ratio = Sales / Net assets
      Total asset turnover ratio = Sales / Total assets

		20X7	20X6	20X5	20X4
Sales	£,000	290	190	160	90
Net assets	£,000	420	340	280	190
Total assets	£,000	1140	950	880	680
Net asset turnover	%	69	56	57	47
Total asset turnover	%	25	20	18	13

Asset usage efficiency:

The ratios indicate that the company has progressively become highly efficient in the use of its assets. By 20X7 the company had increased sales by 222%, while having increased its asset base by 68%. It will be useful to consider why such efficiency has transpired due to the increase in the company asset base. This exercise will continue to enable the company to maintain and improve its operations and processes.

9.4   Cash operating cycle
     = Days sales outstanding + Inventory days outstanding - Payable days outstanding

Cash operating cycle
= 60 + 90 - 70
= 80 days

Using the cash operating formula, the company has an 80-day cash operating cycle. This result by itself is of limited use. It is not possible to make a judgment on the cash operating cycle for this or any company without knowledge of the operating business sector or any comparative benchmarks for the sector or previous year's results for the company. Management would be advised to assess this result against any comparative benchmark for the sector for the current year, or against the company's past performances or against the budgeted cash operating cycle. The results of these comparisons will enable management to take the appropriate course of action.

Chapter 10 – Analysis and interpretation of accounts 2

10.1 a   Earnings per share (EPS) represent the profit attributable to ordinary shareholders divided by the weighted average number of shares in issue during the year.

   b   A bonus share is essentially a free share given to current shareholders in a company, based on the number of shares that the shareholder already owns. While the issue of bonus shares increases the total number of shares issued and owned, it does not increase the value of the company.

   Although the total number of issued shares increases, the ratio of number of shares held by each shareholder remains constant. An issue of bonus shares is referred to as a bonus issue. Depending upon the constitutional documents of the company, only certain classes of shares may be entitled to bonus issues, or may be entitled to bonus issues in preference to other classes. It is also important to note the likely fall in share price per share, pro rata to the bonus rate.

   c

	20X2	20X1
	£,000	£,000
Basic earnings per share (EPS)		
Profit for the year	64,000	48,000
8% preference share dividend (£100m × 8% = £8m)	(8,000)	(8,000)
Profit attributable to ordinary shareholders	56,000	40,000
Shares in issue	30,000	30,000
Bonus issue 1 for 5	6,000	–
Total shares	36,000	30,000
Basic EPS	£1.56	£1.33
Re-stated EPS for 20X1: £1.33 × 5/6		£1.11

   d   Dilution to earnings per share (EPS) can arise due to a number of factors, as follows.
   Conversion of debentures, preference shares and other financial instruments will have an impact on wealth effects due to the number of shares issued if the conversion is offered at less than market value of the shares. However, there are other situations which may give rise to diluted earnings per share, such as warrants and options. Presently share ranking does not exist, but it may do in the future for dividend purposes. This might also lead to dilution of EPS if such share-ranking instruments had conversion rights to ordinary shares.

e		20X2
Diluted earnings per share (DEPS)		**£,000**
Earnings		56,000
Savings on interest		36,000
		92,000
Reduced tax savings on foregone interest: £36m × 33% = £11.88m		(11,880)
Adjusted net earnings		80,120
Calculation of debenture:		
£36,000,000 × 100 / 12% =		300,000
Shares in issue		36,000
£300,000,000 / £300 × 20 =		20,000
Total shares		56,000
Diluted EPS: £80,120,000 / 56,000,000		£1.43

10.2 The DuPont analysis is a technique for analysing the three components of return on equity (ROE):

$$\frac{\text{Net income}}{\text{Sales}} \times \frac{\text{Sales}}{\text{Assets}} \times \frac{\text{Assets}}{\text{Equity}}$$

$$\frac{3,300}{19,600} \times \frac{19,600}{135,000} \times \frac{135,000}{9,500}$$

$$16.84\% \qquad 14.52\% \qquad 1421.05\%$$

= 34.74%

Return on equity = 34.74%

10.3 a

Rights issue price £1.50	
Premium per rights share:1.50 - 1.00	0.5
Closing share premium account	£13,500
Opening share premium account	£6,000
Premium on rights issue	£7,500
Number of rights issue shares (7,500 / 0.50)	15,000
Proceeds from rights issue (15,000 × £1.50)	£22,500

b

Share issues		
Opening shares in issue		25,000
Bonus issue: 25,000/5	5,000	
Number of shares under rights issue	15,000	
Total new share issues		20,000
Total weighted number of shares		45,000
Profit for 20X4		**£**
Closing reserve (as stated in the question)		16,200
Add: Bonus issue		5,000
Add: Dividends paid		6,750
		27,950
Less: Closing retained earnings		(19,000)
Profit for the period (20X4)		8,950

Chapter 11 – Limitations of published accounts

11.1 Creative accounting is the term used to explain the activity known as earnings management. This is a process that can arise intentionally or unintentionally through the choices made by management during the reporting of an entity's financial performance.

11.2 Earnings management can arise from four possible sources within the process of reporting on the financial statements and performances of an entity:
1. Accounting system – the system of accounting does permit the use of choice and judgment which may be exploited by those responsible for the reporting on the financial performance.
2. Accounting choice – the existence of choice between accounting methods may give rise to earnings management.
3. Accounting judgment – accounting includes the use of estimation and as a direct result this personal judgment element may trigger earnings management.
4. Accounting transaction – some of our transactions are not definitive and include estimation and judgment which can contribute to earnings management.

11.3 a   Luboil has incorrectly credited to sales a £10 million contract entered into with Seeder Ltd. This is not the correct procedure. Luboil should divide the contract over five years and post, subject to price variation as agreed with the customer, Seeder Ltd, as to the price variation. Formal recognition of the agreement on price variation should be available to the auditor for inspection. Additionally, a fair value approach to price variation should be used and the contract should be explained in the narratives to the financial reports.

     b   There will be some impact on changes to sales having made the proper treatment of the account. As the contract is based on supply, there may be legal issues with stopping supply to Seeder Ltd. This has to be taken into consideration.

         However, performance ratios such as EPS, ROA, ROE and ROCE will fall, perhaps considerably once accounting adjustments are made and only £2 million revenue is accounted for rather than £10 million.

Chapter 12 – Financial reporting within the business environment

12.1 a   XBRL is a web-based technology that facilitates the electronic communication of economic and financial information in a manner that cuts down costs, provides a greater level of efficiency of use, and provides improved reliability to users and suppliers of information.

         XBRL uses the XML (eXtensible Markup Language) syntax and related XML technologies, which are the standard in communicating information between businesses and the internet. Data can be converted to XBRL by appropriate mapping tools designed to convert electronic data to XBRL format, or data can be written directly in XBRL by suitable software.

     b   XBRL works on a system of tags. Instead of treating financial information as a block of text, as in a standard internet page or a printed document, XBRL provides an identifying tag for each individual item of data. This is computer readable. For example, company revenues and items of expenses and net profit have their own unique tag. This enables manipulation by users, through query forms, to generate data and information in the required format.

     c   Most companies employ the computer desktop and laptop systems as a means for data capture, analysis, and output. A company would need to ensure that its web technology is up to date or otherwise invest in new computer systems. XBRL works on the internet, hence software tools would need to be procured that allow conversion between applications such as accounting software systems, Microsoft Doc files and Excel spreadsheets, which can be used to transfer base data into a useable format for the XBRL system. Comparatively, costs are low; however, maintenance and dedicated staff may need to be employed to provide expert services to staff and employees.

d   The common platform for XBRL is the internet. XBRL codes are embedded in HTML source codes and the system works from dedicated websites.

e   XBRL is web-based, hence the running costs of XBRL are quite low and maintenance costs are relatively cheap. However, the functionality of XBRL-based systems is very powerful, allowing easy access and conformity to company requirements. Proprietary software can be used in conjunction with XBRL to manage changes, enhancements and amendments.

12.2 Pressure on companies to comply with modern business practices demands that they reflect upon and take appropriate action on environmental and social issues using a pro-active approach to business activities management. Waste and toxic emissions are dealt with by law in the UK such as the Environmental Law Act 2006. It may be that current legislation does not require companies to disclose certain relevant information that may be useful to users; however, a growing number of entities across all sectors make their corporate social responsibility public on their website and via other media to communicate with stakeholders. These actions may range from the simple reminder on an e-mail, reminding recipients to reflect upon whether they need to print an email, to much grander pronouncements and actions.

This has a positive impact on the credibility, integrity, and reputation of a company. In being proactive, companies can demonstrate to stakeholders their commitment to social and environmental needs.

A less favourable perspective may regard the engagement with social reporting as the new and effective marketing tool deployed by entities in the twenty-first century.

a   James is under an obligation as the environmental compliance officer to bring existing environmental issues to the attention of senior management. He needs to provide practical solutions as to how the toxic waste could be better managed by investing in new and improved technology.

By offering alternative courses of action and a carrying out a cost–benefit analysis, James could demonstrate the future benefits of the investment. Additionally, he needs to underline the ethical and environmental importance of taking proactive steps and disclosing this to stakeholders, thereby adding reputational capital to the company.

b   The company could take a series of practical steps to comply with environmental issue at hand. The company could:
  - identify areas of concern and draw up policies relevant to the company using appropriate audit tools, such as GRI or TBL;
  - use external experts to advise on best and future course of actions;
  - have effective monitoring and audit policies in place that are regularly updated;
  - provide training for relevant employees on environmental and social matters; and
  - disclose systematically and regularly in annual reports the targets and achievements to date, being clear and honest in doing so.

c   There are many ways a company can report its initiatives. The most common procedure is to disclose its green and social policies through its corporate report. The company should develop stand-alone reports that concentrate on social, environmental and ethical issues, explaining how these are achieved or what processes are in place. This gives a clear indication of targets and timelines.

12.3 a   Company disclosure on listed companies usually features a report on corporate social responsibility (CSR). This report is separate from the financial report and indicates company policy towards social, environmental and ethical issues. The CSR report will also indicate policy, procedure and lines of responsibility. Additionally, it will discuss targets set and achieved, any deficiencies in policy and practice, and the pragmatic steps taken to ensure the company complies with legal and ethical requirements.

b   Within the financial report, companies will report on product lines and geographical operations. This would indicate the exposure the company faces in sourcing its raw material and the markets to which it sells its products.

The directors' and CEO's reports will provide additional information as to the progress the company is making on CSR issues such as ethical trading and its impact on the environment. Reports from relevant third parties such as the external auditor will feature in the financial reports or as part of the wider CSR report giving independent verification.

Commitment to certification and standards and how they have been applied will also be indicators of company commitment to the social agenda.

Glossary

Accounting policies Accounting policies are the specific principles, bases, conventions, rules and practices applied by an entity in preparing and presenting financial statements.

Accruals Provisions for goods and services received but not yet paid for. Accruals are one of the main accounting principles.

Agency theory A theory concerning the relationship between a principal (shareholder) and an agent of the principal (managers).

Asset An asset is a resource controlled by the enterprise as a result of past events and from which future economic benefits are expected to flow to the enterprise.

Associate A business entity that is partly owned by another business entity in which the stake holding is at above 20% but below 51%.

Capital and capital maintenance Concept of financial and physical capital maintenance. Financial capital relates to equity, while the physical capital relates to the increase in capital at the end of the year.

Cash and cash equivalents The mostly liquid assets found within the asset portion of a company's statement of financial affairs. Cash equivalents are assets that are usually ready to cash within three months.

Companies Act A set of legal and regulatory requirements that business entities, particularly limited liability entities, must adhere to in the course of business.

Consolidated accounts When a number of business entities belong to a parent either directly or indirectly, the parent entity prepares a set of consolidated accounts. This has the effect of showing the financial affairs of the group as though it were a single business entity, hence intra-group transactions are cancelled out.

Convergence Reducing international differences in accounting standards by selecting the best practice currently available, or, if none is available, by developing new standards in partnership with national standard setters.

Convertible loan Loan stock that can be converted into ordinary shares at a set date or dates at a predetermined price. The conversion price is the price of ordinary shares at which loan stock can be converted. The number of ordinary shares received by a loan stock holder on conversion of £100 nominal of convertible loan stock is £100 divided by the conversion price.

Convertible preference shares Preference shares that can be converted into ordinary shares. A company may issue them to finance major acquisitions without increasing the company's gearing or diluting the earnings per share (EPS) of the ordinary shares. Preference shares potentially offer the investor a reasonable degree of safety with the chance of capital gains as a result of conversion to ordinary shares if the company prospers.

Corporate governance The system by which companies are directed and controlled. In the UK, the corporate governance system is based on the UK Code on Corporate Governance 2010.

Cost of capital The cost to a company of the return offered to different kinds of capital. This may be in the form of: interest (for debt capital); dividends and participation in the growth of profit (for ordinary shares); dividends alone (for preference shares); or conversion rights (for **convertible loan** stock or convertible preference shares).

Current asset In the entity's normal operating cycle, a current asset is held primarily for trading purposes. It is expected to be realised within 12 months of the statement of financial position. It can also be cash or a cash-equivalent asset.

Current cost Assets are carried at the amount of cash or cash equivalent that would have to be paid if the same or an equivalent asset were currently acquired. Liabilities are carried at the undiscounted amount of cash or cash equivalents that would be required to settle the obligation currently.

Current liability This is expected either to be settled in the normal course of the entity's operating cycle, or is due to be settled within 12 months of the statement of financial position.

Debentures A type of debt instrument that is not secured by physical asset or collateral. The loan may or may not be repayable. If a debenture is not repayable, it may be offered to debenture holders as a convertible loan (see convertible loan).

Debt Long-term capital consisting of money lent by investors. Can be called loan stock, loan notes or debentures. Return on debt consists of interest (usually at a fixed rate), which is payable irrespective of the financial performance of the company. Secured loan stock holders rank before ordinary shareholders for repayment of capital if the company goes into liquidation.

Directors' report An aspect of the annual financial report produced by the board of directors of a business entity required under UK company law. It details the state of the company and its compliance with a set of financial, accounting and corporate social responsibility (CSR) disclosures.

Discontinued operations A component of an enterprise that has either been disposed of, or is classified as 'held for sale'.

Discount rate Cost of capital used to define interest rates or to discount cash flows to find present values.

Dividends A portion of a company's earnings that is returned to shareholders.

Double-entry bookkeeping System of debits and credits that measures assets and liabilities (profit or loss).

Earnings management The manipulation of financial transactions to give a better perspective of a business' financial affairs (e.g. increased revenue or misrepresentation of certain type of expenses).

Earnings per share (EPS) The amount of earnings per each outstanding share in a company. In the case of share movement in a period, the EPS is stated on a weighted average shareholding basis.

Elements of financial statements Assets, liabilities, equity, revenues and expenses.

Equity shares With equity shares the payment of dividends is not guaranteed, and the amount of dividends depends on the company's financial performance. Equity shareholders are last in line for payment of dividends and for repayment of capital if the company goes into liquidation. Equity shareholders accept these risks and disadvantages because they are the legal owners of the company, have voting rights and own any remaining funds after other claims have been met. They expect to benefit, through growth of dividends and share prices, from the company's future success.

External audit A verification process conducted by a third party on the verification of the financial reports. The external audit is carried out by a registered external auditor.

Fair presentation The faithful representation of the effects of transactions in accordance with the definitions and recognition criteria for assets, liabilities, income and expenses set out in the Framework and can be defined as 'Presenting information, including accounting policies, in a manner which provides relevant, reliable, comparable, and understandable information'.

Fair value The measurement of an asset or liability or a financial transaction that best reflects its price. The price may be on a market basis or other means acceptable to a body of users. Fair value must be based on IFRS guidelines.

Faithful representation The principle that reported financial figures that convey to the user the underlying economic reality of the business entity.

Finance lease A resource controlled by a business entity for the substantial part of its life, from which future benefits will flow to the company.

Financial ratios A means of evaluating a company's performance or health that uses a standard of comparisons of items on the company's financial statements. Ratios can be calculated in financial and non-financial terms (e.g. debtor days outstanding, which is measured in days).

Framework This conceptual framework sets out the concepts that underlie the preparation and presentation of financial statements for external users.

Gains or losses In the course of business, an entity will make gains or losses on certain types of transactions such as sale of items of PPE classified as being 'held for sale' or profit or loss on currency translations etc.

Generally Accepted Accounting Principles (GAAP) Refer to the standard framework of guidelines for financial accounting used in any given jurisdiction.

Going concern An accounting concept under which financial reports are prepared on the assumption that a business will not be liquidated within the next 12 months.

Goodwill The difference between the consideration (price paid for an asset) and its carrying value.

Harmonisation Reconciles, to a certain extent, with national differences and provides preparers of accounting information a common framework and the opportunity to deal with major issues in a similar manner globally.

Historical cost The amount of cash or cash equivalents paid for an asset, or the fair value of other considerations given to acquire it.

International Accounting Standards Board (IASB) The body that sets IFRS. The IASB may make amendments to existing accounting standards or issue new standards with reference to new accounting issues or to ensure more clarity for existing and new accounting matters.

International Financial Reporting Standards (IFRS) Set of accounting standards that provide the basis for reporting accounting and financial information.

Integrated reporting (IR) is a clear, concise reporting document used to communicate how an organisation's strategy, governance, performance and prospects lead to the creation of value in the short, medium and long-term, to improve decision making and risk assessment of businesses by stakeholders.

Inventory Is the stock in trade of a business entity. Inventory is either raw material or finished goods. It must be valued at the lower of cost or net realisable value.

Liability Obligation of an entity arising from past transactions or events, the settlement of which may result in the transfer or use of assets, provision of services or other yielding of economic benefits in the future.

Net present value (NPV) The sum of the present values of all the cash flows associated with an investment project.

Non-controlling interest If a parent company owns, say, 80% of another business entity, and the other 20% belongs to minority shareholders, the latter is the non-controlling interest.

Offsetting The concept of reporting separately assets, liabilities, expenses and revenue to give users a clearer picture of a company's transactions.

Operating lease A lease whose term is short compared to the useful life of the asset or piece of equipment.

Preference shares Non-equity shares, with a (usually fixed) dividend paid – subject to the availability of distributable profits – before ordinary share dividends can be paid. Preference shares do not normally have voting rights, but rank before ordinary shares for distribution of capital in the event of liquidation.

Present value The amount of money at today's date that is equivalent to a sum of money in the future. It is calculated by discounting the future sum to reflect its timing and the cost of capital.

Principal financial statements These include the statement of comprehensive income, statement of financial position, statement of changes to equity and the statement of cash flows.

Property, plant and equipment Items of non-current assets, land and buildings held for use that are stated in the statement of financial position at their cost, less any subsequent accumulated depreciation and subsequent accumulated impairment losses.

Realisable value Assets are carried at the amount of cash or cash equivalent that could currently be obtained by selling the asset in an orderly disposal. Liabilities are carried at their settlement values – that is, the undiscounted amounts of cash or cash equivalents expected to be required to settle the liabilities in the normal course of business.

Relevance Accounting information should be able to influence the economic decisions of users. Relevant accounting information should have predictive and/or confirmatory value.

Reporting entities Business and some non-business entities that are required to prepare and submit to a relevant government agency the results of their financial transactions (e.g. sole traders, partnerships and limited companies).

Retained earnings Profits reinvested in the business instead of being paid out as dividends. They belong to the shareholders and form part of shareholders' funds, together with equity capital subscribed by shareholders and reserves. The cost of retained earnings is the same as the cost of other forms of equity capital included in shareholders' funds.

Revenue The gross inflow of economic benefits (cash, receivables, other assets) arising from the ordinary operating activities of an entity.

Rights issue An issue of shares to existing shareholders, usually at a discount to the market price.

Segmental reporting Financial reporting of revenues generated based on either geographical or product basis.

Stakeholders Parties to a company who have a vested interest in that company (e.g. employees, management, customers, suppliers and lenders).

Standardisation The process by which rules are developed for standard setting for similar items globally.

Subsidiary A business entity wholly or partly owned (e.g. 51% or more) by another business entity, where the majority shareholding belongs to the 'parent' company.

Sustainability Also known as social and environmental accounting and incorporating elements of corporate social governance, provides stakeholders with a report on an organisation's performance at an economic, ecological and social level for informed decision making.

True and fair view Used to describe the required standard of financial reporting but equally to justify decisions that require a certain amount of arbitrary judgment. It is the principle that is used in guidelines ranging from auditing and financial standards to the Companies Act.

Value-in-use The discounted present value of the future cash flows expected to arise from the continuing use of an asset, and from its disposal at the end of its useful life.

XBRL A web-based language that serves as a platform for business reporting using common Internet language tools. Referred to as eXtensible Business Reporting Language, it is embedded in the Hypertext Markup Language (HTML).

Directory

References

ACCA Ethical Framework for Professional Accountants – www.accaglobal.com.

ACCA Guide on Environmental and CSR reporting – Guide to Best Practice: www.corporateregister.com/pdf/Guide.pdf.

Accountingweb – www.accountingweb.co.uk.

Auditing Practices Board: 'Scope of an audit of the financial statements of a UK publicly traded company or group' – www.frc.org.uk/apb/scope/UKP.cfm.

Adams, W. M., 'The Future of Sustainability: Re-thinking Environment and Development in the Twenty-first Century.' Report of the IUCN Renowned Thinkers Meeting, 29–31 January 2006.

Bebchuk, L., Cohen, A. and Ferrell, A., 'What matters in corporate governance?' Unpublished working paper, Harvard Law School.

Becker, C., De Fond, M., Jiambalvo, J. and Subramanyam, K. R. 'The effect of audit quality on earnings management', in *Contemporary Accounting Research*, 15: 1–24 (1998).

Benedict, A and Elliott, B., *Practical Accounting* (Prentice Hall, 2001).

Berle, A. A. and Means, G. C., *The Modern Corporation and Private Property* (Harcourt, Brace & World, [1932] 1968).

Blewitt, J., *Understanding Sustainable Development* (Earthscan, 2008).

Bloomberg: http://topics.bloomberg.com/database-software.

Blowfield, M., *Corporate Responsibility*, 2nd edition (Oxford University Press, 2011).

Bonner, S. E., 'A model of the effects of audit task complexity', in *Accounting, Organizations and Society* 19(3): 213–44 (1994).

British Standards Institute (BSI) – Certifications: www.bsigroup.co.uk.

Cadbury Committee, *Report of the Committee on the Financial Aspects of Corporate Governance* (Gee, 1992).

Calder, A., *Corporate Governance: A Practical Guide to the Legal Frameworks and International Codes of Practice* (Kogan Page, 2008).

Copeland, T. and Weston J. F., *Financial Theory and Corporate Policy*, 3rd edition (Addison-Wesley, 2008).

Copnell, T. (July 2016) Audit Committee Institute: https://assets.kpmg.com/content/dam/kpmg/pdf/2016/07/CRT065495A_Brexit_financial_reporting_ACI_final.pdf

Deegan, C. and Unerman, J., *Financial Accounting Theory*, European edition (McGraw Hill, 2008).

DeFond, M. L. T., Wong, J. and Li, S. H., 'The impact of improved auditor independence on audit market concentration in China', in *Journal of Accounting and Economics*, 28: 269–305 (2000).

Deloitte IAS Plus – IFRS and IAS Standards: www.iasplus.com/standard/standard.htm.

Dharan, B., 'Earnings management: accruals vs. financial engineering', in *The Accounting World*, February 2003.

Dine, J. and Koutsias, M., *Company Law*, 7th edition (Palgrave McMillan, 2003).

Drobetz, W., Schillhofer, A., and Zimmermann, H., 'Corporate governance and expected stock returns: evidence from Germany', in *European Financial Management*, 10(2): 267–93 (2004).

Drury, C. *Cost and Management Accounting: An introduction*, 7th edition (Cengage, 2011).

Eco-Management and Audit: http://ec.europa.eu/environment/emas/tools/index_en.htm.

Elliott, B. and Elliott, J., *Financial Accounting and Reporting*, 13th edition (Prentice Hall, 2011).

Francis, J. R. 'What do we know about audit quality?', in *The British Accounting Review*, 36(4): 345–68 (2004).

Glautier, M. W. E. and Underdown, B., *Accounting: Theory and Practice*, 7th edition (Pitman Publishing, 2010).

HMRC *Money Laundering Guide*: www.hmrc.gov.uk/MLR/getstarted/intro.htm.

Hopwood, A. J., 'Understanding financial accounting practice', in *Accounting, Organizations and Society*, 25(8): 763–66 (2000).

IASB *Part A & B: International Financial Reporting Standards* (2011).

Institute of Chartered Accountants of England and Wales (ICAEW) Code of Ethics: www.icaew.com/en/technical/ethics/icaew-code-of-ethics/icaew-code-of-ethics.

Institute of Integrated Reporting Council: www.theiirc.org/resources-2/framework-development/discussion-paper/.

Jensen, M. C. and Meckling, W. H., 'Theory of the firm: managerial behavior, agency costs, and ownership structure', in *Journal of Financial Economics*, 3(4): 305–60 (1976).

Kaur, R., *Lease Accounting: Theory and Practice* (Deep and Deep, 2004).

Khan, Y., 'Cash flows as determinants of dividends policy in mature firms: evidence from FTSE 250 and AIM-listed firms'. Available at SSRN: http://ssrn.com/abstract=1365367 (2009).

Khan, Y. and D'Silva, K. E., 'Audit Fee Modelling and Corporate Governance in a South Asian Context', *Making Corporate Governance Work: Towards Reforming the Ways We Govern Conference*, January 2010. Available at SSRN: http://ssrn.com/abstract=1942393 (2010).

Kothari, J. and Barone, E., *Advanced Financial Accounting* (Prentice Hall, 2011).

Li, Y. and Stokes, D., 'Audit quality and the cost of equity capital', Second Workshop of Audit Quality, EIASM (2008).

Libby, R. and Luft, J., 'Determinants of judgment performance in accounting settings: ability, knowledge, motivation and environment', in *Accounting, Organizations and Society*, 18(5): 425–50 (1993).

Lloyd, B., 'The influence of corporate governance on teaching in corporate finance', in *Long Range Planning*, 39: 456–66 (2006).

Meek, G. K. and Saudagaran, S. M., 'A survey of research on financial reporting in a transnational context', in *Journal of Accounting Literature*, 9: 45–182 (1990).

Melville, A., *International Financial Reporting: A Practical Guide*, 3rd edition (Prentice Hall, 2011).

Myers, S. C., *Principles of Corporate Finance*, 10th edition (McGraw Hill, 2010).

Nobes, C and Parker, R., *Comparative International Accounting*, 11th edition (Prentice Hall, 2010).

Nobes, C. W., 'Towards a general model of the reasons for international differences in financial reporting', in *Abacus*, 34(2): 162–87 (1998).

Reynell, C., 'Corporate governance: killing capitalism?', in *The Economist*, 367(8318–30) (2003).

Soloman, J., *Corporate Governance and Accountability*, 3rd edition (Wiley & Sons, 2010).

Spreckley, F., 'Social audit: a management tool for co-operative working', see www.locallivelihoods.com/Documents/Social%20Audit%201981.pdf (1981).

Stickney, C. P., Weil, R. L., Schipper, K. and Francis, J., *Financial Accounting: An Introduction to Concepts, Methods, and Uses*, 13th edition (Cengage, 2009).

Tricker, B., *Corporate Governance: Principles, Policies and Practices*, 2nd edition (Oxford University Press, 2012).

Weetman, P., *Financial Accounting – An Introduction*, 5th edition (Prentice Hall, 2011).

World Commission on Environment and Development, *Our common future* (Oxford University Press, 1987).

Whittington, G., 'The adoption of international accounting standards in the European Union', in *European Accounting Review*, 14(1): 127–53.

Further reading

Basioudis, I. G., *Financial Accounting – A Practical Guide* (Prentice Hall, 2010).

Holmes, G., Sugden, A. and Gee, P., *Interpreting Company Reports and Accounts*, 10th edition (Prentice Hall, 2008).

Scott, L., Adomako, A. and Oakes, D., *International Accounting: A Compilation* (Pearson, 2011).

Magazines, journals and newsletters

Reading any subject specific matter will advance your vocabulary as well as your knowledge. It is imperative that you immerse yourself in your subject, be interested and curious about all aspects of financial reporting from the scandals to the triumphs.

Economia
This is the monthly journal of the ICAEW. It covers a wide range of topics. www.economia.icaew.com or download the free Economia app for your mobile devices.

CA Today
This is the monthly magazine of the ICAS.

Accounting and Business (AB Magazine)
This is the monthly magazine from ACCA. It covers business and professional developments worldwide including technical updates. Or sign up for a free weekly newsletter, AB Direct e-zine, aimed at accountants and business professionals at www.accaglobal.com or download the free app Student Accountant SA for your mobile devices.

Financial Management
This is CIMA's professional magazine. It focuses on management accounting methods and technology, and has good coverage of some of the topics in the ICSA course (e.g. capital investment appraisal). It is available online via www.cimaglobal.com or download the free CIMA FM app for your mobile devices.

Public Finance
This is the monthly magazine on public sector financial management from CIPFA.

Financial Times newspaper

PQ Magazine
This is a free monthly magazine discussing current accounting issues and technical updates with exam answer techniques and tips. www.pqaccountant.com

Professional bodies and useful organisations

The specialist financial accounting bodies in the UK are the Institute of Chartered Accountants in England and Wales (ICAEW) and the Institute of Chartered Accountants of Scotland (ICAS). Other professional accounting bodies are the Association of Chartered Certified Accountants (ACCA), the Chartered Institute of Management Accountants (CIMA) and the Chartered Institute of Public Finance and Accountancy (CIPFA).

All these accounting bodies include financial management elements in their examination schemes and many of their members are employed in financial management roles in industry, commerce and the public sector.

All the organisations listed below post additional information and resources on their websites. Many of the professional bodies also have international sites and offices that can provide students with additional local or regional material.

Institute of Chartered Accountants in England and Wales (ICAEW)
Chartered Accountants' Hall, Moorgate Place
London EC2R 6EA
Tel +44(0)20 7920 8100
www.icaew.com

Institute of Chartered Accountants of Scotland (ICAS)
1, Kings Street
London EC2V 8AU
Tel +44(0)20 7839 4777
www.icas.com

Association of Chartered Certified Accountants (ACCA)
The Adelphi, 1-11 John Adam Street
London WC2N 6AU
Tel +44(0)20 7059 5701
www.accaglobal.com

Chartered Institute of Management Accountants (CIMA)
The Helicon, 1 South Place
London EC2M 2RB
Tel +44(0)20 8849 2251
www.cimaglobal.com

The Chartered Institute of Public Finance and Accountancy (CIPFA)
77 Mansell Street
London E1 8AN
Tel +44(0)20 7543 5600
www.cipfa.org

Index